William H. Osborne

The History Of The Twenty-Ninth Regiment Of Massachusetts Volunteer Infantry

In The Late War Of The Rebellion

William H. Osborne

The History Of The Twenty-Ninth Regiment Of Massachusetts Volunteer Infantry
In The Late War Of The Rebellion

ISBN/EAN: 9783337116187

Printed in Europe, USA, Canada, Australia, Japan

Cover: Foto ©ninafisch / pixelio.de

More available books at **www.hansebooks.com**

THE

HISTORY

OF THE

TWENTY-NINTH REGIMENT

OF

MASSACHUSETTS VOLUNTEER INFANTRY,

IN

THE LATE WAR OF THE REBELLION.

By
WILLIAM H. OSBORNE,
A MEMBER OF THE REGIMENT.

BOSTON:
ALBERT J. WRIGHT, PRINTER, 79 MILK STREET.
(CORNER OF FEDERAL.)
1877.

Entered, according to Act of Congress, in the year 1877, by
WILLIAM H. OSBORNE,
In the office of the Librarian of Congress, at Washington.

PREFACE.

At the outset, I desire to thank all who have rendered me any assistance in connection with this work. To His Excellency, Governor Rice, I am indebted for a very liberal subscription and many words of encouragement; to my friend and townsman, Honorable Benjamin W. Harris, for copies of orders from the War Department; to General James A. Cunningham, Adjutant-General of Massachusetts, for facilitating my investigations of his records, and granting me unusual privileges in his office; to Major S. B. Phinney of Barnstable and Honorable William T. Davis of Plymouth, for loan of papers, and reports of their towns; to Mr. Charles H. Edson and Millard E. Brown, Esq., of East Bridgewater, for assistance in copying numerous papers; to my comrades, General Joseph H. Barnes, Colonels Thomas William Clarke, Henry R. Sibley, and Willard D. Tripp, Majors Charles T. Richardson and Samuel H. Doten, Captains William D. Chamberlain, Jonas K. Tyler, and James H. Osgood, Lieutenants Thomas Conant, J. O'Neil, and John Lucas, Sergeants Samuel C. Wright, John H. Hancock, and Walter A. Kezar, and Samuel Wells Hunt and Preston Hooper, for indispensable aid in preparing rolls and imparting valuable information.

PREFACE.

In the course of my researches, I have freely consulted the diaries and letters of several of my brother soldiers, the records of the Adjutant-General of Massachusetts, the excellent reports of the Committee of Congress "On the Conduct of the War," several works of Southern authors, the "History of the Civil War in America," by the Count of Paris, a large number of pamphlets, newspapers (Northern and Southern), beside many other publications, collecting, in the course of the seven years in which I have been engaged in this self-imposed task, a very large and varied assortment of the literature of the war.

Where radically different versions of the same event have been given me, I have generally adopted that of the officer who had the responsible command at the time, or of the soldier whose relations to the event were such as to afford him the best means of accurate knowledge. In other cases, I have used my own judgment in the premises, adopting or discarding the version that seemed to me most in harmony or at variance with the truth.

Knowing the sensitive nature of most soldiers, and not wishing to excite new or revive old jealousies, I at first resolved to avoid the bestowal of praise upon any one connected with the regiment. But I soon found that this plan was as difficult of execution as it would be unjust in its operation. I therefore abandoned it, and I desire it to be distinctly understood that I assume the entire responsibility for all I have said in the following pages, commendatory or otherwise, of any person, having had no motives of favoritism or feelings of prejudice, that I am aware of. My position in the regiment being that of a mere private soldier, rendered me naturally neutral, especially toward the officers; what I have said in praise of them, therefore, I have said from a sense of justice alone.

One of the most difficult parts of my task has been that of preparing the rolls of the regiment; and I am compelled to admit, much to my sorrow, that here I have failed to overcome certain difficulties that existed from the first, and which must increase in magnitude with every passing year. After the most careful investigation, I have not, in most instances, been able to give more than the name of and the highest rank attained by each soldier. My failure to accomplish more than this, is owing to the imperfect condition of our rolls at the War Department, and the impossibility of holding personal conferences or having communication with many of the living members.

In attempting even what I have indicated, it is possible that I have made errors; but if these be not more serious than mistakes about rank or the right spelling of a name, I shall be grateful, for I have had fears that, after all, the names of a few who served faithfully in the regiment have been omitted altogether. On the other hand, it is more than probable that the names of soldiers appear upon our rolls who deserted, or who never joined the regiment for service. I concluded, however, not to drop the name of any man from the rolls that had ever been properly put there, and to give no lists of deserters, for the reason that some so reported upon our official rolls were not deserving of such a record, and that others who did desert had previously been most excellent soldiers; and believing that they themselves must regret having yielded to this temptation, often pressing, I have no desire to add to their shame or their sorrow by anything which I might say.

Of the general plan of this work, but little need be said. I have made no attempts at word-painting or fine writing, have endeavored to give as many pertinent anecdotes as space would permit, and tell the story of the regiment in a simple, straightforward way.

The liberal space given in the first part of the volume to the actions of cities and towns and private individuals in connection with the formation of the several companies, I regard as justifiable, on the ground of the unquestionable historical value of such facts. If, however, I have devoted more space to one city or town than another, or to one company than another, it is because I had in the one case more material to select from, and because some comrades have taken more pains than others to furnish me facts in regard to the organization of their companies.

Several of my comrades to whom I appealed for aid seven years ago, when I sent out a circular letter announcing my intention to write the regimental history, comprehended better than myself the magnitude of the undertaking, and consequently had but little faith in its final success. That they were slow at first to respond to my request for assistance, and were reluctant to confide to me their journals and letters, — to them precious mementos of the war, — I do not now marvel. Two years later, however, I convinced them of my well-settled purpose to perform faithfully this work, and from that day to this they have seconded all my efforts in a manner that causes me to feel very grateful.

If I have succeeded in writing a truthful history of the old regiment,— one that will be treasured by my brothers in arms and valuable to the future historian, — I shall feel rewarded for all the many hours of labor that I have bestowed upon it.

W. H. O.

East Bridgewater, Mass.,
August 4, 1877.

HISTORY.

CHAPTER I.

PRELIMINARY REMARKS — EARLY WAR ACTION IN MASSACHUSETTS — BIRTH OF THE REGIMENT, AND HOW IT CHANCED TO BE DESIGNATED THE TWENTY-NINTH.

The Twenty-ninth Regiment of the Massachusetts Volunteers had its origin in some of the earliest war actions of the people of this patriotic Commonwealth, though its numerical designation would seem to suggest a state of facts quite the contrary.

The citizen who finds the name of his ancestor on the "Lexington Alarm List" of the 19th of April, 1775, considers himself richer than before in all that constitutes a proud family record, and feels that an honor has been conferred upon him by reason of this early and honorable military service of his progenitor. In a war waged for the defence of the Republic established by the toils and sufferings of our revolutionary fathers, at Lexington and on later fields, it is an honor not to be lightly esteemed to have one's name recorded and borne upon the roll of those who were the first to enlist in a cause so worthy.

This honor belongs in a peculiar sense to those volunteer soldiers who composed the seven companies that formed the nucleus of the Twenty-ninth Regiment; for they were not only among the first to enlist, but were the first in Massachusetts and all New England to be mustered into the service of the United States for a term of three years.[*]

---

[*] There is but one other military body that can claim a share of this honor, to this extent; viz., Capt. P. A. Davis's company of Lowell, an independent company of infantry called the "Richardson Light Guards," afterwards organized as the Seventh Massachusetts Light Battery. This company was mustered originally May 21, 1861.

As the history of the regiment, therefore, begins with the beginning of hostilities, we must preface our account of its organization with some pertinent remarks concerning the earliest efforts to raise troops in Massachusetts.

The first official act relating to the war was the somewhat famous General Order, No. 4, by direction of the Governor, dated January 16, 1861, requiring the Adjutant-General to ascertain with accuracy the number of the officers and men of the volunteer militia who would instantly respond to any call of the President of the United States for troops. On the 23d of January, 1861, the Legislature passed a Resolve, tendering the aid of the Commonwealth to the President of the United States, in enforcing the laws and preserving the Union. On the 15th of February, an Act was approved, providing for the retention in the service of all volunteer militia companies then existing, and for the organization, "as the public exigency may require," of additional companies of cavalry, artillery, and infantry, the same to be formed, on petition to the Commander-in-Chief, by the mayor and aldermen or selectmen of cities and towns. The first appropriation which seems to have been made for war purposes was by an Act, approved April 3, 1861, the text of which we here give because of its importance:—

"*Resolved*, That the Adjutant and Acting Quartermaster-General be, and he is hereby authorized, under the direction of the Governor and Council, to provide, either by contract or otherwise, a sufficient number of overcoats, blankets, knapsacks, haversacks, and other articles of equipment, camp utensils, and trenching tools, as may be required to equip two thousand troops for active service; and a sum not exceeding twenty-five thousand dollars is hereby appropriated for that purpose." [*Chap. 67, Acts of 1861.*]

Other Acts were passed subsequently to these already named, though not so directly pertinent, but all having the same object; namely, the preparing of the militia for active service, and providing the means of carrying on the war, then so soon expected to burst upon the country. Of these several Resolves, none are perhaps more noticeable for the strong spirit of patriotism that pervades them, than those of May 21 and May 23, 1861. The first was an Act entitled "An Act in addition to an Act to provide for the maintenance of the Union and the Constitution," and is preceded by the following preamble:—

"*Whereas*, The people of Massachusetts regard with like feelings of loyalty and affection the Government of the United States and that of their own Commonwealth, and deem it fit that the arms of each should be strengthened by all which the other can give;

"*And whereas*, Some emergency may arise, during the recess of the Legislature, in which the aid of Massachusetts may be of service to the General Government in its financial arrangements; therefore, *Be it enacted*," etc.

By this remarkably patriotic Resolve, the Governor, with the advice of the Council, was authorized to issue scrip, or certificates of debt, in the name of the Commonwealth, for such sums, not exceeding seven millions of dollars, as he, with the advice of the Council, might deem needful. The scrip so issued was to be sold, and the proceeds loaned to the United States Government, or expended in purchasing its treasury notes, or "delivered to the Secretary of the Treasury of the United States, in exchange for obligations of the United States Government, of corresponding amount."

The second Resolve referred to was entitled "An Act in aid of the families of volunteers, and for other purposes," by which cities and towns were permitted to raise money by taxation, and apply the same in aid of the wife and children of any of their inhabitants who, as a member of the volunteer militia, enlisted into the service of the United States. By the same Act, it was provided that the State should reimburse towns and cities for all aid furnished in pursuance of this law, to an extent limited therein; and by section four of the Act, any city or town was authorized "to organize an armed police or guard," whenever danger from an attack by sea was apprehended.*

For nearly three months before the first act of hostilities, the militia of the Commonwealth were busily engaged in drilling in their several armories; almost nightly, throughout the long, memorable winter of 1861, the patriotic soldiers of the State assembled and received from their instructors, les-

* Chap. 222, Acts of 1861.

sons in the manual of arms and other military matters, and prepared themselves as best they could to answer the first summons to the field.

Finally, as the winter waned, and the signs of war began to thicken, these citizen-soldiers became clamorous for active service, and on the 13th of April, the Adjutant-General addressed a letter to the Secretary of War, asking permission to garrison forts Warren and Independence, in Boston Harbor, with two regiments of the militia. "I believe," said the Adjutant-General, "that our troops would like to do garrison duty until called upon by the President for active service. The regiments might alternate every four or six weeks, and thus they would learn much that would be of service to them, and hold the forts against attack or surprise." * In this letter, it was stated that we then had five thousand infantry, properly officered, armed, and equipped, though only three thousand of them were armed with rifled muskets, the others having "the old smooth-bores," that had "been changed from flint-lock to the percussion."

The desire of the volunteers to enter upon active service was soon gratified. On the 15th of April, only two days after the date of this letter, a telegram was received from Senator Wilson at Washington, requesting twenty companies to be sent to Washington to act in the defence of that city. This was followed on the same day by a formal demand by telegraph from the Secretary of War, calling for two full regiments of militia. This demand was at once complied with, for, on the same day, Special Order No. 14 was issued by the Governor, "directing Colonel Jones of the Sixth Regiment, Colonel Packard of the Fourth, Colonel Wardrop of the Third, and Colonel Munroe of the Eighth, to muster their respective commands on the Boston Common forthwith." The order was transmitted by mail and special messengers to the various colonels, who severally resided at Lowell, Quincy, New Bedford, and Lynn. The companies composing these regiments were scattered throughout the cities and towns of the counties of Essex, Plymouth, Bristol, Norfolk, and Middlesex. But during the day and following night,

* Adjutant-General's Report, 1861, page 7.

nearly every man was notified, and on the morning of the
16th the regiments arrived in Boston. The Third and
Fourth regiments were ordered to proceed "forthwith" to
Fortress Monroe, Va., while the Sixth and Eighth were
sent to Washington. The Fourth left Boston on the 17th
of April, and the Third on the following day, the two
regiments arriving at Fortress Monroe on the 20th of April,
and becoming a part of the garrison at that post. Neither
of the last two commands contained the maximum number
of men; the Third Regiment having, both officers and enlisted men, only 450, while the Fourth, somewhat stronger,
numbered 636.

It appears from the Report of the Adjutant-General of
1861, that from the 13th of April to the 20th of May, —
the former being the date of the attack on Fort Sumter,
— one hundred and fifty-nine applications for leave to raise
companies were granted. These applications were not in
every instance made in pursuance of the Act of February
15, 1861 (Chap. 49), but were often, and perhaps in the
majority of instances, made by private individuals and
the persons who desired to enlist. We have before us a
copy of one of these rolls, the agreement of enlistment
being as follows: —

"We, whose names are hereunto affixed, do severally consent, and, by
our signatures hereunto made, do agree to be enrolled into a company
of volunteer militia, to be raised in the town of   and vicinity, subject to orders of the Commander-in-Chief; and we do hereby agree to
serve for the period of five years, unless sooner discharged agreeably to
law, and this enlistment we enter into with the full understanding that
we are liable at any moment to be ordered into active service under the
Government of the United States."

These enlistment papers were prepared by the Adjutant-
General, issued at his discretion, and accompanying each
paper was a copy of General Order No. 8, dated April 22,
1861, announcing the conditions upon which enlistments
would be received. These were substantially as follows:
That when the requisite number of men to form a full company had enrolled their names, and the authorities of the

cities or towns where such companies were formed had attested the roll and certified their approbation of the application, an inspection of the men by a competent surgeon was to be ordered.

By this order, it was also announced that the "companies organized in the vicinity of existing regiments which at the present time have not ten companies, will be annexed to said regiments until they are full."

The laws of the Commonwealth made no provision for the pay or subsistence of these volunteers until they were ordered by the Governor into active service, yet this proved no hindrance to the work of enlistment, which went actively on. To such of these companies as were likely to be called into active service, arms were issued by the State, while the uniforms were provided by the local authorities, and in some instances by private individuals.

It was under the circumstances which we have just narrated, and at this time, that the seven original companies of the Twenty-ninth Regiment were formed.

The company commanded by Captain Chamberlain, raised in Lynn, was gathered as early as April 18; the companies commanded by Captains Tyler (afterward Wilson) and Clarke, raised in Boston, were recruited April 19; the companies commanded by Captains Leach, Chipman, Barnes, and Doten, raised, respectively, in East Bridgewater, Sandwich, East Boston, and Plymouth, were all formed about April 20. There was no concerted action among the officers and persons who recruited these companies, nor was it understood at the time of their formation that they were to be united in the service, their subsequent union being one of the many accidental occurrences of the war.

The original term of enlistment of these commands was five years in the State's service; but before they could be put in preparation to take the field, the President had concluded not to accept any more militia troops.

On the third day of May, the National Executive issued a call for a force of volunteers, "to serve for a period of three years, unless sooner discharged." Nearly every man of these companies at once enlisted under the new call.

Governor Andrew concluded to make up the deficiency of men in the Third and Fourth regiments, then at Fortress Monroe, with these three years' troops, and accordingly, on the 10th of May, the companies commanded by Captains Tyler and Chamberlain were despatched to Fortress Monroe, where they were assigned to duty with the Third Regiment.

On the eighteenth day of May, the commands of Captains Leach, Doten, Barnes, and Chipman were ordered to the same place, where they were assigned as follows: Captains Doten's and Chipman's companies to the Third, and Captains Leach's and Barnes's companies to the Fourth Regiment. Four days later, the company commanded by Captain Clarke was ordered to Fortress Monroe, and, upon arrival, was attached to the Fourth Regiment. These companies served in the Third and Fourth regiments from the dates of their respective assignments till the expiration of the three months' term of the latter commands, when, on the sixteenth day of July, 1861, they were, by order of General Butler, commanding the department, organized as the "*Massachusetts Battalion*," retaining the latter organization until December 13, 1861, at which time, upon the addition of three new companies, commanded, respectively, by Captains Sibley, Richardson, and Tripp, they became the Twenty-ninth Regiment.

This delay in forming the battalion into a regiment resulted in depriving it of the honor of being the First Regiment of Massachusetts Volunteers; for while it was toiling upon the ramparts of Fortress Monroe, mounting guns under the withering rays of a July sun, throwing up earthworks at Newport News, fighting and marching, and thereby obtaining for the Government a foothold upon the soil of rebellious Virginia, twenty-eight regiments of infantry had been organized in Massachusetts and sent to the seat of war.

By this explanation, it will appear to the general reader how the first three years' volunteers of Massachusetts chanced to be designated the Twenty-ninth Regiment.

There are many curious and interesting facts connected with the raising and formation of these companies, which cannot be better given than by devoting a brief chapter to each. The history of the organization of these commands forms an important part of the history of Massachusetts in the earliest days of the war; and while the tracing of that history may expose to criticism the unmilitary ideas of our people, at the same time it cannot fail to exhibit, in strong colors, their deep love for the Union, and their willingness to make the greatest of sacrifices for its salvation.

CHAPTER II.

CAPTAIN THOMAS W. CLARKE'S COMPANY, "WIGHTMAN RIFLES." ["M" IN THE FOURTH REGIMENT, "RIFLES" OF THE MASSACHUSETTS BATTALION, AND "A" OF THE TWENTY-NINTH REGIMENT.]

On the nineteenth day of April, 1861, a day memorable in the history of the war, Thomas William Clarke, a member of the Suffolk County bar, threw from an office-window on Washington Street, Boston, near the corner of State Street, a recruiting flag, and opened a roll for a company of militia.

So strong was the war spirit of the people then, that in the course of that and the succeeding day, Captain Clarke secured a full complement of men.

On the 21st of April, there was an election of officers, presided over by Brig. Gen. W. W. Bullock of the First Brigade of Militia.

Thomas William Clarke was chosen Captain ; John Critcherson, Jr., of San Francisco, Cal., First Lieutenant ; and Joshua Norton, 3d, of Bridgewater, Second Lieutenant.

Subsequently, and before the muster of the company into the service of the United States, Lieutenant Critcherson was discharged, Norton promoted to First Lieutenant, and John E. White was chosen Second Lieutenant.

May the 9th, the company was ordered into the service of the State, and was paid and rationed by the State from this time till May 21.

During all this time, and as long as it remained in Massachusetts, the company had its quarters in a hall in Bowdoin Square, Boston. Here the men were lodged and fed, and here they held daily drill. It is an interesting fact, as illustrating how meagre were the preparations for war even in Massachusetts, that this company of soldiers, though raised for the public service, was chiefly uniformed by the city of Boston. This uniform consisted of a gray chasseur tunic trimmed with red, gray trousers, and three-cornered gray felt hats trimmed with red. The arms were furnished by the State. A part of these were Harper's Ferry rifles, and a part Winsor rifles (all calibre 54), better known as Mississippi rifles, and were provided with the sabre bayonet.

These arms were formerly used by and were taken from Major Ben: Perley Poore's Battalion, an independent body of militia.

Beside these arms, the company received from the State, red blankets, cartridge-boxes, and the somewhat historic gray overcoats.

While the company was quartered in Boston, the Chauncey Hall School of that city presented it with the quarterly prize-money of the school, amounting to about one hundred and twenty-five dollars, which sum was set apart as a company fund for the benefit of all its members.

The determination of the Government not to accept any more militia troops, announced in War Department orders on the 9th of May, produced a change in the term of enlistment of this company from five years in the State's service to three years in the United States service; and on the 21st of May it was mustered into the service of the United States, at West Roxbury, by Lieut. T. J. C. Amory of the regular army (afterwards Colonel of the 17th Mass. Vols.).

It is a fact worthy of special notice, that after this company had been enrolled for active service under the United States Government, it was ordered into the service of the Commonwealth, and from the time it was so enrolled till the date of its muster (21st), its members were paid out of the State treasury.

The day following the muster of the company into the United States service, it received its long-expected order to leave for the seat of war. Embarking on the steamer "Pembroke," together with an independent company of volunteers from Lowell, under Captain Davis, it sailed for Fortress Monroe, Va. (May 22).

Before leaving the State, Captain Clarke filed with the Adjutant-General a muster and descriptive roll of the company, and accounted for all the ordnance and clothing received from the Commonwealth.

The voyage to Fortress Monroe was by no means devoid of interest. The steamer, which was armed with two nine-inch guns, cleared for action several times during the trip, upon view of suspicious-looking crafts, supposed at the time to be Confederate war-vessels, and on all these occasions the men were beaten to quarters.

The "Pembroke" arrived at Fortress Monroe May 26, and on the following day the company was assigned to duty with the Fourth Regiment of Massachusetts Militia, and ordered to accompany that regiment to Newport News.

Upon joining the Fourth Regiment, the company took the letter "M," and was assigned to the left of the regimental line.

After the return of the Fourth Regiment to Massachusetts, this company was reported and known as the "Rifles" of the Massachusetts Battalion at Fortress Monroe. The letter "A" was given it upon the formation of the Twenty-ninth Regiment, by order of Governor Andrew.

The commission of Captain Clarke bears date of April 20, 1861; that of Lieutenant Norton, May 7, 1861; Second Lieutenant White resigned, and was succeeded by Second Lieutenant George H. Taylor, whose commission bears date of July 31, 1861.

CHAPTER III.

CAPTAIN JONAS K. TYLER'S COMPANY, AFTERWARDS COMMANDED BY CAPTAIN ISRAEL N. WILSON. ["M" IN THE THIRD REGIMENT, "M" OF THE MASSACHUSETTS BATTALION, AND "B" OF THE TWENTY-NINTH REGIMENT.]

As early as the first of March, 1861, Jonas K. Tyler, Esq., a member of the Suffolk bar, and who had seen service in the war with Mexico, offered his services to Governor Andrew in raising a body of troops to serve either the State or National governments in the impending war. But in a letter dated March 8, 1861, the Governor declined these services, on the ground that no call had been made upon the State for troops, and that he possessed no legal authority to raise troops except upon an order issued by the President of the United States.

A month later, when it became apparent that a call would be made for troops, Captain Tyler readily obtained permission from His Excellency to raise a company of militia, with the understanding that they were not to be mustered unless such a call should issue.

On the 17th of April, a roll was opened by Tyler at his office, and by the night of the 18th it was filled with the names of young men, principally residents of Boston.

On the 19th of April, the company was organized by the choice of Jonas K. Tyler of Boston, Captain; Samuel A. Bent, First Lieutenant; Albert Blakeslee, Second Lieutenant; E. Dexter, Third Lieutenant; and Thomas H. Adams, Fourth Lieutenant.

As no quarters were provided by the State, the men were lodged in hotels and boarding-houses, and were drilled daily by a competent drill-master in the school of the soldier and company evolutions. The expense attending the organization of the company and quartering the men was borne by the officers and men, for which they have never been reimbursed.

On the 3d of May, the President having made an actual demand upon the State for troops, the Governor consented to the issue of arms to the men, and on the following day Captain Tyler obtained a requisition for a partial supply of underclothing.

On the 9th of May, Captain Tyler received orders to leave for the seat of war on the 10th; but at this time not a member of the command possessed a uniform, and, what was still more embarrassing, the State had none to furnish.

How was the outfit to be obtained in so short a time? Happily, Boston possessed a mayor, the Hon. Joseph M. Wightman, whose whole heart was enlisted in the cause of the country. In this emergency, Captain Tyler turned to him for assistance, and the promptness with which that aid was furnished reflects the greatest credit, not alone upon the Mayor himself, but upon the city of Boston.

It was well into the evening when the Captain called upon Mayor Wightman and made known the wants of his men. The Mayor comprehended the nature of the situation at once, and in company with Tyler, immediately commenced the search for clothing. Going upon School Street, a number of hacks were found in front of the Parker House, and these were at once secured. The first person called upon was Mrs. Harrison Gray Otis, who furnished them with a large number of useful articles not included in the list of military equipments. From thence the two gentlemen went to the various depots of clothing belonging to the city, where were obtained a sufficient number of coats, trousers, shoes, and stockings. These articles were quickly loaded into the hacks and conveyed to the hall on Washington Street, where the company had assembled upon its brief notice to march.

At eight o'clock the next morning, May 10, the command reported at the State House, ready for service, and were here joined by Capt. William D. Chamberlain's company from Lynn. The men of both companies engaged to serve for three years without hesitation, were inspected by the Adjutant-General, and ordered to embark at once on the steamer "Pembroke." The commissions of both captains bore date of April 19, but Captain Chamberlain having at one time held the rank of major in the militia, was given the command of the battalion, and, at the same time, sealed orders, with instructions not to open the same till the vessel had passed beyond Boston Light. On the march to Rowe's Wharf, where the "Pembroke" was lying, the battalion halted at a place on Federal Street, and there received the gray overcoats.

The short notice to march made it impossible for Captain Tyler to warn all his men, some of whom lived out of the city, and consequently about twenty were left behind; these, however, afterward joined the company at Fortress Monroe.

The "Pembroke" was at this time in the service of the Commonwealth, was armed with two 42-pounder Dahlgren guns, had a guard of armed seamen, and flew both the State and National colors. As she passed the forts in Boston Harbor, she was saluted by them, and the men, being gathered upon deck, returned the salutes by rounds of cheers. It was not until the vessel had passed beyond Boston Light that either officers or soldiers learned their destination. Then the sealed orders were opened, revealing the fact that they were bound for Fortress Monroe, Va., and were to be assigned to the Third Regiment.

There were few events of the trip that were of much moment, though the voyage under such circumstances was necessarily different from any which the soldiers (some of whom had been sailors) had ever before taken. They were going to war, — to the rescue of the nation's most important fortress, which was already being besieged by the traitorous militia of Virginia.

About midnight of the 12th of May, when, by the judgment of the officers, — all lights on that part of the coast having been extinguished, — it was calculated that the steamer was about forty miles from her destination, suddenly from the south, and directly in her course, "*shone out what seemed nothing less than the light of a heavy bombardment. Within a narrower space, as it appeared to us, fierce flashes broke forth, and from the opposite quarter were as fiercely answered again.*" * That Fortress Monroe was being bombarded, was the belief of all on board, and the soldiers kept the deck

---

* Letter of Captain Tyler.

nearly all night, watching and speculating upon these novel scenes. As the steamer sped on her way and neared the scene of the apparent battle, hugging the shore closely, the view increased in splendor, and occasionally there came wafted over the water the low, hollow sound of a distant gun. When morning broke, leaden-colored, though wasted, clouds in the south showed that the soldiers had been watching from a distance a terrific thunder-storm. A little after sunrise, the form of a frigate was observed approaching the steamer from seaward, which in the course of an hour came up and spoke the "Pembroke." The frigate proved to be the "Minnesota," then engaged in cruising off the coast.

On the 13th of May, the "Pembroke" reached Fortress Monroe, the battalion entered the fort, and both companies were attached to the Third Regiment, Captain Tyler's company receiving the letter "M." On the following day, May 14, both commands were mustered into the service for three years by Lieut. C. C. Churchill, U. S. A.

Captain Tyler's company served with the Third Regiment till the term of the latter expired, and then became a part of the Massachusetts Battalion, retaining its letter "M" till the formation of the Twenty-ninth Regiment, when, by order of Governor Andrew, it became a part of that regiment, and its letter was changed to "B."

The number of officers chosen at the time of the organization of the company was greater by two than that authorized by the laws of the United States, and the only officers who accompanied the command to the seat of war were Captain Tyler, First Lieutenant Samuel A. Bent of Boston, and Second Lieutenant Thomas H. Adams of Boston. Captain Tyler resigned on account of ill-health, July 18, 1861, and Lieutenant Bent the same day. Israel N. Wilson of Billerica, who was a First Lieutenant in Capt. P. A. Davis's company, was commissioned Captain July 24, 1861, and succeeded Tyler. On the same day, Ezra Ripley of Cambridge, an able lawyer, was commissioned First Lieutenant, and assigned to this company, joining it soon after, and while it was doing duty at the "Rip-Raps."

CHAPTER IV.

CAPTAIN LEBBEUS LEACH'S COMPANY. ["L" IN THE FOURTH REGIMENT, "L" OF THE MASSACHUSETTS BATTALION, AND "C" OF THE TWENTY-NINTH REGIMENT.]

This company, raised almost wholly in East Bridgewater, Plymouth County, was the direct outgrowth of a series of war meetings, the first of which was held April 20, 1861, the day after the Baltimore affair. At this meeting there was a very large attendance of the citizens of the town, who, after listening to several stirring speeches, adopted a resolution for the formation of a company of volunteers; an informal roll was prepared, and received the signatures of thirty-eight young men.

A second mass meeting was held on the evening of the 24th of April, and, like the first, was largely attended and enthusiastic, resulting in thirty-one additional enlistments.

In the meantime, a legal meeting of the voters of the town had been called for the afternoon of the 27th of April, to take formal action concerning the impending war, for at that time every town and city in the Commonwealth made the cause of the General Government its own, imitating the practice of the colonists in the days of the Revolution, by raising troops and providing for their equipment and payment.

There was never a more thoughtful or solemn assemblage than this meeting; party lines had been wiped away by the bloody events of the 19th of April; the political differences of the late campaign seemed by common consent to have been buried and forgotten, and every voter felt that a part of the responsibility of saving the then disrupted Union rested upon him. In this meeting, it was unanimously resolved, "That this town will raise what money is necessary to uniform a volunteer company, and to properly provide for the family of each member." The sum of $4,000 was appropriated, and it was voted to pay each volunteer of the proposed company $10 each month while in active service, it being supposed at the time that the soldiers were to serve a term of three months.*

There were but few citizens of the town who possessed even the slightest knowledge of military matters, and these were mostly old men who had served in the war of 1812, or had trained at old-fashioned musters. At a time like this, they were naturally looked to for advice; but they had little to give, for their experience as soldiers had been a bloodless one. Wisely estimating, however, the importance of their new position, they furbished up all their well-worn yarns of camp-life at the "Gurnet" and "South Boston Flats," and told them over again with scarcely enough of exaggeration to make them interesting.

The majority of these old worthies had forgotten the most of their drill, and had they remembered it, it would have been of little value to the volunteers of 1861, for the tactics of Steuben had been replaced by those of the gallant old Scott.

The volunteers were compelled, therefore, to depend upon themselves, and in order to prepare as much as possible for active service, held nightly drill-meetings at the town-house, using muskets that had been procured from the State Arsenal.

The company had not been accepted by the State as a part of the militia, and the selectmen of the town for a while were compelled to act as quartermasters-general and commanders-in-chief. As quartermasters, they provided the uniform under the vote of the town, and fixed upon its style, which was very odd, being a sort of cross between the dress of an artilleryman and a common sailor, but not having the comforts or beauty of either. This uniform consisted of gray hip trousers trimmed with red, a blue shirt with a rolling collar ornamented with red braid, and a gray fatigue-cap; shoes, stockings, and underclothing were also furnished, while the patriotic women of the town provided each soldier with a neatly-arranged case of thread, needles, yarn, pins, towels, and other articles of use.

* This vote was faithfully carried out, each original member of the company receiving three months' extra pay, amounting to $30.—AUTHOR.

On the first day of May, a meeting of the company was held for the election of commissioned officers (in the building now occupied by the Catholics as a church), presided over by Captain William C. Lovering of the State militia.

At this meeting, Thomas Bates was elected Captain;* Nathan D. Whitman, First Lieutenant; Josiah E. Richmond, Second Lieutenant; Elisha S. Holbrook, Third Lieutenant; and Lucius D. Burbeck, Fourth Lieutenant.

Eight days after this, Captain Bates received an order from the Adjutant-General of Massachusetts, directing him to proceed to Boston with his company on the following morning. The news that the company had been ordered away spread over the town in the course of a few hours, so that when it took up its march for the depot on the morning of the 9th, nearly the entire population gathered to witness this novel sight, for the like had not been seen in the old town since the year 1814, a period of nearly fifty years.

The ardor of the volunteers was destined to encounter a severe check. Arriving in Boston, they were met by Colonel Horace Binney Sargent of the Governor's staff, who ordered them to repair to the hall in the depot-building of the Old Colony Railroad Company, where was assembled Captain Chipman's company from Sandwich. Here the men of both commands were addressed by Colonel Sargent, who told them that the Governor had received instructions from the War Department that no more militia troops would be accepted by the United States Government, and that unless they were prepared to re-enlist for the term of *three years*, they must give up their arms and go home.

There was no doubt about the patriotic intentions of these men; but many of them had families, and none had made, before leaving their homes, suitable preparations for so long a period of absence, and accordingly both companies voted not to enlist at that time for the long term of three years.

This action made it necessary for them to endure the humiliation of returning home, from whence they had

---

* The commission of Captain Bates described him as a "Captain of Company C, Third Regiment of Infantry, Second Brigade, First Division of the Militia of this Commonwealth," and was dated May 4, 1861.

marched in pride only a few hours before, where they had been wept over by the kind-hearted women, and hundreds of their neighbors had bidden them affectionate adieus.

But to return disarmed was to their minds a great disgrace, and not being willing to endure it, the volunteers from East Bridgewater appealed to their stanch friend, Hon. Benjamin W. Harris, who had accompanied them to Boston, to interpose his influence to obtain a reversal of the latter order.

This was accomplished, and when the time arrived to take the returning train, each man seized his musket, and one of them took two, as a partial offset to what he considered unfair treatment toward him and his comrades; and, to the great amusement of those who were present, the indignant volunteer, who was of gigantic stature, stalked sullenly through the hall, down several flights of stairs, along the platform to the cars, grasping the muzzle of a gun in each hand and dragging the pieces after him, his face plainly indicating extreme rage and a feeling of bitter disappointment.

In the course of a few days after the return of the company to East Bridgewater, a reorganization of it was effected upon the basis of three years' service.

On Sunday, May 12, the company attended, in uniform, divine service, at the Unitarian Church, where a sermon was preached by the Rev. Timothy O. Paine, from the text: "He loveth our nation, and he built us a synagogue." Luke vii. 5.*

May 14, the company held a second meeting for the election of officers, and chose Lebbeus Leach of Boston for Captain, reaffirmed their choice of Nathan D. Whitman as First Lieutenant, and elected Elisha S. Holbrook as Second Lieutenant. Captain Leach was born in Bridgewater, and belonged to one of the oldest families of the ancient township, being a lineal descendant of Giles Leach of Weymouth, who settled in the West Precinct as early as 1665; and one of his paternal ancestors lost his life in the French and Indian

---

* This sermon was afterward printed in pamphlet form, with the motto, "Stand by the Flag!" and circulated among the volunteers at Fortress Monroe, Va.

war. Captain Leach was fifty-nine years old at the time of his election, and had seen some service in the militia.

Lieutenant Whitman was likewise of a very old and respectable Colonial family, from whence have sprung a long line of able and distinguished men. His first ancestor in this country was John Whitman of Weymouth, the first military officer of that town, and his ancestor Thomas (son of John) came to East Bridgewater in 1662.

Lieutenant Holbrook was a native of Braintree, Mass., had resided several years in East Bridgewater, and was very active in the formation of the company.

A large majority of the members of the company were also natives of Plymouth County, whose ancestors were among the early or first settlers of the Old Colony. We speak of these things, not from a feeling of boastfulness, but to show to the reader how purely American was this command, and how directly allied with the history and traditions of the ancient colony were these volunteers.

On the afternoon of the 17th of May, the company received orders to proceed to Boston on the day following. Night messengers were despatched to all parts of the town and adjoining towns where the members resided, and at an early hour the next morning every man reported for duty at the town-house.

Though it was barely six o'clock in the morning when the company reached the flagstaff (then standing in front of J. Folsom's house), from which the Stars and Stripes were flying, and where they were addressed by Mr. Harris, yet a large majority of the inhabitants of the town had assembled there; and so intense was the war spirit that pervaded the community, that many of the male spectators freely offered the volunteers considerable sums of money for their chance to serve as soldiers.

Upon reaching Boston, the company proceeded to Faneuil Hall, where the members signed a formal enlistment-roll for a term of three years' service; from Faneuil Hall, they marched to the State House, receiving here canteens, haversacks, and other equipments; and here, also, they met Governor Andrew, who seemed to take a deep personal interest in each one of them.

Dinner had been prepared for the company at the Hancock House, Court Square, at the expense of the town of East Bridgewater, under the direction of Mr. George Bryant and Hon. B. W. Harris, both of whom were present and dined with the soldiers at two o'clock in the afternoon. At the conclusion of the dinner, the company marched to Federal Street, where each man received a knapsack, one of the gray overcoats, a rubber and woollen blanket, tin cup, plate, spoon, knife, and fork; and when these articles had been distributed, marched to Commercial Wharf, where it went on board the "Cambridge," a screw steamer, then in the service of the State. This was about four o'clock in the afternoon; and here assembled Captain Barnes's company of East Boston, Captain Doten's company from Plymouth, Captain Chipman's company from Sandwich, and a body of recruits for the Fourth Regiment, — all to take passage in the same steamer for Fortress Monroe, Va.

At about five o'clock, the steamer hauled out of the dock and passed down the harbor, receiving and returning a salute from Fort Warren. By the time Provincetown was reached, it was quite dark, and the air becoming cold, the soldiers sought shelter below, where they passed the night in much discomfort; for crowded between-decks were nearly five hundred men, and with no adequate means of ventilation, the air soon became overheated and foul.

Sunday the 19th of May was very fine; but as the sun went down, threatening clouds gathered in the east. Soon after dark, the storm burst upon the vessel, then off the coast of Delaware, with great fury. She was ill-adapted to ocean navigation, and being heavily loaded, labored greatly with the sea. Before the storm began, the men had been singing, telling funny stories, and bandying jokes; but a few rolling motions of the steamer made the large majority of them less mirthful, and gulps and groans were heard in every quarter of the dark apartment.

The steamer was armed with two heavy guns, mounted between-decks. At about midnight, one of these pieces broke away from its fastening and began plunging against the side of the vessel. Every soldier not utterly prostrated by sea-sickness sprang to his feet, manned the gun-ropes, and by hard work brought the gun into position and secured it; — not a moment too soon, for perhaps another blow against the side would have made a ragged hole, through which the merciless sea would have rushed unchecked, engulfing boat and passengers.

The storm continued till the noon of the 21st, during which time the steamer had passed south of the entrance to Chesapeake Bay and reached a point in dangerous proximity to the sunken reefs off Hatteras Inlet, on the coast of North Carolina. The "Quaker City," a United States steamer cruising in that vicinity, hailed the "Cambridge," just in season, it is confidently believed, to save her from being stranded upon the then inhospitable coast of that region.

Fortress Monroe was reached about noon of the 21st, and with but slight delay the volunteers were landed, those not wholly disabled by the voyage bounding ashore with the glee of escaped prisoners. When the men left their homes, the grass there had scarcely put off its seared and gray coating of winter; here nature had all the vernal appearance of midsummer, the trees were in full leaf, and the air laden with the rich perfume of roses that bloomed about the officers' quarters in the fort and the many attractive residences outside the walls. Captain Leach's company and the East Boston men were assigned camping-ground in the midst of a group of beautiful live-oaks, in the southerly part of the fortress, and were furnished new and commodious tents and a liberal supply of clean fresh straw.

On the day after the arrival, May 22, the company was examined by the Surgeon of the Post, and Privates Francis C. Bryant, Oliver H. Wade, Henry B. Rogers, Edmund Reed, and R. H. Quinley were rejected; the others being sworn into the service for three years, and the company assigned to duty with the Fourth Regiment of Massachusetts Militia.

The arms of the men, which had been furnished by the State, were old smooth-bores, altered from flint-lock to percussion; but no ammunition was supplied by the State, nor was any issued to them by the United States Government till late in the summer of 1861.

This chapter being designed to trace the history of the company from its organization to its entrance into the service, it is only necessary to add, that it took the letter "L" in the Fourth Regiment, served in it till July 16, 1861, then became a part of the Massachusetts Battalion (still retaining the letter "L"), and on the 13th of December, 1861, of the Twenty-ninth Regiment, in which it was designated as "C" company.

CHAPTER V.

Captain Charles Chipman's Company, "Sandwich Guards." ["D" in the Third Regiment, "D" of the Massachusetts Battalion, and "D" of the Twenty-ninth Regiment.]

With a notice of only a few hours, a very large meeting of the inhabitants of Sandwich, Barnstable County, was held on the evening of Saturday, April 20, 1861. The news of the assault upon the Sixth Massachusetts Regiment, in Baltimore, had reached the town, and produced extreme excitement. The meeting was called "to devise ways and means for the raising a company of troops for the defence of the country," and was called to order by Theodore Kern, Esq. Dr. Jonathan Leonard was chosen to preside, and E. S. Whittemore, Secretary. After appropriate remarks upon the objects of the meeting, Dr. Leonard introduced to the people, Major S. B. Phinney, editor of the "Barnstable Patriot," who made a stirring address, ". . . declared his unwavering fidelity to the Union, and determination to sustain the National Administration in its efforts to crush out treason and rebellion."

Addresses were also made by Dr. I. N. Swazey, E. S. Whittemore, Nathaniel F. Fessenden, and Otis Freeman.

"On motion of Theodore Kern, Esq., it was voted, that the sum of $20 be immediately raised by subscription, as a bounty to each man who should enlist in the campaign, and by a subscription-paper the sum of $626 was pledged in the course of the evening, in sums varying from $5 to $70; Major Phinney contributing $70, and promising a stand of colors to the company when formed." *

An informal enlistment-roll was opened at this meeting, receiving the signatures of a large number of young men, among whom was Charles Chipman, who had served in the

---

* "Sandwich Advocate," April 22, 1861.

regular army as a sergeant. A committee of nine gentlemen was chosen "to thoroughly canvass the town and raise the balance of the bounty money," while another committee of three was appointed to wait on the Governor and offer the services of the company to be raised; also to make arrangements for equipping it.

Nothing that we could say would so well serve to show the good spirit and patriotism of the people of Cape Cod, excited by the then recent acts of treason on the part of the South, as the language and tone of the local papers of that period. A copy of the "Barnstable Patriot" (the chief paper of the Cape) of May 23, 1861, is before us as we write, and by its loyal utterances, calls back freshly to our memory those days when the great free North was preparing itself to strike a blow for liberty and the Union.

The paper of which we have spoken, as indeed were most of its issues of that period, is principally devoted to war news, its principal editorial column being headed by these familiar lines,—

"And this be our motto, 'In God is our trust!'
And the Star Spangled Banner in triumph shall wave
O'er the land of the free and the home of the brave."

Following these words was a picture of the American flag, and beneath, this motto,—

"Our flag floats to-day, not for party, but for country."

The work of recruitment progressed so rapidly, that on the 6th of May the company was ready to complete its organization by the choice of commissioned officers. The election was presided over by the selectmen of the town; namely, Mason White, Seth B. Wing, and Isaiah Fish. Charles Chipman was chosen Captain; Charles Brady, First Lieutenant; Henry A. Kern, Second Lieutenant; Alfred E. Smith, Third Lieutenant; James H. Atherton, Fourth Lieutenant; and the company adopted the name of the "Sandwich Guards."

Two days later, May 8, in obedience to orders from Governor Andrew, Captain Chipman proceeded with his company to Boston, with the assurance from headquarters that he was to be sent to Fortress Monroe, Va., on the steamer "Pembroke," then lying in Boston Harbor. The departure of this body of soldiers was of course a great event in the history of the town, as well as that of Cape Cod; for it was the first volunteer company raised in that section of the State, and a great multitude of people gathered at the railway station to bid the soldiers farewell, and to strengthen by kind words their purposes of duty. The kind feelings of the citizens prompted several of them to follow the company to Boston, among them Major Phinney, and provide for the men a bountiful supper at the United States Hotel. On the night of the 8th, the soldiers were quartered in the hall of the Old Colony Railroad Company's depot, on Kneeland Street, and during the evening were visited by Adjutant-General Schouler, who addressed them upon the state of the country and the nature of their duties as soldiers, but gave them no intimation of the disappointment that was in store for them on the following day.

The company had enlisted for the term of five years in the State's service, and with the understanding that it was to be attached to the Third Regiment of Massachusetts Militia, then at Fortress Monroe. On the morning of the 9th, each member of the company was provided with a full Third Regiment uniform, and, later in the day, when they had been joined by the company from East Bridgewater (Captain Bates), Colonel Horace Binney Sargent, aide-de-camp to the Governor, visited them, and without making any explanation, informed them that, in order to be accepted as a part of the volunteer forces of the United States, they must enlist for the term of three years. This was a great blow to the enthusiasm of the men; for while they were willing to enlist for this term, yet they had left their homes and their families without making adequate preparations for so long a time, and they thereupon quite unanimously determined to return.

On their arrival in Sandwich, on the evening of the 9th, they proceeded at once to the Town Hall, to which they were escorted by a large body of citizens. Here, after an eloquent speech by Hon. J. M. Day, Judge of Probate for Barnstable County, who explained to them the military reasons for changing the term of enlistment, Captain Chipman called the roll, and, with a single exception, the men engaged to serve for three years.

As an essential and deeply interesting part of the early history of this command, we now come to the action concerning it of the town of Sandwich, in its capacity of a corporation, such actions being always more solemn than those of individuals, because more deliberate, and taken after more mature consideration.

The voters were summoned to meet at the Town Hall on Saturday, the 11th of May, 1861, "then and there to act on the following articles : —

"1st. To choose a Moderator to preside at said meeting.

"2d. To consider the duty of the town in the present condition of the country, and to take any action that may be thought expedient to assist in the defence of the national honor, and to see if the town will vote to raise the sum of four thousand dollars, or such other sum as may be agreed upon, to be applied to the support and maintenance of the families of such persons as may volunteer and act in the service of the United States, to aid in the defence of our country and the preservation of our Union, and to act upon all matters relating to the above." . . .

The following is a transcript of the records of this meeting:

"SANDWICH, May 11, 1861.

"Pursuant to the warrant, the inhabitants of the town of Sandwich assembled in the Town Hall, and proceeded to the business named in said warrant.

"1st. Chose Charles B. Hall, Esq., Moderator.

"2d. The second article in the warrant coming up, viz., 'To consider the duty of the town in the present condition of the country, and to take action thereon,' it was voted that a committee of five (5) be chosen to retire and make a report, and present the report to the meeting.

"The following persons were chosen said committee: Theodore Kern, Dr. Jonathan Leonard, Charles Dillingham, Charles Southack, and Benjamin F. Bourne; and the following is the report of the committee : —

"'*First*, That the treasurer of the town, with the consent and at the discretion of the selectmen, be authorized to borrow a sum not exceeding four thousand dollars ($4,000), in sums as shall be needed, for the benefit of the families of those persons from this town who may enlist in the service of the Government in defence of our constitutional liberties. *Second*, That the sum so borrowed shall be disbursed by the selectmen in the following manner : A man that leaves a wife shall receive two dollars per week; a wife and child, three dollars per week; and fifty cents per week for each additional child under fourteen years of age. *Third*, That the selectmen be authorized and instructed to assist such families who are dependent upon any volunteer for their support, to which in their judgment the above rule does not apply. *Fourth*,

That the town furnish the company, when called for, a suitable uniform, with this condition: when the company is officially accepted.

"'THEODORE KERN.
"'J. LEONARD.
"'CHARLES SOUTHACK.
"'B. F. BOURNE.
"'CHARLES DILLINGHAM, Sec'y.'

"The foregoing report was read and accepted.

"The several parts of the report were then taken up separately, and, after discussion, were unanimously adopted.

"*Voted*, That all citizens of Sandwich volunteering in companies out of Sandwich, having families, — and also all persons from other towns volunteering in this company, having families, — be included in the above appropriation, provided there should not be an appropriation for them by the towns from which they come, or in which our citizens have volunteered.

"*Voted*, To raise the sum of five hundred dollars ($500), to defray the expense of purchasing uniforms for the company.

"*Voted*, That a committee of four be chosen to purchase the material for uniforms. The following were chosen as that committee: Captain Charles Chipman, Joseph B. Hersey, Charles Southack, J. Henry Peirce.

"*Voted*, That the families of volunteers receive their money once in two weeks."

Under this action of the town, uniforms were furnished the officers of the company; but, as already appears, the State provided clothing for the enlisted men. As in other communities, the ladies of Sandwich contributed with loving hands to the patriotic work of equipping these volunteer soldiers, fitted them out with cases of thread, needles, towels, etc., and provided each man with comfortable underclothing and other articles of necessity.

On the 16th of May, Captain Chipman received an order from Adjutant-General Schouler to report with his command, in Boston, on Saturday, May 18, to leave for the seat of war. At nine o'clock on the morning of the 18th, the company, with full ranks, assembled at the town-house, and, in the presence of a large audience, Major Phinney presented the company the flag he had promised them, accompanying the presentation with a well-considered and eloquent speech. The flag was a beautiful and costly gift, was of fine blue silk, bearing —

". . . on one side, in the centre, . . . the figure of an uplifted right arm grasping the sword of Liberty. Above this figure were the words, in golden letters, 'The Right Arm of Old Massachusetts,' and below it the motto, 'God Speed the Right,' the whole being enclosed in a circle of gold stars. On the reverse side was an American eagle, grasping in one talon a sheaf of arrows, and in the other the olive-branch of peace, and holding in its beak a ribbon-scroll, bearing the words, 'E Pluribus Unum,' and below it the motto, 'Our Whole Country,' all surrounded by gold stars."*

Captain Chipman accepted the flag, and responded for himself and his command, promising to protect both the flag and the Union to the extent of their ability. Hon. George M. Marston of Barnstable was the last to address the soldiers, speaking of the company as "the representative of Cape Cod, the first and perhaps the only company from the old right arm of the Commonwealth that will be mustered into the service of the United States." He fitly concluded his remarks by "a generous offer of personal or professional service to each or all of themselves or families who might need such service."

Upon the conclusion of these deeply-interesting exercises, the company formed, and, escorted by a band of music and nearly the entire population of the town, and large numbers of people from the surrounding towns, marched to the railway station and proceeded to Boston, where they were generously entertained by Sewall H. Fessenden, Esq., agent of the Boston and Sandwich Glass Company. At about five o'clock in the afternoon of the same day (May 18), the command, together with those of Captains Leach, Barnes, and Doten, embarked on the steamer "Cambridge" for Fortress Monroe, arriving at this post on the 21st. They were mustered into the service for three years on the 22d, by Lieut. C. C. Churchill of the Third Artillery, U. S. A., and at once assigned to duty with the Third Regiment, M. V. M., taking the letter "D," and retaining it throughout their whole term. In July, 1861, when the three months' term of the Third Regiment expired, and that regiment returned to Massachusetts, Company D became a part of the Massachusetts Battalion (formed of this and the six other three years' companies spoken of in this work), and, in December, 1861, a part of the Twenty-ninth Regiment of the Massachusetts Volunteers.

* Letter in "Barnstable Patriot," May 21, 1861. This flag was for a time carried by the company, and is now in the possession of Mr. Samuel Wells Hunt of Sandwich, an honored member of that company, who has taken great pains in preserving from forgetfulness the record of the deeds of his comrades.—AUTHOR.

CHAPTER VI.

CAPTAIN SAMUEL H. DOTEN'S COMPANY, "PLYMOUTH ROCK GUARDS."
["E" IN THE FOURTH REGIMENT, "E" OF THE MASSACHUSETTS BATTALION, AND "E" OF THE TWENTY-NINTH REGIMENT.]

The honored old Pilgrim town of Plymouth was among the first in the State to take an active part in the work of furnishing troops for the Union army. Here was an organized body of militia known as the "Standish Guards," commanded by Captain Charles C. Doten. The company was "B" of the Third Regiment of Militia, and left for the seat of war on the 16th of April, 1861. On this occasion, the town was stirred as it had not been since the days of the Revolution; hundreds of the townspeople — among whom could have been found some of the most ardent and intelligent patriots in the country — gathered at an early hour in the morning to witness the departure of its first soldiers of the war.

The company had received its orders to march during the night of the 15th, by a messenger from New Bedford, who had ridden horseback from Wareham, through the dark, pine forests that lay between that town and Plymouth, and in the midst of a storm of rain. The departure of the soldiers was so sudden, that the majority of them went away without having made any preparations for the care and maintenance of their families. But the good people of Plymouth were not unmindful of this fact, and, on the 20th of April, a large public meeting assembled, under a call of the selectmen of the town, "to take such steps as may be necessary to secure ample provision for the families of those who have enlisted for the defence of their country."

The meeting was presided over by Hon. William T. Davis, and the following resolutions, offered by John J. Russell, Esq., were adopted:—

"*Resolved*, That it is our pleasure, as well as our duty, to see to it that our brave volunteers be encouraged by the knowledge that the welfare of those near and dear to them is made the care of their fellow-citizens who remain at home.

"*Resolved,* That the selectmen be requested to apply and distribute, at their discretion, a sum not exceeding two thousand dollars, towards the assistance of those families who, by the sudden departure of the troops, are left in need of pecuniary aid, — such sum to be raised by borrowing, in the name of the town, or in such other way as the selectmen shall deem expedient."

On the very day of this meeting, Samuel H. Doten, a brother of Captain Charles C., was busily engaged in forming a volunteer company in this town, and had already secured nearly a full complement of men. The public meeting referred to was not a regularly-warned town meeting, and the resolutions that had been adopted by it could not be carried out, except they received the sanction of the voters, legally called together for that purpose. On the 11th of May, therefore, in pursuance of a call dated May 4, the town assembled in meeting, chose Moses Bates, Esq., as Moderator, and, upon motion of Hon. Charles G. Davis, adopted the suggestions of the citizens' meeting, and made the following provision for the three years' volunteers of Captain Samuel H. Doten's company: —

"*Voted,* That the sum not exceeding fifteen hundred dollars is hereby appropriated for clothing and equipping such volunteers, for three years' or more service, as are citizens of this town.

"*Voted,* That six dollars per month to each citizen of this town having a family, and four dollars per month to each citizen of this town who is single or unmarried, excepting commissioned officers, who shall enlist in the service of the United States for the war, shall be paid, and the same is hereby appropriated by the town, as extra compensation for the term of actual service during one year, from the first day of May current, to be paid in money in such manner . . . as the selectmen shall deem expedient."

At the same meeting, the treasurer of the town was authorized to borrow "such sums of money, under the direction of the selectmen, as shall be necessary to carry the above votes into effect." It was known that the company now forming would soon be ordered away, and the work of preparing them for the field at once began. The selectmen purchased the materials for the uniforms, and the women met together and cut and made them, and also, with the assistance of the people generally, provided each volunteer with shoes and stockings.

In order to give the record of this company correctly, we must go back a little, and name the dates of the several acts and measures that concern its formation. April 24, the first drill-meeting was held, followed on the 6th of May by an election of officers, under Captain Lovering of the militia. Samuel H. Doten, a gentleman considerably advanced in years, was chosen Captain; John B. Collingwood, First Lieutenant; and Thomas A. Mayo, Second Lieutenant.

At a later date, and before the company was ordered away, the people presented each of the officers with swords and other equipments. The uniform furnished the enlisted men was similar to that worn by the Third Regiment, and consisted of a full suit of reddish gray clothes, the coat reaching to the hips, and the whole — coat, trousers, and cap — trimmed with red braid. This uniform, and other articles furnished, cost the town $1,025.49.

On the 17th of May, Captain Doten received an order from Adjutant-General Schouler to report, with his company, in Boston, on the morning of the 18th. The people of the town were soon apprised of this fact, and early in the morning of the 18th, as soon as the soldiers began to assemble at their headquarters, the citizens — men, women, and children — flocked by hundreds from all parts of the town, to witness a repetition of the scenes of April 16. The spirit of patriotism and kind feeling never ran higher, or displayed itself in a more beautiful and touching manner, than on this historic morning. The men were going to the field, and the fact was not only realized by those who gathered to watch their departure, but it touched a chord of sympathy in their hearts, that at once overcame all selfishness, and led to deeds of generosity that moved the soldiers to tears. As the company stood in line, waiting for the final order to march, one after another of the citizens approached them, and, seizing their hands, left in them sums of money varying from five dollars to one hundred, accompanying each gift with a hearty " God-speed " and an affectionate " farewell."

A band of music and a company of militia, appropriately called the "Home Guards," performed escort duty on the march of the volunteers from their quarters to the railway station, where there was a repetition of hand-shaking and utterance of kind words. The swift train that bore them toward the metropolis — not a few of them never to return — was eagerly watched by the thronging multitude till it was lost to sight, some of the soldiers standing upon the platforms of the cars and exchanging greetings with their neighbors and friends by waving their hats as they whirled away on their sad and eventful journey.

At South Abington, they were met by Captain Leach's company from East Bridgewater, which took the same train to Boston, where the two commands marched to Faneuil Hall, there signing a more formal enlistment-roll than the one previously signed by them, and from thence to the State House, receiving at the latter place arms and the gray overcoats prudently provided by Governor Andrew, at a time when the great mass of the people regarded the threats of war as idle bluster. As stated in former chapters, this company left Boston for Fortress Monroe on this day (May 18), with the three companies of Leach, Barnes, and Chipman, arrived at its destination on the 21st, and was mustered into the service for three years on the 22d. The company had been designated as a part of the Third Regiment, by Governor Andrew, before it left Massachusetts, and immediately upon its muster, took quarters with that regiment, then forming a part of the garrison of Fortress Monroe, and served with it as long as the latter remained in the service, namely, July 16, 1861, when it became a part of the Massachusetts Battalion. The company took the letter "E" upon joining the Third Regiment, and retained it ever afterward, both in the battalion and in the Twenty-ninth Regiment, of which it also became a part on the 13th of December, 1861.

The company left Plymouth with seventy-four enlisted men and three commissioned officers, sixty-seven of whom were citizens of that town. The commissions of the officers are dated May 6, 1861.

CHAPTER VII.

CAPTAIN WILLIAM D. CHAMBERLAIN'S COMPANY, "UNION GUARD." ["I" OF THE FOURTH REGIMENT, "I" OF THE MASSACHUSETTS BATTALION, AND "I" OF THE TWENTY-NINTH REGIMENT.]

On the 17th of April, 1861, William D. Chamberlain of Lynn received authority from the Governor to raise a company of militia, to form a part of the Eighth Regiment of Militia, then under orders to proceed to Washington.

The day following (April 18), a room having been procured in Hill's Building, in that city, a roll was opened, and, in the space of a few hours, was signed by one hundred men.

On the 19th, a meeting of the company was held at the armory of the Lynn Light Infantry, presided over by the mayor of the city, the Hon. Hiram N. Breed, and the following officers chosen: William D. Chamberlain, Captain; Abram A. Oliver, First Lieutenant; John E. Smith, Second Lieutenant; Moses B. Tufts, Third Lieutenant; and John Alley, Fourth Lieutenant. (The last two officers were never mustered.) At this meeting, the company adopted the name, "Union Guard."

The news of the firing upon the Sixth Massachusetts Regiment, on its passage through Baltimore, hastened the departure of the Eighth Regiment from Boston, on the morning of the 20th.

Captain Chamberlain's company was not in readiness to leave for the field at this time, and hence lost its chance to accompany that regiment.

The company improved the additional time furnished by this accidental relief from active service, by holding frequent meetings for purposes of drill. These meetings were held nearly every evening, and were continued till May 3, at which time the President issued his proclamation calling for a force of three years' volunteers.

The uniform consisted of gray frock coats, the gift of the "Empire Fire Company" of Lynn, Kossuth hats, looped at one side, and light blue trousers. The hats and trousers were furnished by the State.

May 5, Captain Chamberlain marched with his company to Boston, and presenting his command to the Governor, offered its services.

An interesting scene took place at the State House on this occasion. Hannibal Hamlin, Vice-President of the United States, His Excellency Governor Andrew, Adjutant-General Schouler, and several other distinguished gentlemen, were present, and the Vice-President and Governor addressed the men. The Governor thanked the commander and his soldiers for the love of country which had led them to offer their services to the Government in the darkest hour of its existence, and assured them that as soon as an opportunity offered, they would be accepted.

The march of the company to Boston was one continued ovation. At Chelsea it was entertained by the militia of that city, and in Charlestown and Boston the citizens vied with each other in showering upon the volunteers numberless favors and courtesies. The company returned to Lynn on the same day, by the Eastern Railroad, and, upon arrival, every man engaged to serve for three years.

May 9, the company was ordered to report at the State House, on the following morning, at nine o'clock.

Promptly at the hour named, the command presented itself to the Adjutant-General, at the State House, here received Springfield rifles and other equipments, and were ordered to report on board the steamer "Pembroke," together with Captain Tyler's company, sailing on this day (May 10) for Fortress Monroe. Before embarking, a committee of the citizens of Lynn presented the company with nearly three hundred dollars in money. The same committee had previously given the officers a complete outfit.

The facts concerning the sealed orders and the voyage to Fortress Monroe have already been given in Chapter IV.

Upon arriving at Fortress Monroe, the company was assigned to the Third Regiment, in which it was designated as Company I, served with that regiment till July 16, and then composed a part of the Massachusetts Battalion, and, in December, 1861, a part of the Twenty-ninth Regiment. Captain Chamberlain's commission, as also those of Lieutenants Oliver and Smith, bear date of April 19, 1861; and the members of this company, together with those of Captain Tyler's command, were the first volunteers in New England who enlisted for a period of three years.

CHAPTER VIII.

CAPTAIN JOSEPH H. BARNES'S COMPANY, "GREENOUGH GUARDS." ["K" IN THE FOURTH REGIMENT, "K" OF THE MASSACHUSETTS BATTALION, AND "K" OF THE TWENTY-NINTH REGIMENT.]

On the 20th of April, 1861, Joseph H. Barnes, a citizen of East Boston, and a native of Hingham, Plymouth County, having been authorized by the Governor, raised a company of infantry, chiefly composed of East Boston men.
On the 25th of April, there was an election of officers, conducted by General Bullock of the militia, resulting in the election of Joseph H. Barnes, Captain; James H. Osgood, Jr., First Lieutenant; William T. Keen, Second Lieutenant; Albert H. Townsend, Third Lieutenant; and Joseph D. Ellis, Fourth Lieutenant. The commission of Captain Barnes, dated April 27, was as a " Captain of company of infantry in the First Division of the Militia of the Commonwealth." By an order accompanying the commission, the company was assigned to the First Regiment of Militia, then commanded by Col. Robert Cowdin of Boston, and the following order was also received by Captain Barnes: —

"HEADQUARTERS FIRST REGIMENT INFANTRY,
"FIRST BRIGADE, FIRST DIVISION, M. V. M.,
"BOSTON, April 27, 1861.
"ORDERS, NO. 14.

"By Special Orders, No. 100, of this date, from the Commander-in-Chief, transmitted by Division Special Orders, No. 48, of the same date, and Brigade Special Orders, No. 27, of the same date, this regiment is detailed for active duty in the service of the United States. Commandants of companies are hereby ordered to report at the Hancock House, on Sunday, the 28th instant, at 9 o'clock, A. M., for orders. They will assemble their commands at their armories forthwith, ready to march at a moment's notice.
"By command of
COL. ROBERT COWDIN.
"GEORGE W. BEACH, Adjutant."

The company assembled as directed, but, by reason of a change of affairs, the regiment did not leave the State as soon as expected. Subsequently, they were mustered into service as the First (three years) Regiment, and left for the field, June 15, 1861. We give this order, however, as a part of the record of Captain Barnes's company, and as showing at how early a date it was ordered into the service; also, its connection with the First Regiment. In the course of a few days after the company organized, it took quarters at the Maverick House, East Boston, and continued to occupy them till the eighteenth day of May. The citizens of the "Island Ward" paid, by voluntary contributions, the chief part of the expense attending the quartering of the volunteers, and, in common with the other citizens of Boston, provided them with a uniform consisting of a full suit of gray clothes, the jacket being trimmed with red braid. The arms were Springfield rifle-muskets, furnished by the State.

May 17, the company was detached from the First Regiment of Militia, and the following order issued: —

"COMMONWEALTH OF MASSACHUSETTS.
"ADJUTANT-GENERAL'S OFFICE,
"BOSTON, May 17, 1861.

"CAPT. JOSEPH H. BARNES.

"SIR: You are directed by His Excellency the Commander-in-Chief to report yourself and command at headquarters, on Saturday, May 18, at 10 o'clock, A. M., for actual service. You are required to sign, and have your men sign, an enlisting paper, to serve for three years. You will proceed from Boston in the steamer 'Cambridge,' for Fort Monroe.

"Respectfully yours,
"WILLIAM SCHOULER, *Adj. Gen.*"

The words of this order, "You are required to sign, and have your men sign, an enlisting paper, to serve for three years," probably were not intended to convey the idea that the Governor had the power to compel the officers and men to sign such a paper, but that their acceptance as soldiers was on the condition of their enlistment for the term named therein. Captain Barnes reported at the State House with his company, numbering seventy-three enlisted men, at the hour named, where all willingly engaged to serve for three years. They then returned to East Boston, and the men were dismissed for a hurried dinner. Early in the afternoon, the company again assembled at its quarters, and were escorted to the ferry by a body of militia and an immense throng of people, the latter so crowding the streets, that it became difficult for the command to reach the wharf; and so eager were the people to follow the soldiers, that large numbers of them crossed over on the ferry.

Before Captain Barnes and his men left the Maverick House, William W. Greenough, Esq., whose name the company had adopted, and who performed a great variety of services for its members, both before and after they entered the service, presented them with the sum of two hundred and fifty dollars, in gold.

This worthy gentlemen was not the only warm friend which the soldiers of this company left at home. When the command assembled at its quarters in the afternoon of this day, a large number of the ladies of East Boston, together with several of the teachers of the public schools, gathered at the Maverick House, and presented the volunteers with a great many useful articles, including rubber blankets, underclothing, knives, forks, spoons, and cases containing thread, needles, yarn, and towels; a fine pocket-bible was also given to each officer and man.

The combining the gift of a Bible with that of clothing and other articles of physical comfort, was a faithful and touching compliance with one of the injunctions which the holy book itself contained. These Christian women did not say to the soldiers, "Depart in peace; be ye warmed and filled," but gave them ". . . those things which are needful for the body." Nor did the kindness of these gentle ones end here; for as long as the company remained in the service, they continued in this work of love, sending to the field many well-filled boxes of clothing and other needed supplies.

Upon the arrival of the company at the steamer, later in the afternoon, Captain Barnes received the following order:—

"COMMONWEALTH OF MASSACHUSETTS.

"ADJUTANT-GENERAL'S OFFICE,
"BOSTON, May 18, 1861.

"CAPT. JOS. H. BARNES:

"As senior officer of the Massachusetts troops embarked to-day on board the ship 'Cambridge' for Fortress Monroe, you will detail such guards and sentinels as may be necessary for proper discipline and for the care and safety of the ship, under the direction of the captain of said vessel.

"Company from Plymouth, Capt. Doten; company from Sandwich, Capt. Chipman, which are to be attached to the Third Regiment, Col. Wardrop, now at Fortress Monroe; company from East Bridgewater, Capt. Leach; company from East Boston, Capt. Barnes; together with 32 men belonging to Co. H of Quincy; 37 men belonging to Co. I of Hingham; 12 men belonging to Co. F, Foxborough; 22 men belonging to Co. D, Randolph; and 45 men belonging to Co. A, Canton, severally of the Fourth Regiment, Col. Packard, now at Fort Monroe, will be attached to the regiment upon their arrival at their place of destination. You are to have command of the troops until you report yourself to the officer in command of Fort Monroe.

"You are to take good care of the men, and to use your best efforts to cause discipline and harmony.

"By order of His Excellency, Governor and Commander-in-Chief.

"WILLIAM SCHOULER, *Adj. Gen.*"

May 21, the "Cambridge" reached Fortress Monroe. The company having been assigned to the Fourth Regiment, received the letter "K," and was made the color-company of the regiment. It was mustered into the service for three years, on the following day (May 22), and, five days later, went with the Fourth Regiment to Newport News. It retained the letter "K" throughout its service, became a part of the Massachusetts Battalion, July 16, 1861, and, in December following, was incorporated with the Twenty-ninth Regiment.

The gentlemen who were elected to the offices of third and fourth lieutenants upon the first organization of the company, could not, under the laws of the United States, be mustered with that rank. Lieutenant Ellis, however, accompanied the command to Fortress Monroe, but soon afterwards returned to Massachusetts. Charles Hewett, one of the original members, was rejected upon the surgical examination at Fortress Monroe, being the only one of the command rejected, and was furnished by General Butler with transportation to Boston.

The commissions of the two lieutenants, Osgood and Keen, bear the same date as that of the Captain; namely, April 27, 1861.

CHAPTER IX.

THE THIRD REGIMENT OF MASSACHUSETTS MILITIA — ITS SERVICE AT FORTRESS MONROE AND HAMPTON, VA. — DESTRUCTION OF VESSELS AND OTHER PROPERTY AT PORTSMOUTH — SPEECH OF COLONEL DIMICK — ITS RETURN TO MASSACHUSETTS.

The author has given, in the preceding chapters, detailed accounts of the formation of the seven companies of the Twenty-ninth Regiment which earliest enlisted. Pursuing the narrative of this corps in the order of time, he will, at the proper time and in the proper place, give like accounts of the formation of the companies of Captains Sibley, Tripp, and Richardson, which, in December, 1861, were made a part of that regiment, and thus completed its organization.

It will be observed by the reader who has perused the foregoing chapters, that four of these seven companies were assigned to duty with the Third Regiment of Massachusetts Militia. Apart, therefore, from the history of their formation, these commands have a history in connection with the Third Regiment which is alike interesting and important. The Third Regiment left Boston on the steamer "S. R. Spaulding," April 17, 1861, and arrived at Fortress Monroe April 20. It was composed of seven companies; namely, "A" of Halifax, Capt. Joseph S. Harlow of Middleborough; "B" of Plymouth (Standish Guards), Capt. Charles C. Doten; "C" of Cambridge, Capt. James C. Richardson; "G" of Freetown, Capt. John W. Marble; "H" of Plympton, Capt. Lucian L. Perkins; "K" of Carver, Capt. William S. McFarlin; and "L" of New Bedford, Capt. Timothy Ingraham.

The regiment was one of the oldest militia corps of Massachusetts. Company "A" of Halifax was organized as early as 1792. One of its past commanders, Captain Asa Thompson of Halifax, who was living at the breaking out of the war, and who joined it when it was first formed, commanded the company in the war of 1812. As four of its seven companies were from Plymouth County, the regiment has always been considered as belonging chiefly to the Old Colony. Its aggregate membership at the time of its leaving for the field was about four hundred and fifty.

The field and staff of the regiment were as follows: Colonel, David W. Wardrop of New Bedford; Lieutenant-Colonel, Charles Raymond of Plymouth; Major, John H. Jennings of New Bedford; Adjutant, Austin S. Cushman of New Bedford; Quartermaster, Edward D. Allen, Fairhaven; Surgeon, Alexander R. Holmes, New Bedford; Assistant Surgeon, Johnson Clark, New Bedford; Sergeant-Major, Alberti C. Maggi, New Bedford; Quartermaster-Sergeant, Frederick S. Gifford of New Bedford.

It is not our purpose or province to write a complete history of the Third Regiment; but the fact is eminently worthy of notice, that it rendered some of the most important service performed by any body of militia that went into the war from Massachusetts. It is also a noticeable fact, that many of its officers and men, subsequently to their three months' service at Fortress Monroe, filled high military positions. Thus its Colonel was commissioned Colonel of the Ninety-ninth New York Regiment; Lieutenant-Colonel Raymond was appointed to the same office in the Seventh Massachusetts Infantry; Sergeant-Major Maggi became Colonel of the Thirty-third Massachusetts Infantry, and distinguished himself as a soldier; Captain Doten was made Captain in the Thirty-eighth; and Captain Ingraham, a superior soldier, was promoted to the coloneley of the last-named regiment.

When the Third Regiment was despatched to Fortress Monroe, the tenure of the Government there was decidedly precarious. There had been no open hostilities on the part of the insurgents in that department, but they were everywhere carrying forward the most active war measures. A battery of seven guns had been erected at Sewall's Point, at the mouth of the Elizabeth, and obstructions had been placed in the channel of the river. Forts Norfolk and Nelson, which commanded the approaches to the cities of Norfolk and Portsmouth, were in the hands of the Confederate Militia; but still lying in the river, near these cities, were the United States vessels "Pennsylvania," "Cumberland," "Merrimack," "Germantown," "Dolphin," "Raritan," "Columbia," and "Plymouth." The Norfolk navy-yard was one of the most extensive and valuable naval depots in the United States. The grounds, three-fourths of a mile long and about a quarter of a mile wide, were filled with machine-shops, foundries, storehouses, and dwellings for officers. There were three large shiphouses, and a dry-dock built of granite. The whole property of the yard was estimated at about nine millions of dollars.

On the 18th of April, the Confederate General Taliaferro arrived at Norfolk, and took charge of the insurgent militia, whereupon a large number of naval officers resigned their commissions and at once entered the Confederate service. Commodore McCauly, who commanded the yard, was wavering and uncertain in his convictions of duty, but Commodore Pendegrast and Captain Marston of the "Cumberland" were fixed in their determination to serve their Government.

At about six o'clock in the afternoon of April 20, the Third Regiment, which had arrived at Fortress Monroe a few hours before, was ordered on board the United States gunboat "Pawnee," commanded by Commodore Paulding. After passing Sewall's Point in safety, the steamer neared Fort Norfolk, then in the hands of the enemy. The channel lay near the shore, and it was expected the Confederates would fire upon the gunboat the moment she came within range of their guns. The soldiers were ordered to lie down upon the deck, the marines paraded the quarter, and the sailors were at battery. The moon was shining brightly; it was clear and calm; the fort was plainly visible; even the suppressed tones of its garrison could be heard on board. When just abreast the fort, some one called aloud from the parapet, "What ship is that?"—"what ship is that?" No reply was made, and the soldiers who heard the hail whispered to each other, "Now it will come!" and their hearts beat quick and fast as they lay, faces downward, expecting every instant to hear the crash of guns and the howling of cannon-balls. But it did not come; the war had scarcely begun; there was still lingering in the hearts of the enemy some respect for the old flag, and a wholesome dread of firing upon it. Nearer the navy-yard lay the United States ship "Pennsylvania," broadside across the stream. The "Pawnee" approached her, and was hailed as before. The hail was answered, but apparently not heard, and in a moment the black and gloomy-looking sides of the "Pennsylvania" were illumined. The ports had been opened. At the same time a voice from her gun-deck, "Shall I fire, sir?" caught the ears of those on the "Pawnee." A watchful old gunner on the latter vessel stepped up to the executive officer, and said, in slow and measured words, as though it was the most commonplace affair in the world, "They are going to fire on the 'Pawnee,' sir!" The officer at once leaped into the rigging, and, with his trumpet, cried, "Pawnee! Pawnee! Pawnee!" in a voice that was heard far and near, and echoed over the waters and silent town. "Pawnee! Pawnee! Pawnee!" was shouted back from gun-deck and quarter, and then loud cheers and hearty cries of welcome came out of the open ports of the "Pennsylvania." This was a similar mistake to that which arose in the early morning of this day, at the fortress, as to the identity of the steamer "State of Maine," that had on board the Fourth Massachusetts Regiment, and came even nearer proving fatal, for the lanyards were already in the hands of the gunners of both vessels, and but for the prompt action of the executive officer of the approaching steamer, there would have been a bloody encounter between these soldiers and sailors of the Union.

Upon arriving at Norfolk, about nine o'clock, the whole regiment was ordered ashore into the navy-yard, and, under the commands of the officers, began immediately in the work of destruction, which was already in full progress. Twenty men were detailed from Company B of Plymouth to mine the dry-dock, while the balance of the force, aided by the sailors and yardmen, went to work throwing into the river shot, shell, revolvers, carbines, and stands of arms.

There were nearly three thousand heavy guns in the yard, many of them columbiads and fine Dahlgrens. These were spiked as best they could be, but very imperfectly, as the Confederates afterwards managed to use them. At midnight, the barracks in the yard were set on fire, and then the shiphouses, in one of which was the partially-completed ship "New York."

The "Pawnee," taking the "Cumberland" in tow, and having on board the Third Regiment and all the men from the yard, except those who were left to fire the trains, started down the river, and sent up a rocket, which went high into the air, and then "burst in shivers of many-colored lights."

This was the signal to fire the trains. Simultaneously, flashes of fire were seen running about on the decks of the deserted ships "Pennsylvania," "Merrimack," "Dolphin," "Germantown," "Plymouth," "Raritan," and "Columbia," and in a few seconds they were wrapped in flames. Says an eye-witness: —

"I need not try to picture the scene of the grand conflagration that now burst like the day of judgment on the startled citizens of Norfolk, Portsmouth, and the surrounding country. Any one who has seen a ship burn, and knows how, like a fiery serpent, the flame leaps from pitchy deck to smoking shrouds, and writhes to their very top, around the masts that stand like martyrs doomed, can form some idea of the wonderful display that followed."

The old, dismantled ships "Delaware" and "Columbus" were sunk, and several of the vessels that were fired had also been scuttled. The "Merrimack," having sunk before the flames did her much damage, was, as is well known to our readers, afterwards raised by the Confederates, and constructed into a shot-proof steam-battery.

The total value of these vessels, as estimated by the Chief of the Bureau of Construction, was $1,980,000, while the total value of all the public property lost by this catastrophe is estimated at $9,700,181.93; and the report of Commander Alden to the Secretary of the Navy shows, that, by a wiser and more vigorous action on the part of the commandant of the yard, a large portion of this dreadful loss might have been prevented.

The "Pawnee" reached Fortress Monroe at six o'clock Sunday morning (April 21), having in tow the sloop-of-war "Cumberland," now so famous in the annals of naval warfare.

The men of the Third Regiment had a severe experience on this expedition, having toiled nearly all night, and been eighteen hours without food. Their introduction to one of the most dreadful experiences of war was indeed a very sudden one, and this was followed by nearly three weeks of privation, caused by the scanty supply of food at the fortress, and by three months of almost ceaseless toil.

Included in the plot of the enemy to capture Norfolk, was also the scheme to capture Fortress Monroe.

At this time an irregular body of Confederate militia, variously estimated as to number, occupied the village of Hampton, about two and a half miles from the fortress, while their pickets held a drawbridge over Mill Creek, not more than a mile distant. The flags of the insurgents could be distinguished at the fortress, flying from the roofs of private and public buildings in Hampton. On the 13th of May, Colonel Dimick made an advance with a body of infantry and a piece of artillery, and forced the enemy from his position at the bridge. The bridge was thereupon occupied by the Federals; but no attempt was made to pursue the enemy beyond this point.

This condition of affairs continued till May 23, when, the garrison having been materially strengthened by the arrival of the First Vermont Militia, under Colonel J. W. Phelps, and several New York regiments, General Butler, then being in command, ordered Colonel Phelps to make a reconnoissance in Hampton and vicinity. Upon approaching the bridge over Hampton Creek, Colonel Phelps discovered that the enemy had fired it. The flames were partially extinguished, but the bridge was so nearly destroyed, that the troops were obliged to cross the river in scows and flat-boats. Upon the arrival of the Vermont troops, the Confederate militia and all the inhabitants, save the negroes and one white family, fled the town, leaving behind them, in many instances, their household furniture and other personal effects.

On the afternoon of the same day, General Butler, with Company B of the Third Regiment and Captain Tyler's company, proceeded some seven miles into the enemy's country, in the direction of Yorktown. This was the first reconnoissance which the volunteers had made, and consequently proved very interesting to them.

There was no lack of work for these troops, and every day

found them engaged in some highly necessary, though not always pleasant, service.

The summer was at its height, the days were hot and sultry, while the nights were often cold and damp. The men were frequently obliged to engage all day in the most laborious occupations, and at night go on guard.

The work was indeed severe. Through the treachery of arch traitors while in government office, the fortress had been dismantled to a great extent of its customary armament. These ravages had to be repaired, guns mounted upon the high parapet, and others, whose carriages had gone to decay, remounted.

Of draught-horses or mules, there were few, if any, in the department; but there were plenty of wagons, and into these the men were harnessed, drawing heavy loads of ammunition and stores from the wharves into the fortress. While one party was doing this labor, another was engaged in unloading vessels and steamers at the piers, and still another employed in the very severe work of mounting heavy guns, a work which consisted in slinging the gun (oftentimes a large columbiad, weighing several thousand pounds) between two heavy iron wheels, dragging the whole from the ordnance-yard into the fort, up the steep embankment, and then placing it in position. This labor was often performed while the mercury was ranging in the vicinity of 100°, and was not seldom followed by a drill.

On the first day of July, the regiment was ordered to Hampton Village. Here it occupied a number of deserted houses, and picketed the country for several miles around the town. On the 4th, it marched from the village to Camp Hamilton, where, in connection with other troops, it was reviewed by Hon. Simon Cameron, Secretary of War.

Returning to its quarters in the town, it remained there till July 16, the latter date making the expiration of its term.

On this day, the regiment was ordered to Fortress Monroe. Here it and the Fourth Regiment, whose term expired the same day, were reviewed by General Butler and Colonel Justin Dimick. Colonel Dimick was in command of the fortress at the time of the arrival of these regiments. He was an old soldier, having seen service in Mexico and in several Indian wars. Like most professional soldiers, he rarely indulged in speech-making; but the trying circumstances under which he had been placed during the early days of the Rebellion; the timely and almost Providential arrival of these troops, which enabled him to hold the fortress against the machinations of several of his former associates in arms, who had resigned their commissions in the regular army and espoused the cause of the Confederacy; the intelligent appreciation of the situation which the volunteers had manifested, and their willingness to do any service required of them, no matter how menial or severe, had touched very deeply the heart of this old officer, and he could not suffer them to be dismissed without expressing to them his sense of gratitude for what they had done. Mounted upon his little dapple gray, with uncovered head, and voice as tremulous with emotion as that of an aged father taking leave of a beloved son, he recounted the exciting events in the early service of the regiments at that place, the confusion and distrust that prevailed at the time of their arrival, bore eloquent testimony to the manner in which they had performed their duties, and concluded by thanking them in the name of the Republic which they had helped to save.

When the old hero turned away, his eyes were suffused with tears, and the troops sent up cheer upon cheer as their only response.

The reception tendered these regiments upon their arrival in Boston proved that their services were as well appreciated by the people of Massachusetts as by their veteran commander.

CHAPTER X.

THE FOURTH REGIMENT OF MASSACHUSETTS MILITIA AT FORTRESS MONROE — THE SERVICE IT RENDERED THE COUNTRY — ORDERED TO NEWPORT NEWS — BATTLE OF GREAT BETHEL — RETURN TO MASSACHUSETTS.

For the reasons already stated, it seems necessary to give a brief account of the doings of the Fourth Regiment while in the field, embracing as they do a part of the record of the companies of Captains Barnes, Leach, and Clarke, of the Twenty-ninth Regiment.

The Fourth Regiment was originally composed of nine companies. Of these, Norfolk County contributed four: Company "A" of Canton, Captain Ira Drake; "C" of Braintree, Captain Cephas C. Bumpus; "D" of Randolph, Captain Horace Niles; and "H" of Quincy, Captain Franklin Curtis. Bristol County, three: Company "B" of Easton, Captain Milo M. Williams; "G" of Taunton, Captain Timothy Gordon; and "F" of Foxborough, Captain David L. Shepard. And Plymouth County, two: Company "E" of South Abington, Captain Charles F. Allen; and "I" of Hingham, Captain Luther Stephenson, Jr.

The regiment mustered for duty, at the time of its departure from Massachusetts, 636 officers and enlisted men.

Its field and staff were as follows: Colonel, Abner B. Packard, Quincy; Lieutenant-Colonel, Hawkes Fearing, Jr., Hingham; Major, Horace O. Whittemore, Boston; Adjutant, Henry Walker, Quincy; Quartermaster, William H. Carruth, Boston; Surgeon, Henry M. Saville, Quincy; Surgeon's Mate, William L. Faxon, Quincy.

As was the case with nearly all the militia regiments that entered the service of the United States in 1861, the Fourth Regiment afterwards furnished from among its officers and men, a large number of officers, some of them of high rank, for the various three years' regiments of Massachusetts and other States.

For instance, Captain Charles F. Allen of South Abington became Major in the Thirty-eighth Massachusetts. Lieutenant-Colonel Fearing subsequently became Colonel of the Eighth New Hampshire; Major Whittemore, Lieutenant-Colonel of the Thirtieth Massachusetts; Captain Luther Stephenson, Jr. (Co. I), Lieutenant-Colonel of the Thirty-second Massachusetts; and Corporal W. D. Tripp (Co. G) became Captain of Company F of the Twenty-ninth Regiment.

While waiting at the State House, on the 17th of April, where the regiment had reported itself for duty upon only twelve hours' notice, it was addressed by Governor Andrew in the following manner: —

"*Officers and Soldiers of the Fourth Regiment:*

"It gives me unspeakable pleasure to witness this array from the good Old Colony. You have come from the shores of the sounding sea, where lie the ashes of Pilgrims, and you are bound on a high and noble pilgrimage for liberty, for the Union and Constitution of your country. Soldiers of the Old Bay State, sons of sires who never disgraced their flag in civil life or on the tented field, I thank you from the bottom of my heart for this noble response to the call of your State and country. You cannot wait for words. I bid you God-speed — an affectionate farewell!"

A special train conveyed the regiment to Fall River, where it arrived on the afternoon of this day, and embarked upon the steamer "State of Maine," for New York. Quite late in the afternoon of the 18th, it reached the latter city, and on the following morning sailed for Fortress Monroe on the same steamer.

At the time of the departure of the regiment from New York, great fears were entertained for the safety of this fortress. It was known that Colonel Dimick, its commander, had but a meagre garrison; that the fort was in a poor state for defence, and was being closely besieged by the hostile militia of Virginia, then under cunning and able officers, formerly of our regular army, who knew every weak point about the works. The fortress was momentarily expected, therefore, to fall into the hands of the enemy, and when the steamer "State of Maine" hove in sight, on the morning of the 20th of April, it was not considered prudent by the officers of the regiment to attempt a landing, till daylight should solve the troublesome mystery.

The steamer lay off and on for an hour or more; the men were all on deck, looking anxiously in the direction of the fortress, waiting with throbbing hearts for the first gleam of approaching day; questioning, doubting, the while, which flag — that of their country or the insurgents — would reveal itself to their sight.

Meanwhile the dark form of the steamer had been observed from the fortress, and doubts as to the character of the vessel, not less troublesome than those of the volunteers on board, had seized fast hold upon the garrison. The guns of the "Water Battery" were shotted and manned, and every preparation made to repel the attack of the possible foe.

At last the morning sun lighted up the low walls and green parapets of the fort, and from its tall flagstaff the Stars and Stripes were seen floating gracefully in the wind. The old flag flying from the peak of the steamer caught the watching eyes of the garrison at the same moment; the grim guns in the "Water Battery" were unshotted, and, instead of angry defiance, sent out loud peals of welcome. The men on board the steamer replied with hearty cheers; the boat hauled up to the wharf; the men immediately disembarked and marched into the fortress, where they were received with every manifestation of joy. The safety of the fort was now assured, confidence took the place of dark doubts, and the cause of the Government in that department wore a brighter hue.

By this opportune arrival of the Fourth Regiment, and the Third also, which came a little later in the day, Fortress Monroe was undoubtedly saved to the Government, and for this almost priceless service to the country, the people are largely indebted to the unsleeping vigilance of John A. Andrew, and to the ardent patriotism of the volunteers of the Third and Fourth regiments of Massachusetts Militia. From the time of the arrival of the Fourth Regiment till the 27th of May, its men were almost constantly on duty in and about the fortress, mounting cannon, and having an experience similar to that of the Third Regiment.

On the 21st of May, the steamer "Cambridge" arrived from Boston, bringing, among other troops, the companies commanded by Captains Doten, Leach, Chipman, and Barnes.

Captains Leach's and Barnes's companies, and, subsequently, that of Captain Clarke, were assigned to the Fourth, and the others to the Third Regiment.

The number of troops in and about the fortress was now sufficient to justify the occupation of a greater extent of territory. On the 26th of May, an order was issued, directing the establishment of a camp at the mouth of the James River, at a place known as and properly written "Newport's News," though more commonly written Newport News,* which spelling we adopt, as it is better known to our soldiers by that name. Newport News was a cultivated plateau of nearly two miles in length, extending back from the river a distance of half a mile, where it bordered upon an extensive forest of pine. The banks of the James here rose to a height of thirty feet, from the sides of which bubbled out numerous springs of pure water.

Colonel John W. Phelps was given charge of this expedition. He was a celebrated artillerist. Born in Vermont in 1813, he graduated at West Point in 1836, and was brevetted to the Fourth Artillery. A First Lieutenant in the Mexican war, he served with distinguished gallantry on Scott's line. At Contreras and Churubusco, in command of a company in the storming brigade of Riley, his services were conspicuous and exceptionally brilliant. For this he was brevetted a Captain, but declined the distinction. He was the originator of the text-books for heavy artillery in use before the war, and commanded a battery in the Utah expedition of Albert Sidney Johnston, and at one time commanded Fort Brown, Texas. He was an uncompromising enemy of human slavery, and, becoming dissatisfied with what he regarded as the pro-slavery sentiment of both the army and the administration, in 1859, resigned his commission and at once settled in Brattleborough, Vt. In the spring of 1861, he was made

---

* So called (as the author has learned, from an ancient tradition among the inhabitants of that region) from the fact, that, about the year 1609, the starving colonists of that place were succored by the timely arrival of a fleet of vessels, laden with provisions, under the command of Admiral Newport of the English navy. The worthy admiral brought the pinched colonists *good news*, and in honor of the event, and as an expression of their gratitude, they called the place *Newport's News*.

Colonel of the First Vermont Militia, and shortly afterwards came to Fortress Monroe, as has already been stated. Colonel Phelps was a superior soldier, and a most valuable acquisition to the army in any department.

The troops which composed the expedition to Newport News were the Fourth Massachusetts Militia, First Vermont Militia, and Colonel Bendix's Seventh New York (German),— all infantry. Captains Barnes's and Clarke's companies went with the Fourth Regiment, while Captain Leach's company was, by order of General Butler, retained in the fort to perform garrison duty. The troops embarked at an early hour on the morning of the 27th. As the steamboat which had on board the Fourth Regiment was passing into the mouth of the James River, the Confederate batteries on Sewall's Point opened a brisk fire upon it. One of the shots, a huge missile, passed over the decks, just above the heads of the men, while the others fell short.

The Fourth Regiment was sent from Fortress Monroe to this distant post with a very small supply of ammunition. Captain Barnes's company had only twenty rounds of cartridges and ten percussion-caps to each man; while Clarke's company, which had a kind of arm different from the rest of the command, had brought from Boston a large supply of ammunition, about 14,000 rounds of ball-cartridges and 20,000 extra percussion-caps. No tents were supplied the troops that went to Newport News until about a week after they reached there. In the meantime, the men lived in huts made of rails and covered with branches of trees and bushes.

As soon as Colonel Phelps arrived, he began the erection of earthworks. These were of semi-circular form, terminating at either extremity on the bank of the river, and were nearly half a mile long. In the ditch in front of the works were placed obstructions of the nature of *chevaux-de-frise*. On the main works commanding the plain and forest were mounted a number of heavy guns, while on the bluff facing the river was a battery of five large pieces, and among them a Sawyer and James rifle. Upon these works the men of the Fourth Regiment and those of Barnes's and Clarke's companies labored for many days, and at a time when the weather was extremely hot. The men were wholly unaccustomed to such work, being compelled, from the scarcity of draught animals in the department, to draw from the adjacent forest the logs which were used on the fortifications.

On the 5th of June, the troops here had an opportunity to witness for the first time a battle. The United States gunboat "Harriet Lane," a low side-wheel steamer, came up the river and attacked a Confederate sand-battery on Pig Point, directly opposite Newport News. The fight was a lively one, though of short duration, in the course of which the vessel was several times struck, and a number of her men badly wounded. During the affair, the steamer captured a supply-sloop of the enemy, and towed it down to the fort.

June 6, a body of mounted Confederates made a sudden dash upon a working party near a place afterwards known as "Number Nine Picket," in the forest, in front of the centre of our main works. The long roll was beaten, and the camp quickly put under arms. Captain Barnes was ordered out with his company, but the enemy had fled before his arrival at the place of attack. The company then went forward on the main road to "Lee's House." On the way out, one of Barnes's scouts saw one of the enemy leading his horse along a road that ran near the edge of the forest. The scout fired upon the enemy, who, unhurt, mounted and fled. At Lee's House, a large number of negroes were congregated, old and young, and considerable information was obtained from them in relation to the movements of the enemy in that vicinity, and especially in regard to the mounted men that had made the assault upon our working party. While here, and just as the company was returning, Captain Luther Stephenson of the Fourth Regiment came up rapidly with his company, having been ordered by General Phelps to go out to Barnes's support. After a brief pause, both companies returned to camp. The information obtained was reported to the General, and Barnes and Stephenson were ordered to return after dark that night to Lee's House with their commands, with directions to use their discretion as to how far they should proceed into the country. The two commands spent the night at this place, throwing out pickets into the fields and on the edge of the woods. The next morning, the companies of Captains Barnes and Stephenson reconnoitred in the direction of "Smith's Farm," about six miles up the river.

During the day, small bodies of Confederates were several times seen, but no collision occurred. When the companies were near Smith's place, a negro was observed skulking in the bushes. He was brought before the officers and questioned by them concerning the country and the location of the enemy's camp. From this negro the Captains obtained very valuable information relating to the enemy's works at a place called Great Bethel. The colored man was taken to Newport News, where he was examined by Colonel Phelps and one of the staff officers of General Butler. In a few days after this reconnoissance, General Butler issued his orders for the expedition against Great Bethel.

The movement on Great Bethel occurred on the 10th of June, 1861. Great Bethel was the name of a church located in the midst of a sparsely-settled country, about nine miles on the road leading south from Hampton, in the direction of, and some twelve miles from, Yorktown, in York County. Here, and also at another place near by called Little Bethel, were bodies of Confederate troops, being a part of the command of Colonel J. Bankhead Magruder.* The latter place was an outpost or picket-station of the camp at Great Bethel. The Federal movement was made in two columns: one from Hampton, consisting of Colonel Townsend's Third New York Infantry, Colonel Duryea's Fifth New York (Zouaves) Infantry, with two mountain howitzers; and the second column from Newport News, consisting of one field-piece (6-pounder), under Lieutenant Greble of the United States army, three companies of the Seventh New York † Infantry, under Colonel Bendix, three companies of the Fourth Massachusetts Militia Infantry, namely, Companies "G" of Taunton, "F" of Foxborough, and "H" of Quincy, the companies commanded by Captains Clarke and Barnes, and five companies of the First Vermont Militia Infantry.

* "First Year of the War," by Pollard, page 77.
† General Butler's report to Lieutenant-General Scott, published in New York "Tribune" of June 14, 1861.

The last-named ten companies formed a battalion, and were commanded by Lieutenant-Colonel Washburn of the First Vermont, assisted by Major Whittemore and Adjutant Walker of the Fourth Massachusetts and Adjutant Hiram Stephens of the First Vermont. The expedition was commanded by Brigadier-General Ebenezer W. Pierce of the Massachusetts Militia. The column from Newport News marched at about midnight of the 9th, and the column from Hampton earlier in the evening, the distance being greater. The two columns were to form a junction in the vicinity of Little Bethel early on the following morning.

The advance of the column from Hampton, consisting of Duryea's Zouaves, passed the junction of the road from Newport News with the main road from Hampton, the point designated for the two columns to unite, shortly before daybreak, moved rapidly forward, and surprised the enemy's outpost at Little Bethel.

Immediately afterwards, at about daybreak, the column from Newport News arrived at the point named for uniting, and in the absence of any knowledge that the Zouaves had already passed the point, turned to the left, and entering upon the main road, moved rapidly forward toward Little Bethel, with the view of accomplishing what had already been done without their knowledge.

At this stage of affairs, the Vermont and Massachusetts troops being all upon the main road, following the Zouaves and the rear of the Newport News column, consisting of the three German companies (Seventh New York) and a piece of artillery, dragged by hand, being just at the junction, not having made the turn into the main road, the head of Colonel Townsend's regiment, the rear of the Hampton column, made its appearance over the top of the hill, on the main road from Hampton, rapidly approaching the junction. A small belt of woods, without undergrowth, at the intersection of the two roads, lay between the three German companies and the main road, on which Townsend's men were moving. At the head of Colonel Townsend's column rode General Pierce and many other mounted officers, giving it the appearance, "in the magnifying dusk of the early morning," of a body of cavalry. Colonel Bendix, supposing from these circumstances that the approaching column was a body of Confederate cavalry, and the column from Hampton being under a similar delusion as to the character of the Germans, partially hid as they were by the woods, the two columns immediately fired upon each other, and a brisk · interchange of musketry ensued, to which the Germans added the fire of their 6-pounder, as soon as they could run it into position on the main road.

The column from Hampton then fell back behind the crest of the hill to form, leaving several of their number killed and wounded on the field. The heads of the two columns moving toward Little Bethel, as already indicated, at once countermarched on the double-quick to the scene of action. Upon arriving there, the firing had ceased. Colonel Townsend's regiment was not in sight, and the Germans were in line of battle in an open field, having moved through the belt of woods toward their supposed enemy. The Vermont and Massachusetts troops of the advanced column, being nearest, reached the place first, and formed in line in front of the German companies, with the exception of Captain Clarke's company of this command, which, as support to Lieutenant Greble's gun, moved with that officer up the road to the brow of the hill. Lieutenant Greble, who was in advance, mounted, came upon the wounded of Townsend's regiment, and the fatal error was at once apparent. Meantime Townsend's regiment had formed behind the hill, and on the appearance of the troops at the brow of the hill, discharged their howitzer, happily without effect. Duryea's Zouaves had also returned and taken position.

The mistake having been discovered, the several bodies united and proceeded toward Bethel. A surprise was now out of the question, the enemy having undoubtedly been alarmed by the firing.

It was well into the forenoon when our troops arrived in front of the enemy's works at Great Bethel. As our column was moving slowly by the flank, on the main road, an officer from the front came up and informed each company commander that they were near the enemy, and directed them to keep their men well closed up. Shortly after, while our force was still on the main road and not yet in sight of the enemy's works, a heavy gun was fired from that quarter, and the shot passed over the heads of our men, through the tops of the trees. The column at once halted, and the several regiments quickly moved out of the road. Duryea's went to the right and halted, while the battalion of Colonel Washburn moved to the left into an open field, and formed in line of battle near a fence, a belt of woods in front shutting off a view of the enemy. Soon after this, the Zouaves were ordered forward; they went by the flank through the woods on the edge of the road, and came suddenly upon the enemy's works, which proved to be quite formidable, being nearly a fourth of a mile in length, mounting several guns, and defended by a body of infantry and a battery of field-pieces. There was but one direct approach, and this was across a narrow wooden bridge that spanned a brook in front of the works, about three feet deep and from twelve to fifteen feet wide. The right of the enemy was protected by an impassable morass or swamp, and their left by fallen timber and other obstructions. The Zouaves attempted to charge directly across the bridge, but encountering a terrible fire of both artillery and musketry, fell back with a loss of four killed and eleven wounded, and, among the latter, Captain Kilpatrick (afterwards General Kilpatrick of cavalry fame).* Colonel Washburn's battalion remained in the position we have indicated for nearly thirty minutes, during all of which time there was heavy firing at the front, and was then moved by the right flank across the main road into the woods on the right of the road, and halted just inside of the edge of the woods, an open field being in their front; and although from this position the enemy's works were still invisible, yet their bullets were coming into the woods literally in showers. To this point a considerable number of the Zouaves had retired, and were seen lying flat upon the ground. In the near vicinity was Lieutenant Greble, with his gun, actively engaged with the enemy, Captain Clarke's company being his main support. The battalion was again put in

* Letter to the New York "Tribune," June 14, 1861.

motion, and after passing a short distance to the right, came to "a sort of dry ditch, with a high embankment in front," opposite the left of the enemy's position, with an open field between them and the enemy. Only three Massachusetts companies were now with the battalion; namely, Captain Barnes's company, Company G of Taunton, and Company H of Quincy (Fourth Regiment). Captain Shepard's company ("F") had been left at Little Bethel as a guard. Soon the order came from Colonel Washburn to charge. The Massachusetts men climbed the embankment, and sprang forward toward the enemy's works in their immediate front, under a severe though wild and random fire of both musketry and cannon. The ground was somewhat descending, and after a rapid run of a few minutes, the men came to the brook before referred to. Captain Barnes led his company, and jumped at once into the brook, Lieutenants Osgood and Keen doing likewise; and the men following their brave example, all were quickly on the enemy's side, at the very foot of the works. Here they were greeted with a severe volley of musketry, mingled with grape; but our men were unharmed, and, rising from the ground, ran up the embankment and discharged their pieces among the enemy, who were now considerably confused, and in some parts of their works apparently falling back. Our soldiers were also much excited, and probably fired wildly, doing little execution, for this was the first time they had faced a hostile gun; but they kept at it till ordered to stop, running up the bank to fire, and then dropping back to load. This was the golden moment in the battle, which, had it been improved by the commanding officer of our forces, would have unquestionably resulted in the capture of the works; but instead of seconding the brave efforts of our assaulting party, all the rest of the Federal force (excepting Greble and his gun) were allowed to remain inactive. This state of things continued for several minutes, — perhaps fifteen, — when Horace Colby of Barnes's company was instantly killed, and Frank L. Souther of Company H (Fourth Regiment) mortally wounded. There were less than two hundred men across the brook, these being mainly Massachusetts men of the companies of Barnes, Gordon, and Curtis. Colonel Washburn, Major Whittemore, and Adjutants Walker and Stephens were also there. The enemy observing the utter cessation of hostilities at all other points, had recovered from their first surprise, and now held all parts of their works. Finally, Colonel Washburn, perceiving that he was not to be supported, and that his men on the breastworks were liable at any moment to be flanked or driven into the ditch and captured (for the enemy greatly outnumbered them), gave the order to withdraw. The East Boston men seized the dead body of Colby and attempted to carry it off, but found it impossible to do so. The men fell back more deliberately than veterans, for veterans would have run; while these proud and inexperienced soldiers of Massachusetts, thinking it unmilitary to run, walked steadily backward to the woods, often pausing to load and fire. One of them, Stewart (Barnes's company), whose gun was so foul that it could not be discharged, showed his pluck by snapping caps at the enemy as he went away.

About this time, Major Winthrop of General Butler's staff was killed, and, shortly after, Lieutenant Greble, at his gun. No further effort was made to capture the works, and the order to retreat was given to our whole force, which now retired in good order, no pursuit whatever being attempted by the enemy. Lieutenant Greble's gun was hauled from its exposed position into the woods, and the body of that gallant officer was lashed to it and conveyed to Fortress Monroe, where it was received with many manifestations of grief. The body of Major Winthrop, together with several others killed and wounded, were left upon the field.

The casualties among the Massachusetts troops were as follows: Horace Colby of Captain Barnes's company, and Matthew Fitzpatrick of Captain Clarke's company, were killed; Sergeant A. H. DeCosta of Captain Clarke's company, and Frank L. Souther of the Fourth Regiment, were wounded, the latter mortally.

The total Union loss in this battle has been variously estimated at from twenty-five to forty, killed and wounded. The loss of the Confederates was small, one authority giving it as one killed and seven wounded. A few days after the battle, a flag of truce was sent out from our lines, to discover the condition of our dead and wounded. Major Cary of the Confederates met our flag, and informed the officer in charge that our dead had been properly buried upon the field, and our wounded suitably cared for. The personal effects of Major Winthrop, including his gold watch, were given up to our officer in charge of the flag.

The contemporary estimate of the importance of this affair is very ludicrous, when viewed in the light of the subsequent events of the war. General Butler comforted himself by saying, "Our troops have learned confidence in themselves under fire, the enemy have shown that they will not meet us in the open field, and our officers have learned wherein their organization and drill are inefficient."* The Northern press regarded it as "a severe engagement"; while in the South it was spoken of as "a brilliant victory," and was even made the subject of a spirited lyric published in the New Orleans "Delta." One Frank I. Wilson of Raleigh N. C., in 1864, published a pamphlet of twenty-eight pages, mostly devoted to a description of this skirmish, prefaced by various heroic mottoes and quotations from Halleck and other authors. The book contains many extravagant statements, and besides giving the names of some of the officers and troops engaged, is of little value as a contribution to the history of the war, which statement is well illustrated by the assertion of its author, on page 19, that the loss of the Federals "was about three hundred killed and as many more wounded."

Some of the statements of Northern writers are nearly as much at variance with the truth as those above quoted. Mr. Abbott, in his "History of the Civil War" (Vol. I., p. 151), says of Major Winthrop, that "he fell dead nearer the enemy's works than any other man"; while Mr. Parton says, quoting from the report of the Confederate Colonel, D. H. Hill ("Butler in New Orleans," page 146), that Major Winthrop "was the only man in the Union force who displayed even an approximation to courage." While the author has no desire to

---

* General Butler's report to Lieutenant-General Scott, printed in New York "Tribune" of June 14, 1861.

detract from the fame of Major Winthrop, who was unquestionably a brave man, yet these statements are grossly false, and cruelly unjust to the other officers and men who took part in the battle. Colonel Duryea's men charged the enemy's works with great bravery, as did also the Massachusetts troops under Lieutenant-Colonel Washburn; and had there been proper concert of action, these assaults would have doubtless led to victory. Horace Colby of Captain Barnes's company fell on the slope of the enemy's works, and his comrades, in endeavoring to recover his body, were obliged to drag it off by the legs; while, according to the best authority, Major Winthrop fell thirty yards from the enemy's works, being shot while standing on a log viewing the Confederate position on their right.

Since the author has had the subject of this battle under consideration, he has consulted *very high* and *reliable* Confederate authority in regard to it, from which he has obtained the following facts: On the 8th of June, 1861, the First North Carolina Regiment of Infantry, under Colonel Daniel H. Hill (General D. H. Hill), moved down from Yorktown, where it had been in camp, to the near neighborhood of Great Bethel. On the 9th of June, Colonel Magruder (General Magruder) came from Yorktown and ordered Colonel Hill to move before day of the 10th, to rebuild a bridge near Hampton, that had been destroyed by the Federals. Colonel Hill did not like the movement, and requested Colonel Magruder, his senior, to accompany him. Magruder consented, and before daylight on the 10th, the Confederate troops, consisting of Hill's regiment, 700 strong, some Virginia companies of infantry under Lieutenant-Colonel Stewart, about 200, a company of Virginia Howitzers (Richmond Howitzers), numbering about 100 men, started on their march. After having gone three or four miles, day broke upon them, when they met a Mrs. Trumbell, who informed them that the Federals had been at her house that morning, and but for an accident which had occurred, whereby they had fired upon one another, they would have reached Bethel by daylight. Upon receiving this information, Magruder ordered the troops to halt, and then ordered them to fall back toward Great Bethel. Upon reaching the ground on the south side of the intersection of the two roads, between Little and Great Bethel, Colonel Magruder thought he would divide his force and send a portion of his command, together with the Howitzers, down the Back River road; but Colonel Hill, who was an excellent soldier. suggested that they had better keep together, occupy their works at Great Bethel, and wait for the approach of the Federals. This was finally agreed upon, and the wisdom of such a course is apparent from what followed.

When the movement was made by the Federals on the enemy's left flank, "it created some alarm"; and when the movement on their right flank was made by Townsend's regiment, "Magruder ordered the Virginians, who were holding the pits in advance of the creek, to abandon them"; but Colonel Hill sent Captain Bridger, with his company, to reoccupy them, which he did. About this time, Magruder, supposing his whole right flank to be enveloped, ordered a retreat of all his forces on Yorktown. This order was, however, recalled, when, soon after, Colonel M. discovered his mistake.

The Federal movement on the enemy's left flank. "which created some alarm," referred to by our informant. and spoken of above, was unquestionably that of the battalion of Lieutenant-Colonel Washburn, one of our Massachusetts officers engaged in it having always insisted that the enemy were retreating when our men reached their works. That the works charged by the battalion were the enemy's main works, is beyond dispute; and the fact that the Confederates temporarily retired from them, is distinctly stated by Mr. Pollard, in his book entitled the "First Year of the War," page 77.

The author has not gone into the numerous details of this battle with any erroneous idea of its importance, but simply because it was the first pitched battle of the war, and the facts concerning it have been much in dispute, and because it shows how the raw troops of both armies fought at that very early period.

General Butler thought the enemy cowardly because they fought behind works; but the fact that they did so, proves that they were commanded by good officers, who knew something about fighting; while the fact that General Butler failed to place some experienced officer — like General Phelps, for instance — in command of the expedition, shows that he had quite as much to learn as his troops, and even more than some of his lieutenants. The battle was, perhaps, well planned, but was fought by the Federals with very little skill. There was something of the same assurance of easy victory on our part which characterized the battle of Bull Run, that so soon followed.

On the 29th of June, a scouting party went out from Newport News and captured four of the enemy, who were in full zouave uniform, and belonged to a Louisiana regiment. On the same day, the Fourth Regiment was ordered to embark, but for some reason its departure was delayed until the second day of July, when, in pursuance of orders from General Butler, it proceeded by steamer to Hampton, and occupied that town with the Third Regiment.* In the forenoon of the 4th, both regiments marched to Camp Hamilton, were reviewed by General Pierce, and in the afternoon by General Butler and Secretary Cameron. On the 11th of July, the regiment marched to Fortress Monroe, preparatory to embarking for home, and there exchanged their Springfield muskets "for old, altered, flint-lock guns." † While stopping at Fortress Monroe, the men were addressed by General Butler and Colonel Dimick.

On the 15th, the regiment went on board the steamer "S. R. Spaulding," and after a passage of about fifty-six hours, reached Boston Harbor, landed on Long Island, and there remained till the 22d; on the latter day proceeding to the city, and being reviewed on Boston Common by Governor Andrew.

The disaster of Bull Run had so far depressed the feelings of the people, that the reception in Boston was not attended with that degree of enthusiasm which the soldiers had reason to expect; but every loyal heart was sorrow-stricken then, and the appearance of the bronzed faces of the men, and their well-worn uniforms, served only as a reminder of the sad realities of war. The local receptions given the various com-

---

* Statement of Adjutant Walker, "Mass. Military Record," page 158.
† Statement of same officer, ibid., page 169.

panics were, however, most cordial: bells were rung, flags displayed, and speeches of welcome were made.

These and other soldiers of our militia performed, in the early days of the war, a part similar to that of the Minutemen of the Revolution, and the gratitude of a liberty-loving people will ever be accorded to them.

CHAPTER XI.

The Review in Fortress Monroe — A Fourth of July Battle — Formation of the Massachusetts Battalion — Captain Leach's Company Sent to the Rip-Raps — Guarding Prisoners — Burning of Hampton by the Confederates — The Battalion Sent to Newport News.

We have already spoken of the presence in the department of the Secretary of War, and his review of the Third and Fourth regiments at Camp Hamilton. On the fourth day of July, the garrison of Fortress Monroe was reviewed by that officer, General Butler, and Colonel Dimick. At that time Captain Leach's company was stationed at the fort, and was reviewed with the rest of the troops. Probably no member of that company will soon forget the chagrin which he and all his comrades experienced that day on account of the shabbiness of their uniforms. There was not one soldier in ten of the company whose trousers were not in tatters, and whose shirt — for they had neither dress-coats nor blouses — was not faded to a dingy yellow and out at the elbows. The grotesque style of their uniforms, which are particularly described in a previous chapter, and the poor quality of their arms, added to their generally ragged condition, made them disagreeably conspicuous, especially as they formed on the immediate left of the regulars, a well-drilled and finely-uniformed and equipped body of soldiers. When the inspecting party, in full dress, came riding down the line, and their eyes fell upon the shabby-looking Massachusetts boys, Secretary Cameron was so much surprised, that he turned to General Butler and asked, " What terribly ragged troops are these?" The General was greatly mortified to be compelled to state in reply, that they were Massachusetts volunteers. When the equipments of the men were inspected by one of the staff officers, he found that their cartridge-boxes were empty, although they had been on duty there for more than a month.* The public disgrace which the men were compelled to suffer on this occasion was partially compensated on the following day, by an issue to them of a full suit of United States infantry uniform, including the dress-hat and coat.

Beside this inspection, the Fourth was attended by two other incidents of an entirely different nature. A little after noon, the United States gunboat "Pawnee" weighed anchor, and, steaming across the Roads, commenced a spirited attack upon the Confederate land-batteries at Sewall's Point. The fight took place in plain view of the whole garrison, the troops off duty lining the parapets and watching every movement and every shot with the most intense interest. The steamer was very rapid in her movements, and managed to expose but little of her hull to the enemy's gunners. Her shell were often seen to explode in the tree-tops and about the shore, while those of the hostile batteries frequently passed through her rigging and plunged into the water near her, throwing up beautiful jets of silvery spray and foam.

Towards night a threatening black cloud arose in the south, while a fresh wind was blowing from the opposite quarter. There were a number of war-vessels in the Roads, and among them the brig "Perry," a very snugly-rigged and peculiarly trim-looking vessel. About six o'clock, the latter was observed to be making sail, and in the course of a few minutes was heading towards Cape Henry, speeding before the breeze like a bird. It was but a short time before the hull of the vessel was lost to view; but against the dark background of the clouds, from out of which there frequently came flashes of lightning, the snowy sails of the brig were for a long time plainly visible.

At short distances apart, along the shore near which she was passing, were Confederate sand-batteries. As the brig approached them, suddenly a flash of flame was seen to dart out of the woods on the shore, and quickly in response a flash from under the white sails of the vessel, — for her hull was

---

* Some fellow, in a spirit of fun-making, had filled the cartridge-box of an unsuspecting comrade with white beans; an incident that greatly amused the inspecting officer, and led him to inquire of the soldier if he had mistaken his cartridge-box for his haversack.

still invisible, — and then, after the lapse of a few seconds, came reverberating across the dark water the sullen boom of a gun, mingled with a peal of thunder. This fine display continued till some time after it was quite dark, when the rain began to descend in large drops, driving the spectators from the parapets. There was a succession of heavy rainstorms, accompanied by severe thunder and lightning, lasting nearly all night.

When the Third and Fourth regiments retired from the service, the seven three-years' companies became so many unattached and independent commands, the necessities of whose members, as well as the true interests of the Government, demanded that they should speedily become an organized body, having a responsible commander and such other officers as the actual needs of field life always require. General Butler, appreciating the situation of these soldiers, promptly issued the following order: —

"HEADQUARTERS DEPARTMENT OF VIRGINIA,
"FORTRESS MONROE, VA., July 16, 1861.
"SPECIAL ORDERS, No. 144.

"Captain Barnes, Massachusetts Volunteers, is assigned to the command of the companies of Massachusetts Volunteers now in the department and not organized into a regiment. Captain Barnes will appoint from the subalterns of his command an officer to perform the duties of an Acting Assistant Quartermaster and Acting Assistant Commissary of Subsistence.

"(Official.)   By command of Major-General Butler.
               "(Signed)   T. J. HAINES, A. A. A. G.
               "(Signed)   WM. D. WHIPPLE, A. A. G."

Captain Barnes, upon assuming command of these troops (which were designated by Adjutant-General Schouler, in his reports, as the First Battalion of Massachusetts Volunteers), appointed First Lieutenant John B. Collingwood, Adjutant; First Lieutenant Joshua Norton, 3d, Acting Assistant Quartermaster; and Sergeant Henry S. Braden, Sergeant-Major.

By an order from General Butler, also dated July 16, Captain Leach was directed to proceed with his company to the little island in Hampton Roads known as the Rip-Raps, to relieve a detachment of the Third Regiment there stationed. Here, some years before, the Government had begun the erection of a fortification called Fort Calhoun, the name of which was changed during the war to Fort Wool. Several guns had been mounted about the partially-completed works, and on the wharf a rifled cannon of heavy calibre, known as the Sawyer rifle. The island was then being used as a place of confinement for Confederate prisoners and Federal soldiers under sentence of court-martial, though at the time Captain Leach took command, there were only four or five prisoners at the place, and those civilians, who had been captured by the Union gunboats in the act of transporting from the eastern shore of Virginia to the enemy's camp at Yorktown, arms and munitions of war; but, later in the year, a part of the prisoners captured by General Burnside in his Hatteras expedition were sent here, swelling the number to about sixty. These prisoners were comfortably quartered in a part of one of the barracks occupied by Captain Leach's men, and were provided with the same rations as the soldiers, which were ample and wholesome, being treated in many respects by our men more like companions than prisoners; they were usually allowed the liberties of the island, subjected to little if any restraint, passing the long summer days in fishing from the wharf, and watching the movements of our war-vessels.

On the 26th of July, Captain Tyler's company, then commanded by Captain Wilson, was also ordered to Fort Wool. With the exception of mounting cannon, a work never regarded by the soldiers with much favor, the duties imposed upon the garrison here were very light, the limited size of the grounds making it impossible to conduct any military evolutions, beside a simple dress-parade, and hence the men were exempted from drill duty, an immunity, however, that was not at all to their advantage.

A short time before the transfer of Captain Leach's company to this post, a number of the privates and non-commissioned officers of his command had been detailed for guard duty on board the United States gunboat "Anacosta," then commanded by Commander Collins, U. S. N., the same officer who afterwards, while in command of the "Wachusett," so distinguished himself by the capture of the Confederate war-steamer "Florida," in the Bay of San Salvador.

The operations of the enemy in the vicinity of Sewall's Point, at the mouth of the Elizabeth River, about two and a half miles from the Rip-Raps, rendered it essential to maintain a close watch of that locality, as a successful night attack upon the little garrison at Fort Wool was entirely feasible. The duty performed by the "Anacosta" was that of watching at night the hostile shore, and warning our fleet in Hampton Roads of the approach of fire-rafts and floating torpedoes. Some time in August, the "Anacosta" was relieved, and the guard ordered to return to their company.

The country which lay between our lines and those of the enemy was to a great extent heavily wooded, was from ten to twelve miles in length, and extended from the shore of the Chesapeake Bay to the James River. Here and there throughout this wild region, in little clearings in the forest, often miles apart, were farm-houses and a few acres of cultivated land, and threading the whole country were numerous roads and horse-paths. This whole region was a common scouting-ground for both armies, and a love of adventure often led our soldiers to advance, in squads of ten or twenty, far into the country.

On the night of the 18th of July, a party composed of Major Rawlins, an officer of a Pennsylvania regiment, a Mr. Shurtleff, an artist, Major Halliday, Captain Jenkins, and two others, started from the vicinity of Fortress Monroe, and proceeded some eight miles toward Yorktown. This foolish adventure had a very sad termination, for while the party were picking their way along the dark forest road, they were fired upon by a body of the enemy, who lay concealed. Major Rawlins was killed, Jenkins and Shurtleff were captured, while Halliday and the rest of the party, by a hasty flight, managed to escape. This sad affair tended to check these ill-advised excursions, and to teach all who had a passion for reckless adventure a timely lesson.

The five companies under Barnes remained in Hampton, after the departure of the Fourth Regiment, until about July 30, when they were ordered back to the fort, and garrisoned a redoubt that during the summer had been erected just outside the water battery of the fortress, on the sand-beach. The Battalion remained here till August 5, when it was ordered by General Butler to take post at Camp Hamilton, about one mile distant from the fortress, and in the direction of Hampton. The number of troops in the department had been materially decreased since the battle of Bull Run, and it was doubtless considered imprudent for a small force to occupy Hampton, and accordingly the troops had all been drawn in from the town, and were now stationed at Camp Hamilton.

For several days there had been indications of an advance by the enemy in the direction of the town. Deserters and others who came into our lines reported that such a movement was in progress; but it was not till the 7th of August that these stories were confirmed. On that day, it became evident to all that the enemy in force were actually moving forward, and apparently directly towards Hampton. The purpose of this movement at this time could not be understood by our officers. Our troops were not occupying Hampton, and the small force at Camp Hamilton could, if necessary, be easily retired into the fortress; besides, the enemy could not expect to be able to occupy and hold either Hampton or Camp Hamilton, under the guns of the fort and our fleet. It was therefore thought that the movement towards the town was a ruse, and that the real attack would be made on the camp at Newport News. At sundown of the 7th, the position of affairs remained unchanged. One thing was clear: the enemy was advancing, and rapidly approaching Hampton. To guard against surprise, General Butler had directed that a number of transports be held in readiness to convey troops up the James, to Newport News, if necessary, and the reserve commands were ordered to be prepared to move at a moment's notice.

Besides the five companies of our Massachusetts Battalion, there were stationed at Camp Hamilton, Col. Max Weber's Twentieth New York Regiment and a portion of the Naval Brigade (Ninety-ninth New York Regiment).* A strong picket-line was posted on the bank of Hampton Creek; and at the bridge, which had been partially destroyed, was stationed a guard from the Battalion under Lieutenant Mayo of Company E. In the evening, General Butler visited the camp, for the purpose of ascertaining any new developments.

* Also called Union Coast Guard.

All was quiet, no sound came from the pickets, and the town was silent. The General, after imparting to the several battalion commanders such information and directions as he deemed essential, returned to the fort. The night was black, and the wind blew freshly from the south. At about nine o'clock, our pickets were suddenly startled by the shouting of the negroes (who still remained in the village), and presently the regular tramp of marching soldiers was heard by our men. Then appeared two long rows of torches, lighting up the dark, narrow ways and the windows of the deserted houses. Suddenly the column halted, and the flaming torches were seen dancing about wildly in all directions, like so many will-o'-the-wisps. And now the quiet of the night was broken by loud yells, the houses were entered and fired, and soon the whole town was enveloped in flames, casting a bright light over the bay, and revealing to our soldiers the forms of the enemy as they moved about the streets. Our Massachusetts men at the bridge soon began to fire, and the sharp crack of rifles was added to the roar of the flames. The fire of our soldiers became very galling to the enemy, and he sought to dislodge them, making a bold dash for the bridge, at the head of which stood our men, behind a hastily-constructed barricade. The bridge was long and narrow, and the enemy came on at a quick run. They had advanced but a short distance, when a sharp fire from our lines drove them back with some loss. Several other, though feeble, attempts were made to drive our men from the bridge; but each attempt signally failed, and the picket-firing was kept up at intervals throughout the night.

That was indeed a memorable night in the history of the Battalion. The loud roar of the flames, the cries of the terrified negroes as they were being driven from their huts by the enemy and marched off under guard into their lines, all combined to make up a wild scene the terror of which was not a little heightened by the presence of our gunboats in the Roads, which kept up a vigorous bombardment of the fields and woods about the town, and occasionally threw a huge shell into the burning village, scattering the fragments of the buildings, and carrying consternation to the enemy.

There were not lacking acts of brutality on the part of those who were guilty of this wicked deed. Living in the village were an old white gentleman and his aged wife, who had many times befriended the Union troops, and whose son was a major in that portion of the Confederate army that destroyed the town. This major led the burning party which fired the place; but not satisfied with this work, he must needs visit upon his parents, whom he suspected of harboring sentiments of loyalty to the old flag, an act of vengeance as cowardly as it was revolting. Going in the darkness to their house, which was on the outskirts of the village, in harsh tones he ordered them to leave it in fifteen minutes, or, to use his own language, "I'll burn it over your heads." These aged persons, having on scarcely any clothing save their night-garments, rushed out into the gloom of that awful night. The son, now filled with frenzy, heedless of the cries and supplications of his parents, applied the torch with his own hand to the home that had sheltered him in youth. In the light of their burning dwelling, the horror-stricken pair hastened to the river, and jumping into a small skiff, gained the Union camp.*

From sundown of the 7th till late into the forenoon of the following day, the Battalion remained in position on the easterly side of the creek, picketing its banks, closely watching the town, and successfully resisting every attempt of the enemy to cross over. Quite early in the morning of the 8th, the Confederates withdrew, driving before them a horde of panic-stricken negroes, and carrying away a considerable number of their own killed and wounded.

The result of that night's insane work was the burning of nearly five hundred buildings, and the destruction of property to the value of many thousands of dollars; and the only reason ever assigned for this piece of vandalism, was, that the town might not furnish winter cantonments for the Federal troops. But the burning of the village inflicted no material injury upon the Federals; it rather relieved them of the grave responsibility of guarding it, and protecting from plunder the many articles of great value left there by its former occupants. Hampton, which was settled in 1705,

* These facts were related by the father and mother to members of the Battalion, and were afterwards substantially admitted by the officer referred to, to whose credit be it said, that he "very deeply regretted it."—AUTHOR.

contained at the time of its evacuation in May, 1861, a population of about 1,500 souls, and was one of the finest towns in the Old Dominion. A creek, called Hampton Creek, spanned by the long wooden bridge before mentioned, divided the town unequally, the village proper being on the westerly bank, and containing about five hundred buildings, among them several churches, one an ancient brick structure, ivy-clad, in the burial-yard of which were the graves of several distinguished Virginians. In the belfry of this church (one of the oldest in the State) hung a bell cast in England, and connected with it were many historic associations. In the war of the Revolution, and again in 1812, it had been desecrated by British soldiers and sailors. "It ought to have been spared," says a writer, "as a venerable and sacred relic"; but all its worth and antiquity were not proof against the barbarity that consigned it to ruin.

On the Fortress Monroe side of the creek were many fine buildings and elegant private residences, all of which were spared, through the efforts of our men. Near the fort was the Chesapeake Female Seminary, and nearer the village was the residence of ex-President Tyler, the once honored owner of which deserted it at the time of the general exodus of the people; but as a token of his sympathy with the cause of the insurgents, left the "Stars and Bars" flying from the roof. These, however, were taken down soon after by the stalwart standard-bearer of the Fifth New York Regiment, who put in their place the "Stars and Stripes," an emblem far more fit to float over the home of one who had held the highest office in the gift of the people.

The day previous to the burning of Hampton (Aug. 6), a party of the Battalion, consisting of Lieutenant Oliver, Sergeant Atwood, a corporal, and sixteen men, were detailed to embark on board of a small steamer, for the purpose of cruising on the "Eastern Shore," so called, to board all crafts of a suspicious character. The men took with them one week's rations, but were absent ten days, and for the last few days, subsisted mainly on sea-crabs. They met with several exciting incidents, and returned to camp in a half-famished condition. On the 18th of August, Captain Barnes was ordered by General Butler to proceed to Newport News with the five companies of the Battalion under his immediate command, but Captains Leach's and Wilson's companies were retained at the Rip-Raps till November.

Two of the New York regiments stationed at Camp Butler (Newport News) during the latter part of August, became involved in a sad difficulty, which grew out of the discontent of their men. There had been some misunderstanding, in the first place, about their term of service, and for some cause they had, up to this time, received no pay, nor had the local authorities at home, as was contended by them, paid to their families the aid promised at the time of their enlistment. The feeling of dissatisfaction which resulted from this state of things finally culminated in open mutiny, and nearly five hundred of the enlisted men of these regiments laid down their arms and refused to do duty. By order of General Butler, they were placed under arrest, and sent, under guard, to the Rip-Raps, where, for several days, they were kept in close confinement. About this time, General Butler was succeeded in the command of the department by General Wool, a veteran officer of the regular army, and thereupon an order was issued, directing Captain Leach to subsist these men upon nothing except bread and water as long as they continued to harbor a spirit of mutiny. The sympathy of Leach's and Wilson's men toward these prisoners was very strongly excited, and the guard stationed over them systematically, but slyly, evaded the orders from head-quarters, and freely shared with them their rations of meat and coffee. Finally, about the first of September, the prisoners having become convinced of the folly of their conduct, asked permission to return to duty; and that wish having been made known to General Wool, they were ordered to Fortress Monroe, severely reprimanded by the General, and, with the exception of three or four of their number,* who were charged with being ringleaders in the revolt, were par-

---

* As an example of the discipline at this time enforced in the department, we will state in brief the sentence of one of these unfortunate soldiers. By the sentence, he was to forfeit all pay and allowances during the remainder of his term; to be confined, at hard labor, during that time on one of the Tortugas islands; to wear a twelve-pound ball attached to his right ankle by a chain three feet long; and for a certain number of days in each year be kept in solitary confinement on bread and water.—AUTHOR.

doned of their grave offence, and ordered to their respective commands. It is but just to these men to say, that they subsequently became most excellent soldiers, and that their grievances were by no means fanciful.

The four months spent at the Rip-Raps constituted one of the "soft times," to use a soldier's phrase, in the service of these two companies, and one to which their members have often alluded with evident pleasure. The men were here required to perform but little duty, were liberally supplied with good food and clothing, and their many unoccupied hours pleasantly spent in fishing, catching "soft crabs," a very delicious shell-fish, shooting porpoises, watching the movements of our rapidly-accumulating navy, discussing gravely the situation of the country, planning campaigns, and fighting imaginary battles. If all the military and political lore eliminated by these camp-fire debates, the queer pranks and comic sayings of the witty ones, could be reduced to print, the result would be a large and by no means uninteresting volume. These idle days gave birth, also, to much letter-writing: some specimens of which, still in the author's possession, exhibit traces of wonderful imaginative powers, and show that their composers were not in all respects very devout converts to truth.

CHAPTER XII.

THE BATTALION AT NEWPORT NEWS ONCE MORE — THE GARRISON AND
OFFICERS — ANECDOTES OF GENERAL PHELPS — THE FAMOUS DRILLS —
GUARD DUTY — "PARISH" AND "BRICK" HOUSES — THE NEGROES —
THE SOLDIERS TEACH THE BOYS TO DRILL — COUNTING THE RAILS —
SCOUTING.

The time which was spent by the Battalion at Newport News after it was last ordered here (Aug. 18, 1861), covering as it did the remainder of the term of service as such an organization, and embracing nearly five months of its service as a part of the Twenty-ninth Regiment, seems to demand a full account of the operations at this post during this period; for although the place never possessed much significance after the beginning of the Peninsular campaign, in May, 1862, yet it was here that the members of the Battalion and regiment were thoroughly schooled in their duties.

During the summer of 1861, Phelps (who was still in command here) had been deservedly advanced to the rank of brigadier-general. The brief account heretofore given of the early military career of this officer scarcely furnishes our readers with anything more than a general knowledge of him; for, although a soldier of the strictest sect, he employed certain peculiar methods of discipline which most professional military men would regard with disfavor, but which were none the less wholesome, and admirably adapted to the volunteers, whose character he seemed thoroughly to understand. All his orders of prohibition were directed against the enlisted men, though he expected the officers to take the hint and always set a good example.

A good illustration of this system of discipline is furnished by the following incident: During the warm months, the soldiers were much in the habit of bathing upon the beach, which was sandy and smooth, and it was by no means infrequent that several hundreds of these bathers were seen enjoying together the refreshing waters of the James. What was chiefly objectionable about this was the practice of the men in bathing at all hours of the day, and in large numbers; and the habit was not wholly confined to the men, some of the officers of lesser rank doing the same thing. Finally, an order was issued forbidding bathing upon the beach between the hours of guard-mount in the morning and retreat at night. Not long after the publication of the order, the General, while sitting in front of his quarters, a little cottage that overlooked the river and shore, observed two young officers preparing to bathe in front of his house. Waiting till they had undressed, he called to the Sergeant of the Guard, and ordered him to arrest the two officers and bring them naked to his quarters. The Sergeant, with good relish and alacrity, obeyed the order, and locking arms with the nude officials, who begged loudly for their clothes, conducted them (a highly-amused crowd of soldiers looking on from the camp) into the presence of the Commander, who, though inwardly pleased, presented a stern countenance.

"Have you heard of the order about bathing?" asked the General. "Yes, General," replied one of the culprits; "but we are officers, and the order applies only to enlisted men." "Very true, gentlemen," says Phelps, in his peculiar tone and Yankee accent; "but how is a soldier to know an officer except by his dress? If you choose to bathe naked, and expect to be recognized as officers, pray have your shoulder-straps buttoned on to you. Go to your quarters."

This ingenious and witty reprimand had all the effect of one of greater severity, while it furnished the garrison with a good joke to laugh over; and it showed, also, the democratic spirit in which the laws of the post were to be administered.

Phelps was a superior drill-master, and it was to the rigid system of drill inaugurated by him, and continued by his worthy successor, General Mansfield, that the troops constituting the garrison at Newport News owe much of the proficiency which they displayed in the battles and campaigns of a later date. Any narrative of the life of the Battalion at this place would be imperfect unless it embraced some mention of the drills to which allusion has been made. The ground was very favorable for extensive movements; the long plain was covered with a thick coat of velvety grass, and very little broken. General Phelps almost invariably took personal charge of these drills, though he sometimes intrusted them to his colonels, a number of whom were very able officers. The spectacle presented by these manœuvres was often grand. The troops, consisting of four full regiments, three large battalions, and a light battery, were exercised in all the varied field movements, creating an interest among the troops that was sometimes intense, and giving rise to a most wholesome rivalry among the officers and men of the different regiments. An amusing incident occurred in connection with one of these drills, which shows, perhaps, even better than the anecdote just related, the eccentricity of Phelps, and his novel methods of reproving delinquency.

A regiment belonging on the right of the line was late one day, and the rest of the brigade was kept waiting several minutes for it to arrive. At last the slow ones made their appearance, coming out of their camp on the double-quick, in the hope of making up for their tardiness; but when they were about two hundred yards off, the General gave an order which swung the brigade by battalions, in mass, to the left and rear, and then another that turned it end for end. The unfortunate regiment was then in front of the line, double-quicking to its place. Phelps, flinging the right wing of the brigade to the rear again, and the left wing forward, kept the regiment trotting around the outside of the field a full hour, with the massed battalions swinging on their centre, away from them. At last he deployed in line again, by extension from the left, and allowed the "double-quickers" to get to their place, and when they had supported arms, the facetious old General promptly raised his hat and dismissed the drill. The laggards had been suitably punished for their lack of punctuality, and the General and the rest of the soldiers had enjoyed a good joke.

Having spoken of the Commander of the Post, it seems proper to make some allusion to his troops, and his most able subalterns, as a part of the description of the personnel of the

camp. After the departure of the Fourth Massachusetts and
First Vermont militia, and later the Ninth New York, all of
which regiments were made up of a fine class of men, the
permanent garrison here consisted of the First, Second, and
Seventh New York regiments, the remnants of the Eleventh
New York, Ellsworth's old regiment, a portion of the Twentieth New York, the Massachusetts Battalion, and Captain
Loder's U. S. Light Battery. The First New York was an
orderly body of troops, commanded by Colonel Dyckman,
and occupied a portion of the works on the extreme left of
the brigade line. The Second was raised chiefly in Troy, and
became a good fighting regiment; its colonel, Carr, was a
talented officer, who afterwards won a brigadier's stars. The
Seventh was, for a part of the time, commanded by Colonel
Bendix, the Eleventh by Lieutenant-Colonel Losier, a well-drilled officer, and the Twentieth, German, by Max Weber,
later in the war a brigadier-general. The Seventh New York,
composed wholly of Germans, was a superior regiment in
every respect, and several of its officers had held, and some
of them then held, high rank in the army of Prussia. Early
in the autumn of 1861, Colonel Bendix resigned, and was
succeeded by Lieutenant-Colonel Kappf. Major Caspar Keller
became Lieutenant-Colonel, and Captain George Von Schack
of the Prussian Guards was made Major. Not long after,
Kappf resigned, and Von Schack was promoted to the
coloneley, Keller very generously waiving his claims. Von
Schack was a soldier of high breeding and of the best
blood of Prussia; his father, General Von Schack, was the
chief of staff to Prince Frederick Carl in one or more campaigns of the army of Prussia. When Colonel George Von
Schack came to us, he was a lieutenant of the Prussian
Guards, and had been chamberlain to the Prince. Of all
the colonels of foreign, and particularly of continental, lineage or extraction, in the early part of the war, Von Schack
was the most earnest in his efforts to learn the American
way. From the first, he gave his commands in English, and
tolerated no innovation upon the prescribed tactics of movements. He seemed exceedingly desirous of learning the
habits and traits of character of the Americans, and soon
proved himself a very apt student; for, beside learning to

appreciate those with whom he was fighting, he soon learned to appreciate and love the cause for which he was fighting, and the Union army contained no more ardent patriot than he. He was an excellent drill-master, and the "Steuben Seventh," under his command, acquired a name and a fame for discipline and efficiency in the volunteers equal to that of the "Fancy Seventh" in the militia. He served throughout the war with distinction, was several times severely wounded in battle, and at the close of the Rebellion held the well-earned rank of brigadier-general.

A camp so isolated as that at Newport News, being about twelve miles from Fortress Monroe, and having no safe communication with it except by water, required the establishment of an outpost and the maintenance of a strong picket. To ensure immunity from an attack by sea, one or more vessels of our navy were kept constantly anchored in the river. At one time, early in the summer, the ship "Savannah" was on duty, but she was soon after relieved by the frigate "Congress" and the sloop-of-war "Cumberland," the latter vessels remaining till the disastrous battle of the 8th and 9th of March, 1862, when both were destroyed. The picket line was very long, and for the most part located in the deep forest which bordered the plain. Roads and foot-paths penetrated the woods in every direction, furnishing so many avenues of approach to our lines, rendering necessary not only the utmost vigilance, but a strong guard. More than once, during the dark nights of the summer and autumn, scouting parties of the enemy crept stealthily along these covered ways, and attempted to surprise our sentinels. Several of these picket stations were considerably remote from the camp; that of "Brick House Station," a large brick mansion standing in the midst of an open field, and more properly an outpost, was the most distant from the main camp; but the most isolated, and certainly the most exposed of these stations, was the "Parish House," occupied by an infirm and aged Virginian, who claimed to be a Unionist, and who owned some thirty slaves of all ages. His plantation was very large, and skirted the shores of Hampton Roads. At this place, the small force of three men and a corporal usually constituted the guard, which was generally composed of members of the Battalion. The old planter was very nervous, and always complaining of some real or fancied injury; his swine and poultry, of which he had large numbers, frequently came home at night with diminished ranks. But his chief and more serious affliction was caused by the voluntary departure of his able-bodied negroes; they would hover about the Union camp in spite of all the old man could do or say. The few that remained with him consisted chiefly of faithful old women and helpless children. Among the latter was a bright-eyed, well-favored mulatto boy, about ten years old; he soon became the favorite of our soldiers, who shortened an old musket for him, and taught him the manual of arms. The youth became very proficient in the exercise, and imparted his military knowledge to the other young negro boys upon the plantation, who, providing themselves with sticks and brooms, frequently drilled under their little chief in the presence of the guard.

When the cool nights of September and October came, service upon the picket line was by no means agreeable; to keep themselves warm, the men would build fires, and, although there was scarcely any part of the line destitute of material for a fire, yet the rail fences, composed of well-seasoned wood, were usually taken for this purpose. When this practice became known at headquarters, General Wool issued a very stringent order forbidding it. Each field-officer of the day was instructed by General Phelps to use his utmost endeavors to cause this order to be complied with, but it was far more easy to give such orders than to enforce them. Some of the stations could not be reached at all by this officer at night, and many of them not oftener than once in twenty-four hours; the result was, that this order was practically a nullity.

On a certain occasion, during the time of which we have spoken, Captain Clarke of the Battalion was field-officer of the day. As was always the case, he received special instructions from General Phelps to enforce the order relative to the burning of rails. Clarke was relieved by Major Gaebel of the Seventh New York, and the two officers, as is customary, proceeded to the headquarters of General Phelps just after guard-mount, Captain C. having turned over to his successor the orders received by him on the day previous. The General stated to Major Gaebel that there were no new orders relative to the duties of the officer of the day, and if he had received the orders from Captain C., he was sufficiently informed concerning them, though he considered it necessary to call his attention to the particular order about burning rails, — that it "must be enforced." Major G. replied that Captain Clarke had already called his attention to that matter, and he "would see that it was enforced." Phelps, well aware of the practice of the guards, replied, "O, yes, you will see that it is enforced; all officers are willing to do that"; and then, turning to Clarke, said, "Now, yesterday morning, Captain, I called your attention specially to this subject; but it was very cold last night, and you may depend upon it the men did not suffer for want of rails, order or no order." This seemed to Clarke like a reflection upon his official conduct, and, without considering the effect of his words, he promptly answered, "There were no rails burned last night, sir." "O, indeed!" said Phelps; "then it is true, is it, that no rails were burned last night?" "No, sir; not a rail," said Clarke, with an air of increased assurance and injured dignity. "O, indeed! And pray, Captain, how do you know?" With this question, the dialogue had reached an interesting point; sure enough, how did he know? and what would he say to this? There were miles of rail fences, and almost an infinite number of rails. "Why," said the quick-witted Captain, now fairly driven to the wall, "when I received your orders yesterday morning, I proceeded to count the rails, and just before coming off duty this morning, I again counted them; and they were all there, General, every one." This answer was evidently unexpected by Phelps; it would have been unmilitary to question the veracity of his subaltern; but he evidently didn't believe the absurd statement, though uttered with great apparent candor, and with every show of good faith. The General's countenance suddenly changed; it was a terrible test of his courtesy not to say something disagreeable, and, with a look of undisguised astonishment, he turned from Clarke to Gaebel, and said, "Major, count the rails! Good morning, gentlemen!"

Whether the Major ever counted the rails, we do not know,

but it is reported, that, upon leaving the office of General Phelps, he expressed his regrets for having had imposed upon him, through Clarke's intemperate statement, a duty that would consume the remainder of his term to perform.

On the 21st of October, the Battalion had a little affair with the enemy, on the Warwick Road, about five miles from Newport News, by which it earned considerable praise and reputation for steadiness. A bakery having been established at Camp Butler (Newport News), large quantities of fuel was required. At various points throughout the vast forest, which, with slight interruptions, stretched from Hampton Roads to Richmond, were piles of seasoned wood; one of these, containing several hundred cords, was located near the bank of the James River, and on the road before mentioned. On the morning of the day named, Captain Barnes received orders from General Phelps to take the teams of the post (twenty-one wagons and eighty-two mules and horses) and go into the forest for wood. Barnes took with him two hundred officers and men. Lieutenant Mayo had the immediate supervision of the train, Chamberlain had the advance, and Clarke the rear of the column; and a small body of scouts, under a corporal of Company I, was thrown out some distance in advance of the head of the column. The road for most of the distance lay through a dense wilderness. When the little band had reached a point about a mile from its destination, the scouts came suddenly upon an ambuscade of the enemy, on the right of the road, where the forest was deep and dark. The Confederates rose up quickly from behind some logs and bushes, where up to that moment they had lain concealed, discharged their pieces, and at the same moment made a rush for our scouts, capturing one of the number, Augustus A. Blaney, and then hurrying away with him into their lines. The companies were ordered up immediately, filed to the left of the road, and formed in line of battle. There seemed to be quite a number of the enemy in the woods, and although our men could only here and there catch a glimpse of them as they skulked behind the trees, yet they fired a volley or two, whereupon the enemy fled. The train then proceeded to the wood-pile, the wagons were filled and started homeward, meeting on the way the Seventh New

York Regiment and Loder's Light Battery, which had been sent out by General Phelps, after the firing began, to render aid to the Battalion. This affair, though really very trifling, caused considerable excitement at the time, and the officers and men were highly complimented by both Generals Phelps and Wool; the conduct of the Battalion on this occasion acquiring some additional importance from the fact that every previous attempt of our troops to obtain wood in that locality had been frustrated by the enemy, and had resulted in the capture, in more than one instance, of several of our men and teams.

One of the unsuccessful efforts to gather wood at this place was the origin of a good story, which was often told in Camp Butler; and though the author does not vouch for its entire accuracy, yet he gives it as another specimen of Phelps's wit, and as a camp story, whatever its worth.

The German officer who had charge of this expedition, as the story goes, reported to the General an encounter with the enemy, and the loss of four mules. "Did you lose any men killed?" asked Phelps. "No, sir." "Any wounded?" "No, sir; but, mein Gott, Scheneral, they carry off four jackass." "Very well, Captain, you will charge those four jackass to yourself on the next pay-roll," quietly answered the General. In the course of a few days, the same officer came to head-quarters and reported another skirmish, the capture by his command of two or three of the enemy and a pair of horses, and one or two slight casualties in his company. The officer stood before Phelps with dilated eyes, as he made his report, his face glowing with enthusiasm and pride at the thought of his gallant performance, and the expectation of being cordially commended for it by his superior; but his ardor was somewhat abated by the following congratulation: "I am very glad, Captain, you have got those horses, for now you needn't pay for but two of the mules you lost."

The Battalion having acquired a reputation for bravery, and won the confidence of General Phelps, by its success on the Warwick Road, that officer was very naturally led into again selecting it for the same service; and in the course of a few weeks from that time, Captain Barnes received orders to go for wood. The five companies, with a large number of teams, marched up the river to the wood-pile which has just been mentioned, and loaded all the wagons without being molested by the enemy. When this was accomplished, the teams were headed toward camp, accompanied by a strong guard, the balance of the Battalion following slowly in the rear.

The train had gone but a short distance, when the advance guard reported that the enemy were visible in the woods in front, apparently in large numbers. The teams were at once stopped, and it was soon found that the report was correct, and that a considerable force of the enemy's cavalry were evidently moving into position, for the purpose of intercepting our train. The situation of the Battalion was rather serious in its nature. It was readily seen by the officers that it would be a difficult undertaking to force a passage with the long line of wagons loaded with wood, with their mules and horses. Prompt action was required. A forest road was fortunately discovered that led toward the James River, and gradually towards camp; and this road was found to terminate near the river, at a stream which flowed into the James. From the other side of this stream, the road continued toward camp; but this rivulet, which was probably fordable at certain seasons of the year, was at this time impassable for teams. Our skirmishers were directed to occupy the attention of the enemy if necessary, while the head of the train was turned into the forest road, and a strong detail of men, under Captain Doten, made to throw a bridge across the stream. With great celerity, rails and logs were gathered, and a rude bridge constructed, over which our wagons all managed to cross with safety, and were no sooner on the other side than they struck the open lands on the banks of the James River, and moved rapidly toward camp.

The enemy, who were some distance away, and between whom and the main body of the Battalion there intervened a dense woods, were wholly ignorant of these movements, evidently supposing that the wagons could move to camp only on the main road, which they were guarding. They had not even deemed it necessary to attack our skirmishers, until they saw our wagons a long distance away, moving across the open country. They then, for the first time, realized that they had been outwitted, and immediately moved forward to attack the Battalion. The skirmishers fell back, and the Battalion formed in line of battle.

The whole situation had been changed. The wagons were now safe, and were on their way toward camp; and this having been happily accomplished, our men were unhampered, and in a condition to give the enemy a warm reception. This the Confederates seemed to realize fully, and after exchanging a few shots, withdrew, the Battalion marching leisurely to camp. At the "Brick House Picket," they were met by General Phelps, who had been already informed of the affair by the officer in immediate charge of the train. When the General learned how the movement had been conducted, he was greatly pleased, and bestowed warm commendations upon the officers and men of the Battalion.

As, in the course of this narrative, we are soon to speak of a change in the command of the post, and hence to take leave of General Phelps, we feel that we cannot do so without giving a few more instances of his sparkling wit.

One day, a young artillery officer, fresh from civil life, was observed to have the wrists of his new white gauntlets covered with tables written with ink. He was asked by the General what these figures were, and why he had them written upon his gauntlets. The young officer explained that his memory of ranges and elevations was poor, and he had hit upon that plan of having them always before him. "Now, that is very ingenious," said Phelps; "a West Point officer, I dare say, would never have thought of that." "Yes," said the officer, delighted by the General's apparent approval of his plan, "I thought it was a most excellent idea." "I see but one drawback to it," said the General; "if you should happen to lose your gloves, you would have to let your sergeant command the battery." Those gauntlets were never seen on drill afterwards.

An acting adjutant of one of the regiments at Newport News made, while on drill, several humiliating blunders. The General thought it an opportunity for a moral lecture to all the officers. "Adjutant," said he, "if you spent more time over your books, and less time in drinking and carousing, you would appear far more creditably on drill." "Excuse me, General, but I don't drink," replied the officer.

"Well," said Phelps, "I am very sorry for it. There's no excuse whatever, then, for your blunders; 'tis sheer stupidity."

The General understood all the peculiarities of volunteer soldiers, and where they operated to the disadvantage of good discipline, he sought to correct them, not as would most officers, by punishment, but by some ingenious device, often mirth-provoking, but none the less salutary in its effects. One of these traits of the volunteers, the outgrowth of their free American life, and their habits of study and self-reliance, was a keen desire to know the object and reason of every order given them, and, if not told the object, to guess at it, and then execute the order with sole reference to its supposed intent. This propensity had annoyed General Phelps exceedingly. To effectually break up this habit, and to substitute for it the obedience of the regular, was his desire, and he watched for some good opportunity to teach the lesson to all his officers. The opportunity soon presented itself. A Confederate tug-boat, armed with a gun of long range, came down the James one day and commenced firing at the United States ship "Savannah." The General ordered a gun to be fired at her with 14° of elevation. The officer in charge of our battery, who was a member of the Battalion, thought 16° would be better, and giving the gun that range, made a superb shot, sending a ball directly through the smoke-stack of the tug. "Now you have the range, Lieutenant, fire away," was the General's sole remark, as he turned and left the battery. The tug turned and steamed away up the river, and was soon out of range. The Lieutenant thought himself highly complimented by the General, exerted himself to the utmost to fire rapidly, and at mess that night related the incident to his brother officers with great gusto, not hesitating to assert that his knowledge of artillery practice was even superior to that of the commanding general. At midnight, General Phelps sent for Captain Barnes, commanding the Battalion. On his reporting, the General began afar off, "I was wakeful to-night, and thought you might be willing to relieve me of my uneasiness by giving me a little of your company," and then he began talking in this wise. "The officers and men are all good, but they are volunteers; they are better than regulars in one respect, — they are zealous, — but they are very bad in another: they think of the object of an order, and execute it zealously in the direction of the object they imagine is intended. Now, there is Lieutenant —— of your command, a capital officer, very zealous and intelligent; he has a first-rate notion about artillery; he makes excellent shots. I told him to fire at the tug to-day, and to give the gun 14° elevation, but he gave it 16°, and made as good a long shot as I ever saw; he hit the boat; his zeal carried him away; he didn't obey his orders; he thought I wanted him to hit the boat; I wanted, instead, to tole her down nearer, when I could have easily blown her out of the water. Your Lieutenant thus spoiled my whole plan. Now, go back to your quarters, call the Lieutenant up, and tell him this, that I have just told you; make him understand it. That is all the punishment I think he will need."

Lieutenant —— was duly summoned, and received his reprimand. While he never again boasted of his skill as an artillerist, and was compelled to endure the jests of his brother officers, he nevertheless learned a lesson of implicit obedience to orders, that proved very valuable to him during the remainder of his honorable service in the army.

CHAPTER XIII.

CAPTAINS LEACH'S AND WILSON'S COMPANIES LEAVE THE RIP-RAPS — ORDERED TO NEWPORT NEWS — GENERAL MANSFIELD RELIEVES GENERAL PHELPS — THE DRILLS CONTINUED — TARGET PRACTICE — WINTER QUARTERS AND BUILDING OF BARRACKS — THE ORGANIZATION OF THE TWENTY-NINTH REGIMENT — DISSATISFACTION ABOUT THE APPOINTMENT OF NEW OFFICERS — COURT-MARTIAL OF COLONEL PIERCE — BURSTING OF THE SAWYER GUN AND DEATH OF TWO OF THE MEN.

On the 3d of November, 1861, the companies commanded by Captains Leach and Wilson were ordered to join the Battalion at Newport News, and were relieved at the Rip-Raps by two companies of the Union Coast Guard under Major Halliday.

Upon arriving at Newport News, these commands were assigned camping-grounds inside of the breastworks, and with the Battalion. This was the first time that all the companies had been together; the uniting of them made an increased membership of nearly two hundred, and a total membership of between five and six hundred, which, at a later period in the war, would have far exceeded the numerical strength of even our largest regiments.

Toward the last of November, General Phelps was ordered to the department of the Gulf, and Brigadier-General Joseph K. F. Mansfield was assigned to the command of Camp Butler. General Mansfield was a native of Connecticut. He graduated at West Point, at the age of eighteen, second in a class of forty members. In the Cadet Battalion, he had served in every grade, and, on graduation, was appointed to the Engineers. From that time till the Mexican war, he was on sea-coast fortifications, and was principal constructing officer of Fort Pulaski, an experience that enabled him to give very valuable advice to General Gilmore, in his approaches to that place. In 1838, Mansfield was a captain, and in 1846 was assigned to General Taylor as chief engineer, when he directed the fortifications of Fort Brown, opposite Matamoras, and afterward assisting in its defence, won his major's brevet for gallant conduct. In September, 1846, he was in charge of the reconnoissance of Monterey, and the battles which ensued around that place scarred him with seven severe wounds, and brevetted him a lieutenant-colonel. In the battle of Buena Vista, he was conspicuously engaged; so much so, that his services were rewarded by the brevet rank of colonel.

In 1853, he became Colonel and Inspector-General of the army. At the time of the inauguration of President Lincoln, he was stationed in Washington, and on the increase of the army in 1861, was made Brigadier-General, and assigned to duty about the city, supervising the construction of the fortifications there with his great skill as an engineer, and after the disastrous battle of Bull Run, contributing to the reorganization of the volunteers. Upon the appointment of General Wool to the command of Fortress Monroe, General Mansfield was sent thither, and after commanding for a short time the district of Hatteras, and subsequently Camp Hamilton, was ordered, late in November, to relieve General Phelps at Newport News. Here he remained till May, 1862, participated in the expedition against Norfolk, afterwards commanded at Suffolk, and, in September, was ordered to Washington on the McDowell Court of Inquiry, and while there was promoted to be Major-General of Volunteers, and assigned to the command of the Twelfth Corps, reaching his command just before the battle of Antietam. As we shall have occasion to speak of him in connection with that battle, we will not at this time follow his history further in that direction.

The same stern sense of duty which the General manifested while in the field was daily impressed by him upon the men under his command at Newport News. He was not a preacher nor a martinet; he was a plain, shrewd, well-educated gentleman, with a fine sense of humor, great practical talent, inexhaustible tact, and had an intimate knowledge of human nature. He was familiar with the men, always had a kind word for the sentinel at headquarters, and when the sentinel had once properly saluted him, he would say, "You will oblige me by not saluting me again to-day, as I have to be constantly going out and coming in, and I don't care for it."

One of the first orders issued by him, after taking command of this post, was to institute target practice, at ranges of 200, 400, 600, and 1,000 yards. By this order, a record of shots was to be kept; each company was to shoot three times a week, and the ten best marksmen of the regiment, every week, were to be selected and allowed a day's liberty at Fortress Monroe; and as this included a sail on the steamer of some twenty miles (both ways) and a visit to one of the most interesting places in the department, being, as it were, a sort of metropolis, the reward thus offered was highly prized and eagerly sought for by all the men. By the same order, officers were encouraged to compete with the men in this exercise. No man was to fire less than ten shots each week; guards, on relief, were to discharge their pieces at a target, and be marked for it; and the best marksman in the guard got a day's liberty. The targets used were pieces of old tents, stretched on frames six feet high and two feet wide, with a black cross four inches wide on them, the horizontal arm at a height of four and a half feet.

Volley firing was also practiced, by which means an excellent knowledge of the capacity of the musket was acquired, a knowledge that served all the regiments at Newport News in good stead, at a later period in the war. The officers always afterward knew their marksmen, and could at any time detail a few sharpshooters for special work when needed.

One of General Mansfield's drills was a march in campaign order, and he was very particular to describe what things a soldier should carry in campaign, permitting what was forbidden in the army of the Potomac at one time, — photographs and letters, — and not encouraging a superfluity of blacking brushes. Upon the first marching drill, the staff-officers were sent round to say, that at route-step it was usual to allow the men to smoke and talk in campaign; and he desired the officers to encourage it then, as it would be necessary to allow it in the future. The drills thus inaugurated were continued as long as the weather would permit, and were all chosen with special reference to active service in the field.

The following anecdote shows the dry humor of General

Mansfield, and his efficient tact in the management of citizen-soldiery. One day a man neglected to salute him. He stopped his horse, and said, "My man, did you know it was my duty, by the army regulations, to touch my hat to you every time I meet you?" "No, sir: I am sure I never thought of such a thing." "Yes; but it is yours to touch your hat to me first. I hope you will never allow me again to fail in my duty to you." Civility at Newport News, after that, was not so often forgotten.

When the cold weather approached, early in December, a general order was issued, directing the erection of barracks for winter quarters. Each regiment, and each company of a regiment, were required to build their own houses. All who could be spared from duty were provided with axes, and, under the charge of an officer, marched daily into the neighboring pine forest, where they cut the tall trees, and fashioned them into proper shapes for building purposes; the logs were hauled into camp by the mules and horses; and as each company had its complement of carpenters and other mechanics, a village of comfortable log-houses soon covered the plain, promising the troops ample protection from the biting blasts and drenching rains of the coming winter storms.

About this time, an effort was being made in Massachusetts to raise three companies of infantry, which were to be united with the Battalion, and thus form a full regiment.

Sometime in October, 1861, Dr. Henry B. Wheelwright of Taunton received permission from Governor Andrew to raise a company of infantry, and succeeded in enlisting a number of men. On the 2d of November, 1861, the Governor issued an order, that the men raised by Dr. Wheelwright, which were then in charge of Willard D. Tripp of Taunton, a corporal of the Fourth Regiment, be sent to camp at Assonet, a village of Freetown, to report to Brigadier-General E. W. Pierce, and be there merged, so as to form a company, with the men recruited by General Pierce. By the same order, Dr. Wheelwright was authorized to raise another company "immediately, ten days being allowed for that purpose," from the 4th of November, and directing that all men recruited by him be sent to Assonet, and be under the command of General Pierce. The Quartermaster-General and Commissary-General were ordered to "furnish clothing, transportation, and rations" for the men, upon requisitions made upon them by General Pierce.

During the time the men were at Assonet, they were quartered in an ancient building known as the "Old Post-office"; they were lodged in that part of it called "Pierce's Hall," while their food was cooked in the basement. This old house was erected about the year 1745, and at the commencement of the Revolution, was owned and occupied by Colonel Thomas Gilbert, a captain at the siege of Louisburg. Gilbert was a Tory at the breaking out of the Revolution, and this house was confiscated and sold, he having gone into the English army. In April, 1775, a large body of Whigs assembled to tear down the house, but for some reason refrained from doing so.

The recruits remained in Assonet till the middle of November, and were then ordered to Pawtucket, where was established a rendezvous for recruits, under Captain Milo M. Williams of the Fourth Regiment. By the middle of December, ninety-eight enlisted men had been secured for this company, representing nearly every county in Eastern Massachusetts, and on the 13th of December, Tripp was commissioned Captain, and the following order issued:—

"COMMONWEALTH OF MASSACHUSETTS.

"HEADQUARTERS, Boston, December 13, 1861.

"SPECIAL ORDER, No. 627.

"Willard D. Tripp of Taunton, having been commissioned as Captain in the Twenty-ninth Regiment of Massachusetts Volunteers, will forthwith assume command of recruits stationed at 'Camp Pierce,' in Pawtucket.

"Captain Tripp will make daily reports to the Adjutant-General of the number and condition of recruits under his command.

"By order of His Excellency John A. Andrew, Governor and Commander-in-Chief.

"WILLIAM SCHOULER, *Adj. Gen.*"

The lieutenants of this company, whose commissions bear date of December 13, 1861, were First Lieutenant Alfred O. Brooks and Second Lieutenant Thomas H. Husband, both of Boston.

Two other companies were raised about this time,—one

by Charles T. Richardson of Pawtucket, and the other by Henry R. Sibley of Charlestown. Richardson's company was recruited mostly in Pawtucket and neighboring towns in Rhode Island. He secured a good class of men, who afterward became excellent soldiers, and, what was better, none were bounty men, nor secured by promise of additional pay.

On the 16th of December, Richardson was commissioned Captain, and this order issued:—

"COMMONWEALTH OF MASSACHUSETTS.
"HEADQUARTERS, BOSTON, December 17, 1861.

"Charles T. Richardson of Pawtucket, having been commissioned as Captain in the Twenty-ninth Regiment of the Massachusetts Volunteers, will report forthwith for orders to Colonel Ebenezer W. Pierce, commander of said regiment, at Freetown, Mass.*

"By command of His Excellency John A. Andrew, Governor and Commander-in-Chief.

"WILLIAM SCHOULER, *Adj. Gen.*"

The lieutenants of Captain Richardson's company were William Pray, a sergeant of Captain Barnes's company, promoted to be First Lieutenant, and Charles D. Browne of Boston, commissioned Second Lieutenant January 1, 1862 (formerly a private in Co. B, Thirteenth Mass. Regt).

As early as October 31, 1861, Henry R. Sibley of Charlestown was authorized by a special order from the Adjutant-General's office, "to raise a company of infantry, to be mustered into the United States service for three years or during the war, and to form a part of the Massachusetts Volunteers." The order further provided, if the company was recruited within ten days, it "would be accepted as a part of a regiment to be formed of the Massachusetts companies now at Fortress Monroe." If not recruited within ten days, the enlisted men were to be put into such other companies and regiments as the Commander-in-Chief might direct.

The mention of ten days in this order as the limit of time allowed for the formation of this company seems to have been prompted by a purpose to stimulate the energies of those to whom the recruitment was confided; for while the

* Colonel Pierce was commissioned December 13, 1861.

time was materially exceeded, yet the company was unhesitatingly accepted as a part of the regiment referred to: namely, the Twenty-ninth.

The men who formed this command represented nearly every section of the Commonwealth, though, as no one nor half-dozen other towns contributed so large a quota as Charlestown, and as its Captain and First Lieutenant were citizens of that city, it has always, and with propriety, been spoken of as the " Charlestown company of the Twenty-ninth Regiment." The men were all volunteers ; some were recruited by Sibley, others by D. W. Lee (First Lieutenant), and a few by the State recruiting officers. No bounties beyond the United States bounty of $100, promised after two years' service, were held out as an inducement to enlist ; and though there was not that amount of enthusiasm, exhibited in rapid enlistments, which characterized the raising of troops in April and May, yet there was an utter absence of any of the fallacious ideas about the cowardly character of the enemy, and every man who placed his name upon the roll fully realized all the grave consequences that might follow. The material thus secured was most excellent, and the " Bay State Guards," the proud name adopted by this company, proved a worthy member of the regiment, and an honor to the "Old Bay State." Something of the touching and revered spirit of the 19th of April was manifested by the people of Charlestown toward this company of volunteers. The Bunker Hill Soldiers' Relief Society of that city, an organization composed entirely of ladies, early sought to express their sympathy, by providing each soldier with many articles of comfort ; while the men contributed money, reimbursing Captain Sibley for the expenses he had incurred, and presenting the officers with uniforms and side-arms.

The militia system of the election of officers by the enlisted men was permitted in this case, and not abused. Henry R. Sibley was elected Captain ; Daniel W. Lee, First Lieutenant ; and William R. Corlew (of Somerville), Second Lieutenant.

In view of the fact that the company was soon to leave for the seat of war, appropriate services were held on the afternoon of Christmas Day, at the First Baptist Church in Charlestown. where addresses were made by several distinguished clergymen. The company attended in a body, and the occasion was one of much solemnity, "and also of gratification to the many friends of the company who thronged the house. . . . In the evening of this day, the Guards were the recipients of an ovation at the City Hall, a collation being provided for them by the city, at which the Hon. Richard Frothingham presided."* On this occasion was a presentation, with appropriate speeches, of two beautiful swords, with sashes and belts, to Captain Sibley and Lieutenant Lee, together with a revolver each to Sergeants Pippey and Kellam; and the Rev. Dr. George E. Ellis, who was present, stated that he would give to the enlisted man of the company, who at the end of the term of service should be adjudged by the Captain to have been the best soldier, a hundred-dollar United States bond.†

Shortly after this, the company was ordered to Camp Cameron (Mass.), where it was under the general command, for the most of the time, of the Colonel of the Twenty-eighth Regiment, there recruiting for the field; and after that regiment left, guarded the public property, of which there was a large amount, and for the faithful care of which the company was publicly thanked by the Governor.

It is apparent, from what has already been written, that Governor Andrew was endeavoring to carry out the long-neglected plan of erecting the Battalion into a regiment; but the official order, which we here give in full, was not issued till the 13th of December.

"COMMONWEALTH OF MASSACHUSETTS.

"SPECIAL ORDER, NO. 626.   "HEADQUARTERS, BOSTON, Dec. 13, 1861.

"The companies of Massachusetts Volunteers, commanded by Captains William D. Chamberlain of Lynn, Thomas W. Clarke of Boston, Joseph H. Barnes of Boston, Charles Chipman of Sandwich, Samuel H. Doten of Plymouth, Lebbeus Leach of East Bridgewater, Israel N. Wilson of Billerica, now in the service at Fortress Monroe and vicinity, together with the company now in camp at Pawtucket, commanded by

---

* "Charlestown Advertiser," December 28, 1861.

† At the proper time the bond was awarded to Sergeant John H. Hancock, who gave one of his arms to the country, and who was a brave and deserving soldier.

Captain Willard D. Tripp of Taunton, will constitute the Twenty-ninth Regiment of the Massachusetts Volunteers. Two other companies will be added to the regiment as soon as organized.

"By command of His Excellency John A. Andrew, Governor and Commander-in-Chief.

"WILLIAM SCHOULER, *Adj. Gen.*"

We have not pursued this subject strictly in the order of dates, as the above order really ante-dated the formation of Richardson's and Sibley's companies; but they were in process of formation before this order was issued, and, to prevent confusion in the narrative, we have chosen to complete the story of each company before treating of the organization of the regiment, of which there is much to be said.

On the same day of the foregoing order, Brigadier-General* Ebenezer W. Pierce of Freetown was appointed by Governor Andrew Colonel of the Twenty-ninth Regiment; on the same day, also, Captain Joseph H. Barnes was commissioned Lieutenant-Colonel, and Captain Charles Chipman Major. The staff and non-commissioned staff were as follows: Orlando Brown of Wrentham, Surgeon; George B. Cogswell of Easton, Assistant Surgeon; Lieutenant Joshua Norton, 3d, of Captain Clarke's company, Quartermaster; Lieutenant John B. Collingwood of Captain Doten's company, Adjutant; Sergeant Henry S. Braden of Captain Barnes's company, Sergeant-Major; Sergeant William W. Davis of Clarke's company, Quartermaster-Sergeant; John B. Pizer, of Tripp's company, Commissary-Sergeant; John Hardy of Clarke's company, Hospital Steward. Rev. Henry E. Hempstead of Watertown was chosen Chaplain in January, 1862.

On the 4th of January (1862), there were several promotions among the officers and men of the Battalion. First Lieutenant James H. Osgood, Jr., was made Captain of his company, in place of Barnes, promoted; First Lieutenant Charles Brady, Captain, in place of Chipman, promoted; Second Lieutenant William T. Keen of Captain Barnes's

---

* Brigadier-General of the militia.

company. First Lieutenant, vice Osgood, promoted; Sergeant William Pray of Barnes's company, First Lieutenant, and assigned to duty in Captain Richardson's company; Second Lieutenant Henry A. Kern of Chipman's company, First Lieutenant, vice Brady, promoted; Sergeant John P. Burbeck of Barnes's company, Second Lieutenant, vice Kern, promoted.

The lettering of the several companies, by no means an unimportant part of the work of organizing a regiment, was determined by the following order:—

"COMMONWEALTH OF MASSACHUSETTS.

"SPECIAL ORDER, No. 2.

"HEADQUARTERS, BOSTON, Jan. 2, 1862.

"The companies comprising the Twenty-ninth Regiment of the Massachusetts Volunteers will be lettered as follows:—

"The company commanded by Captain Clarke, 'A'; by Captain Wilson, 'B'; by Captain Leach, 'C'; by Lieutenant Brady, 'D'; by Captain Doten, 'E'; by Captain Tripp, 'F'; by Captain Richardson, 'G'; by Captain Sibley, 'H'; by Captain Chamberlain, 'I'; by Lieutenant Osgood (Barnes's company), 'K.'

"Colonel Pierce, commanding Twenty-ninth Regiment, will promulgate this order.

"By command of His Excellency John A. Andrew, Commander-in-Chief.

"WILLIAM BROWN, *Asst. Adj. Gen.*"

The companies of Captains Richardson, Sibley, and Tripp, together with Colonel Pierce, Surgeon Brown, and Assistant-Surgeon Cogswell, taking with them the colors of the regiment, left Boston for Newport News on the 13th of January, 1862, by the Stonington line to New York. At Philadelphia, they received the same bounty which the ladies of that noble city were giving to all the volunteers who passed through it. From Philadelphia, the command proceeded to Baltimore, and from thence by steamer to Fortress Monroe, reaching Camp Butler on the 17th of the month, and joining the Battalion there stationed.

Beside the proper officers of the three new companies, there were commissioned about this time, and assigned to the regiment, Second Lieutenant Augustus D. Ayling, First Lieutenant Freeman A. Taber, and First Lieutenant John

A. Sayles. None of these officers had ever been connected with the Battalion, nor, with the exception of Ayling, had any of them seen service. The case of Company E of Plymouth gave rise to the most complaint. The lieutenants of this company were (First) John B. Collingwood and (Second) Thomas A. Mayo. Collingwood was made Adjutant of the regiment; but instead of promoting Lieutenant Mayo, who was a deserving and efficient officer of mature age, First Lieutenant Freeman A. Taber, a beardless boy, possessing very slight qualifications for his office, was placed over, and outranked, Mayo. The fact that this company was composed of a superior class of men, and contained not a few who were even capable of commanding a company, causes the wrong and slight thus put upon it to be still more apparent. Second Lieutenant Henry A. Kern of Company D was promoted to be First Lieutenant to fill the vacancy caused by the promotion of First Lieutenant Brady to the captaincy of that company, and Augustus D. Ayling, a most excellent soldier, formerly of Captain P. A. Davis's company of Lowell, was assigned to the position of Second Lieutenant. The claims of Second Lieutenant George H. Taylor of Clarke's company were overlooked, and Sayles, a gentleman of no military training or experience, was allowed to outrank Taylor in his own company, with which he had served since July, 1861.

It would be useless to attempt to conceal the fact that the appointment of the colonel of the regiment was exceedingly distasteful to the officers and men of the Battalion. No fault was found with the manner of organizing the three new companies, and the appointment of officers of these companies, for the good reasons that these officers had been active in the recruitment of their commands, and were doubtless acceptable to their men. The chief cause of grievance of the members of the Battalion, therefore, was, first, the colonelcy of the regiment, and, secondly, the action of Governor Andrew in filling the vacant offices in the seven old companies with new men, and ignoring the just claims to promotion of the old officers and enlisted men of those companies. The well-nigh unanimous sentiment of the Battalion would have dictated a very different selection of the chief field-officer, and of several of the new officers of the line. All the new appointments would have been made from among the officers and men of the Battalion, of which there was abundant good material to select from; and on the score of actual service of nearly a year's duration,—a service beginning at a very early period in the war, when all was darkness and doubt,— it cannot be denied that this sentiment was founded upon the plainest principles of equity. All the bickerings and heart-burnings which subsequently arose in the regiment can be directly traced to this action of our State officials; and to those who are familiar with the facts concerning this matter, it is cause of no little surprise, that the feeling of dissatisfaction thus produced did not result in far graver consequences.

During the winter of 1862, charges of improper conduct were preferred against Colonel Pierce. A court-martial convened,* and, upon trial, he was found guilty, and sentenced to dismissal from the service. General Mansfield approved of the findings of the court-martial; but General Wool, his superior, disapproved them, and Colonel Pierce was reinstated in his command of the regiment. With the feeling of a faithful historian, to record the facts as he finds them, the author, in telling the story of the regiment, has found it necessary to present this state of affairs, the responsibility for which would seem to rest upon the appointing power.

Some reference has been made to the Sawyer rifle at Camp Butler, in the course of this narrative, and now we are called upon to record a very serious accident in connection with this gun, which occurred on the 11th of February. The guns, of which there were two in the department, were the invention of a man named Sawyer. "His system consisted of cutting in the bore of the gun six radial twisted grooves half an inch deep and rather more than an inch wide from muzzle to

---

* This court-martial was composed of the following officers: Colonel Brown, Twentieth Indiana; Colonel Schley, Fifth Maryland; Colonel Dyckman, First New York; Colonel Von Schack, Seventh New York; Lieutenant-Colonel Holland, Fifth Maryland; Lieutenant-Colonel ———, Twentieth Indiana; Lieutenant-Colonel Keller, Seventh New York; Lieutenant Dale, Judge-Advocate.

breech. The twist was uniform, but the grooves were perhaps a trifle deeper near the breech than at the muzzle." The shot was a cast-iron projectile, cylindro-conoidal in shape, and plated with lead. Both this gun and the one at the Rip-Raps had been frequently fired during the summer and autumn, and were found to possess great range and power. On the day referred to, a very distinguished party were visiting Newport News, consisting, among others, of the Secretary of War, Hon. Simon Cameron, Senator Henry Wilson, and Secretary Seward. For the entertainment of these visitors, the Sawyer gun, of which so much had been said, must of course be fired. It was for the last time, however, and the shot was to be a test one for extraordinary range. The gun was given its extreme elevation, 30°. This almost nullified the recoil, and caused the greatest possible strain on the walls of the gun. Officers, soldiers, and civilians had clustered around the bastion where the gun was mounted, with field-glasses in hand, to watch the opposite shore, in the expectation of seeing the shell burst there. The explosion was terrific. A portion of the breech, weighing several hundred pounds, was sent high into the air, but so slowly as to be visible in its ascent; and still another piece, weighing nearly three hundred and fifty pounds, which, in falling, struck Private James W. Sheppard of Company B, who but the day before had returned from his wedding furlough, and crushed him to the earth, killing him instantly. Smaller fragments of the gun struck and severely wounded Lieutenant Smith of Company I, and Privates John F. Hall and Seth W. Paty of Company E. Private Charles E. Jones of Company D, who was one of the gunners, was also instantly killed. Others still were injured by the concussion caused by the explosion, and made temporarily deaf. Captains Wilson and Clarke were standing at the time upon the parapet, about ten yards off, and a piece of the gun, weighing as much as a thousand pounds, flew over them, knocking off the hat of one of them, and striking the earth some twenty yards from the battery, partially buried itself in the ground.

Two morals were drawn from this sad affair by two of the officers of the regiment, the one mechanical and the other military. The mechanical moral was, that rifled cast-iron guns, on the Sawyer plan, were a failure, and that, everything considered, it was fortunate that the gun burst at the time it did, for, had this accident occurred in battle, the calamity would have been far more dreadful. The military moral was, that it is a piece of extreme folly to shoot for the amusement of visitors.

CHAPTER XIV.

THE SINKING OF THE "CUMBERLAND" AND DESTRUCTION OF THE "CONGRESS"—FIGHT BETWEEN THE "MERRIMACK" AND "MONITOR"—THE "MERRIMACK" AND OTHER CONFEDERATE VESSELS ENTER HAMPTON ROADS AND CAPTURE THREE OF OUR VESSELS IN BROAD DAYLIGHT—OUR FLEET SHELL THE CONFEDERATE BATTERIES—BOMBARDMENT OF THE RIP-RAPS—ADVENTURES OF CAPTAIN DRAKE DEKAY—THE ARMY OF THE POTOMAC LANDS AT HAMPTON—EXCITING SCENES IN THE DEPARTMENT.

The Federal naval force present in Hampton Roads and James River, on the 8th of March, 1862, consisted of the "Minnesota," a steam-frigate, commanded by Captain Van Brunt, carrying fifty guns; the frigate "Congress," a sailing-vessel of fifty guns, commanded by Captain Smith; the "Roanoke," a steam-frigate of the same class of the "Minnesota," carrying fifty guns, commanded by Captain Marston; the "St. Lawrence," a sailing-frigate, twelve guns; the sloop-of-war "Cumberland," twenty-four guns. Beside these were two armed tugs, the "Whilden" and "Zouave," and a small gunboat called the "Dragon."

The "Minnesota," "St. Lawrence," "Roanoke," and the tugs and gunboat lay off Fortress Monroe, while the "Congress" and the "Cumberland" were anchored in the James; the former nearest the mouth of the river, and the latter about three-fourths of a mile from the shore, and directly opposite the camp at Newport News. Sometime in November, 1861, the "Roanoke" broke her shaft, and was in this disabled condition at this time. The crew of the "Congress" had, early in March, 1862, been discharged, and the vessel manned by three companies of the Naval Brigade.

The war-vessels of the Confederates in these waters were the "Merrimack," also known in history as the "Virginia," carrying ten guns, eight broadside and one at each end; the "Patrick Henry," six guns; the "Jamestown," two guns; the "Raleigh," "Beaufort," and "Teaser," each one gun.

The "Merrimack" had been raised by the enemy during the summer of 1861, and constructed into a shot-proof steam-battery, with inclined iron-plated sides and submerged ends. "The eaves of the casemates, as well as the ends of the vessel, were submerged, and a ram was added as a weapon of offence." This novel vessel of war was commanded by Captain Franklin Buchanan, formerly of the United States Navy.

At about two o'clock in the afternoon of the 8th of March, the long roll startled the garrison at Newport News. The men were quickly in line, and in a few minutes the cry of, "The 'Merrimack'! The 'Merrimack'!" resounded throughout the camp. A dense volume of black smoke was now seen at the mouth of the Elizabeth River, and in the course of fifteen minutes the dark form of the foe was distinctly seen. The day was bright and warm; not a breeze rippled the surface of the river. The "Congress" being nearest the enemy, began making preparations for the battle. Her masts and spars soon whitened with her sails, and the four thousand soldiers in Camp Butler stood mute, but with intense anxiety, waiting the opening of the contest. The painful silence that brooded over that strange scene was at last suddenly broken by a sharp, angry "bang!" from one of the larboard ports of the "Cumberland." The shot struck within a few yards of the "Merrimack," sending the water in silvery spray high into the air. The signal for the assault thus given was quickly followed by a whole broadside from the "Congress." For a short time both "Congress" and "Merrimack" were veiled from sight by the clouds of curling smoke. To the surprise and alarm of the garrison, the cloud rose, revealing the "Merrimack" still afloat and apparently unharmed, still approaching. The "Congress" now began a rapid and continuous fire upon the enemy. The "Merrimack," without replying to this fire, passed close alongside the frigate, and when within a few hundred yards of her, across her bows, opened on her with a rifled gun. The shot entered the frigate, raking her from stem to stern, dismounting several of her guns, and killing and wounding many of her crew, among them her brave commander.

The "Congress" was fairly disabled by this shot; her commander was killed, confusion reigned supreme, and now the Stars and Stripes were hauled down, and the white flag of truce run up to masthead. The frigate slipped her cables and floated helplessly away, the "Merrimack" continuing on her course toward the "Cumberland."

It was reserved for the latter vessel to make the bravest fight of that terrible and eventful day. As soon as the "Merrimack" was within easy range, the sloop-of-war opened with a whole broadside; but the shot glanced harmlessly from the mailed sides of the foe; and now, with full head of steam, the enemy made a desperate and angry plunge toward his plucky antagonist, sending his ugly prow crashing through her timbers. The prow struck the "Cumberland" under her starboard fore-channels, making an enormous hole. For a few minutes, both vessels seemed to be sinking. The prow had wedged itself so firmly in the timbers as to render it difficult for the enemy to withdraw and save himself from the same fate he had designed for the ship. After a few trials, he succeeded, however, and backing off, took up a position directly across the bows of the "Cumberland," and opened on her at very close range, the two vessels almost touching each other. In this position the "Cumberland" could only use her bow guns (some three or four); but these were worked with great energy, sending their heavy shot directly at the enemy's ports.

The shell and canister of the "Merrimack" were sweeping the gun-decks of the "Cumberland" with fearful slaughter. At times, nearly every gun was unmanned, but other brave sailors came upon the bloody deck and renewed the unequal contest. The flag of the "Cumberland" was still flying defiantly from her mizzen-mast; the shouts and cries of friend and foe, the angry and excited commands of the officers, could be distinctly heard on shore.

The sick-bay of the "Cumberland" was filled to suffocation with blackened and bleeding victims, and, what added greater terror to the scene, she was now rapidly sinking. Despite the vigorous plying of the pumps, the water rose to the main hatchway in less than ten minutes after she was struck, flooding her forward powder-magazines, and rendering them useless. The noble ship now canted to port. Many sprang to save the wounded, while other brave tars still stood at their guns, delivering their last fire as the inrushing waters closed over them. Like a creature of flesh and blood in the agonies of death, the sloop-of-war trembled and creaked, her bows plunged into the dark water, her stern mounted high into the air, and down she went, with a roaring, rushing sound of the waves.

The water was now filled with struggling men striking for the shore. The beach was lined with enraged and pitying soldiers. Logs and planks were seized by them and thrown into the water, to aid the swimmers, and others rushing into the water to their arm-pits, seized the half-drowned sailors and brought them to the land. Others of the sailors were rescued by the steam-propeller "Whilden," Capt. William Riggins, which put off to the scene of the disaster in the midst of the fire of the "Merrimack," and thus saved the lives of many who would otherwise have found a watery grave. About one hundred of the dead and wounded of the "Cumberland" went down with the ship, and among them the Chaplain, the Rev. J. Lenhart.

The land-battery in Camp Butler, which was chiefly manned by members of the Twenty-ninth, and which mounted some five guns, — among them two 42-pounder James rifles, — was very active during the entire contest between the "Merrimack" and "Cumberland." When the "Cumberland" sunk, the Confederate ram was a fair target for our men, but their shots were wholly powerless to do her harm. The "Merrimack" replied to several of our shots, one of her shells striking the parapet, and throwing the earth in clouds of dust over the gunners.

The river now presented a scene of great interest. The "Jamestown" and "Patrick Henry," two Confederate steamers, had arrived, and taking up a position about two miles from our camp, began shelling it with great vigor. One of these missiles passed through a barrack of the First New York, while others cut off the tops of the pines about the camp. These two steamers divided their attentions about equally between the camp and the floating "Congress," firing at the latter with murderous effect, and in shameful and savage violation of the rules of civilized warfare, the "Congress" displaying all the while her flag of truce.

An attempt was now made to capture our frigate, and tow her off, a prize of war. The steam-tug "Zouave" (Union) immediately ran down to her and towed her to our shore, fairly beaching her, before the Confederate steamers "Beaufort" and "Raleigh" arrived. Upon reaching the "Congress," these steamers immediately hauled alongside. General Mansfield, observing this movement, ordered Captain Howard, with a section of his light battery, and Colonel Brown, with two companies of the Twentieth Indiana Regiment, to open fire upon these steamers. The order was promptly obeyed, and in a few moments our shot were striking the Confederate steamers, and whistling about the ears of their men, as they were attempting to clamber up the sides and into the ports of our ship, causing them to withdraw, and killing and wounding several of their number. Among the wounded were Buchanan, the commander of the "Merrimack," who received a severe gunshot wound in the thigh, and Lieutenant Minot of the "Beaufort." The crew of the "Congress," her dead and wounded, and some of the valuable movable articles on her, were landed under a fire from the Confederate fleet. Early in the afternoon, the steam-frigate "Minnesota," the "Roanoke," and "St. Lawrence" (anchored near Fortress Monroe) attempted to come to the relief of our fleet in the James. The machinery of the "Roanoke" was out of order, and she was towed by two tugs; the "St. Lawrence," not being a steam-vessel, was also towed. In order to enter the James, these vessels were obliged to pass within easy range of a battery on Sewall's Point, which did them considerable damage. After passing into the mouth of the James, the "Minnesota" and "St. Lawrence" both grounded. The entire fleet of the enemy, headed by the "Merrimack," now quitted the disabled "Congress" and steamed down to attack the "Minnesota" and "St. Lawrence." The "Merrimack," being of deep draught, could not approach nearer than a mile to either of these ships; and her firing being very inaccurate, she only succeeded in striking the "Minnesota" once. For awhile, the small Confederate steamers, armed with rifled cannon, and having the choice of both distance and position, did considerable damage to the "Minnesota," but eventually the frigate drove them away.

By this time the day was far spent, the sun having already set; and when everybody on shore had begun to consider the sad day's work ended, the huge monster, the "Merrimack," was again observed approaching Camp Butler. This time she took the inner channel, and as she came along, her immense chimney towering up among the branches of the trees that overhung the river bank, belching forth volumes of smoke and sparks, her appearance was simply appalling. Arriving at a point where the channel winds in nearest to the shore, the camp was fairly within range of her bow gun. A sudden burst of light, a dismal, deafening roar, and the crashing of boards and timbers were heard almost simultaneously. The large shot passed entirely through the post hospital and the headquarters' building of General Mansfield, tearing down the chimney of the latter, and nearly burying that venerable officer in the ruins. He was, fortunately, but little hurt, and soon emerged from the house white with plaster. This ended the hostilities of the 8th of March. The "Merrimack" now withdrew, and darkness soon settled down upon both land and water.

The night was one of great gloom and excitement in Camp Butler, as well as in all the Federal camps in the department. Mounted orderlies were riding in every direction, and rumors were rife of a land attack by the enemy's troops under Magruder. In anticipation of such a movement, the garrison was re-enforced early in the evening by a body of infantry from Camp Hamilton, and every preparation was made to repel the assault.

While the day, which had just closed, had been rendered famous in history by its unexampled occurrences, the night which followed was destined to usher in scenes that will never fade from the memory of those who witnessed them. The frigate "Congress," which lay hard aground on the sand-beach near the camp of the Twentieth Indiana Regiment, had been set on fire late in the afternoon, and the lurid flames now lit up the bay and strand with a brightness rivaling that of the day itself. Many of her guns were still shotted, and as the fire coiled about them, they began to discharge; a shot from one of them, skimming the surface of the water, entered and sank a schooner lying at our wharf. The flames had mounted each mast and spar, and were leaping out at every port with angry tongues. Heaps of shells, which had been brought from the magazines for the afternoon's encounter, lay on the gun-decks; these now began to explode, and ever and anon they would dart up out of the roaring, crackling mass, high into the air, and course in every direction through the heavens.

At twelve o'clock, the magazines blew up with a terrific noise. This event had been anticipated by the garrison, and the shores and adjacent camps were crowded with awe-struck gazers. The whole upper works of the frigate had, hours before, been reduced to ashes by the devouring flames; the masts and spars, blackened and charred, had fallen into and across the burning hull; these were sent high into the air with other *debris*, and as, blast succeeded blast, were suddenly arrested in their descent and again sent heavenward. The spectacle thus presented was awfully grand; a column of fire and sulphurous smoke, fifty feet in diameter at its base and not less than two hundred feet high, dividing in its centre into thousands of smaller jets, and falling in myriads of bunches and grains of fire, like the sprays of a gigantic fountain, lighted up the camp and bay for miles.

The yards and rigging of the "Minnesota" and "St. Lawrence" were filled with men armed with fire-buckets, lest the falling sparks should ignite the tarred ropes of these vessels, and unite them in one general conflagration. The sides of the hapless "Congress" were thrown open by the last explosion, and the next morning, all that could be seen of the once proud ship were a few blackened ribs, a short distance above the surface of the water.

When the soldiers of Camp Butler turned away from that scene to retire to their quarters, it was with heavy hearts. The recollection of the harrowing events of the afternoon was still fresh in their minds; they had now witnessed the total destruction of another vessel of our navy, the loss of which gave joy to the South, a new lease of life to the Rebellion, and operated to postpone the day when they would be permitted to doff the blue and return to their homes.

Sunday the 9th of March dawned, finding the frigate "Minnesota" still aground, her consort, the "St. Lawrence," having more fortunately drifted into deep water. The day broke fair, and so calm was everything upon both water and land, that it seemed very like a preparation for the funeral of the two hundred brave men who had tasted death on the preceding day. The Confederate fleet could be distinctly seen lying at anchor under their batteries at Sewall's Point. A column of white steam was issuing from the pipes of the "Merrimack"; it was evident that she was preparing to set out on her second day's exploits, and attempt to deal the final blow to our navy in Hampton Roads. At about seven o'clock, the "Merrimack" was discovered to be moving, and following her were the other vessels of the Confederate fleet. Upon rounding the Point, the iron-clad shaped her course directly towards Fortress Monroe, but she had not proceeded far before she suddenly turned and steered toward the mouth of the James. The drums of the "Minnesota" were heard beating her anxious crew to quarters. When the "Merrimack" had arrived within fair range, she fired a shot from her bow gun. The shot struck the frigate under her counter, doing her not a little damage. The fire was quickly replied to by the frigate, and now Captain Van Brunt, her commander, signalled the "Monitor," which up to that moment had lain close alongside of the ship, and which had arrived from New York the night before, to attack the enemy.

This diminutive craft had not until this time been seen by our men on shore, although rumors of its arrival had spread through camp; and as it steamed out upon the bay, wonder as to what it was, and what it would be likely to accomplish, seized fast hold upon all. With apparent confidence in its ability to contend with the monster iron-clad of the enemy, the "Monitor" steamed directly toward it, and when within one hundred yards, opened fire. The report of that gun rang out so loud upon the still air of the morning, as to immediately create a feeling of confidence in the ability of the little boat to contend successfully with the enemy. In less than five minutes from that time, the two vessels were hotly engaged with each other, belching out fire and iron in each others' faces.

The other vessels of the enemy were by this time fairly engaged with the "St. Lawrence," "Minnesota," and the Federal gunboats, and were soon put to flight, keeping well off toward the opposite shore. Shortly after the "Merrimack" had fired her first broadside at the "Monitor," and had seen her shots glance harmlessly from the revolving turret, she tried the experiment of sinking her, and after backing off slowly, ran at her, head on. The prow of the "Merrimack" struck the "Monitor," but glanced, and the little vessel swung around, delivering in this position several of her most effective shots in rapid succession. After this the combatants parted, and a brief truce followed, at the close of which the two vessels again neared each other, and a second duel, fiercer and more desperate if possible than the first, ensued.

At one time during the battle, the Confederate steamer "Jamestown" ventured to interfere on the side of the "Merrimack," but received from the "Monitor" a shot that pierced her sides, and disabled her to such a degree as to cause her to haul off. During much of the time that the two iron-clads were actively engaged, they were scarcely visible from the shore, being enveloped in clouds of smoke; but occasionally the garrison were disagreeably reminded of what was going on by a huge shot from one or the other of the vessels missing its mark and reaching the land. Several of these huge missiles went bounding over the long plain, casting the dust high into the air, and plowing up the earth in deep, irregular furrows.

At about twelve o'clock, while the "Monitor" was apparently resting, being separated by the distance of a mile from her antagonist, the "Merrimack" made a sudden movement towards the "Minnesota." The tide being at its height, it was doubtless supposed by the enemy that he could reach the frigate, and give her a death-blow with his prow. The "Minnesota" opened upon the enemy with all her broadside guns and ten-inch pivot; "a broadside," says Captain

Van Brunt in his report, "that would have blown out of the water any timber-built ship in the world." The "Merrimack" replied with her rifled bow gun "with a shell which passed through the chief engineer's stateroom, through the engineer's messroom amidships, and burst in the boatswain's room, tearing four rooms all into one; in its passage, exploding two charges of powder, which set the ship on fire."*. . . The fire was quickly extinguished; but the alarm of fire having reached the ears of the men, great consternation prevailed for several minutes. A second shot from the ram went through the boiler of the gunboat "Dragon," which lay near the "Minnesota," exploding it, and badly scalding and wounding a number of our sailors. The position of the enemy was now such as to enable the "Minnesota" to concentrate upon him a heavy fire from her gun-deck, spar-deck, and forecastle pivot-guns; and it was stated by the marine officer of the frigate, who was stationed on the poop, that at least fifty solid shot struck the slanting side of the "Merrimack" during this fire, but without producing any apparent effect.

By the time the "Merrimack" had fired her third shot at the "Minnesota," the "Monitor" had reached the scene of action, and immediately ran in between the two vessels, covering by her turret, as far as possible, the already badly-injured frigate. This movement of the "Monitor" caused the "Merrimack" to change her position, in doing which she grounded. Again the frigate, aided by the "Monitor," poured into the ram every available gun; but the staneh iron-clad withstood the combined fire of both our vessels, and in the course of a few minutes floated, shaping her course down the bay, being closely followed by the "Monitor." In the course of this pursuit, the "Merrimack" suddenly turned, and with full head of steam, struck the "Monitor" for the second time with her prow; but the blow produced no effect, while the "Monitor" fired a solid shot that plunged into the enemy's roof. Then followed a cannonade more desperate, if possible, than any which had preceded it. The "Merrimack" brought four of her guns to bear upon the "Monitor's" turret and pilot-house. In the latter was Lieutenant Worden,

---

* Report of Captain Van Brunt

watching the progress of the battle. An immense solid shot struck the house with such force as to loosen the cement about the inside of the structure, and set in motion a fragment of it, which struck the gallant lieutenant in one of his eyes. The concussion and the blow completely stunned him, rendered him senseless, and disabled him for further duty during the battle. Soon after this accident, the "Monitor" stood down for Fortress Monroe, when the "Merrimack" and two of her consorts again turned toward the stranded frigate. Captain Van Brunt had nearly expended all his solid shot, his ship was already badly crippled, and his officers and men worn out by their excessive labor. It is no wonder, therefore, that when he saw the near prospect of another terrible struggle with the invulnerable enemy, that the thought of burning his vessel came into his mind, for, to use his language, "I determined never to give up the ship to the rebels." Fortunately the "Merrimack" was satisfied that her efforts to further cripple our fleet could not succeed, and being herself more or less disabled, headed toward Norfolk, the "Monitor," to the unspeakable joy of the spectators, starting in pursuit. The chase, which was continued for several miles, and then abandoned, was not attended with any firing on the part of either vessel. This was the closing scene of this remarkable battle.

The excitement in Camp Butler was not to end just here. The men had hardly swallowed their dinner, before a number of horsemen came riding into camp, their horses flecked with foam and themselves covered with dust. They had come from the outposts to inform General Mansfield that the enemy in large numbers were advancing, and that an attack was imminent. The long roll was again beaten, and the excited men mustered with no less alacrity than on the previous day. The Twenty-ninth Regiment formed in line of battle just inside the breastworks, and as it stood there anxiously gazing in the direction of the forest, Lieutenant-Colonel Barnes, then in command, rode to the front, and uttered these words: "Men, we may be called upon to meet the enemy in battle this afternoon, the most of you for the first time. Remember that you are the only Massachusetts troops in this camp!" The emotion of pride and sense of responsibility which these simple words awoke in the breasts of the men was manifested by a hearty cheer all along the line. Things looked very much like a fight at that moment; the entire garrison was under arms, and General Mansfield, mounted, was moving briskly about the camp, speaking cheering words to the troops. This was his speech to the Twenty-ninth: "My men, Magruder is up the river with ten thousand troops. I have in camp six thousand men with muskets and a million rounds of cartridges; and so long as there is left me a man, a musket, or a cartridge, I'll keep that flag flying!" pointing to the post flag flying near his quarters.

The Twentieth New York Regiment was despatched to the "Brick House," where it threw up entrenchments and remained during the night. The enemy expected that our entire fleet would be destroyed in this fight, and with the "Merrimack" on the river and a large force in front, they hoped for an easy victory; but finding that our fleet still existed, they concluded not to attack, and toward night retired.

The repose and quiet which had reigned so constantly during the long winter of 1861-62, in Camp Butler, were ended by the tragic occurrences of these two days. As long as the regiment thereafter continued to remain at Newport News, scarcely a day passed without its exciting incident; and not infrequently the slumbers of the men at night were rudely broken by the ominous sound of the long roll and the sudden screech of a shell thrown from the "Teaser," an insolent little nondescript of the enemy's fleet, which sailed down the river occasionally, and amused herself by firing into our camp.

Ever after the 9th of March, the mails were irregular, the "Merrimack" at times blockading the mouth of the river, and rendering water communication between Newport News and Fortress Monroe difficult and hazardous. The passenger-boat "Express," which had run regularly twice a day between the fort and camp, was obliged to suspend her trips during the time the "Merrimack" remained at the mouth of the Elizabeth, as she could not enter the James without the risk of being blown out of the water by the terrible guns of the iron-clad, and a small boat of light draught was put on the route in her place. Even this little steamer was obliged, in passing the Point, to hug the shore closely in order to avoid the enemy, and to make her trips after nightfall or before daylight in the morning. In the course of a few weeks our naval force in the Roads began to increase considerably, and the Confederate ram withdrew farther up the river, only occasionally showing herself, and then rarely below Craney Island.

An affair occurred on the 11th of April that was very humiliating, and caused great indignation and alarm throughout the North. During the forenoon of this day, the "Merrimack," "Jamestown," and "Patrick Henry" steamed slowly down the Elizabeth into Hampton Roads, directly under the guns of Fortress Monroe and some dozen large Federal vessels. Near the mouth of Hampton Creek were anchored a brig and two schooners, supply-vessels. The Confederate steamer "Jamestown" deliberately ran up to these vessels, boarded them, and towed them off toward Norfolk without the slightest opposition being made by the navy or the fort; and while this disgrace was being visited, unrebuked, upon our flag, several of the sailing-vessels of our navy were hoisting sails and making all possible haste seaward, actually running before they were hurt.

A crowd of highly-exasperated soldiers were looking upon this scene from Newport News, filled with amazement by the strange and unexplained conduct of our navy, and of the Commander of Fortress Monroe. It was impossible that men who had witnessed the brave fight which the "Cumberland," about a month before, had made with the iron monster of the enemy, — who had seen our noble ship go down with the flag flying, and who had exposed their own lives to save those of her crew, — who had themselves manned the land-batteries, and done whatever lay in their power to destroy the foe, — could look upon this scene without having their soldierly pride stung to the quick, and their feelings of love for the flag severely wounded.

The enemy's fleet lay in the Roads till near dark, inviting an attack from our vessels, but not venturing to make one. Just as the "Merrimack" was leaving, she bade our fleet good night by firing three shots into it, which were replied to by the "Naugatuck" and "Octorora."

Not long after this, an attack was made by our fleet upon

the enemy's shore-batteries, extending all the way from Ocean View to Sewall's Point, a distance of ten miles or more. The shore was heavily wooded, and these works, in which were stationed small bodies of troops, were erected in the edge of the timber, commanding all the available landing-places. At Sewall's Point, where there was a large Confederate camp, were several very powerful works, containing one or more bomb-proofs. The movement began about one o'clock in the afternoon, and the line of battle, which was led by the "Monitor," was made up of about twelve vessels. Beginning near Ocean View, the fleet commenced raining a shower of shot and shell upon the beach and woods. Presently a puff of white smoke was seen rising among the trees, and at the same moment a huge shell exploded just over the masts of one of the gun-boats. This was followed by another and another in rapid succession; but the fire from the boats was too severe for the little sand-battery: its guns were silenced and its garrison dispersed in less than fifteen minutes.

While this battle was in progress, some of the leading vessels had stirred up several other works, and a fierce contest ensued, ending, as did the first, in the course of a few minutes. In this manner, the fleet continued along the shore, silencing every battery as it was reached, until it came to the end of Sewall's Point, where it encountered the bomb-proofs, and met with a more determined resistance. Here the chief part of the fighting was done by the "Monitor," which, being of lighter draught than the other vessels, lay in near the beach, and shelled the forts at comparatively close range, while the other boats shelled the woods and camp.

The view of this battle from "Signal Station Point," so called (Newport News), was very grand. The large shot of the "Monitor" would strike the sides of the earthworks, and throw up vast columns of dust and sand high into the air, while the shells from the frigates and gunboats were exploding rapidly among the branches of the forest-trees, tearing away great pieces of their trunks, and scattering the fragments in all directions. At short intervals, a long flash of flame and column of smoke would dart out of the embrasures of the hostile works, showing that the enemy was not disposed to yield his position.

After this bombardment had been going on for an hour or more, the "Merrimack" was seen coming down the Elizabeth, and when within a mile of the Point, every vessel of the Federal fleet turned suddenly and went toward the fortress. The ram attempted no pursuit, but sailed down toward the Point and remained stationary for a few moments; when, as suddenly as they had retreated, the Federal vessels began to return, whereupon the "Merrimack" retired, and the bombardment of the land-batteries was renewed, continuing till well into the evening, but with no decisive results.

A few days after this event (April 19), an affair of some interest occurred, being an attempt on the part of the Confederates to shell out the garrison at the Rip-Raps. By means of a gun of remarkable range, stationed on Sewall's Point, the enemy was able to throw shell entirely over the little island, which he did more frequently than to hit it. The shelling began late in the afternoon, in the midst of a severe thunder-storm, and lasted until some time after dark, the batteries at the Rip-Raps replying with vigor. It is not probable that either party inflicted any injury upon the other; but the display afforded by the passing shells, made visible by their burning fuses, making graceful curves, sometimes almost meeting each other in the heavens, and bursting in the darkness, was grand and startling.

The department of Fortress Monroe had now assumed greater importance than it had ever possessed before. The attention of the whole world had been turned thither because of the great battles of the 8th and 9th of March, which had revolutionized the system of marine architecture, and furnished examples of human bravery unsurpassed in the annals of naval warfare. But the department was to be the starting-point of one of the greatest of our many military expeditions, and for a brief season the rendezvous of one of the finest armies that ever took the field; namely, the Army of the Potomac. "The council, composed of four corps commanders, organized by the President of the United States, at its meeting on the 13th of March, adopted Fort Monroe as the base of operations for the movement of the Army of the Potomac upon Richmond."*

* General McClellan's "Report and Campaigns," page 150.

The first arrival of troops was about the middle of March, and from that time till the middle of April, transports were constantly arriving in the Roads, loaded with soldiers, horses, and all the munitions of war.

Fortress Monroe and Hampton soon assumed the appearance of great mercantile ports; the wharves were filled with vessels and steamers, and long trains were constantly engaged in transporting the cargoes of these vessels to the headquarters of the army, then established in the vicinity of Hampton. The increased activity in the military affairs of the department was manifest at Newport News, for occasionally troops were landed at this camp, and among them the entire division of General Casey, numbering five or six thousand men, and containing several light batteries, which paraded upon the field near the works. On the 2d of April, the transport steamer "Hero" arrived, bringing a Maine and Pennsylvania regiment. As the steamer was nearing the landing, she was fired at from the enemy's works at Pig Point, and narrowly escaped being hit. About this time, there came several Western regiments, all of which bivouacked on the plain, and later the camp was largely increased by the arrival of other troops. A part of these were destined to go to New Orleans, and during the latter part of April, took passage on the transport steamer "Constitution," at that time the largest in the service. When the "Constitution" steamed out of the James, she was exposed to a very severe fire from Sewall's Point. It was broad daylight, and as she approached the hostile shore, being compelled to keep in the main channel because of her great draught, the enemy opened on her with shell, several of which exploded among her rigging and inflicted upon her some damage; but fortunately none of the troops were hurt, though they were all on deck. Events of this nature, and the daring exploits of Captain Drake DeKay, a very gallant young officer of General Mansfield's staff, furnished abundant material for camp talk, and kept up a constant excitement. DeKay formed a crew from among the members of companies A and B of the Twenty-ninth Regiment, manned one of the large barges of the "Cumberland," saved from the battle, and made nightly excursions up the river, capturing on one occasion a schooner, and setting her on fire; and at another time landed on the opposite shore, and reconnoitred the enemy's position. When the Army of the Potomac began to move up the Peninsula, and rumors thick and fast of great battles and severe skirmishes reached the rear, the excitement was increased tenfold. Among these rumors, which no one, however ingenious or industrious, could have traced to their source, especially to any authentic source, were reports, frequently circulated, that the regiment was to cross the river and attack Pig Point, to join the Army of the Potomac, march on Norfolk, and to do a great variety of other things; and, strangely enough, many of these predicted movements were eventually made by the regiment.

CHAPTER XV.

DEPARTURE OF THE REGIMENT FROM NEWPORT NEWS — CAPTURE OF NORFOLK AND PORTSMOUTH — THE "MERRIMACK" BLOWN UP — THE OCCUPATION OF THE CAPTURED CITIES — CAMP HARRISON — THE REGIMENT CHARGED WITH KILLING PIGS — IT GOES TO THE MARINE HOSPITAL — PATROL DUTY IN PORTSMOUTH — THE UNIONISTS OF PORTSMOUTH — THE REGIMENT LEAVES THE CITY — CAMP ANDREW — CAMP OF ADVANCED POST — AN ATTEMPT TO MAKE THE MEN SLAVE-CATCHERS FAILS — THE LONG MARCH TO SUFFOLK — ORDERED TO JOIN THE ARMY OF THE POTOMAC — SAIL UP THE YORK — THE REGIMENT LANDS AT "WHITE HOUSE."

Early in May, the following order was issued :—

"HEADQUARTERS DEPARTMENT OF VIRGINIA,
"FORTRESS MONROE, May —, 1862.
"GENERAL ORDERS, No. 40.

"The troops of this command being about to march into the country occupied by the enemy, they are warned that plundering and depredating upon private property will not be tolerated for a moment. *The penalty of death will be executed upon any soldier found violating this order.*

"By command of Major-General Wool.
"(Signed) WM. D. WHIPPLE, *Asst. Adj. Gen.*"

This order, and the movements which soon followed, clearly indicated that a more active life was in store for the troops here, who had performed little else than camp duty for nearly a year.

On the 8th, the new iron-clad "Galena," accompanied by the "Aroostook" and "Port Royal," — the latter vessel under the command of the brave Lieutenant Morris, and manned by the survivors of the "Cumberland," — came up the James, and passing up toward City Point, engaged several of the enemy's works.

On the 9th, Captain Howard's Light Battery left the camp and went to Fortress Monroe, and at midnight orders were received for the Twenty-ninth Regiment to march to the same place. The men were aroused from their slumbers, ordered to pack knapsacks, and be in readiness to march at four o'clock the next morning. This was indeed a very brief notice for the men to prepare to quit their old home, to which, because of the numerous comforts they had enjoyed there, they had become strongly attached. Every barrack was a little museum in itself, and each soldier had collected a great variety of useful, and to him, valuable articles. Knowing that he could carry but a few things with him, it became a painful struggle to decide what to take and what to abandon. The regiment was promptly in line at the hour named, but did not march till eight o'clock in the morning.

The distance by land to Fortress Monroe is about twelve miles. The day was warm and cloudless, and the men, not having had at that time much experience in marching, trudged along over the dusty roads, panting from the heat, and reached Camp Hamilton at two o'clock in the afternoon, somewhat jaded. Towards evening, when they had refreshed themselves with a meal made of such rations as they took with them in their haversacks and some hot coffee, they were ordered to "fall in"; and after marching out of a large wheat-field, where they had rested for a couple of hours, proceeded on the road to Fortress Monroe, reaching there a little after sundown, halting on one of the wharves, and in the course of an hour embarking on a small steamboat which was waiting to receive them. A number of other transports were lying in the Roads, filled with troops, all bound on the same expedition. When the steamer cast off from the wharf, the troops on the various boats began to cheer, and cries of "Norfolk!" and "Richmond!" sounded out on the still air of the mild and pleasant evening.

After a delightful moonlight voyage of an hour, the boat approached the shore at Ocean View, where a pontoon wharf, formed of canal-boats and planks, had been constructed. The boat was made fast to this floating structure, and the regiment immediately landed by companies, marching up upon the white sand-beach and forming in line. Just above the beach, on a grassy lawn of several acres, stood the remains of a large building, windowless and dark and deserted; close about this cleared space was the edge of the forest, which stretched as far inland as the eye could see in the dim moonlight. After the regiment had formed on the beach, it marched up to this grass-plot and halted. The men were already weary, and in a few moments they began to lie down on the grass, and soon fell into a sound sleep. At last, after nearly an hour spent here, the men were aroused, and the regiment took up its line of march into the woods, a squad of cavalry going in advance. The road was narrow, rough, and muddy, the branches of the towering trees meeting overhead and forming an arch, shutting out even the light of the stars, and rendering the way blinding dark. The discomforts of the march were much increased by the numerous obstructions the enemy had placed in the road, consisting chiefly of large pine-trees that had been felled across it, through the branches of which the men were obliged to crawl, tearing their clothing, and scratching their faces and hands. The result was, the marching was very slow and exhausting, it being nearly midnight before the halting-place was reached. The bivouac was made in a deserted cavalry camp of the enemy, formed in a little clearing in the forest; on two sides of the enclosure were rows of very comfortable board huts, and on the third, a long line of horse-sheds. All about the camp, fires were burning brightly, indicating recent occupation.

By the time the halt was made, both officers and men were about worn out, and every one shifted for himself, seeking some unoccupied house or sheltered place. "Tattoo" was not sounded that night; the owlish propensities of the mischievous ones were thoroughly overcome by fatigue, and in a few moments the camp was as quiet as a bed-chamber.

After a sound and refreshing sleep, the men awoke bright and early on the morning of the 11th of May. The forest in which they had reposed seemed primeval and boundless. Shaggy green moss hung in long, graceful locks from the boughs of the gigantic pines; the woods were vocal with the music of merry birds; it was one of the most genial days of all the spring. But the boys had not long to tarry here; Norfolk was to be taken, and as soon as breakfast was had, the regiment was to march.

While waiting here, a tremendous explosion was heard; the noise seemed to come from the direction of Sewall's Point, and the rumor immediately spread through the camp that the "Merrimack" had been blown up. Though the person who started this report doubtless guessed at it, yet such proved to be the fact, and the guess was founded upon the general belief that the Confederates would be certain to destroy the iron-clad as soon as a movement was made on Norfolk.

The regiment "fell in" about seven o'clock, and the march to Norfolk was at once commenced. The road for most of the distance lay through the forest and a country that was almost destitute of habitations. The men were in light marching order, having left their knapsacks at Camp Hamilton on the day previous. Many of the soldiers who performed that march will remember the unsatisfactory statements of the negroes met on the road, as to the distance to Norfolk. "How far is it to Norfolk?" was the oft-repeated inquiry made of these grinning contrabands. "I s'pose dis eighteen mile, massa," and "a heap of a way off," were the invariable answers made to these questions. And the same statements were made by them when the regiment was actually within a mile of the city.

At noon, the regiment arrived at a line of breastworks, two miles from the city, enclosing a deserted camp of the enemy, known as Camp Harrison. Intelligence had been received while on the march that Norfolk and Portsmouth had capitulated the night before; and when the long line of works, bristling with guns, some sixty-five in number, greeted the eyes of the soldiers, they inspired no emotions other than surprise that the enemy should have abandoned a position of such great strength, and wonder as to how the city could ever have been taken, if the Confederates had made a determined stand here.

After a brief halt at this place, the regiment was again ordered to "fall in," and in the course of a half-hour was in the heart of the captured city. The march through Norfolk proved very interesting to the men, though few, if any, demonstrations were made by the people. A solitary house displayed the American flag, and this was greeted with cheers. The regiment marched to the City Hall, from the dome of which the Stars and Stripes were flying. From this point a view of the river, was obtained, and, lying at anchor, were seen a number of our gunboats, together with the "Monitor," all making a liberal display of bunting, and reminding one of a Fourth of July celebration.

At night, the regiment returned to Camp Harrison, where it remained till the 14th of May. The enemy had burned the barracks at this place, and our men, not being provided with tents, were obliged to resort to a great variety of methods to shield themselves from the cold air and dense fogs at night. Rails were taken, placed against the breastworks, and covered with grass and green boughs, under which squads of five and six would sleep; others found lodging in the magazines, which were formed by deep excavations in the earth, covered with logs and sand; others still made them little huts of brush and reeds, while not a few had no other covering than a single blanket. The ground was low and marshy, and the exhalations from the neighboring swamp (the Dismal Swamp) and the accumulated offal of the camp, gave the whole air a foul odor, that eventually would have resulted disastrously to the health of the troops. On the morning of the 14th, however, the regiment received orders to march; and although the men knew nothing of what was in store for them, the order was joyfully received, because any change could not be otherwise than for the better. The regiment marched again to Norfolk, and crossing the ferry, entered the city of Portsmouth. After arriving here, it proceeded to the United States Marine Hospital, and went into camp, being supplied with Sibley tents, which were pitched upon the beautiful green lawn bordering upon the water, the officers taking up their quarters in the hospital.

A report reached General Wool, at this time, that members of the regiment had killed a number of swine while on their march from Ocean View to Norfolk, and the result was the following order: —

"HEADQUARTERS DEPARTMENT OF VIRGINIA,
"FORT MONROE, VA., May 12, 1862.

"BRIG. GEN. EGBERT L. VIELE,
"*Military Governor of Norfolk.*

"SIR: It has been reported at these headquarters that certain soldiers of Colonel E. W. Pierce's Twenty-ninth Regiment Massachusetts Volunteers yesterday killed a number of hogs, private property of citizens living near Ocean View, Va. You will use every endeavor to ascertain who are the offenders, and, if you succeed, you will place them in close confinement and report them to these headquarters. If it should be ascertained that this report is true, you will cause the owners to be paid for the hogs at the rate of five dollars for each hog. If the money is not immediately paid, you will order the regiment to return to Newport News forthwith, and send the offender or offenders prisoners to Fort Monroe.

"By command of Major-General Wool.

"(Signed)   WM. D. WHIPPLE, *Asst. Adj. Gen.*"

The Colonel of the regiment was called upon by General Viele to explain the matter mentioned in the order. The affair was thoroughly investigated; but no evidence could be obtained to show that any member of the regiment killed the hogs, and the name of the person who gave the information to General Wool was requested. Here the whole affair ended; no one of the regiment was executed, nor was the regiment sent back to Newport News in disgrace on account of two or three defunct pigs, that probably belonged to the enemy's camp, and not to private individuals.

This was a good season for orders. No sooner had the Major-General recovered from his wrath about the hog affair, than he began to think about his "skilful and gallant movement" on Norfolk, and the result was General Order No. 47, as replete with egotism and self-praise as it was long and gusty. The Major-General took great credit to himself for having "captured" Norfolk and Portsmouth, the fact being that these cities were *evacuated* by the Confederates in consequence of the movement of General McClellan on Richmond, and simply *occupied* by the troops under General Wool. Not a drop of blood was shed in the movement, and not the slightest resistance made by the Confederate commander. Indeed, the movement did not originate with General Wool, but was commenced upon the suggestion of President Lincoln.

The regiment remained at the Marine Hospital till the 20th, during which time it was almost constantly on duty. The duties performed were those of patrol, provost, and guard. The night-patrol service was sometimes exciting and amusing. The city was filled with dogs, mostly of the species known as "cur"; and as the patrol wended through the dark streets and narrow alleys, the canines would set up their howlings and yelps. Occasionally a large pack of these animals would make a sudden sally from out of some yard upon the passing soldiers, and then would follow a charge with fixed bayonets, from which the insolent dogs generally came off "second best," leaving some of their pack stretched lifeless in the street.

Some of the women of Norfolk and Portsmouth were quite as spiteful towards the soldiers as were the dogs. The scene was not infrequent of a bevy of finely-dressed ladies parading the streets with small Confederate flags pinned to their breasts, and, on passing a soldier, gathering their skirts closely about their bodies, lest they should touch the hated "vandal." And not seldom these fiery women would indulge in insulting and taunting language. Another, and, if possible, still more fiendish manifestation of hatred of the soldiers, consisted in politely presenting them with beautiful bouquets, filled with needles. The giver would station herself at some convenient point of observation after doing this, and wait patiently for the soldier to press the flowers to his face, when up would go a loud shout of exultation. Few, if any, indignities were visited upon the perpetrators of these petty, though annoying, insults, the good breeding of our men usually preventing them from indulging in either harsh or insulting language, though their ingenuity generally enabled them to do or say something in return that made their fair assailants feel any way but pleased with the result. There were, however, among the people of Portsmouth, and especially among the former employés at the navy-yard, those who still loved the Union, and who remembered with gratitude that for many years they and their children had enjoyed a comfortable support from the labor which the Government had regularly furnished them. One day, when Captain Leach's company was on guard duty at Newtown (a part of the city), in the vicinity of the navy-yard, the loyal people there welcomed them by a display of American flags. The whole settlement was radiant with bunting — streamers, ships' flags, jacks, and pennants — which had been saved from the yard in April, 1861, when the place was abandoned by the United States officers. How these poor people had managed to keep these emblems of loyalty during the year that had elapsed, was something of a mystery, considering how strict was the surveillance under which all suspected Unionists had been placed. But they had hidden them under carpets, in attics, and cellars; and one old gentleman stated that his had been boxed up tightly and buried in his garden, and the musty, soiled appearance of the flags showed plainly these statements were true.

On the 20th of May, the regiment broke camp at the Marine Hospital, and marched through Portsmouth to the Gosport Navy-Yard, near which it went into camp. The camping-ground was by no means pleasant, nor the means of comfort there afforded great. On the following day, the Quartermaster reduced the number of tents, at which there was considerable fault found; but by this time the majority of the men had arrived at that desirable point in a soldier's life, where they treated every discomfort and privation as a necessary part of their military experience. Only four days were spent here, when the regiment again moved, this time some five miles from the city, encamping in an extensive clover-field, that was named by Colonel Pierce "Camp Andrew."

While here, the men were kept quite active in drilling, and in the performance of guard and picket duty. The location of the camp was only a little less unhealthy than that of Camp Harrison. On the 26th, the regiment moved again, going just outside of a line of earthworks that had been thrown up by the enemy during their occupation. At this place, which was called "Camp of Advanced Post," were also the Twentieth New York and a Pennsylvania regiment. The latter manifested a strange fancy for animals; a black bear, a score or more of dogs and cats, and a troop of monkeys making up the list. On the night of the 30th, occurred a severe thunder and rain storm; the camp was flooded, and the lightning lit up the neighboring forest at every flash.

It was at this place that an attempt was made by a slave-master to pursue his runaway negroes into the camp of the regiment. Captain Samuel H. Doten was officer of the day on the first occasion; the master requested of the Captain, permission to search the camp for his two negroes, whom he suspected were concealed there, having followed the regiment from Portsmouth, but his request was flatly refused. The planter being satisfied that he could not succeed without some authority from headquarters, called on General Viele, and after telling his story, had no difficulty in obtaining from that officer an order directed to the Colonel of the Twenty-ninth Regiment to immediately produce the negroes in question and turn them over to their owner. Armed with this order, the citizen appeared the next day, and demanded of Captain Thomas W. Clarke (who had succeeded Doten as officer of the day), in the arrogant plantation style, permission to search the camp for his missing servants, at the same time exhibiting the order from General Viele. Like his predecessor, Clarke refused to grant the request, but on the ground that it was improper to allow citizens to search the camp, and especially in an enemy's country, and that, moreover, the order did not give the bearer any such authority. The citizen was therefore retained on the guard line, and the order taken by Clarke to headquarters, where a consultation with the Colonel was had. The order demanded the giving up of the slaves, and thus rendered a search imperative; but it was concluded that the search should be made, not by the citizen, but by the non-commissioned officers of each company. Curious as it may seem, notwithstanding a most thorough hunt was made, and that there were a large number of negroes in camp, the particular negroes inquired for were not found, and the citizen was compelled to return without his slaves.

The officers and men of the Twenty-ninth Regiment never felt a very deep interest in returning refugee negroes to their masters, and had never been educated up to the point of believing it to be any part of their duties as soldiers, in fighting for the restoration of the Union, to aid the slavemasters who were attempting to destroy it. To have felt otherwise, would have been as unjust as unnatural, for the poor negroes were the best, and in many instances the only, friends which the so'diers found throughout the Southern land. Whenever they came into our camps, they communicated to our officers whatever information they possessed about the movements and plans of the enemy; and although this information was seldom reliable, yet it was conscientiously given, its imperfections being mainly attributable to the utter incapacity of the negro to comprehend number or distance.

They were faithful and devoted servants to the soldiers, never demanding or expecting pay for their labor; were made supremely happy by the gift of a pair of blue trousers or a blouse; would follow a regiment on its longest and hardest marches; relieve the weary soldier of his knapsack or gun, and if the soldier was sick or overcome by the heat, save him from falling on the road and suffering the fate of a straggler. Scarcely a soldier of Company C will fail to remember the faithful "Toney," who came to them from North Carolina through the wilds of the Dismal Swamp, and followed their fortunes to the end of the war.

On the 1st of June, the Paymaster arrived in camp, and paid off the men. At midnight of the 2d, orders came for the regiment to march early the next morning; it was in line and moved out of camp at six o'clock on the morning of the 3d. The place of destination was Suffolk, a post-village, capital of Nansemond County, Va., distant from Portsmouth about thirty-five miles, and the distance actually marched by the regiment, from its encampment to the village, not less than twenty-five miles. The day was extremely hot and sultry; the roads for much of the distance half submerged in water, and everywhere muddy. The men were in heavy marching order, each man's burden consisting of his rifle, three days' rations, forty rounds of cartridges, a canteen, and a knapsack. The men had not had much practice in marching, and it was easy enough to foresee the result of such an undertaking. Long before noon they began to straggle; instances of sunstroke were quite numerous: and all during that boiling, blistering day, no halt exceeding fifteen minutes was permitted. It was *a forced march of the most aggravated character, and that, too, without the slightest demand or necessity.*

At this time, the Sixteenth Massachusetts Regiment, under Colonel Powell T. Wyman, was at Suffolk, and the post was in command of that officer, who was a soldier of superior qualities. When the Twenty-ninth Regiment straggled into

Suffolk, on the night of the 3d of June, with about half its numbers, and the circumstances became known to Colonel Wyman, he expressed great indignation at the manner in which this movement had been conducted, asserting that the order to Colonel Pierce did not contemplate a forced march.

The regiment had outmarched its baggage-wagons, and when it arrived in the town it was consequently destitute of tents; and without any orders or arrangement on the part of the commanding officer, the men were left to shift for themselves. The majority slept in the open air, and among them a veteran captain of sixty, who wrapped himself up in a blanket and lay down upon the field. During the night, it rained heavily, and a more sorry-appearing body of soldiers was never mustered for roll-call than the Twenty-ninth on the following morning. Quite a number were made seriously ill by sunstrokes.

Captain Howard's Light Battery, largely made up of detailed members of the regiment, arrived here on the 4th. The entire Federal force in and about Suffolk at this time was less than 2,500 men all told, and consisted of the following troops: Sixteenth Massachusetts, Twenty-ninth Massachusetts, Captain Howard's Light Battery, a section of Captain Follett's Battery, and two companies of cavalry. The enemy in large force were in the near neighborhood, the picket duty was not a little hazardous, and the isolated situation of the troops, and the constant danger of attack, rendered the responsibilities of this command of the gravest character. It was fortunate for the cause of the Government, therefore, that its interests here were confided to the charge of so brave and skilful an officer as Colonel Powell T. Wyman.

The Twenty-ninth Regiment, as also the Sixteenth, were destined to remain here but a short time. At two o'clock in the afternoon of the 6th, the Twenty-ninth received orders to march, and striking tents, it proceeded to the Suffolk Station of the Seaboard and Roanoke Railroad, where it took the cars for Portsmouth, arriving at the latter place at five o'clock in the afternoon of the same day. The night of the 6th was spent in the depot at Portsmouth, none of the enlisted men being permitted to leave their quarters.

On the morning of the 7th, the regiment embarked on the

steamer "Catskill," for White House Landing, at the head of navigation on the Pamunkey River. The pleasure of this trip, which occupied the entire day, was in striking contrast with the numerous discomforts and hardships which the soldiers had experienced during the four weeks preceding, and which they were destined to encounter in the eventful campaign upon which they were about to enter. The day was exceedingly fine, and the course of the steamer lay along the banks of the Elizabeth River, Craney Island, Hampton Roads, and the shores of the Chesapeake Bay, — some of the finest water and land scenery to be found in the Old Dominion. The mouth of York River was reached about noon. There were few, if any, on board the "Catskill" who were ignorant of the historic associations that clustered about the two points of high land that form the mouth of the York. All eyes were busy obtaining a view of these places, — Yorktown on the left and Gloucester on the right. Here was encamped but recently the army of General Magruder; here on the 19th of October, 1781, Lord Cornwallis surrendered to General Washington his sword, an event that practically terminated the war of the Revolution. Still standing in Yorktown was the house of General Thomas Nelson, who commanded the Virginia militia at the capture of Cornwallis.

The sail up the York and its larger branch, the Pamunkey, occupied the remainder of the day. The country was in its finest dress; broad green meadows skirted the stream as far as the vision could extend; the meadows landward were bounded by high banks, covered with flowering trees and climbing vines; and beyond all were the dense pine forests, so common to the Peninsula. Here and there along the banks were comfortable, peaceful-looking farm-houses, about which clustered groups of colored people, who waved their hands as the large white steamer glided by.

White House Landing was reached just as the sun was going down. The river here was filled with transports, gunboats, and vessels of all sizes and descriptions. White House was a busy place in those days. There were to be seen large stacks of bread-boxes, immense numbers of barrels of beef and pork, army wagons, and ordnance supplies; and droves of horses and mules and large herds of fat cattle were grazing among the green fields of General Fitz Hugh Lee, who owned the place. Here, also, were arriving and departing long trains of wagons, engaged in transporting these supplies to the front, some ten or fifteen miles away, and close at hand was a locomotive attached to an extensive train of cars, the engine bearing the familiar name of "Mayflower." *

Upon leaving the steamer, the regiment marched the distance of a mile from the wharf, into a fine grass-field near the wagon-road. By this time it was quite dark; the night was warm, and the men made few complaints at being compelled to sleep without tents. Just as they were going off into a sound sleep, some wag, whose love of fun was still active, cried out to the guard, "Put up the bars there, by the road; if you don't, we shall all catch our death-colds before morning!" This was the signal for a hearty laugh, the merriment of the occasion being heightened by the actual putting up of the bars.

* Formerly, this engine was the property of the Old Colony Railroad Company of Massachusetts, but had been purchased by the Government.

CHAPTER XVI.

MARCH TO THE FRONT — FAIR OAKS — ASSIGNED TO THE IRISH BRIGADE — HARD SERVICE — SHARPSHOOTING — THE AFFAIR OF JUNE 15, AND DEATH OF BROWN — THE WOODCHOPPING AFFAIR — BATTLE OF GAINES' MILL. — THE RETREAT — BATTLES OF PEACH ORCHARD AND SAVAGE'S STATION — DESTRUCTION OF STORES — BURNING OF THE TRAIN OF CARS.

On the morning of the 8th of June, the regiment was for the first time supplied with shelter-tents. These consisted of two pieces of cloth, each about six feet long and three and one-half feet wide, so made as to button together, the two parts overlapping and thus shedding water. One tent was issued to every two men, each man carrying his half in his knapsack. There were no ends to this slight covering, and hence the name *shelter-tent*. At about four o'clock in the afternoon of this day, the regiment started for the front, marching a distance of some seven miles on the Richmond and York River Railroad, halting at night, and going into camp on a slight elevation of ground near the track. After breakfast on the following morning, the march towards the front was resumed. The destination of the regiment was Fair Oaks, about seven miles from Richmond. Fair Oaks was the centre of the Union line, and was held by the corps of General Sumner. The march was performed on the railroad, a distance of about thirteen miles, and was accomplished by two o'clock in the afternoon. Upon reaching the lines, the regiment was halted in a piece of plowed ground, some thirty yards or more in front of the grove of graceful oaks that gave the place its name, and just on the edge of the forest in which were stationed our pickets.

This was the battle-ground of June 1, one of the severest battles of the campaign, the effects of which were still apparent. The trunks of the trees were literally filled with bullets, while the little white cottage then occupied by General Sumner was perforated with shots of various sizes. Many of the enemy's dead in the adjacent forest were still unburied, and the sickening odors that came from it were almost unendurable. The regiment had some days before been ordered to join General Sumner's corps, and on this day it was, by the following order, attached to Brigadier-General Thomas Francis Meagher's brigade :—

"HEADQUARTERS RICHARDSON'S DIVISION,
"CAMP AT FAIR OAKS, VA., June 9, 1862.
"SPECIAL ORDER NO. —.

"The Twenty-ninth Regiment Massachusetts Volunteers is hereby assigned to the brigade of General Meagher.

'By command of Brigadier-General Richardson.

"JOHN M. NOWELL, A. A. G."

This brigade was better known as the "Irish Brigade," and was composed of the Sixty-third, Sixty-ninth, and Eighty-eighth New York regiments, — all Irish. The Brigade had fought gallantly at Fair Oaks on the first of June, where it had lost heavily; and the Sixty-ninth, now commanded by Colonel Robert Nugent,[*] a fine soldier, had distinguished itself at Bull Run. At the time of the assignment of the Twenty-ninth Regiment to this brigade, the latter was in need of recruitment, having lost a good many of its men by battle and disease; but it had been desired by its officers to fill up its depleted ranks by the addition of another Irish regiment. Although the Twenty-ninth was essentially an American regiment, very largely composed of and officered by men who were direct descendants of the early settlers of the Plymouth and Bay colonies, — one of its members, indeed, being a lineal descendant of Miles Standish, — yet it was cordially welcomed to the Brigade by its old officers and members.

The night of the 9th of June was cold and stormy; at sundown the men pitched their tents; but an order soon came directing that they be struck at once, as they had already been seen by the enemy, and had attracted his fire. The storm lasted all night, and the men were compelled to lie exposed to a pelting rain, upon a bed of mud. No rations were issued to the regiment till the night of the 10th, its

* Now Major Twenty-fourth United States Infantry.

members in the meantime being obliged to depend for food upon the generosity of the other regiments of the Brigade. The levelling effect of field life was curiously apparent here. It was an honor, but not a material advantage, to be an officer under these circumstances. The writer remembers seeing the lamented Major of the regiment sitting on his horse some time during the second day, at the front, wet to his skin, shivering from the cold, and asking and receiving from a more fortunate private, a drink of hot coffee from a very black-looking tin dipper.

The two armies were very near each other at this place, only a half-mile of woods intervening; and in these woods were the Union and Confederate pickets, stationed behind trees and logs; in some places the hostile lines being less than twenty yards apart. The nearness of the pickets to each other resulted in almost constant firing, which was very destructive, hardly an hour elapsing from sunrise to sunset without some poor soldier being borne from the forest reeking in blood, and not seldom pallid and lifeless. To add to the horrors of this life, the sharpshooters of the enemy, stationed in tall pines and in their rifle-pits, fired with almost unerring aim at every moving object; and at irregular intervals, during both night and day, the enemy's batteries threw shot and shell into our lines.

Neither was all the shelling and sharpshooting done by the enemy. The Federals were by no means on the defensive, but were besieging Richmond, and neglected no opportunity to worry the enemy, or wrest from him even so much as a foot of ground. Directly in front of Sumner's headquarters, at the edge of a large field, were the remains of an old house, and near it an apple-tree, behind which there was usually stationed one of our sharpshooters, who amused himself in exchanging shots with a Confederate rifleman who had a lodge in the branches of a large pine on the farther side of the field. The elevated nature of the ground in the rear of this tree afforded the troops there encamped an opportunity of witnessing these practices, and when a particularly good shot was made, they would usually manifest their appreciation of it by a loud cheer.

These days at Fair Oaks, as well as those that followed,

embracing the whole period from the 9th of June till the time when the Army of the Potomac was finally settled down at Harrison's Landing, were among the most exciting in the history of the regiment. In the first place, the men were not only exposed to some of the worst dangers of war, but also suffered intensely from the hot weather, unhealthy location of the camps, and severe labor. From some mistaken notion, they were ordered to leave their overcoats and blouses at White House Landing, the want of which was keenly felt, as the nights were cold, and the fogs, especially after nightfall, so dense as closely to resemble rain, while the days were broiling hot. The dress-coat worn by them, being a close-fitting garment, was ill-adapted to fatigue duty, and not sufficiently thick to protect them from the chilling night air.

The standing order requiring all troops at the front to quit their tents at three o'clock in the morning, and remain standing, nearly motionless, in line of battle till sunrise, proved very exhaustive; and all these hardships combined, to which should be added the impurity of the water and the poisoned air of the battle-field, produced many cases of fever and other equally fatal diseases. On the afternoon of the 14th of June, companies C and E were ordered on picket in the swamp at the left of the railroad, nearly in front of Hooker's division. This place was considered one of the worst on the whole picket line, for several reasons; skirmishes there were more common than at any other point, and the swamp was very wet, being in places little better than a morass, and everywhere filled with a dense undergrowth of bushes and briers. The pickets were stationed behind trees, which in many instances were scarcely large enough to cover the body, and about them no footing save a few hussocks or uncovered roots.

The night of the 14th was unusually mild and beautiful; the moon shone brightly, throwing here and there a beam of its soft light down through the branches of the pines, and relieving the place of some of its natural gloom. There seemed to be some sort of a festival or celebration in the camp of the enemy, as several of their bands played merrily all the evening. Not a shot was fired during the whole night, and this peaceful order of things continued nearly all the succeeding day (Sunday), which was warm and sultry. At about three o'clock in the afternoon, a violent thunderstorm came up, accompanied by a strong wind. When the storm was at its height, and our guards were crouching under the trees and bushes to shield themselves from the pelting rain, the crackling of the brush in their front was heard, and presently the heads of the enemy were seen through the undergrowth. This was to be a raid upon our pickets, and the time was chosen in the hope of finding them unprepared, and confused by the tempest; but our men were vigilant, and as soon as the enemy were seen, began to fire. The latter replied by a loud screech and a deafening volley of musketry, showing that they were present in large numbers, and immediately after charged. Our pickets fell back from their posts to the edge of the woods, firing as they retired, and upon reaching the reserves under Captains Leach and Doten, formed in line. The Confederates, to the number, apparently, of a full regiment, followed slowly on, till they came to within a few yards of the edge of the wood, when they paused, and again fired several volleys; but by this time the swamp was being shelled by our batteries. The shells bursting among the trees, and throwing down large fragments, caused a sudden termination of the assault, and the retirement of the enemy. During this fight, which lasted about fifteen minutes, some soldiers of Company E captured one of the enemy in the swamp, while attempting to retreat with his comrades. In this affray, also, George D. Brown of Company C, a very faithful and intelligent soldier, was killed; and Charles Kleinhans of Company E, fatally wounded. The body of Brown was found by his comrades, when they returned to their posts, in a most shocking condition; he had apparently been shot through the vitals and afterward bayoneted through the lower jaw and neck; his clothing had been stripped from his body, and every article of value he had upon his person carried away.

On the 16th of June, the Brigade was relieved of its post at the extreme front, and ordered into the grove of oaks, in the rear, where the ground was much higher. The 18th of June was a day of great excitement. In the afternoon, our pickets at the centre advanced, bringing on a sharp engagement, which lasted for several hours ; and this was followed by a very determined advance of a large body of the enemy's infantry on the Nine Miles Road, which ran directly through our camp. They came along in fine style, and in full view of our troops, until they reached a point about eighty yards from one of our outworks, on the edge of the forest, when its battery opened on them with shell and grape. The column was at once thrown into confusion, a wild flight soon following, the dead and wounded being left in the road. After nightfall, the wounded were gathered up by our men and brought into camp, and the dead buried in the field near by.

On the 19th, the Sixteenth Massachusetts Infantry, forming a part of General Hooker's division, encamped at the left of the railroad, near the famous twin houses, had a severe engagement with the enemy, in the swamp before referred to, losing thirty-four of its number killed and wounded. The regiment was ordered to advance through the thick woods, and when well into them, encountered a superior force of the enemy posted behind the trees.

June 20, companies C, E, and D, together with several companies of the Sixty-ninth and Eighty-eighth New York regiments, were detailed to work in the trenches in front of General Hooker's division. A little after noon, the enemy commenced shelling the working party, keeping it up for nearly two hours. There were no casualties. On the 23d, several companies of the regiment were again detailed to go on picket in the swamp, and, with a portion of the First Massachusetts Infantry, advanced through the woods to the enemy's rifle-pits on the farther side. A sharp skirmish was the result, lasting till near nightfall, dwindling into picket-firing, and in this form continuing all night.

An unusual and strange proceeding was attempted by a certain staff-officer of the corps, on the night of the 26th, in which companies C, E, and G participated. Toward dusk, these commands marched to the headquarters of the Brigade Quartermaster, where each man was given a new axe and helve, and told to put them together. This was a piece of work to which most of the soldiers were quite unaccustomed; but they contrived to do it in a rude manner, and then, under the aforenamed staff-officer, were marched down the railroad, in the direction of Richmond. The men were sent into the forest on either side of the track, and ordered to cut down the trees. It was an insane performance. The woods were thick and inky dark; the soldier could with difficulty discern the tree he was at work upon; the axes were insecurely attached to the helves, constantly coming off; and, worse than all else, the men were at work outside of our pickets, and within a few yards of the enemy. This farce was kept up not longer than ten minutes, when the Confederates suddenly closed it by firing several volleys among the workmen. Mr. Staff-Officer thereupon concluded to cease operations at this point, and take his command farther to the right of the line. Here the same droll proceeding was repeated, and with the same results, except that this time the men barely escaped capture. Nearly the whole night was occupied by this movement, the companies reaching camp at four o'clock the next morning.

There had been, for several days prior to this, many indications of a great movement on the part of the enemy. Firing on the picket lines had greatly increased, and in many places quite formidable attacks had been made. Some of the guards had reported having heard the rumbling of artillery and baggage-wagons within the enemy's lines, the noise indicating a movement of the trains towards our right. All during the 26th there had been heavy firing in the direction of Porter's corps, and at night of this day the news of the battle of Mechanicsville reached our camp at the centre.

About noon of the 27th, loud and continuous firing, growing hourly more severe, was heard from the same quarter, and at five o'clock in the afternoon, the order came for the Brigade to march, each man being supplied with three days' rations, and told to take his blanket. At the time the order was received, companies A and I of the regiment were on picket, and could not be recalled. The brigade line was promptly formed at the hour named, and the regiments at once moved out of camp, in the direction of Gaines' Mill. Proceeding a mile on the main road, the troops were halted, where, after pausing a few moments, they were joined by French's brigade.

The day was one of the hottest of the summer, the roads were dusty and rough, and the march for most of the distance was performed at the double-quick,—the gray-haired Leach, then sixty-four years old, going with his company. He was advised by his brother officers to remain in camp ; but he indignantly refused to do so, declaring that he entered the army to fight, and that he should go with his men into every place of danger, so long as he had the strength to walk. Every moment, as the troops neared the field, the noise and tumult of the battle grew louder and louder, and at last, when a point had been reached within a mile of the place, the men began to witness some of the effects of the terrible struggle which was there going on. First a few stragglers were met, who, panic-stricken, gave doleful accounts of what had happened at the front ; a little farther on, and a number of wounded men were seen lying by the roadside, looking deathly pale, and presently the road ahead seemed filled with ambulances, and mingling among them was a crowd of crippled and maimed soldiers, hobbling along by aid of their muskets; officers, wounded and dead, were being borne away in the arms of their trusty men. The road was so much obstructed by these means, that the onward movement of our brigades was greatly retarded, and it was nearly seven o'clock before they reached a wooden bridge that spanned the Chickahominy, about a half-mile from Gaines' Mill. Here the Fifth United States Cavalry were seen deploying on the edge of the woods and river a short distance in advance, while about the base of the hill, in front, were large masses of disorganized troops, whose excited officers were using vain efforts to rally. This proved to be the most critical moment in the battle, which had raged with fury since noon. General Porter, with not more than thirty-five thousand men, on an extended line reaching all the way from New Cold Harbor to the Chickahominy, had been opposed from the first by a superior force ; and shortly before the arrival of our brigades, the enemy had been re-enforced by the army of Jackson, making a combined force of about sixty thousand. Nearly all the great military leaders of the Rebellion were on the field,— Lee, Jackson, Longstreet, D. H. Hill, A. P. Hill, Ewell, Hood, Whiting, Stuart, and even Jefferson Davis, who had come down from Richmond to witness the destruction of McClellan's right wing. A crushing and fearful charge of the Confederate columns had just been made all along Porter's attenuated and sadly-thinned line; and as our two brigades were rapidly moving toward the hill, the remnants of the last Federal battle line on that part of the field made its appearance upon the crest, shouting wildly,— some of the men with and others without arms,— and then rushed in confusion through the well-formed lines of the brigades, to the rear. As soon as the fugitives passed, the ranks of these troops closed, and giving three hearty cheers, they began to ascend the hill. Just then several pieces of the enemy's light artillery made their appearance upon the brow of the hill, and unlimbering, began to prepare to fire. The advancing troops of Meagher and French caught the enemy's sight; he paused a moment, looked astonished, and then with great celerity limbered up his guns and disappeared without firing a shot.

This act of the fresh troops, in driving the enemy from the hill and deliberately facing their cannon, had the effect of reanimating Porter's jaded and dispirited men. They began to form at once in the rear of Meagher's and French's lines: and on a neighboring elevation was the glorious old Ninth Massachusetts, rallying around its colors for the last time that day.

When our men reached the summit of the hill, the enemy had crossed over the field, and was seen forming on a long ridge nearly opposite our position. The smoke had now risen to the tops of the trees, and beneath this pall lay the ground, formerly a grass-field, but now a dusty plain, where the principal part of the fighting had taken place; the Confederate and Federal dead, wounded and dead horses, knapsacks, muskets, clothing, wrecked caissons and cannon, were scattered in wild confusion over this space, while here and there were the wounded of both armies, crawling and staggering towards their respective lines to escape capture. It was a scene that presented at a glance all the ruin of a terrible battle; but, fortunately, the advancing troops had but a moment to contemplate it. The brigades were at once hurried down the hillside toward the enemy's new line; several of the field-officers of Porter's corps going along with them, and uttering words of encouragement. Among these officers was General Butterfield, who was without a command. Catching sight of the State flag carried by the Twenty-ninth Regiment, — it was the only Pine-tree flag then on the field, — he went dashing up to the color-sergeant, and cried out, "Give me the white flag of Massachusetts, and I'll lead you against the enemy." The Sergeant (Horace A. Jenks of Company E) tightened his grasp on the colors and gave a look of inquiry to the Lieutenant-Colonel of the regiment, who was but a few feet distant. That officer quietly replied, "Keep your colors!" which he did, carrying them bravely forward in the face of a bitter fire. The brigades moved over the field in matchless order, and reaching the rising ground upon which the enemy was posted, began to ascend. The enemy's infantry again fell back, while his batteries remained on the ridge, continuing to fire an occasional shot, until the darkness of night rendered all hostilities impossible. When half-way up the ridge, the men were ordered to lie down, remaining here for nearly two hours. Standing behind the colors was Lieutenant Thomas A. Mayo, watching calmly the movements of the enemy, when a cannon-shot, doubtless aimed at the flags, struck him about the neck and sent him heavily to the ground, lifeless. His body was left on the spot where he fell. The darkness that settled down over the field was simply intense; an object ten feet distant could scarcely be seen. Several times during the night small reconnoitring parties were sent out, and in several instances almost stumbled upon the enemy's soldiers, who were very near us, resulting in an exchange of shots. At one time the regiment, in moving to the left, approached within a few yards of the edge of the timber in which apparently a large number of the enemy were assembled: fires were burning brightly through the woods, around which were gathered groups of Confederates, and so near were our men to this bivouac of the enemy, that the conversations of the latter could be distinctly heard. They seemed to be summing up their losses, recounting the exciting incidents of the battle just ended, and speculating upon the events of the coming day.

The following incident will serve to show the close proximity of the enemy: Major O'Neill of General Meagher's staff was sent forward with certain directions to the regiment; groping his way in the darkness to the position that he felt sure the regiment occupied, he suddenly came upon a body of men. "Is this the Twenty-ninth Massachusetts?" said the gallant Major. "No," was the reply, "this is the —th Virginia, and you are our prisoner," and the Major found himself in the hands of the enemy.

The regiment remained on the field till about two o'clock in the morning, when the order was given to fall back. There were many exciting incidents connected with that night's stay at Gaines' Mill, the precarious situation rendering it necessary for our troops to be active and constantly moving to different parts of the field. The men were very weary, and whenever they were ordered to lie down upon the ground, — as was the case whenever they halted, — they would fall into a slumber. One of the field-officers stated that upon rising from the ground, where he had reclined for a few minutes, he found a snake clinging among his beard.

Our dead had been left unburied upon the field, and our wounded gathered together in small groups about an old building on the side of the hill, near the river. The fate that loomed up before these wounded men, was neglect, capture, and perhaps death. This they keenly realized, and as the retiring columns filed past them, they all joined in earnest supplications to be taken away. The words of one of these unfortunate men are still fresh in the mind of the writer. "Is this what a man gets in fighting for the Union?" said the bleeding, abandoned soldier, as he turned in his pain to listen to the tramping of the retreating troops.

The army of General Porter had crossed the Chickahominy during the night, and his exhausted soldiers were seen lying by the roadside; long trains of wagons were moving away toward the James; the eventful retreat had already begun; but the soldiers knew it not, and well was it that they did not know, or realize the real nature of the situation. When the regiment reached Fair Oaks, which was near daybreak in the morning, it found its tents occupied by other troops. An hour before, the enemy had made an attack in force upon General Sedgwick's front, and these troops had been called to aid in repelling the assault, which was effectively done, for the number of Confederate dead found in the woods in front of Sedgwick's line furnished substantial proof of a bloody repulse.

The brigades had performed important service at Gaines' Mill, and their very slight loss furnishes no evidence of the amount of work actually done by them. The last assault of the enemy would have proved extremely disastrous but for the opportune arrival of these fresh troops. General McClellan, in his "Report and Campaigns" (pages 248–9), speaking of the last assault of the enemy, says: "French's and Meagher's brigades now appeared, driving before them the stragglers, who were thronging toward the bridge. These brigades advanced boldly to the front, and by their example, as well as by the steadiness of their bearing, reanimated our own troops, and warned the enemy that re-enforcements had arrived. It was now dusk. The enemy, already repulsed several times with terrible slaughter, and hearing the shouts of the fresh troops, failed to follow up their advantage."

The Count of Paris, in his "History of the Civil War in America" (Vol. II., pages 103–4), after speaking of this assault, says: "At this instant, Richardson and Meagher arrive on the ground with the two brigades sent by Sumner. The second is composed exclusively of Irishmen,* the green flag, ornamented with a golden harp, floating in their midst. They arrive shouting vociferously, and displaying all that vivacity and dash for which the children of this ancient warlike race are noted when marching to battle. Their comrades, on finding themselves thus supported, respond with loud hurrahs, by which they seek to gain fresh courage. In the meantime, the enemy has re-formed his ranks and is again in motion; but instead of a routed crowd, he beholds a body of resolute troops, who seem to be calmly waiting for him. . . . At this sight he hesitates, and approaching night puts an end to the sanguinary struggle."

June 28. The day passed by very quietly. It was the usual calm that follows a terrible battle, and the silence that generally precedes a great movement. As the day closed,

---

* The Count makes a mistake as to the composition of this brigade, though the Twenty-ninth Regiment, which was a part of the brigade, can still claim a share of this high compliment.—AUTHOR.

however, the signs of retreat began to thicken. The formidable earthworks, upon which the men had toiled during so many blistering days, were being rapidly dismantled, some of the large pieces spiked, and others buried in the ground. At sundown the men were ordered to pack knapsacks and prepare to march. The company cooks were directed to destroy all rations not required for immediate distribution, while the sick and wounded in the hospitals were packed off in ambulances and sent to the rear.

At nine o'clock that evening, the men were ordered to "fall in," and the Brigade started across a stubble-field, in the rear of the camp, and striking the railroad, marched down the track toward "White House," halting on a little hill near Savage's Station. The night was very dark and uncomfortable, a cold, drizzling rain continuing till near daybreak.

On the afternoon of the 28th, companies F and G, Captains Tripp and Richardson, beside one or two other companies of the Brigade, were placed on picket at the right and left of the railroad, in front of Fair Oaks, and were not recalled when the army fell back on the evening of that day. At one o'clock in the morning of the 29th, the field-officer of the day visited the pickets, and informed Captain Tripp that they were to hold the line till daylight and then withdraw down the railroad, if they could do so without the enemy following them too closely. If they found this impossible, they were nevertheless to fall back, but in doing so, make all the resistance in their power, so that our army might be fully alarmed. At four o'clock, A. M., Captain Tripp communicated his instructions to the other officers on his part of the line, and soon after an attempt was made to withdraw the pickets; but the enemy, who were unusually vigilant, immediately advanced, whereupon our pickets were sent back to their posts. When all was quiet again, another attempt was made to call in the pickets; but no sooner had they left their posts, than the enemy began to follow them up. Several other attempts were made to fall back out of the woods, but each time attended with the same results. Finally, one of our officers suggested the plan of going through the ceremony of relieving guard, as a means of deceiving the enemy. Between six and seven o'clock, A. M., the reserves were marched into the woods, and visited every post; but instead of placing a new sentinel on guard, the old picket rose and stealthily left the forest. After passing along the whole line, the reserves also hastened out of the woods, and the entire force at once began to fall back to their old camp at Fair Oaks, where their tents were still standing, barely reaching it before the enemy appeared in sight at the edge of the timber, cautiously advancing in skirmish order. A body of Federal cavalry was drawn up in line of battle just in front of the camp; and when the guards halted there to strike their tents and gather up their personal effects, the commanding officer of the cavalry ordered them to desist, move on at once to the rear, and join their respective regiments; but, to save this property from falling into the hands of the enemy, the tents were immediately burned.

Company G was wholly overlooked by the officer of the day, and received no instructions whatever as to leaving the picket line. Sunday morning, a little before seven o'clock, Captain Richardson and Lieutenant Browne of his company, becoming convinced that there was something wrong in their not having any orders, made a tour of the picket line, and to their surprise found that it was everywhere deserted. Going out of the woods, they met a mounted orderly, who informed Captain R. that all the other pickets had been called in, and said to him, that if he had any men in the woods, he had better get them out as soon as possible. Captain Richardson and Lieutenant Browne hastened back to their lines, and quickly called in their men; but the enemy's skirmishers were soon in their rear, and followed them till they had nearly reached our cavalry.

Sunday, June 29, broke exceedingly warm and sultry. Early in the morning the Brigade started up the track towards Fair Oaks, and after proceeding less than a mile, moved into a field and halted. Here General Meagher called his regimental commanders together and attempted to explain to them the orders under which he was acting; but neither he nor his colonels seemed to comprehend what was expected, and the result was, the Brigade marched deliberately back to the little hill where it had spent the night.

General Meagher was, later in the day, placed in arrest by General Richardson, and remained in arrest till the afternoon of the next day. The Brigade remained at this point for a short time, and was then ordered to the railroad bridge, a distance of about two miles from Savage's Station. This bridge (spanning the Chickahominy at that point) had been burned the day before to prevent the enemy from crossing. They had, however, already effected this purpose higher up the stream, and their cavalry, with a few field-pieces, were now seen moving cautiously down the road, a mile away. A pause of nearly an hour here, and the Twenty-ninth and Sixty-third regiments were ordered to proceed to Savage's. The enemy had come through the woods at a place called Peach Orchard, near the railroad, where they had attacked a small body of our troops. When the two regiments arrived, the enemy, perceiving the re-enforcements, fell back precipitately into the forest and retired. The march to Peach Orchard was made on a rapid run, and though the distance was not great, it was more fatal in its effects than any of the long, hard marches of the succeeding days; for the sun was now high, and poured its nearly vertical rays down into the deep cut through which the railroad ran, and on which the men were compelled to march. The trees and thick foliage that grew along the sides of the ravine effectually shut out the breeze, rendering the place like a heated furnace. One after another both officers and men, even the stoutest and most hardy, fell fainting and senseless from sunstrokes, and among them Captain Leach and Lieutenant Hathaway of Company C, leaving that command without a single commissioned officer, Lieutenant Whitman having been sick with malarial fever for several weeks, and being then in the hospital. From Peach Orchard the regiments proceeded to Savage's Station, and shortly after were joined by the Sixty-ninth and Eighty-eighth, and finally by all the other troops of the division and corps.

Savage's Station was the name of a depot on the Richmond and York River Railroad, deriving its name from the owner of the plantation, near whose grounds it was located, and whose mansion stood on a slight elevation on the northerly side of the track. On the opposite side was a large field, skirted on three sides by a heavy growth of pine timber, along the easterly edge of which ran a road. Mr. Savage's house, and the grounds about it, had been used as a hospital and hospital camp, and at this time there were lying in the house and the numerous tents about it, several hundred of our wounded and sick. Such of these unfortunate ones as could not walk were later in the day abandoned, and captured by the enemy.

Near this place, as also at Fair Oaks Station, a mile farther towards Richmond, were vast quantities of army supplies, which could not be moved. The work of destroying these stores began about noon. Enormous fires were kindled, and into them were thrown boxes of hard bread, bales of clothing, cases of shoes, blankets, fragments of cars, tents, hospital stores, barrels of whiskey, and turpentine. The whole combined made a fire covering an area of nearly two acres. When the flames, mounting above the tops of the trees, were roaring and crackling with intense fury, the workmen, blackened with smoke and wild with the excitement which a vast conflagration always creates, began to pitch into the burning mass kegs of powder and boxes of ammunition. The latter proved a dangerous experiment, and was not repeated. "This destruction of stores," says the Count of Paris, "was a sort of holocaust offered to the god of war." While this was taking place, the troops were hurrying to and fro, taking up the various positions assigned them on the hill and the long plain at its foot, preparing to meet the enemy, who was momentarily expected. The grandeur and awfulness of these scenes cannot be adequately portrayed by language. An army of forty thousand men were mustering for battle; the rumbling of the artillery, as it went from point to point over the field, the excited commands of hundreds of officers, the neighing of horses, the roar of the flames, and the shouts of the men, made up the wildest of all the wild scenes of war. The noise and tumult were, however, of short duration; it was not long before everything had changed. By two o'clock, the lines were formed, the artillery had unlimbered and taken position, and then could have been seen, under the cloudless sky of that June day, the corps of Heintzleman, Franklin, and

Sumner, with their numerous starry flags, quietly and calmly waiting for the storm of battle to burst upon them.

Another, and if possible, a stranger and more unusual scene, was to be witnessed before the serious work of fighting was to begin. On the track near Fair Oaks Station stood a train of nearly fifty baggage-cars, with a powerful locomotive attached to it. Into the cars were put hundreds of kegs of powder, shells, cartridges, and other materials of a highly combustible character. By two o'clock the cars were well loaded with their dangerous freight, and when this was done, each car was set on fire, and the engine, with full head of steam, set in motion. In full view of the waiting army, the burning train swept past Savage's Station with the speed of lightning. The grade from this point to the Chickahominy was descending, greatly increasing the velocity of the train; every revolution of the wheels increased the volume of fire, so that now the form of the cars was scarcely visible. The Rev. Dr. James J. Marks, Chaplain of the Sixty-third Pennsylvania Regiment, who witnessed this event from Savage's house, where he was piously engaged in caring for our sick, thus describes it: "I could not think of anything as a suitable representation of a scene so grand but that of a thousand thunderbolts chained together and wreathed with lightning, rushing with scathing fury and the roar of the tornado over the trembling earth. In a few seconds the engine, cars, and wheels were nothing but one long chain of fire,— a frightful meteor flashing past us." The distance from Savage's Station to the Chickahominy is not far from two and a half miles. When the train had reached the deep forest beyond the station, a deafening explosion burst upon the ears of the troops. The fire had reached the ammunition, and now in quick succession began to burst the shells. The noise thus produced was simply terrific; first the loud, sullen sound of a huge shell rent the air, echoing far and wide through the deep recesses of the forest; now came the explosion of smaller ammunition, sounding like the rattle of musketry. The scene of war seemed transferred for awhile to the upper regions; the shrieking, hissing missiles were coursing in all directions through the clear sky, far above the tops of the tallest trees; columns of white smoke were shooting up in gracefully tapering cones toward the zenith; beautiful circles, well defined, marked the explosion of shells. The rattle and roar of the rushing train were distinctly heard for some minutes, ending at last in a succession of crashing sounds. The cars leaped off the end of the track at the railroad bridge, the engine and tender jumping full twenty feet, and lodging on the top of a tall pier, from which they were afterward taken by the Confederates.

Once more all was quiet. The men, momentarily relieved from excitement, began to think of refreshing themselves with food and water. The Twenty-ninth Regiment was fortunate in being near a well, in the yard of an old farm-house, and though the water was muddy, they managed to slake their thirst with it. True to their soldierly instincts, they embraced this opportunity to make a little coffee; but they had scarcely swallowed it before the booming of a cannon was heard, the sound coming from the direction of Fair Oaks. During the afternoon, several large fuse-shell, fired from this gun, fell about the yard of the house, but none of the men were hurt. As the day waned, the firing of artillery increased. The main body of the Confederates appeared to be advancing from the direction of the Chickahominy, and as they neared our lines, cautiously feeling their way, they opened fire with several field-pieces. This fire was vigorously replied to by our batteries, and continued till five o'clock, when, as if by general consent, it suddenly ceased. A state of almost complete stillness existed for about fifteen minutes, during which a thick cloud of dust was seen rising up among the trees, about a mile in front of our lines, indicating the approach of a large body of troops, for the dust-cloud came nearer and nearer to us every moment. Suddenly the whole mass of the Confederate infantry debouched from the woods on the easterly side of Savage's house, and sprang forward with wild yells and screams toward the open ground in front of the station, filling the ravine at the foot of the hill on which stood the troops of Sumner and Franklin; for Heintzleman had, from some misunderstanding, retreated toward White Oak Swamp early in the afternoon.

General Sedgwick's division, being nearest the railroad,

was the first to receive the fire of the enemy; but his men met it most valiantly, showing a firm front. Not an inch of ground was yielded to the enemy; and now the foe, ranging themselves along the track in an extended but compact line, began firing over the bank into our equally compact lines. The two armies were now face to face, and only a few yards apart. The enemy must be dislodged at any cost of life, no matter how great; and several brigades, among them the brigade of Vermont troops, were ordered to charge them. The Green Mountain boys started from the brow of the hill on a sharp run; the musketry of the enemy swept their whole line from right to left; they staggered and huddled together, as troops are apt to do when exposed to a dreadful fire, and for an instant they nearly paused, dreading to go on. Looking back, they saw the Sixty-ninth New York and other troops pressing on close behind; their line immediately straightened, and again they dashed toward the ravine from which was issuing a sheet of flame. Passing their left flank, the Sixty-ninth New York, with fixed bayonets, ran straight toward the gorge, and with an impetuosity so characteristic of them, and such as few troops can withstand, rushed directly upon the enemy's soldiers. The Vermont troops, and others on their right, followed the brave example of the dauntless Irishmen, and in less than three minutes the railroad was ours; the thoroughly-routed enemy were running wildly and in great confusion for the woods in their rear, their flight being hastened by a shower of shells thrown from our batteries stationed on the crest of the hill. While this remarkable charge substantially checked the advance of the enemy, it did not end the battle; for we were contending with the veteran troops of Magruder, themselves trained in all the most daring feats of war, taught by their fearless commander never to quit a fight as long as the slightest hope of victory survived. At the time the fighting on the railroad was in progress, a body of the enemy made their appearance on the track near Fair Oaks, moving down on our left, and following a locomotive which propelled in front of it a flat car on which was mounted a heavy cannon. As soon as this movement was discovered, the left wing of the Twenty-ninth was ordered through the woods to check it. This was done in a very complete manner, a single volley from our men causing an immediate retrograde movement of the enemy. Dislodged from the railroad, the Confederates, who filled the woods on our right, now appeared in force in that quarter, and began a sharp attack on a por tion of Franklin's corps. This, like the first, was of short duration; but it dwindled into an irregular fire of musketry, and lasted till nearly nine o'clock. As it grew dark, the sky became black with storm-clouds. Vivid flashes of lightning shot through the heavens, followed by deep and sullen peals of thunder, — "nature's artillery." Presently rain-drops began to patter down upon the dusty field, cooling the parched earth and the smarting wounds of the victims of the battle. The storm that followed was tropical in its character and very severe, ending at once all hostilities. In the midst of the drenching rain, when it was near midnight, the jaded troops of Sumner and Franklin quit their field of victory and entered the dark forest on their route to the James.

CHAPTER XVII.

THE RETREAT CONTINUED — BATTLES OF WHITE OAK SWAMP, CHARLES CITY CROSS ROADS, AND MALVERN HILL — THE ARMY FALLS BACK TO HARRISON'S LANDING — GENERAL MEAGHER'S SPEECH TO THE TWENTY-NINTH — PRESIDENT LINCOLN VISITS THE TROOPS — THEIR DESTITUTION — THE ARMY LEAVES THE PENINSULA — THE REGIMENT GOES TO NEWPORT NEWS.

The storm spoken of in the last chapter continued all night. The roads were in a very bad condition; the entire army and trains had passed over them, and this, together with the rain, had served to render them almost impassable. The effects of the retreat were apparent all along the route; lying beside the road were broken wagons and hundreds of sleeping men. These men had straggled from their commands and lain down to spend the night; but as the rear guard passed along, they were aroused and forced to move toward White Oak Swamp. Through this swamp runs a sluggish stream called White Oak Swamp Creek, bounded on both sides by an extensive morass, which, in its natural condition, was impassable for an army and its heavy trains. While the preparations for the retreat were being made, General Barnard and his engineers performed the remarkable feat of constructing a raised corduroy road over the whole space of this swamp and morass, about two hundred yards, throwing across the creek a number of bridges, and arranging for each bridge an independent wagon-road through the forest. When the Brigade reached here, on Monday morning, the 30th of June, a large number of wagons were found waiting for their turn to cross over the stream, and the greatest confusion prevailed. By daybreak, however, the trains had all crossed over the creek, and, shortly after, followed the troops. General Richardson's division was the last to cross, and when over, formed in line of battle, the Irish Brigade and Twenty-ninth Regiment being nearest the creek, and thereby constituting the rear of the entire army.

The men were so weary from the great fatigues they had endured, that many fell asleep as they stood leaning on their guns. Soon after sunrise, the cavalry crossed, driving before them a horde of stragglers; the bridges were blown up, and the necessary disposition made of the troops to repel an attack of the enemy. The Irish Brigade retired a few hundred feet from the stream, and took up a position in a little valley, a short distance from a large farm-house (Nelson's). Here the entire forenoon was passed in quiet; the men made a little coffee, the last of three days' rations, and received a small supply of raw salt pork and hard-tack.

The regiment was here occupying an open country; the opposite side of the creek was heavily wooded. There had been no indications of the enemy during the forenoon, but, as it afterward appeared, the whole of General Jackson's army had approached without the knowledge of our officers, through the woods, and noiselessly placed in position several batteries, one authority giving the number of their guns as forty.

About one o'clock in the afternoon, while our men were asleep upon the ground, the enemy suddenly, without any warning, opened with all their guns a furious fire. There had been gathered here a large number of our wagons and several pontoon trains. Just as the fire opened, these trains were preparing to move on, and the mules, several hundred in number, had been detached from the wagons and driven to the creek for water. The result was a stampede of all these animals; and the men, suddenly aroused from sleep by the firing, found themselves in the midst of a herd of crazed mules, braying and running in all directions. The shot and shell from the enemy's batteries were falling like hail about the troops, and at one time a movement to the rear commenced. This was quickly checked, however, and the Irish Brigade was ordered forward to support our batteries, which were now being placed in position on the crest of a little hill at the left of Nelson's house, to reply to the fire of the enemy. A desperate contest ensued, for the crossing of the stream by Jackson at this time would have been attended by the most disastrous consequences to our army. One of the most famous batteries in Richardson's division was that commanded by Captain Pettit. The enemy's fire was sweeping the brow of the hill, rendering the placing our guns in position a task of great difficulty and danger. The situation was serious; it was necessary to get the trains away; and to do this, the enemy must be prevented from crossing the creek. General Richardson rode up to Captain Pettit and said, "Captain, can you place your battery in position and reply to them?" Pettit answered promptly that he could, and asked the General to give him the Twenty-ninth as a support. Captain Pettit at once started with his guns, the regiment being ordered to follow him; but before the latter had advanced a distance of twenty yards, Colonel Pierce was severely wounded, losing his right arm. At the same time, Captain Pray and Lieutenant Davis were also wounded, and Sergeant Kellam and privates Austin, Smith, and Short were killed.

Colonel Barnes at once took command of the regiment, and stepping to the front, ordered it a little farther to the left; for in the confusion caused by the first fire of the enemy, it got out of the position indicated by General Richardson, who was on the ground directing the movements of both the infantry and artillery. Once in its true position, the regiment lay down upon the ground, a few yards in the rear of Pettit's battery. Pettit was a hero. In the midst of one of the wildest storms of shot and shell, and the tumult of the moment, which alone was almost enough to unnerve a man, he came up with his battery, the horses on a keen run, unlimbered his pieces on the very crest of the hill, and in an incredibly short time was engaged in firing. When Pettit had got fairly in position, General Richardson, who had been sitting on his horse close by, looking on in an admiring manner, turned to the regiment, and said, "Now, men, I think you ought to give Pettit and his boys three cheers." The cheers were given; as much, however, for the brave General, whose life was in constant danger, as for the gallant Captain. Pettit's guns did fine execution that afternoon, at one time silencing several of the enemy's pieces.

With such pauses on both sides as were necessary to give the guns a chance to cool, or to place new batteries in position, the fire was kept up till sundown. Both artillery and infantry suffered greatly from the fire and the extreme heat of the sun. The majority of the enemy's shell exploded near our batteries, but the fragments would scatter many yards in all directions, throwing upon the prostrate soldiers large pieces of turf and masses of earth, and frequently passed through the ranks, causing great havoc. Hazard's battery, which was a little to the left of Pettit's, was almost unmanned. Hazard and many of his men were killed, while others were wounded; and at the close of the fight, a detail was made from the Brigade to drag off his guns.

During the afternoon, Jackson made several determined efforts to cross the creek, but was each time driven back. The house of Mr. Nelson, which was occupied by some members of his family, was several times struck and considerably shattered by random cannon-balls.

While this action was going on, a large force of the enemy, with artillery, coming down the Charles City Road from Richmond, attacked a portion of General Sumner's corps, and other Union troops, about two miles south of the creek, at Charles City Cross Roads. Earlier in the day there had been some severe fighting at Glendale, near this point, where the First and Sixteenth Massachusetts regiments had been engaged; the former losing its Major, Charles P. Chandler, and the latter its brave Colonel, Powell T. Wyman.

The battle at the Cross Roads began about three o'clock in the afternoon. As the day closed, the firing at this point increased greatly. The Pennsylvania Reserves, under General McCall, had been driven from the field with great loss; and many had been taken prisoners, including the General himself and a number of his staff. One of our batteries, known as the "Dutch Battery," had created a considerable panic by cutting their horses from the guns and posting pell-mell through the lines of our infantry. When matters had reached this pass, General Sumner sent for the Irish and French's brigades at the creek. The march to the Cross Roads was performed at a rapid run; the men were already overheated and weary, and now they threw away even their blankets, having already parted with their knapsacks. As they neared the field, our retreating troops sent up a loud cheer, prolonged by "Tigers!" and "Here comes the Irish Brigade! Now we'll have 'em!" The brigades had come, indeed, just in season to enable General Sumner to maintain his position.* The arrival of fresh troops put a sudden termination to the battle. The enemy fell back to their side of the field, and from thence to the woods, the two brigades following them, exchanging a few shots and an occasional volley. It being nearly dark, but little was seen of the field by our men.

The Twenty-ninth was posted on the left, near a Virginia fence, where were a number of field-pieces with their carriages broken; and strewn about the ground, in great confusion, were knapsacks, clothing, and guns. The burial parties and surgeons had not even begun their sad labors, and it seemed doubtful whether they would that night, for the battle was no sooner over, than the army began to retreat towards Malvern Hill. That night's march is memorable. The road ran through a thick forest, and was crowded with stragglers, who, having skulked in the woods all day, and aware of the fact that our army was retreating, were now hastening away to escape capture. These unfaithful soldiers were a sore trial to our more faithful officers and men. They were panicky to the last degree, and, like so many timid children, ran along beside our column, nearly crowding our men out of the ranks.

The Brigade reached Malvern Hill just before daylight, and lay down to rest. It halted on a long plain that runs parallel with the James River, where was also resting a large body of our infantry. The men had had little, if any, sleep since the 27th of June: they had been engaged in battle a considsiderable part of Friday, Sunday, and Monday preceding; had marched nearly the whole of the nights of each of those days, and of the night of Saturday the 28th. During this time the weather had been extremely hot, the mercury ranging all the way from 90° to 100°; and it therefore reflects no discredit upon the Twenty-ninth, that on this morning, after such unexampled hardships and sufferings, many of its most trusty officers and men failed to respond to the roll-call, and were reported "missing." The ranks had been badly thinned by the causes recited, one company being without a single commissioned

---

* General Sumner's testimony before the Joint Committee of Congress on the conduct of the war. See Report on the "Conduct of the War," Part I., page 364.

officer, and reporting only fifteen enlisted men present for duty.

The rest here obtained was very brief. As soon as it was fairly day, the men were aroused and started toward the front. The Brigade took up a position in a field near a road, where it supported several of our batteries. The enemy had already come up, and from a neighboring hill, a mile away, was throwing shell in the direction of our lines: and in the course of an hour the firing became quite brisk, several of the shell falling within a few yards of the Brigade, and in one instance striking a Virginia fence that intersected our line. The fence was pulled down to lessen the danger of the situation, and shortly afterward the Brigade was ordered to the rear, joining its division, which was stationed behind a range of high hills on the extreme right of the lines of our army. A meadow and wheat-field of several hundred acres stretched from the foot of this ridge toward the James River, bounded on the south by a pine forest, into which General Richardson threw a line of skirmishers.

There had been more or less firing at different points since sunrise, but it did not become general till about one o'clock. The regiment, within easy hearing distance of the battle, remained in this position till about five o'clock in the afternoon. A large herd of cattle was feeding upon the meadows; the soldiers being without rations, a detail was made from each brigade, soon after noon, to slaughter a sufficient number of these animals to supply the troops; and when this was done, the meat — scarcely cold — was served out by regiments. When the turn of the Twenty-ninth came to have a "bite," it was late in the afternoon. The slaughtered animals lay upon the grass, and the men by scores swarmed around them, each soldier helping himself to a piece of such size and quality as his fancy dictated.

The meat having been cut, was placed upon the end of a sharp-pointed stick and thrust into the fire to broil. In the process of cooking, being very fresh, it swelled greatly, so that more than one soldier was astonished to find his small ration of meat suddenly grown to a ball of the size of his head. As the men stood about the fire gnawing their beef like so many half-famished dogs, the bugle sounded "fall in!" With his meat in one hand and his gun in the other, each soldier took his place in the ranks. It was amusing to look down the line and observe the disappointment marked upon the countenances of the men at being torn away from their rude but much-relished repast. Fault-finding and severe scolding — soldiers' privileges — were freely indulged in; while some of the witty ones and wags gave the incident a laughable turn by sticking their half-cooked pieces of meat upon the points of their bayonets, declaring their intention of carrying their rations with them. At this moment, however, there was more serious work on hand than fault-finding or joking. The left of the Union line was being severely pressed by General D. H. Hill; and General Sumner — who was that day in command of the field — had sent for the Irish Brigade to re-enforce our troops. As at Charles City Cross Roads, the regiments were started off on a brisk run, hardly slacking their pace till they reached the front. Here was General Griffin's artillery, of nearly one hundred pieces, on the side of a long hill, at the base of which was a cleared grass-field of several hundred acres, flanked on three sides by woods. When the Brigade arrived at this point, the noise of the battle was almost deafening. A thick cloud of smoke overhung the field. The Confederates had just made the last of a series of brave but desperate charges upon the artillery, and the remnant of the Ninth Massachusetts Regiment, which had been in support during the most of the day, was engaged in a severe struggle with the only partially-repulsed enemy. The Twenty-ninth was detached from the Brigade and ordered to move up, under this terrible fire, to the support of the brigade of regulars under Lieutenant-Colonel Buchanan, then on the advanced line supporting several batteries of artillery. The regiment moved briskly forward to the immediate rear of the regulars, where they were ordered to lie down.

Buchanan's troops had suffered severely during the battle, and, with their greatly-lessened numbers, were in imminent danger of being at any moment swept away and captured. In less than an hour from this time it was pitchy dark, and the firing on both sides, save that of our gunboats, ceased.

During the night the artillery hauled off, and all the troops except the regulars and the Twenty-ninth left this part of the field. After the regiment was detached from the Brigade and sent forward to this position, Colonel Barnes received no further orders; but later in the evening the indications were plain that his failure to receive orders to retire was probably due to some mistake on the part of his brigade commander; and these suspicions were more than confirmed upon holding a consultation with Colonel Buchanan, who stated that the brigade of regulars was not to leave the field till the next morning.

The position of Colonel Barnes was not an enviable one; while he received no order to withdraw, he was nevertheless in possession of information that caused him hardly to doubt that it was intended the regiment should join the Brigade; yet, should he retire, he might be censured for moving without orders, and should he remain till morning and hazard his whole command in attempting to retreat in the presence of the entire Confederate army, he might also be blamed severely. In reaching the conclusion he did, therefore, namely, to remain with the regulars and share with them the perils of the service assigned to them, he simply obeyed the instincts of a good soldier, and, as it will hereafter appear, his conduct was duly appreciated.

During the night, the enemy in large numbers, with lanterns and torches, were engaged in succoring their wounded, sometimes approaching almost to the muzzles of our guns, but not a shot was fired at them; their labor was one of love, and in this light our men regarded it. Toward midnight, Buchanan — who had expressed great gratification at having the regiment remain with him — became uneasy because of the wooded nature of the ground on his left, and after stating to Colonel Barnes that he could not spare any men from his attenuated line, intimated his desire that a reconnoissance should be made in that quarter. Thereupon Captain Clarke, with companies A, G, and K, was detailed to explore the aforesaid woods. It was a perilous service, as can readily be conceived, for no one knew, as he entered the dark and secluded spot, but that the next step would arouse thousands of the sleeping enemy. The woods were thoroughly scoured, however, without revealing the presence of the enemy, and, to the great relief of all, Clarke returned in due time, bringing this report.

A novel and yet a frightful feature of that night, was the shelling of the enemy's lines by our gunboats. These, some five in number, lay about two miles in the rear of our army, in the James River. The shells, mostly of great size, plowed through the air with a loud roar, their pathway being marked by the burning fuse; "then, when they entered the forest, great trees were shivered into a thousand fragments, the branches were torn from others and tossed into the heavens, or thrown far into the deep shades, and when they burst, it was with an explosion that shook the earth for miles."* A Confederate officer, with whom the author conversed after the battle, described the confusion in their army, produced by this fire, as being very great.

Near daybreak, Colonel Buchanan informed Colonel Barnes that he was about to move to the rear; it was yet quite dark, and one of the regiments of regulars, which lay just in front of the Twenty-ninth, in moving rearward, passed through the lines of the latter, by which the Twenty-ninth became divided, the two wings separating in the darkness. When it became day, the two wings united near the field, and started for Harrison's Landing. The march to this point, where the regiment arrived toward noon of this day (Wednesday, July 2), was hurried and exceedingly toilsome. Not long after daylight a cold rain-storm set in, which lasted for nearly forty-eight hours. The men were without overcoats, and were consequently thoroughly drenched, many of them taking severe colds, which in not a few instances resulted fatally. The officers were equally as destitute as the men. Everything except what they wore had been lost during the retreat; they were without tents, and when the regiment halted at the Landing, in an old orchard, the soldiers stretched themselves upon the ground thoroughly exhausted, passing the night at this place under a pelting, merciless rain. Many who had straggled during the retreat, joined the regiment here, and kind greetings and personal explanations followed.

* "Peninsular Campaign in Virginia," page 293.

When the regiment reached its destination, and joined the other regiments of the Brigade, already in camp, the supposition as to the error in leaving the regiment on the field at Malvern Hill was fully confirmed; and they were highly complimented by General Meagher for their action in remaining, who addressed them in the presence of the whole Brigade. The General was an orator of rare ability, and in this speech, which will be long remembered by those to whom it was addressed, he pictured in impressive language, the varied scenes and hardships of the retreat, and of the desperate battles that attended it. In the course of his remarks, he took occasion to say some very clever things of the regiment. He was an educated Irishman, possessing a very strong national pride, and was especially proud of the high reputation of his three Irish regiments. He told the soldiers of the Twenty-ninth, that they had proved themselves the equals of any others in the Brigade, and had no superiors in the army. As sons of the Pilgrims and Puritans, and natives of the fair land he was glad to call his adopted country, they had shown themselves worthy of their honorable ancestry and high heritage; his heart had swelled with pride as he had stood upon the various fields and witnessed their sturdy valor.

Although these glowing compliments were duly appreciated, yet they did not cause the soldiers to forget their sufferings, nor to banish from their minds, even during their utterance, the thought that they would much prefer a good meal or a comfortable overcoat to all the compliments in the world. Nor did the General's eloquence overcome the disposition of some of the men to be mischievous, for while he was speaking, certain soldiers of the regiment abstracted from his tent nearly all the whiskey he possessed.

As the arrival of the army at this point was a practical termination of the campaign, it seems altogether proper to pause here in our narrative, and give a statement of the losses sustained by the regiment during this time.

KILLED.

At Fair Oaks, June 15.—GEORGE D. BROWN, Co. C.

Battle of Gaines' Mill, June 27.—Second Lieutenant THOMAS A. MAYO, Co. L

White Oak Swamp (Nelson's Farm), June 30.—HENRY AUSTIN, Co. F; Sergeant ANSEL B. KELLAM and GEORGE W. SMITH, Co. H; and JOSEPH A. SHORT, Co. I.

WOUNDED.

Nelson's Farm, June 30.—Colonel EBENEZER W. PIERCE, right arm shot off.

Fair Oaks, June 15.—CHARLES KLEINHANS, Co. E.

At Savage's Station, June 29.—CORNELIUS L. WHITE, Co. G; AUGUSTUS J. LEAVITT, Co. K.

At White Oak Swamp (Nelson's Farm), June 30.—GEORGE E. WADSWORTH, Co. E (died in hospital August 31, 1863); ALFRED B. WARNER and Sergeant SAMUEL C. WRIGHT, Co. E; Sergeant L. A. HOWARD, Co. A; CHARLES ROSS, Co. A; MINOT S. CURTIS, Co. C; Sergeant WALTER A. KEZAR, Corporal A. A. BLANEY, and JOHN H. SHAW, Co. I. (Sergeant Kezar was wounded in the head, and captured.) Captain WILLIAM PRAY, Second Lieutenant WILLIAM W. DAVIS, and Sergeant HENRY A. HUNTING, Co. K.

At Malvern Hill, July 1.—CHARLES E. MERRIAM, Co. E (died November 12, 1862); IRVING BATES (in the hand), and WILLIAM H. OSBORNE (severely in left leg), Co. C.

A full statement of the losses of the regiment during this period should include the names of those who were disabled by sickness and overwork, but there are no data from which such a list can be compiled.

Assistant Surgeon George B. Cogswell voluntarily remained behind at White Oak Swamp (and subsequently fell into the hands of the enemy), for the purpose of attending to the wounded of his regiment who could not be removed, and while in the enemy's lines, made himself exceedingly useful. He rejoined the regiment about July 19, 1862.

When it had once become understood that our army had retreated, a deep feeling of gloom settled down upon the North, while the South became highly elated and confident. The Richmond "Whig" of July 12, 1862, in an article entitled, "The Tide in Our Affairs," urged upon the Confederate government the necessity of continuing aggressive movements toward the Union army, saying: "The foe should never be allowed to recover from their stunned and bewildered state. We should rain blows upon them so fast and thick that they would have no chance to collect their faculties.

The watchword of Danton should now be ours, '*L'audace! l'audace! toujours l'audace!*'"

The same paper, in an article headed, "Effects of Rain," said: "One of the effects of rain in this city is the appearance of numerous Yankee overcoats in the street. Nearly every Confederate soldier is provided with one; and on rainy days, when they are worn, an imaginative person would fancy that the city was garrisoned by Yankee troops." This was written in order to magnify their victory, and to convey the impression that our soldiers had been virtually stripped of their clothing.

The barbarous sentiment that prevailed among the Confederates is shown by the following extract from a Richmond paper of this period: "What has become of the buzzards? It is a singular fact, that very few buzzards have been seen in this section for some time past. One explanation of their absence is, that they have been driven away by the stench from the carcasses of the slain wretches who came here to desolate our State and murder our citizens."

With all this boasting and blasphemy, it was still apparent that the people of the South had quite as much reason to mourn as had the people of the North. All the Southern, and especially the Richmond papers, were filled with long lists of the slain and wounded in the late battles. One of the Richmond papers published about this time a list of the killed and wounded of the Twenty-sixth Alabama Regiment at Gaines' Mill, June 27, which alone contained the names of over one hundred and fifty. The same paper contained numerous obituary notices of brave officers and men who had lost their lives in these battles; and under the title, "Information Wanted," many inquiries were made of the fate and whereabouts of missing Confederate soldiers.

It would, however, in effect, be falsifying history to speak of the retreat as "a grand strategic movement," as was done by some of the Northern newspapers of those days. That the retreat was skilfully conducted cannot be doubted, nor can it be questioned on the other hand that it was a sore defeat to our army, resulting in the loss of many of our gallant soldiers, in the capture of several thousand, many of whom died, and in seriously depressing the spirits of our troops.*

Harrison's Landing is on the north bank of the James, about fifteen miles from Richmond, and was formerly the property of President Harrison. The river at this point is scarcely a mile in width. The grounds in the vicinity of the Landing had been under a high state of cultivation, and when the army arrived, were covered with golden grain nearly ready for harvest. The grain was soon trampled out of sight, and the earth being soft, was, under the influence of the rain, quickly reduced to a deep bed of mud.

The Fourth of July was a proud day for the regiment. In the afternoon, the Brigade was visited by General McClellan, who addressed the men in relation to the recent movement; thanked them for the valuable services rendered by them during the campaign; and concluded by telling them they would soon be supplied with all things requisite to their comfort. At that moment not one in ten had a change of underclothing, and all were destitute of tents. A soldier's letter, written about this time, speaks in undisguised terms of envy of the sleek and comfortable appearance of Colonel Parker's Thirty-second Massachusetts Regiment, which arrived at the Landing on the 3d. "They looked as fat and well dressed as we when at Newport News," says the writer.

On the 5th, the Brigade marched a distance of nearly two miles, and encamped in the woods, a very comfortable place, but quite destitute of water. Near this forest ran a road, on the river-side of which was an extensive wheat-field. Considerably in advance of the regiment, across this field, was a line of cavalry pickets. In one corner of the field, just outside the line held by the cavalry, was a large stack of wheat, from behind which shots were occasionally fired toward our camp. At last this became so annoying, that an effort was made to capture the daring fellows who had been guilty of

---

* The net losses of the Army of the Potomac, from June 20 to this time, amounted to 15,249 men, of whom 1,582 were killed, 7,700 wounded, and 5,958 missing. The loss of the Confederates during the seven days amounted to 20,000 men, to which should be added 5,000 rendered unfit for service from various causes.—*History Civil War in America, by the Compte de Paris, Vol. II., pages 147, 148.*

the insolence. The next time that shots were fired, a squad of our cavalry dashed toward the stack, but no enemy were to be seen. Supposing they had fled into the forest, our men returned; but no sooner had they got back to their lines, than bang! went four guns from behind the same stack. The cavalry again rushed for the wheat, and seeing no sign of an enemy, concluded as before, that they had skulked into the woods; but this time they determined to destroy the wheat, and accordingly set fire to it. In a few minutes the grain was ablaze, and the troopers, standing near, were looking on with feelings of satisfaction, when suddenly the head of a man, and presently the heads of three more, were seen peeping out at the bottom of the stack. These were the self-same fellows who had done the firing, and finding themselves fairly caught, began begging loudly for mercy. The cavalrymen, not wishing to kill them, but bent on punishing them severely, refused to allow them to come out until they were thoroughly smoked. After sundry jests about the quality of "smoked Confederate hams," and amidst roars of laughter, the cavalry boys pulled the "Johnnies" out from the smoking mass of wheat, and marched them into camp. The "Johnnies" themselves, much elated at their escape, and appreciating the joke, joined in the fun, and laughed as loud as the rest. Under this stack was found an excavation of sufficient size to contain a dozen men.

The promise of General McClellan, who was always keenly sensitive to the wants and comfort of his soldiers, was partially fulfilled on the 6th. On this day each man received one shirt, one pair of drawers, and one pair of stockings. They were so much pleased at this, that they recorded it in their diaries, and mentioned it in their letters home.

On the 8th, President Lincoln visited the army, and, with General McClellan, reviewed the troops. The visit of the good-hearted President, who was regarded as a loving father by the men, had the effect of reviving their spirits greatly.

July 19. The regiment was mustered for pay, the first time in several months. Many were absent, not a few never to return, and as their names were called, and one comrade after another responded for them, "Dead!" "Sick!" "Missing!" a deep feeling of sadness crept over all present.

The enemy had brought a few batteries down the river, and stationed them on Coggin's Point, opposite the Landing, from which place, on the night of August 2, they shelled our camp, creating some confusion, but doing no material damage. In a few days afterwards the Point was occupied by Generals Smith and Sedgwick, and the houses there, which had been used as a cover by the enemy, were burned.

On the 4th of August, the regiment, together with one other regiment of the Brigade, were ordered to the vicinity of Malvern Hill, there to perform outpost duty, in connection with General Pleasanton's command of cavalry and horse artillery, remaining at this place about two weeks, and performing very valuable service. After awhile the Irish regiment was recalled, and the Twenty-ninth constituted the only infantry force there. During this time, by direction of General Pleasanton, the regiment made an important reconnoissance to Malvern Hill, encountering the enemy's pickets, and driving them in; Colonel Barnes submitting to General Pleasanton, on his return, a full report of the condition of the roads and the situation of the enemy's camps.

On the 15th of August, the Twenty-ninth, with the rest of General Pleasanton's troops, were recalled, and marched to Haxall's Landing, the regiment being here supplied with tents, having been without them since the retreat. The Army of the Potomac was about to make another move; the sick and disabled were gathered up among the various camps and sent on board of the transports, as were also the knapsacks of the men and the officers' baggage.

Towards evening of the 16th, Sumner's corps left its camp and started down the river, marching about five miles and halting for the night. The next morning the march was resumed; but the army moved so slowly, that only six miles were travelled during the day. This brought the regiment to the mouth of the Chickahominy, where it empties into the James; and here it crossed on the remarkable pontoon bridge, said to have been over 2,000 feet long. In this manner, by short and easy marches, the corps proceeded to Yorktown; on the 18th, passing Charles City Court-house, and the following day, Williamsburg, the seat of William and Mary College. At noon of the 20th, the regiment reached the heights of

Yorktown and went into camp, affording the men an opportunity of inspecting the fortifications, of which they had heard so much while at Newport News. Among these works were several that had been erected in the war of the Revolution by the English and American armies.

At Yorktown, all the troops save Sumner's took transports for the Potomac, his corps having been ordered to Newport News, where it arrived on the 22d. To the Twenty-ninth Regiment, which were among the first troops to arrive, this seemed very much like going home. They encamped near the "Brick House," where, during the first year of their service, they had often been on guard. Every tree and fence was familiar to them; the long plain near by was the scene of their drilling under Phelps and Mansfield, and the adjacent river-bank their target ground. The arrival here would have been far more pleasant, had it not been attended by very inclement weather and a hard march; but all these discomforts were forgotten the next day, when there reached camp a large mail, the first which had been received since the regiment left Harrison's Landing.

CHAPTER XVIII.

The Regiment Leaves Newport News — Ordered to Fredericksburg — Battle of Centreville — A Drill in the Face of the Enemy — March Through Maryland — Battles of South Mountain and Antietam — The Song of the Dying Soldier — A List of the Killed and Wounded.

During the latter part of August, 1862, Sumner's corps began to leave Newport News and proceed to Fredericksburg. On the 24th, the Irish Brigade broke camp, went on board the steamer "Commodore," and after lying off Newport News about forty-eight hours, steamed down the James, and from thence to Aquia Creek Landing, on the Potomac, where it disembarked. On the 27th, it proceeded by rail to Fredericksburg, and went into camp with its division on the north bank of the Rappahannock. Fredericksburg was then a beautiful town, showing none of those distressing signs of war which marked many other portions of Virginia. The recent showers had imparted an emerald hue to the whole country; the gardens about the town — which stands on a high bluff on the south side of the stream — were filled with blooming plants and trees laden with luscious fruits. Such a scene of peace and plenty as this the sunburnt and destitute soldiers of the Peninsula had not feasted their eyes upon for many months; the place seemed to them like a real Eden, into which they had suddenly and unexpectedly been dropped.

"It is rumored that we are to stay here during the remainder of the season," says a soldier of the Twenty-ninth, in a letter to his friends, little dreaming how soon they were to leave this quiet spot and endure the hardships of another campaign. "It is rumored" was the familiar and stereotyped language with which all false camp stories commenced; and as they generally promised some better or happier experience than that of the present, none labored to dispel the pleasing illusions which they created, though these were repeatedly swept away by sad and bitter events. The soldier alluded to had barely finished his letter before the order came to march. Tents were struck, rations issued, and the men turned their backs on the green hills of Fredericksburg, never again to look upon the town in beauty and tranquillity. Going to the railway station, the Brigade took the cars and returned to Aquia Creek Landing, there embarking on the steamer "Louisiana" for Alexandria, arriving at the latter place on the evening of the 28th. The troops did not land here until the morning of the 29th; and as soon as they touched the shore, marched out to Camp California, about ten miles up the river toward Washington, pausing for dinner. On this march occurred a humorous incident. The Irish Brigade, in moving along the road with its tattered flags, the clothing of its men being almost as ragged as its banners, had occasion to pass the camp of a recently-mustered Pennsylvania regiment. The great contrast between the bright, new uniforms of the Pennsylvania troops and the shabby ones of the war-worn Brigade, led to much bantering, and many severe things were said by both sides. Finally, a soldier of the Pennsylvania regiment, with stentorian voice and in a triumphant manner, bawled out, "What have you done with your knapsacks; thrown 'em away, haint you?" The men of the Brigade were without knapsacks, and this impudent inquiry seemed difficult to answer satisfactorily. Very promptly, however, one of the soldiers of the Twenty-ninth replied, "Thrown 'em away? Yes, ——— you, we've thrown away four sets." This left the victory with the Brigade, and stopped the jangle; for it was an indirect way of saying what could not be denied, that the Brigade was composed of veterans, while the Pennsylvanians had not been long enough in the service to part with even one set of knapsacks, and were therefore very green. The four regiments of the Brigade went into camp that night at Arlington Heights.

General Pope was calling loudly for re-enforcements during these gloomy days, and the Army of the Potomac, the bulk of which was in and about Alexandria, had been ordered forward by General Halleck. Generals Sumner and Franklin were directed to make rapid marches to join Pope. On the morning of the 30th, the Irish Brigade marched, halting for a few hours at Fort Corcoran, only three miles distant from Arlington. As again showing the utter ignorance of the men of the intended movements of the army, and of the experiences in store for them, the brief halt at this fort led to a *rumor* that the regiment was to stay there for a period of thirty days to recruit; and so thoroughly believed was this report, that some of the men went leisurely at work "doing their washing," so that at about three o'clock in the afternoon, when the order to march came, more than one soldier, half stripped, had nearly all his clothes "in the wash," and one unfortunate corporal, who had taken a notion to wash both shirt and trousers, was called away so suddenly, that he was obliged to march all night in his drawers and a thin blouse, carrying his wet garments with him. Even the commanding officer of the regiment, who for the first time in many months was contemplating "a square meal," was so much surprised by the order to move, that he was obliged to quit, leaving his dinner boiling in the pot and two live geese tied behind his tent, having made elaborate preparations for a long stay.

The regiment reached a point about two miles beyond Fairfax Court-house that night, halting beside the road leading to Centreville. Long before reaching here, the noise of the battle of the Second Bull Run was distinctly heard.

August 31, the march was resumed early in the morning, the Brigade reaching Centreville about noon, joining the other troops of General Sumner's corps, and taking its place in the line. Soon after, the whole corps moved up and took the front line of the army, notwithstanding the fact that the men were nearly destitute of ammunition.

The remains of General Pope's army had fallen back to this place in a disorganized condition, and on the following day commenced to retreat toward Washington, Sumner and Franklin protecting their rear. Here our comrades of the Twenty-ninth, who were stationed on a high hill, that afforded them an extended view of the country, witnessed another wholesale destruction of stores and supplies. It was not an exact repetition of Savage's Station, yet so closely resembled it, as to make the sight a familiar one, and call up in their minds many recollections of the retreat from Richmond.

During the afternoon of September 1, General Sumner's corps were the only Union troops that remained on the field. The enemy were close at hand, the Fifth New Hampshire, indeed, being at that moment skirmishing with them only a few hundred yards from the main body of our troops. The order for the corps to fall back had been given; but the brave old commander was in no haste about it, and for the purpose of inspiring his men with confidence, and teaching them habits of coolness, he caused the various divisions to execute the order (to fall back) by the regular tactic formations. The ground chanced to be favorable for this plan. The veteran General sat upon his horse in the midst of his troops, giving his commands in a cool and deliberate manner, that excited the admiration of his soldiers. It was altogether a novel scene,—an army on drill in the face of the enemy; the various movements were skilfully performed, and were so planned as always to keep one of the divisions in line of battle facing the enemy, and covering the other troops in the rear. All the while these evolutions were going on,—which occupied some hours,—the corps was slowly retiring.

It was late in the night before the Brigade commenced to fall back toward Washington. Earlier in the evening, the enemy, under A. P. Hill and Jackson, had attacked a portion of our retreating column; and while the contest was raging fiercely, a violent tempest arose, "the artillery of earth meeting with a response in the still heavier thunder of the skies." This was a repetition of another of the events at Savage's Station, as was also the gloomy, comfortless night and the hardly less gloomy march that followed. While on the march that night, a long ambulance train, filled with wounded, moved along over the road, and in halting to give the train an opportunity to pass, the regiment became divided, nearly an hour elapsing before the two portions managed to unite.

On Tuesday morning, September 2, the Brigade halted two miles west of Fairfax Court-house. The regiment was here thrown out in the rear as skirmishers, and were shortly after attacked by the Confederate cavalry. Pettit's battery, being in position near them, fired a few shots at the enemy, and put him to flight. At three o'clock in the afternoon the regiment was relieved, and at five o'clock marched with the Brigade to Fall's Church, and from there to Langley's, reaching the latter place during the night. The distance marched this day was not far from eighteen miles, and proved to be so severe a strain upon the already overtaxed men, that many were unable to keep up, and not a few were made dangerously sick. Lieutenant Hathaway of Company C falling senseless by the way and never afterward being able to rejoin his command.

On the afternoon of the 2d, the Brigade passed the Potomac on Chain Bridge, marched through Georgetown, and from there to Tenallytown, about six miles from Washington. This was a pleasant little village. The men had a good, clean camping-ground, but no tents. The absence of tents, however, had ceased to be counted as a discomfort. The soldiers had long been in that state of mind which caused them to look upon a green pasture or field with feelings of supreme contentment. The Brigade remained in Tenallytown till Friday the 5th, and then went to Rockville, nine miles distant. The men were compelled to march in the fields, General Banks's corps, the artillery, and trains taking the road. On the 6th, Sumner's corps passed through Rockville, and formed a line of battle two miles north of the town, with Banks's corps on the left. There was some skirmishing during the day between the Union and Confederate cavalry. No further movement of importance was made until the 9th, and then the corps performed a distance of about ten miles, stopping for the night near Seneca Mills. The whole army was moving in the same direction, though by different roads.

The marches were not at this time very long nor forced; the country through which the army moved was very picturesque and fruitful; the fields were filled with corn, and from these the soldiers had many delicious meals, — roasting the milky corn, gathering peaches and apples from the well-laden orchards, and not seldom supping upon fresh pork (purchased of course of the country people).

The towns of Middlebrook, Clarksburg, and Hyattsville were successively passed on the journey between the 10th and 12th, at the latter place being only a few hours behind the rear guard of the enemy. On the 13th, our army marched through Frederick City, and were joyfully received by the people. Only three days before, the city had been occupied by the armies of Lee and Jackson; and notwithstanding the presence of the enemy, the loyal people avowed their sentiments with great freedom. It is reported that the pious General Jackson, while remaining in the city over Sunday of the 7th, attended divine services at the church of the Rev. Dr. Zacharias, and that the undaunted clergyman, in a firm voice, prayed for the President of the United States in the presence of the Confederate General. The treasonable proclamation of General Lee, issued about this time, met with a cold response; and although some recruits were obtained for his army, the majority of them shortly after deserted and returned to their homes. The ragged and filthy appearance of the Confederate soldiers, many of whom were barefooted, tended to disgust even the Secessionists (who had not sufficient moral courage to follow the fortunes of the brave soldiers of the South); and when the Southern army retired, and the Patriot army followed, all classes were about equally jubilant.

Upon leaving Frederick City, the Confederates retreated towards Sharpsburg. Twelve miles from Frederick City, and three from Middletown, is Turner's Gap, through which runs the Middletown Road. This Gap is one of several passes in the South Mountains, here nearly one thousand feet high. At this place a large force of the enemy made a determined stand, and on the 14th, a desperate battle was fought. General Reno's Ninth Army Corps being conspicuously engaged, and that gallant General losing his life. The battle resulted in a complete Union victory.

General Richardson's division arrived at the base of the mountain at nine o'clock in the evening of this day, and the men slept on their arms all night. On the morning of the 15th, the division passed up the mountain, the Irish Brigade being in advance. The enemy had fled during the night, leaving their dead unburied and their wounded uncared for. The ground in many places was thickly strewn with the dead and wounded of both armies; one poor fellow (a Confederate) was still alive, having been shot through the head, the ball coming out at the eye. Thirty-four of the enemy's dead were counted in one spot only a few rods square. The place where the Pennsylvania Reserves ("Bucktails") charged up the precipitous mountain-side, bore sad evidence of the bloody character of the battle. The dead and mangled bodies of both friend and foe were in some places mingled together; the wounded, lying among rocks and deep thickets, were calling aloud to the passing soldiers for water and aid. The summit and westerly side of the mountain, down which the Confederates fled, gave proof of the extreme panic which seized them at the close of the battle; guns, blankets, and equipments were scattered about the ground in great profusion. It was very encouraging to our soldiers to witness these indications of the retreat of their valiant old enemy of the Peninsula, who, less than two months before, had put them in the same awkward plight, and caused them untold hardships.

On this day, the division of General Richardson, with the exception of a few cavalry, was in advance of the entire Union army. The other corps, except Franklin's, followed towards the middle of the day. General Richardson came up with the enemy about three miles from Keedysville. The Confederates were posted on a number of wooded hills, little less than a mile from and on the southwest side of Antietam Creek; their lines extended across the Sharpsburg Road, their right resting on a creek only a mile from the Potomac River. General Richardson did not cross the creek, but took up a position on the easterly side. About three o'clock in the afternoon, other portions of the army came up; Pettit's battery took ground on the hill where the Twenty-ninth was stationed, and shortly after, the battery was joined by two pieces of flying artillery, when matters became lively at once. The enemy had been amusing himself for some hours before, by shelling our unprotected lines. Our artillery at once answered his fire, Pettit's battery especially making some most excellent shots, in one instance driving the Confederate gunners from their pieces. This artillery duel continued nearly the whole day; and at one time, towards the close, the division, in changing its position, became badly exposed to the enemy's fire, but fortunately few lives were lost.

On the morning of the 16th, our army was well up towards

the creek, with well-formed lines. Pettit's battery was relieved in the forenoon by another of twelve 20-pounder Parrotts; and these our Brigade supported all day. The enemy had almost exact range of our position, but his shell not exploding, did little execution. There was, however, some loss, and Corporal Tribou of Company C (Twenty-ninth), who carried the State colors, was severely wounded, losing his left foot above the ankle.

While the exact nature of the situation was not known to any except the officers of high rank, yet, when the day closed, there was probably not a private soldier along the line who did not realize that the army was on the eve of one of the greatest battles of the war.

On the 17th of September, which was one of the many beautiful days of the early Southern autumn, was fought the renowned battle of Antietam. The preceding night had been devoted to watching, manœuvring, and careful preparation by the commanders of both armies. Generals Hooker and Mansfield had crossed the creek with their respective corps during the night, bivouacking on the farm of J. Poffenberger, in the vicinity of the enemy's left;* and at daylight on the 17th, these troops became hotly engaged. While the battle was in progress, General Sumner's corps was ordered to fill a gap on the left of the Union army, where, up to that time, there had been no fighting.

At nine o'clock, General Richardson's division received its order to march. Moving from the position it had occupied during the night of the 16th, the Irish Brigade again in advance, the division made a wide detour to the right, and forded the creek, the men entering the cold water to their hips. General Richardson, with his staff about him, sat on his horse near the creek; and as the various regiments filed past him, addressed the Colonels in his usual stern manner: "No straggling to-day, Colonel! Keep your men well up and in hand." When the troops reached the opposite shore of the stream, they were halted for a few moments, the men seizing upon the chance to empty their shoes, wring their stockings, and adjust their equipments. A flock of sheep

* General McClellan's Report.

quietly grazing on the hillside gave the place an air of peace, and but for the loud peal of artillery on the right, the men would have scarcely imagined themselves amid scenes of war.

Now came the second order to march. The ground was ascending, and the Brigade moved by the flank, the Sixty-ninth in advance, and next to them the Twenty-ninth. No sooner had the troops begun to move, than the enemy opened upon them, from the vicinity of Dr. Piper's and Roulette's houses, a galling artillery fire.

The crest of the hill was soon reached. The order was here given for the Brigade to form "a line of battle, and move forward till they met the enemy." Under a terrible fire, the Brigade formed its line with great rapidity and in fine style, in the following order: Sixty-ninth on the right; next the Twenty-ninth; on their left the Sixty-third; and on the extreme left the Eighty-eighth. About this time, General Meagher was disabled, "his horse having been shot under him." *

In front of the line was an open field, over which the enemy's shot and shell came bounding and crashing incessantly, making great gaps in our line, and strewing the ground with the dead and wounded. "Forward!"—a welcome order; and the Brigade moved rapidly over the field. The enemy increased his fire, but the line moved on. A hundred yards in front was a Virginia fence; on the other side was another field and slightly rising ground; over the crest of the rising ground, a sunken road; and on the farther side of the road, an extensive corn-field and orchard. As the regiments neared the fence, a yell went up from the corn-field, and instantly springing to their feet, a long line of the enemy ran out towards our men, crossing the road and mounting the crest, where they delivered a mighty volley with deliberate aim. In an instant the air seemed filled with hissing bullets and large splinters from the fence.

Our line wavered a little; the fire was frightfully destructive. The field-officers perceiving this, ran through the ranks to the front. Instantly the line stiffened. And now for the fence. "Tear it down!" Immediately two thousand strong

---

* General McClellan's Report, page 382.

hands seize it, and it is flat upon the ground. "Forward!" Everything moves like clock-work. Without firing a shot, the Brigade moved in perfect line toward the sunken road, the enemy all the while firing deadly volleys. "Look at the perfect line of the Irish Brigade as it moves on the enemy!" said General McClellan to his generals, as he sat on his horse, near the creek. "Yes," says the brave old General Mansfield, who was present and watching the movement with intense interest. "I claim the credit of having drilled the Twenty-ninth Massachusetts Regiment of that Brigade."

Two-thirds of the distance across this bloody field was performed before came the order to "halt!" and at the same time the command to "fire!" The volley that played out along the line towards that terrible crest made the hills ring far and wide. It was spitefully done, and very effective, for instantly the Confederates fell back from the summit into the sunken road, receiving as they did so several other volleys. No sooner in the road, the enemy, nothing daunted, commenced to fire over the bank. That part of our line held by the Sixty-ninth and Sixty-third was much exposed, while the Twenty-ninth, its usual "good luck" not forsaking it even here, was protected by a little ridge in its front and a slight depression of the ground upon which it stood. This did not in any way affect their range on the enemy, — the corn-field opened wide before them, their shots cutting off the stalks of green corn as would a scythe, and having their effect upon the enemy who were hiding there.

An hour had nearly elapsed since the front had been reached; several of the captains had reported that the guns of their men were getting so hot that the rammers were leaping out of the pipes at every discharge. The men had already nearly expended their ammunition. Several times during the battle the enemy had undertaken to come forward, but as often as they attempted it, they were swept back by our fire. Since General Meagher had been disabled, there had been no general officer present, each colonel acting upon his own responsibility. The enemy were well covered and determined.

Up to this time neither regiment had known the fate of the others, nor the extent of their respective losses. Colonel Barnes now hastened to the right of the Twenty-ninth, for the purpose of taking a careful survey of the field. To his dismay, he perceived that the Sixty-ninth, though holding on bravely, had lost nearly half their number; the Sixty-third had fared equally as hard, and the officers and men of both regiments were striving to keep up their formation. The Colonel, feeling a deep responsibility, saw at once that something must be done to prevent disaster: he knew, though he had received no orders since entering the fight, that from necessity the Brigade would soon be relieved, and was every moment expecting to hear the welcome shouts of fresh troops. Hastily giving his idea to Major Charles Chipman, his brave and worthy subordinate, he called upon the regiment for three cheers. The Major took the order to the left, and the boys gave the cheers with a will. Colonel Barnes then gave the order. "forward!" Instantly Sergeant Francis M. Kingman, the dauntless color-bearer, sprang to the front, the whole regiment promptly following him. Above the noise of the battle were heard the answering shouts of the brave Irishmen of the Brigade, their warlike spirit gaining fresh impulse as they started forward on the charge.

The crisis was over now; the bold forward movement had saved the Brigade from even one blot upon its bright record of fame. The shouts of our men, and their sudden dash toward the sunken road, so startled the enemy that their fire visibly slackened, their line wavered, and squads of two and three began leaving the road and running into the corn. Now the rush of troops was heard in the rear; now the air was rent with wild yells. It was altogether too much of a shock for the enemy; they broke, and fled for the corn-field. The next moment, Caldwell's brigade, led by General Richardson in person, with Cross, Barlow, and all its other heroes, came sweeping up behind the shattered lines of the Irish Brigade. "The lines were passed by the Irish Brigade breaking company to the rear, and General Caldwell's by company to the front, as steadily as on drill."*

The flight of the enemy was now complete. In a few moments Caldwell's men were in possession of the road, and driving the Confederates through the corn-field and into the

* General McClellan's Report, page 382.

orchard beyond. The Irish Brigade, upon being thus relieved, fell back a short distance to the rear, retiring behind the first hill it had passed upon moving to the front. It had been in battle one hour and fifteen minutes. It was a sad sight to witness the broken and decimated ranks of the Sixty-third and Sixty-ninth, as they halted under the brow of the hill. The Sixty-third had lost very heavily of its officers and men, while the Sixty-ninth suffered even worse. Of seventy-two recruits who had joined the latter regiment a few days before, and who went into the battle with new uniforms, but two of the number escaped unhurt. Even in retiring from the front, the Brigade had suffered greatly from the fire of the enemy's artillery, the Twenty-ninth suffering with the rest, though fortunately escaping the battle with a loss of only forty-four.

Panting from heat and exhaustion, the men at once stretched themselves upon the ground; but the Twenty-ninth had only rested a half-hour before they were again summoned by General Richardson to come to the front. Upon approaching the crest of the hill near the sunken road, the regiment was observed by General Richardson, who was personally directing the fire of a battery in a very exposed position. He beckoned Colonel Barnes to his side, and said, "I pray you, give me a canteen of water; I am dying of thirst." The Colonel going back to the regiment, brought one of the numerous canteens, freely offered; but the General had barely raised it to his lips, when an exploding shell mortally wounded him.

The men, with sad hearts, watched the bleeding officer, as he was being borne away, never to return to his command, and then moved on toward the brow of the famous hill, now being swept by the artillery of the Confederates. Here the Twenty-ninth formed on the left of Caldwell's brigade, and immediately threw out a line of skirmishers into the corn-field, joining the Fifth New Hampshire and other troops of the division engaged in a lively skirmish with the enemy, who was in the orchard, posted behind the trees and a long line of board fence, that ran along the edge of the orchard. The enemy's troops here stationed were the same encountered by the Brigade in the battle of the morning, and were said to be a part of General Pryor's division, the flower of the Confederate army. They were most excellent soldiers, fighting throughout the day with a determination that excited the wonder and admiration of all who encountered them.

The regiment retained the position just described during the remainder of the day and the night which followed. The enemy, with guns stationed in the orchard, and in advantageous positions on the right, enfiladed a part of our line here with murderous effect. General Hancock having assumed command of the division upon the wounding of General Richardson, was everywhere present, and exposed himself frequently to the fire. Hoping to silence the batteries of the Confederates, he sent forward several of our batteries to the hill last mentioned, and among them the "Dutch Battery," so called. The latter came up well, but had fired but four rounds, when the men were driven from their guns, the regiment dragging off the abandoned pieces under the most perilous circumstances.

This part of the line was the scene of some of the most interesting events of the day, and every inch of ground was purchased with blood. The land over which Generals Richardson's and French's divisions fought was irregular in the extreme; "was intersected by numerous ravines, hills covered with growing corn enclosed by stone walls, behind which the enemy could advance unobserved upon any exposed part of our lines." Once during the day the enemy attempted to gain the right of Richardson's position in the corn-field. This movement was happily frustrated by the skilful manœuvres of General Brooks's brigade.

General Caldwell's brigade, after relieving the Irish Brigade in the forenoon. "with determined gallantry," not only drove the enemy in their front. but taking the Confederate line in flank, at the right of the Brigade, captured three hundred prisoners and three stands of colors.

Shortly after the assault on the right, the enemy attempted to turn the left of the division, but were gallantly met by the Fifth New Hampshire (under the famous Colonel Cross) and the Eighty-first Pennsylvania. After a sharp contest and a remarkable charge by these regiments, the enemy fled in confusion, "leaving many killed, wounded and prisoners, and the colors of the Fourth North Carolina, in our hands."

When night came, the Twenty-ninth regiment still lay at the front, in the corn. They were on the skirmish line, and under such a constant fire from the enemy, that it was impossible to relieve them. During all the long hours of the darkness that followed, the men lay upon the ground, listening to the piteous moans and cries for help of the wounded soldiers of the enemy, who were lying about the field between the two lines, and could not be removed nor reached with safety. These sad sounds were occasionally drowned by the crash of musketry and the dismal hissing of bullets. In this manner the night was passed by our soldiers at the front; and the day which succeeded was scarcely less distressing in its experiences.

Although the battle was not renewed on the 18th, yet the two armies lay facing each other during the whole day and a part of the following night. Before light on the morning of the 18th, Company F, under Captain Tripp, which had been on the advanced line in the corn-field since noon of the 17th, where they had been terribly exposed, was relieved by Company C, under First Lieutenant N. D. Whitman, and Company K, under Captain Pray. Even in the darkness, the work of relieving the men at the front was attended with great risk. The two lines were less than one hundred yards apart; the enemy were intensely savage, and kept up a random but almost incessant firing. When the daylight came, matters were much worse; for, beside being more exposed to the fire from the orchard, our men suffered greatly from the heat of the sun, which poured down on their backs, being obliged to lie upon their faces between the rows of corn.

A large number of wounded Confederates were still scattered through the corn-field, some of them only a few yards distant from our pickets. The constant cries of these poor fellows, who were begging our men to remove them and to give them water, excited the sympathy of our soldiers, and many brave, and even reckless, efforts were made during the day to relieve their sufferings. One soldier of Company C*

---

* Charles C. Whitman, a very brave soldier.—AUTHOR.

crawled on his hands and knees a distance of several yards toward the Confederate lines, in order to give a wounded enemy a drink of water from his canteen, the bullets of the Confederate sharpshooters striking close about him, and covering him with dust.

Another of these humane undertakings gave birth to an occurrence much talked of among our soldiers at the time, and which resulted in a temporary suspension of hostilities. Of the several versions given of this affair, the author chooses the following as being probably the most correct: Near the lines of the Fifth New Hampshire (in the corn-field), was lying a wounded Confederate officer. He was suffering greatly, and had been beseeching Colonel Cross's men to take him into our lines. At last, Colonel Cross, moved deeply by these appeals, procured a canvas stretcher, and with the assistance of some of his men, went to the officer's aid. Creeping stealthily along the ground, they neared the spot where the man lay, and pushed the stretcher under him. In doing so, a portion of the white canvas appeared above the tops of the corn. The enemy in the orchard observing it, immediately — and, doubtless, only too gladly — took it for a flag of truce, and at once ceased firing. After a little delay, General Pryor (?) of the Confederate army appeared, bearing a white flag, and General Meagher was ordered to meet him and ascertain his wishes. When the two officers met, each demanded of the other to know why the flag of truce had been raised, and each insisting that the flag had not been raised by their side, a somewhat heated conversation followed, when the two officers parted, and the firing immediately recommenced, Colonel Cross taking advantage of the lull to remove the wounded officer from the corn-field and convey him safely into our lines, where he was kindly treated and his wounds dressed.

During the night of the 18th, the enemy withdrew, but, as is well known, no movement took place during the following day. On the 19th, the last sad duties in connection with the battle were performed by our soldiers; namely, the burial of the dead. The Twenty-ninth was chiefly employed in this work during a greater part of the day, the part of the field assigned to them being the corn-field, sunken road, and orchard. Here the dead of the enemy (our own having been removed during the battle) were very numerous, and in the first stages of decomposition. Many of them had been lying on the field under the scorching rays of the sun for nearly forty-eight hours, and were swollen and black, and emitted a disgusting odor, fairly sickening our burial-party, who dug long trenches three feet deep, in which the dead were placed and covered with earth, as decently as circumstances would allow. In some places, as many as twenty-five bodies were found in a heap; in others, as many as seventy-five mangled and blackened victims were found lying only a few feet apart.

The trees in the orchard showed plainly the fierceness of the strife, which for two days and two nights had raged there with hardly a moment's cessation. The trunks of the trees were literally filled with bullets, and the bark on the exposed sides wholly stripped off to a height of from six to ten feet from the ground.

The wounded of the Twenty-ninth had all been conveyed to a brick house and barn a short distance to the rear, where their more fortunate comrades paid them frequent visits during the 19th, cheering them with kind words, exchanging accounts of the battle, and rendering numerous little services. The dead of the regiment had been carefully buried on the field, and, where practicable, their honored graves were marked.

The numerous praises bestowed upon the regiment for its valuable services in this battle were highly flattering to both officers and men. General Meagher sent a request to Colonel Barnes to visit him at his tent a few days after the battle, and in the most pleasing manner expressed his high appreciation of the conduct of the Twenty-ninth. As the praise bestowed upon the Brigade is justly shared by the regiment, the author deems it but justice to his comrades to quote in this connection the words of General McClellan. In his report of the battle, that officer makes use of the following language:—

"Meagher's brigade, advancing steadily, soon became engaged with the enemy, posted to the left and in front of Roulette's house. It continued to advance, under heavy fire, nearly to the crest of the hill overlooking Piper's house, the enemy being posted in a continuation of the sunken road and corn-field before referred to. Here the brave Irish Brigade opened upon the enemy a terrific musketry fire. . . . The Irish Brigade sustained its well-earned reputation. After suffering terribly, both in officers and men, and strewing the ground with their enemies as they drove them back, their ammunition nearly expended, and their commander, General Meagher, disabled by the fall of his horse, shot under him, this brigade was ordered to give place to General Caldwell's brigade, which advanced to a short distance in its rear. The lines were passed by the Irish Brigade breaking company to the rear, and General Caldwell's by company to the front, as steadily as on drill!"

Honorable mention of the Brigade is made in two other places in the report of General McClellan.

One of the members of the regiment, who was an inmate of the barn which has been alluded to in this chapter, relates the following touching incident: Among the wounded men here, was a poor soldier, both of whose legs had been amputated. He had been told by the surgeons that his case was a hopeless one, and if he had any message to send to his friends in the North, they would gladly transmit the same. Conscious of having done his duty, he spoke often of the battle, and then dictated to the surgeons a brief, but touching, letter to his wife and family. His thoughts now seemed to turn wholly upon his far-off home, and forgetting his torturing pains, his face seemed all aglow with the sweet memories which were floating before his mind. After talking a few moments, he asked those about him to raise his head from the floor. Suddenly summoning all his remaining energies, he began to sing in a clear and very melodious voice, "Home, Sweet Home." All voices save his were quickly hushed in deep and attentive silence. The surgeons and nurses who were on duty among the wounded paused in their labors, and stood spell-bound and fascinated by the sweetness of his voice, and his rich cadences. The appearance of the dying singer, his countenance pallid and bloodless, gave the spectacle a strange, unearthly character, and the effective rendering which he gave to the tender and touching sentiment of the song fairly melted the hearts of all present; and when he finished, breathing out in the utterance of the closing words the last remnant of his strength, and sank almost senseless upon his pallet, "there was not a dry eye in the room." The poor soldier died in the course of the day, but the incident was made a subject of conversation among the inmates for several weeks afterwards.

The following is a list of the killed, wounded, and missing of the regiment in this battle : —

KILLED.

Co. A. — Corporal TIMOTHY D. DONOVAN; Private EDWARD O'DONNELL.
Co. B. — JOHN J. O'BRIEN.
Co. C. — Corporal ELIJAH H. TOLEMAN; Private DAVID H. LINCOLN (from injuries received during battle).
Co. E. — Private LAWRENCE R. BLAKE.
Co. F. — Private EDWARD RATAGAN.
Co. H. — Corporal ROBERT F. GREENOUGH.
Co. I. — Private JOHN C. DOW.

WOUNDED.

Co. A. — Privates MARTIN C. MULLEN, EDWARD KELLEY, ISAAC H. FERRY, JOSEPH S. FARRELL.
Co. B. — Private CHARLES MCNULTY.
Co. C. — First Sergeant THOMAS CONANT; Corporals D. W. TRIBOU,* GEORGE W. ALLEN;* Privates HENRY A. OSBORNE, THOMAS ARNOLD, NEIL MCMILLAN.
Co. D. — Second Lieutenant JAMES H. ATHERTON;* Corporal DAVID D. COLEMAN; Bugler BENJ. C. DALTON; Privates FRANK G. BUMPUS, JOHN FAGAN.
Co. E. — Sergeant JOHN SHANNON; Corporal SAMUEL C. WRIGHT.*
Co. F. — Lieutenant THOMAS H. HUSBAND; Sergeant BELA H. KING; Privates JOSEPH L. WESTGATE, ELISHA WESTGATE; Musician DARIUS BONNEY.
Co. G. — Private JOSEPH DUXBURY.
Co. H. — Musician JAMES A. FORBES; Private WILLIAM STORY.
Co. I. — Privates THOMAS L. GLASS, CHARLES E. HARRIS, BENJ. E. THOMPSON.
Co. K. — Privates ELISHA C. RANKS, THOMAS F. DOLAN.

* Corporal Tribou lost his left foot by a cannon-ball while carrying the State colors; he was a good soldier. Corporal Allen, who was likewise a well-drilled and gallant soldier, received a very dangerous wound in the head, from which he has never fully recovered. Lieutenant Atherton, a brave man and true, who was afterward commissioned a First Lieutenant, received a severe wound in one of his arms. Corporal Samuel C. Wright was one of the brave volunteers to pull down the fence on the morning of September 17. — AUTHOR.

MISSING.*

Co. B. — Corporals H. A. DEAN, THOMAS ——, CHARLES E. GETCHELL, PHILLIP SULLIVAN.

* The Author does not know what finally became of the four missing ones, though he believes they all afterwards joined their company, and were all wounded while entering the fight. The full name of one of the latter soldiers is not known to me. The names of these men, as they appear in the above list, were taken from the "New York Herald" of September 19, 1862.

CHAPTER XIX.

THE REGIMENT LEAVES ANTIETAM — MARCH TO HARPER'S FERRY — THE RECONNOISSANCE TO CHARLESTOWN, VA. — THE LOUDON VALLEY CAMPAIGN — CHANGE OF COMMANDERS — THE GREEN FLAG AFFAIR — BATTLE OF FREDERICKSBURG — WINTER CAMP — DEATH OF CHAPLAIN HEMPSTEAD — CLOSE OF THE SECOND YEAR'S SERVICE — COMPLIMENTARY CORRESPONDENCE CONCERNING THE REGIMENT.

After attending to the sad duties of burying the dead on the 19th of September, the regiment, at three o'clock in the afternoon, was sent to the rear, and remained in the near vicinity of the field till the 22d, during a part of which time it performed picket duty. On the morning of the last-named day, it started for Harper's Ferry, passing through the village of Sharpsburg, fording Antietam Creek at "The Iron Works." The village of Sharpsburg was in the thick of the fight. On the side of the town fronting the Federal line of battle, nearly every house was shattered or marked by balls. The "Dunker Church," or "School-house," as it was called by our soldiers, on the outskirts of the town, and much nearer the field, was a complete wreck. The description given of its appearance by a negro, who lived near the field, is quite as truthful as original: "It was well smashed to pieces; all made like a riddle; you could jest look in and out where you pleased."

When the battle began, on the morning of the 17th, the inhabitants of the village, about one thousand in number, fled from their houses and took refuge at a place some two miles distant, in a forest near the river, where they would have been in a sad plight if our army had followed the retreating Confederates on the 19th. When our troops passed through the town, the most of the houses were still vacant, and our soldiers, somewhat destitute of rations, helped themselves to such articles of food, stray poultry, pigs, and so forth, as the enemy had left untouched. A woman living in this village, being afterwards questioned by a distinguished writer, who visited the place, as to which army did the most pilfering, replied as follows: "The rebels took, but the Yankees took right smart!"

Toward sundown of the 22d, the regiment reached Harper's Ferry, and forded the Potomac River; the water at the point of crossing was in many places nearly waist-deep; the current was strong, and rushed over huge rocks, broken, jagged, and slippery. In crossing, many lost their footing and fell, receiving bruises; while the horses stumbled and floundered so badly that their riders were obliged to dismount.

At Harper's Ferry, the Potomac and Shenandoah unite their waters, and flow through a deep gorge in the Blue Ridge. The land is mountainous and broken for miles around. A little west of the village, on the Virginia side of the river, are Bolivar Heights, while on the north, just across the Potomac, and nearly opposite, on the Maryland side, are Maryland Heights. "No doubt," says Trowbridge, who visited this spot, "there was once a stupendous cataract here, pouring its shining sheet toward the morning sun from a vast inland sea; for the tourist still finds, far up the steep face of the mountains, dimples which in past ages ceaselessly whirling water-eddies made." Upon gaining the Virginia shore of the Potomac, the regiment with its Brigade passed through the town of Harper's Ferry, ascended Bolivar Heights, and encamped near the spot where Colonel Miles, on the 15th of September, disgracefully surrendered his army of over 11,000 men to General Jackson. When the enemy evacuated Harper's Ferry, they burned all the bridges that crossed the river at this place, but on the 24th, our troops constructed a pontoon bridge, and thus re-established easy communication between the two shores.

On the 25th, the Irish Brigade was augmented by the addition of the One Hundred and Forty-fifth Pennsylvania Regiment, and on the 27th, moved its camp down the side of Bolivar Heights to near the Potomac. About this time, Captain Henry R. Sibley, who had a narrow escape from death at Antietam, left for home on sick leave, and the command of Company H devolved upon First Lieutenant Daniel

W. Lee, an efficient and conscientious soldier, who, on the 14th of the following January, was commissioned Captain. Captain Sibley never again joined the regiment; a severe and nearly fatal illness followed his return to Massachusetts. Careful medical treatment so far restored him, however, that in June, 1863, he accepted an appointment as Commissary of Subsistence of Volunteers, with the rank of Captain. Upon receiving this appointment, he was ordered to report at New Orleans, where he served honorably for several months, taking part, while in that department, in the movement to Sabine Pass, and in the second Teche and the Red River expeditions. He afterwards served on the staff of Major-General Emory, in the Shenandoah Valley; and at a later period in the war, upon the staffs of Generals Torbett and Hancock. Early in 1865, he was promoted to be Lieutenant-Colonel, and left the service in December, 1865, with the brevet rank of Colonel of Volunteers. He was a very faithful and intelligent soldier, and since the war has been honored with many positions of trust.

On the first day of October, the Brigade was reviewed by President Lincoln, Generals McClellan, Sumner, and Hancock. From this time till the 16th, the Brigade remained in this position, performing picket and drill duty. The new movement of the army into Virginia was close at hand, and feints, strategic operations, and reconnoissances were now frequently occurring. The march on Charlestown, about ten miles from Harper's Ferry, where the enemy had a small force, was one of the movements preliminary to the grand movement of the whole army.

On the night of the 16th, the entire division received orders to be in readiness to march at daybreak the next morning. On the morning of the 17th, the troops left their camp and started for Charlestown; the day was chilly and the roads muddy. The enemy's pickets were driven out of the town after some sharp skirmishing, and our division marched in and occupied it, the Twenty-ninth Regiment and the rest of the Irish Brigade being thrown out in advance of the other troops into a field on the outskirts of the town, and in the near vicinity of the spot where John Brown was executed. Near at hand, also, was the jail where the old hero had been confined, and the court-house where he had been tried and received his sentence of death; facts which added somewhat to the interest of the expedition, but did not detract from the discomforts caused by the weather, for when the night set in it began to rain. The enemy were close by, and the utmost watchfulness was necessary, giving the men no opportunity to protect themselves from exposure. The soldiers were thoroughly drenched by the storm, and as soon as it was dark, though on the front line, they began to build fires and make coffee; but quickly the order came for all fires to be extinguished. Later in the night, the report was received that General McClellan had dashed into town accompanied by his entire staff, and with the report came an order to rekindle the fires, and for each man to build two. The order was a welcome one, given probably, not out of consideration for the sufferings of the men, but to create the impression in the enemy's lines that McClellan had occupied the town in force; and to help on the ruse, the citizens were permitted to pass out and convey to their friends the report, then current, that our army was moving on Winchester. Suddenly, the next morning, when all were expecting a forward movement, the division was ordered to fall back to Halltown. Here it spent another night, quite as severe as the one which had preceded it, and on the morning of the 19th, returned to Harper's Ferry. No further movement took place till the 29th of October, when the whole army began its march to Falmouth, down the Loudon Valley. On this day, quite late in the afternoon, the regiment left its camp, crossed the Shenandaah on a pontoon bridge, and followed the Potomac down, on the Virginia side, passing over a rough road at the base of Bolivar Heights. The scenery was fine, but the march was mostly performed after dark. Camped in "Pleasant Valley"; weather cool.

October 30. Started at sunrise. The entire Army of the Potomac was moving in the same direction. After a few hours the division divided, the two parts marching in line of battle on opposite sides of the road. Finally the cavalry, batteries, and teams came up, and the camp was formed. Weather fine.

October 31. Regiment ordered for picket, two miles from

camp. The several companies were posted on the different roads to watch the enemy. Mustered for pay.

November 1. Ordered back to camp, and upon reaching it, were ordered to march. Went six miles and halted for the night.

November 2 (Sunday). Called into line at daybreak. After going a short distance, deployed into a field, and marched in line of battle over fields and fences, till opposite the entrance to Snicker's Gap, when a halt was made, and the batteries came up and took position. Just prior to this, as the skirmishers of the Irish Brigade came up with the enemy's cavalry at this gap, a lively fight ensued, in the course of which Major O'Neil, of General Meagher's staff, was captured. Our cavalry, however, followed up the enemy and recaptured the gallant Major, who seems to have been peculiarly unfortunate, having before been captured at the battle of Gaines' Mill.

November 3. The regiment was detailed for ammunition guard. Marched five miles and encamped on a beautiful farm. Weather cool, but fine.

November 4. Drew one day's rations. Pleasanton's cavalry, numbering about six thousand, and ten batteries, started with the regiment on the march this morning, which began very early.

November 5. Marched seven miles and encamped on the side of a rough, broken hill. The wind was high and cold, and at midnight it rose to a gale, accompanied by snow and rain.

November 6. Started early, and marched through Piedmont, where the railroad passes. Travelled ten miles and camped for the night. One hundred men detailed for picket under Captain Doten. Very cold, and toward night it began to snow. Colonel Barnes was officer of the day; the guards were posted in a forest, about a mile from camp; the wind blew a gale, and the night was so dark, that the officers in command of the pickets found it impossible to establish the line. When daylight came, the ground was covered with snow to the depth of several inches. Upon reaching camp early in the morning, it was found that the other regiments in the Brigade were preparing to march, while the men of the

Twenty-ninth, who had remained in camp, were still asleep in their tents. General Meagher observing at this moment the lack of preparation on the part of the regiment, rode down to the camp, and accosting Colonel Barnes, inquired the reason why the regiment was not under arms. The Colonel told the General they had received no orders to that effect, whereupon the Adjutant-General of the Brigade was taken to task, and a disturbance at headquarters seemed imminent. But it afterwards transpired that such orders had been given to a certain officer of the regiment, and that he had neglected to transmit them. This piece of negligence resulted in giving the boys a severe march that day; for while they were preparing to move, the rest of the Brigade started, and was not overtaken till late in the afternoon.

On this day, the news of the death of Major-General Richardson, who formerly commanded the division, reached the regiment. General Richardson died at the house of Mr. Pry, near the battle-field of Antietam, from the effects of the wound received in that battle, and his death cast a deep shadow of gloom over the entire army, and particularly over the Second Corps, in which he had long served, and in connection with which he had won a most enviable reputation as a brave and skilful soldier. The loss of such an officer as General Richardson was an event which might well have called forth a more universal expression of sorrow.

The 7th of November also witnessed a change in the command of the Army of the Potomac, though this was not known to the troops till the 9th, when the fact was promulgated by general order. At this time the army was massed in and near Warrenton; and here the farewell address of General McClellan, and the order of General Burnside, announcing his assumption of the command of the army, were read to each regiment.

The Twenty-ninth arrived at Warrenton on the 9th, where it remained for several days inactive, as did the rest of the army here assembled. On the 15th, it started from its camp, marched nearly nine miles, passed through the village of Warrenton, and halted beside the road to spend the night. The movement of the army was in the direction of Falmouth, and on the following morning the regiment broke camp, being on the skirmish line a part of the time, and marching through morasses and tangled woods. The men had a severe day's work. Water was scarce, and they were hurried along, with but few halts, till near sundown, going nearly twenty miles in the course of the day. When they stopped for the night, they threw themselves upon the ground in a sort of hopeless spirit, believing that the morrow would bring them another hard march. Their prediction proved true, for on the next day they were at the rear of the whole army, and had severe duty as guard of the wagon train, reaching Falmouth toward nightfall, when they found that their Brigade, — from which they had been separated during the day, — having been ordered by General Sumner to cross the Rappahannock to capture one of the enemy's batteries, was rapidly moving towards the river. The regiment, without making a halt to rest, hurried forward to join their brave comrades in this perilous undertaking; but after proceeding a short distance, they learned that the order had been countermanded, meeting the other regiments of the Brigade returning to camp. General Hancock, commanding the division, complimented the Brigade for the quickness with which it moved after the order was given to cross the river, saying to General Meagher, "This is quick work, sir!"

While our army was at this point, Belle Plain Landing, on Potomac Creek, was its base of supplies. This Landing was only ten miles distant; but the railroads had been torn up by the enemy, and all the provisions were hauled over the rough, muddy roads in wagons. The enemy's cavalry were constantly raiding over the country through which the roads passed, and every train went strongly guarded. On the 21st, a detail of fifty men was made from the Twenty-ninth, to guard a train of thirty-five teams, which went to the Landing for provisions; the roads were so heavy, that two days were occupied by the journey, several of the horses and mules dying on the way.

On the 22d, the regiment moved its camp in order to get out of the range of the enemy's guns, which were stationed on the westerly side of the Rappahannock. Half of the term of enlistment of the seven old companies expired this day, and the men did not fail to speak of it, and make it a subject of conversation, recounting the experiences of the past, and speculating as to the year and a half before them.

November 27 was the day appointed for Thanksgiving in Massachusetts, and in most of the loyal States. The men had for dinner, "hard-tack" and salt beef. The Chaplain, Rev. Mr. Hempstead, read the proclamation of Governor Andrew, in which occurred the usual expressions of gratitude and thanks to God, for the bountiful harvests, and so forth. Although the fare of the soldiers had been of the coarsest and simplest quality, and their hardships and privations almost numberless, yet they had indeed much to be thankful for; their lives had been spared through great dangers, and their toils and hardships had been endured, to the end that the Republic might survive the shock of civil war.

About this time a little trouble arose concerning the proposed presentation of a green banner to the regiment. General Meagher and his brother officers of the Sixty-third, Sixty-ninth, and Eighty-eighth New York regiments had very kindly caused a fine silk Irish flag to be made in New York City for the Twenty-ninth Regiment, and had arranged for its presentation by General Sumner. It was intended that the gift should be of the nature of a surprise; but by some means, the project came to the knowledge of Colonel Barnes, who also learned that it was the desire of General Meagher that the flag should be carried by the regiment. While the Colonel would have been proud to receive the flag for the regiment as a token of the respect of their Irish comrades, yet he objected to the flag being *carried* by the regiment, on the ground that it was not an Irish regiment, feeling assured that this was the sentiment of the officers and men of his command. He accordingly made known to General Meagher these objections, whereupon the offer of the flag was withdrawn; and by arrangement of the parties interested, it was afterwards presented to another regiment.

Closely following this incident, — namely, November 30, — the Twenty-ninth was by order of General Sumner transferred from the Irish Brigade to that of Colonel B. C. Christ, General William W. Burns's division of the Ninth Corps, the latter being then commanded by General Orlando B. Willcox.

On the 3d of December, the regiment was sent on picket opposite Fredericksburg. The Confederate pickets, on the opposite shore of the river, were poorly clad, only a small number having overcoats, though the weather was cold. On the next day, at dark, the regiment was relieved, and on the 5th, a detachment was again sent to Belle Plain as a guard to a wagon train ; the weather was very severe, a cold, driving snow-storm lasting nearly all day. The movements of General Burnside, which resulted in the battle of Fredericksburg, were now in progress ; inspections of the troops were frequent ; and on the 9th, Colonel Barnes made an inspection of the arms and equipments of the regiment.

On the 10th, the men were ordered to have three days' rations in their haversacks, and to have on hand sixty rounds of cartridges each.

On the morning of the 11th, the Brigade of Colonel Christ was ordered under arms, but did not march till nearly four o'clock in the afternoon. Upon reaching the river, the order was countermanded, and the Brigade returned to its camp, the men being allowed to enjoy a good night's rest.

At eight o'clock on the morning of the 12th, the Brigade was again ordered under arms, marched to the river, and crossed on a pontoon bridge. The enemy had previously been dislodged from the formidable works on the water-side of the town, and hence no opposition was made to the crossing of the Brigade. The regiment remained near the river all day, and, except a portion of the afternoon, was not under fire. The air was filled with a thick fog, and was intensely cold ; without tents or any adequate covering, the men spent that long, cheerless, winter night on the banks of the river, half paralyzed with the cold, waiting for the day to break, which, as they supposed, was to usher in a terrible battle, and in which it then seemed probable they would take a conspicuous part.

When the day came, the fog-cloud lifted, and the sun shed upon the waiting army its cheering beams of warm light. Soon after sunrise, the order came for the Brigade to form in line of battle, but it did not move till near nightfall. For the first time in its field life, the regiment was on the reserve line all day, but within full view of the battle, which raged and roared from sunrise till far into the night. When it was quite dark, the line was advanced into the outskirts of the town; the men not being permitted to enter the houses, remained in the streets. The battle had gone against us, and during the night some of the shattered regiments, which had been at the front all day, filed sadly through the streets on their way to the river, telling their story of disaster as they passed along.

Early in the morning of Sunday the 14th, the Brigade fell back, but still farther to the left, where they spent the day in quiet. The temptation to visit the deserted houses in the town was too great for many, and though the orders to the contrary were very imperative, yet not a few of the men left the lines upon various pretexts, and went sight-seeing. The effect of our shots upon the buildings was very severe, and the ruin and desolation thereby occasioned, furnished one of the saddest chapters in that campaign. Family portraits were torn from the walls of the dwellings, costly pianos and elegant furniture broken, marble mantles thrown down, and the cherished keepsakes of once happy families strewn about the floors and streets. In some instances huge shells had entered the buildings and exploded, tearing the walls open, leaving nothing but a mass of ruins; while in others, solid shots, speeding with the velocity of lightning, had passed entirely through the buildings, leaving black-looking but smoothly-cut apertures of the size of one's head. "I had no temptation to take anything which I found in my searches through these shattered homes, though filled with many articles of great value. I was so impressed by these sad scenes of war, that I hastened back to my regiment, sorry to have witnessed such desolation and ruin," says a soldier of the regiment, in a letter to his wife. These are the true sentiments of a good soldier, and if they had been more generally entertained by the soldiers of both armies, there would have been far less wanton and needless destruction of property during the war.

It was by a mere accident that the regiment did not become actively engaged in the battle. On the afternoon of the 13th, the division of General Burns was ordered to support General Franklin's corps; in moving towards Franklin's position, it became somewhat exposed to the artillery fire of the enemy, and Lieutenant Carpenter of Company H (Twenty-ninth), was slightly, and James L. Pettis of Company E severely, wounded. The other regiments of the Brigade (Christ's) suffered some loss, the Twenty-seventh New Jersey, which was next the Twenty-ninth in the line, losing seventeen killed and wounded.*

After the Brigade retired from its advanced position, on Sunday the 14th, it formed near the gas-works, on the outskirts of the city. The enemy, from the heights beyond the town, occasionally threw a shot towards our lines, many of which struck the gasometer, — an iron structure, — glanced off with great fury, tearing away pieces of the iron, and throwing them about in various directions.

All during the 15th, the regiment had direct orders to hold itself in readiness to march at a moment's warning. After dark, the men were directed to roll up their blankets, and were cautioned against lighting their pipes or kindling fires. All orders were passed along the line in low tones. It was apparent that some movement of importance was on foot, and it was soon discovered that our army was falling back across the river, a movement that was attended with great danger, inasmuch as the enemy was close at hand, and the river only passable by means of pontoons. Late in the afternoon, after it was decided to recross the river, the regiment was directed to remain until the other troops of the corps had crossed, when it was to remove three small pontoon bridges that had been thrown across a canal or creek which ran between the Rappahannock and the enemy's works, and then emptied its waters into the river. The Brigade commander, Colonel Christ, intimated that he considered the undertaking a hazardous one, and scarcely worth the risk. The corps commenced crossing shortly after dark, the regiment remaining in its position until all were fairly across, and then moved forward a considerable distance to the left, and commenced at once the work assigned to them. A captain, with a sufficient number of men, was detailed for each bridge, and the work went on rapidly and noiselessly, the regiment mean-

* Soldier's diary.

while remaining in line of battle, ready for any emergency. It was remarkable that a work of this nature could be done so quietly; but the men, as well as the officers, fully realized the necessity of stillness. Only once in the course of the labor was any noise made, and this was caused by the falling of a plank against one of the boats. Even this noise was not great; but it seemed to the anxious listeners like a peal of thunder, that was likely to be followed by the crash of the enemy's muskets. Fortunately it did not arouse the enemy; but it called out a large bloodhound, with powerful voice, which came running down to the opposite shore of the creek, and commenced baying and howling, keeping up its savage cries till the work was ended, annoying the men greatly, as they suspected that the next yelp would be followed by the enemy's charging yell. Finally, after what seemed an age, but which in reality was only a short time, the three bridges were all removed, without the loss of a single piece, and the boats successfully floated across the Rappahannock. If the enemy had moved forward, — and it is surprising that they did not, — the result would have been disastrous to the regiment, perhaps cost it its very existence; and had this result followed, the attempt would have been deemed an act of folly. As it was, the plan was successfully carried out, and the regiment was warmly congratulated.

The first streaks of the morning light appeared in the eastern horizon before the men, worn by the fatigues of the night, reached their old camping-ground, on the northerly bank of the Rappahannock. The regiment escaped this battle with but two casualties; but had it remained with the Irish Brigade, which was at the front, and suffered terribly, probably nearly half its members would have been killed or wounded. To this circumstance chiefly, — one over which none of its officers had the slightest control, — it owes this remarkable piece of good fortune.

On the 21st of December, died Chaplain Hempstead, after a short illness. The position of a chaplain in the army was a peculiar one, and by many practical minds the office was regarded as one of doubtful utility, there seeming to be very little natural connection between the sacred and delicate duties of the saving of human souls and the stern and bloody work of man-killing. Neither the Act of Congress which provided for the appointment of chaplains, nor the Army Regulations, prescribed their duties, any further than to provide that they should render to the colonels of their regiments quarterly reports of "the moral and religious condition of the regiment, and such suggestions as may conduce to the social happiness and moral improvement of the troops." Though the duties of these officers were not particularly specified, yet a conscientious chaplain had abundant chances to render great service in both a moral and social way. Such a chaplain was the Rev. Henry E. Hempstead. He was ever at the bedside of the sick and wounded soldier, attended to the distribution and forwarding of the mails (a service more keenly appreciated than most others by the soldiers), and in a thousand other ways endeared himself to the members of his regiment. He was the cherished companion for a long time of the heroic Arthur B. Fuller, Chaplain of the Sixteenth Massachusetts Regiment, and, strangely enough, the tragic death of the latter preceded that of Mr. Hempstead by only a few days.

On the 21st, the entire regiment was detailed for picket service on the river below Fredericksburg. The enemy's pickets were on the opposite shore, and during the night threw up rifle-pits on the bluff. The soldiers of the two armies had been so long together in the various campaigns in which they had been engaged, and so often witnessed each others' bravery and devotion, that a feeling of mutual respect, not to say regard, had grown up between them. Whenever the pickets of the respective armies got within speaking distance of each other, this feeling prompted them to talk and enter into an agreement for a temporary truce. The usual preliminaries for a parley and a chat began in this wise: "Say, Yank, want to talk?" "Yes, Johnny," replies the Union soldier; and then followed a mutual agreement not to fire, and following this, oftentimes, a protracted conversation about their experiences in battle, what they had to eat, the merits of their respective officers, how they liked the service, in which frequently a large number on each side would take part. Sometimes grave questions of state were discussed, and not unfrequently the conversation was enlivened by jokes, stories, and "twitting on facts." These parleys were carried on without the knowledge of the officers on either side, and were finally forbidden. On the night in question, the Twenty-ninth "boys" found the Confederate pickets as friendly as they had been before the battle, and the result was, that they sat down on the shore and had an old-time chat, which was kept up nearly all night.

On the 23d, General Sumner reviewed his grand division, composed of the Second and Ninth corps, the ceremony lasting nearly all day.

The campaign having closed with the battle of Fredericksburg, the work of preparing winter quarters for the army began soon after. Each company was divided into squads, and each squad was charged with the work of preparing its own hut. The prospect of having a comfortable abode at that, the most inclement season of the year, furnished a sufficient incentive for each man to do his "level best": and the amount of Yankee ingenuity displayed in the preparation of these winter homes was as instructive as it was pleasing in its results; logs were cut in the adjacent forests, and these, cut into suitable lengths, formed the walls of the house, while the tent was used for a roof. Inside of these, chimneys and fire-places were constructed, as well as comfortable bunks, and long before the close of the year, Falmouth was a city of log-houses, containing a population of over one hundred thousand veteran soldiers.

On the last day of the year, the regiment was mustered for pay, an event always of deep interest to the men, but peculiarly so on this occasion, as it witnessed the close of another year of their service in the army, and brought them nearer to the welcome day when they would be permitted to bid good-by forever to the hardships, toils, and dangers of army life. The year that expired on that day had been singularly eventful, as must needs be all years of war. The regiment had been engaged in not less than ten pitched battles, besides many skirmishes; it had marched on Norfolk, travelled up and down the Peninsula, navigated the Chesapeake Bay and the Potomac, marched to Centreville, tramped nearly the entire length of the State of Maryland, and, passing down the Loudon Valley, had penetrated almost to the Virginia seaboard. Many of its most cherished and bravest soldiers had fallen by disease and the bullet; but with all these losses and bitter fortunes, it had not lost its flag or its honor. The Twenty-ninth was now in its truest sense a veteran regiment. Its services during the year which then closed had enabled it to spread upon the public military record of the Commonwealth a most flattering testimonial of its bravery from one of the generals under which it had served in the field.

We conclude this chapter by giving the following letter to Governor Andrew, relative to the regiment:—

"HEADQUARTERS IRISH BRIGADE, HANCOCK'S DIVISION,
"SECOND CORPS, ARMY OF THE POTOMAC,
"CAMP NEAR FALMOUTH, VA., Nov. 19, 1862.

"To JOHN A. ANDREW, *Governor of Massachusetts.*

"SIR: In accordance with the desire of the Governor of Massachusetts, and circular received, I have the honor to state that the Twenty-ninth Massachusetts Volunteers joined my command at Fair Oaks, on the 9th of June, 1862; since which time they have been under my command, and are still a regiment of the Irish Brigade. . . .

"In relation to the physique and morale of the men composing the Twenty-niuth Massachusetts Volunteers, I have the honor, and to me a pleasure, to state they are obedient, vigilant, and reliable, ever ready for every duty; while in the field, under my own eye, they have been unsurpassed as soldiers, brave and heroic. Their loss is no indication of their valor, for uncontrolled circumstances and location will favor, or be more fatal, as these circumstances may happen. Of the field-officers of the regiment, I have to state nothing but the most cordial feelings have ever existed between them and me. They severally have my entire confidence and good wishes. They have ever been found at their post, and in readiness for the most arduous duties. Colonel Ebenezer W. Peirce, who lost an arm in the battle of White Oak Swamp, has my sympathy, and in so soon rejoining his regiment for duty, proved his readiness to be where a soldier should be,—at the head of his regiment. Lieutenant-Colonel Joseph H. Barnes is a soldier of the true type, in whom I have a perfect and implicit reliance. Brave and honorable, he is a credit to his State. Major Charles Chipman, likewise, is a soldier of first-rate order, and has borne himself as a true man and a patriot on the field, and as a pattern to the men of the regiment in all times of trial, never flinching from any of the duties or responsibilities of the severest campaigns of modern times. Of the line and staff officers, I can only state they all perform their duty becoming true men and brave. Massachusetts need never be ashamed of such citizens or children. Their identity with the Irish regiments of my command has been most pleasing, cordial, and the fraternity of feeling is admirable in the extreme. Massachusetts shakes hands with her adopted citizens in their devotion to a common country and a common flag. They will stand by them together until victory crowns their endeavors, and harmony is restored to the Union.

"As an incident of the cordial feeling existing in this brigade towards their brother soldiers of the Massachusetts Twenty-ninth Volunteers, I have to state that at a meeting of the officers of the old New York regiments, held some time since, they voted to their brother soldiers of the Twenty-ninth Massachusetts Volunteers a green banner, emblematical of the particular brigade in which they so honorably serve, and of the cordiality of feeling which exists between them. This banner is now on its way, and will shortly be presented to the Twenty-ninth by General Edwin V. Sumner, a commander proud of the Irish Brigade, and a son of old Massachusetts.

"The only way that I know His Excellency can aid this fine regiment, is by filling it up to the maximum standard by her native and adopted sons.

"I have the honor to be, most obediently and respectfully yours,

"THOMAS O'NEILL, *Major and A. A. G.*,
"For Brig. Gen. THOMAS FRANCIS MEAGHER, *Commanding Irish Brigade.*"

CHAPTER XX.

THE WEATHER — ON PICKET NEAR THE RAPPAHANNOCK — THE "MUD EXPEDITION" — THE NINTH CORPS AT NEWPORT NEWS — THE REGIMENT GOES TO KENTUCKY — RECEPTION AT CINCINNATI — LIFE IN PARIS, KY. — SCOUTING — MARCH TO SOMERSET, KY.

January came in with a series of pleasant days, but with heavy frosts at night. On the 10th, however, there was a cold rain-storm, and the weather which immediately followed this furnishes a good idea of the character of a Virginia winter. Before the next morning, the wind changed to the north, freezing hard the wet earth; before noon of the 11th, the sun came out bright and warm, and, in the course of a few hours, the ground was like a quagmire, and the roads almost impassable. The first day of the year was made a holiday for the army.

January 5, a detail was made from the regiment for picket duty on the river, consisting of two commissioned officers and sixty-five enlisted men. Captain Tripp, who had charge of part of the pickets on this day, gives an excellent account in his diary of what he saw of the enemy's lines. With the assistance of a powerful field-glass, the day being fine and the atmosphere free from fog, he could discern the enemy's entire position. As far down the river as the aided eye could reach, were seen their camps and camp-fires: this was the Confederate right wing. Westward were numerous columns of smoke rising up out of the woods, denoting the presence of a large army. As the glass was turned a little farther in the latter direction, the eye fell upon a collection of fresh-looking mounds, under which reposed the gallant dead of Franklin's corps; for this was the spot where his soldiers fought so bravely, and where so many went down in the storm of the battle. Near the place where Franklin crossed the river on the morning of the 13th of December, were long lines of entrenchments, while still nearer the bank were numerous rifle-pits, and, gathered about them, squads of Confederate soldiers, clad in their butternut uniforms, closely watching our lines. Yonder was a brick house, having the appearance of the headquarters of a general, for about it stood a number of horses, and arriving and departing were several mounted orderlies. Directly in front of the building was a battery of brass field-pieces. In the rear of the house, on rising ground, were two redoubts and a line of entrenchments. Then, in another direction, were seen the ruins of the railroad bridge, which once during the battle was gained and held by our troops, but which they finally yielded after a desperate struggle.

A little at the left of the town was a large house, riddled with shot and shell, the red flag placed there by our surgeons still flying from its roof. At some distance in the rear of this house rose a high hill, crowned with a line of entrenchments having embrasures for ten guns, and behind all these, still a higher hill with five redoubts, at the right of which were three more redoubts, with embrasures for four guns, the several redoubts being so arranged as to enfilade the fire of each other. This whole region was, in short, a network of powerful fortifications, intricate and impregnable, — a fact which shows how difficult was the task of General Burnside, and makes still more prominent the bravery of our soldiers of the Army of the Potomac, who, on that cold December morning, moved forward to the hopeless assault with cheers.

During the day of the 5th, some of the pickets belonging to our regiment endeavored to start a conversation with the Confederate pickets, on the opposite bank, but without much success. Finally, one of our soldiers asked the Confederates the name of their regiment; the inquiry was answered by writing on a piece of white paper, in large black characters, "17th Virginia," and holding it up to view. This encouraged another of our soldiers to make a boat of a piece of board, rig it with a rude sail, freight it with coffee and newspapers, and send it across to the enemy's side. After a little delay, the boat was returned, loaded with Virginia tobacco and late Richmond papers.

It often happened, after the first year of the war, that the troops were not regularly paid. This was occasioned chiefly by the unsettled condition of the army, and its frequent movements. At the time of which we are speaking, the regiment had not received any pay for a series of months; and although it may not be readily understood by the general reader how soldiers could make much use of money in the army, where they were provided with food and clothing, yet they were always in need of something which the Government did not furnish, and there were few situations in which the opportunities to spend money were not equal to the soldier's means. The few provident ones who always contrived to save their wages, — some with a view to speculate in a small way, — had plenty of chances, during such times of financial embarrassment as this, to loan money at high rates of interest. This loaning of money was a very common practice among the soldiers, and the careful accounts which they kept with each other, and the character of some of the charges made, were extremely ludicrous. The writer remembers of having seen one of these accounts, which had on a single page twenty charges, none of which exceeded ten cents, and several were as small as one cent. This was not, however, because the soldiers were penurious, but because their pay was small, and each had plenty of uses for the little money he received.

On the night of the 16th, the regiment received orders to "pack up," and be ready, with three days' cooked rations, to move at an early hour on the following morning. Everybody was out bright and early the next morning, completing arrangements for the expected march, for it was no slight task to prepare a regiment to move, especially after it had been long settled in camp. A day of excitement was passed; but yet the order to march did not come. No one knew what was contemplated, though everybody surmised that it was another forward movement, and as usual, when there was a prospect of a fight, the men retired at night singing patriotic songs with new life and vigor.

Sunday the 18th went by in very much the same manner as the day before. During the morning, however, Franklin's grand division moved up the river, all in high spirits. This heightened the excitement in camp, and gave still greater force to the rumor of a forward movement, which was fully confirmed at night by the reading, on dress-parade, of General Burnside's order, announcing to the army that it was once more going to meet the enemy in battle.

Monday morning came, and with it a storm of wind and rain, which increased as the night approached. At three o'clock the next morning, orders were received that in consequence of the storm, the tents would not be struck till specially ordered. There was no improvement in the weather during the three succeeding days; and on the 21st, it was generally understood that the whole movement was abandoned. Such proved to be the fact, and, on the 22d, the trains and troops began to return; that is, that portion of them which managed to get out of the mud, for much of the artillery, and some of the heavy wagons, could not be moved for several days. The enemy in large force were encountered at Banks's Ford, and it was reported that one of their skirmishers hailed one of our skirmishers with the facetious inquiry of why we didn't come before it rained, as they had been patiently waiting for us for several days. This movement was generally known as the "Mud Expedition."

On the 26th, General Burnside was relieved of his command of the army by General Hooker. On the 28th, Major Chipman rejoined the regiment, after several months' absence caused by sickness. On the last day of January, Major M. S. Stone, the new paymaster, made his appearance, for the purpose of paying off the regiment, causing great rejoicing, but for some reason, did not pay the entire amount then due the members.

February 5, the regiment received orders to be ready to embark for Fortress Monroe without delay. Major-General William F. Smith relieved General Sedgwick in command of the Ninth Corps, and was ordered to report with that corps to General Dix. February 8, General Burns was relieved of his command of the division, and was succeeded by General Willcox; on the same day there was a temporary change in the command of two of the companies of the regiment; Captain Brooks being relieved of the command of Company D and ordered to Company G, and Captain Richardson assuming command of Company D.

The departure of the regiment did not take place till the 12th of the month, though each day it had received orders to march, which were as often countermanded as issued. The men were aroused at four o'clock in the morning of the 12th, and at five o'clock marched to Falmouth Station, where, after some delay, they took the cars for Aquia Creek Landing, arriving there before noon. At this place the regiment embarked on the transport steamer "Hero," which also took on board Company B of the Twenty-seventh New Jersey Regiment, a squad of the One Hundred and Third New York Volunteers, several of the corps officers, and for freight fifty horses and several tons of baggage; the steamer also towed down into the bay a schooner laden with mules and army wagons. At night it was rough weather, the wind blew hard, and the transport came to anchor off "Piney Point," starting again the next morning. Before night of the 13th, the steamer had entered Hampton Roads, and come to anchor under the walls of the old fortress. Soon after arriving, Colonel Barnes, then in command of the regiment, went ashore for orders, but received none, making it necessary for the officers and men to spend another night on the crowded transport. On the morning of the 14th, the Colonel again went ashore, and this time received orders to report to General Willcox at Newport News. After some delay, the transport steamed up the James River, and at two o'clock in the afternoon the regiment landed and marched through the fortifications, halting on the banks of the river and forming its camp not far from the old "Brick House." The barracks erected by the Battalion in the autumn of 1861 had been torn down. With this exception Newport News looked very familiar, and one of the officers remarked at the time, "It seems as though the war is over, and we have all at last returned home."

By a strange combination of circumstances, the regiment had now been brought to this distant camp for the third time in its history. Its first service here was in 1861, when it knew nothing of war or its hardships; the second at the close of the exhaustive Peninsular campaign; and this, the third, at the close of three other campaigns, in each of which it had reaped its full share of glory and suffering. Newport News had become a camp of no mean proportions; in the river was lying a formidable fleet of war-vessels, among them the "Galena," and one double-turreted monitor. "Merrimack No. 2," then at Richmond, and occasionally showing itself far up the river, as if it was about to make a raid upon our shipping in Hampton Roads, was doubtless the principal cause of this assemblage of the navy, though a military camp could not safely be maintained here, with the enemy in possession of Richmond and the opposite shore, without the aid of one or more vessels of war. A small burial-yard had been established some months before the regiment left Newport News, in May, 1862; but now it had grown to be a mammoth city of the dead; a large portion of the plain between the old camp of the Twentieth New York Regiment and the signal station was covered with soldiers' graves. Soon after the arrival of the Ninth Corps at Newport News, General Getty's division was transferred to Suffolk, where the enemy under Longstreet were making serious demonstrations. This withdrawal of Getty's division reduced the corps to two divisions,— one under the command of General Orlando B. Willcox, and the other under General Samuel D. Sturgis; and the corps was commanded by Major-General John G. Parke.

While the regiment was here, the following commissions were issued: First Lieutenant Abram A. Oliver as Captain, from January 10, 1863; Second Lieutenant J. O'Neil as First Lieutenant, from November 1, 1862; Second Lieutenant John M. Deane as First Lieutenant; Sergeant-Major Hunting as Second Lieutenant. The reception of a commission was made the occasion of a pleasant social gathering among the officers, and certain things were done in connection with the affair which in the army were termed "pinching the commission." Although our knowledge of the nature of these proceedings is somewhat limited, yet we should judge that some term of a liquid nature would express their character better than "pinching." There had been several changes among the officers of the regiment prior to this, that should be mentioned at this time. Surgeon Brown left the regiment early in 1862; Assistant Surgeon Cogswell was made Surgeon, August 7, 1862, and Albert Wood of Tewksbury, Assistant Surgeon, July 31, 1862; James C. Bassett, Assistant Surgeon, August 20, 1862; First Lieutenant Alfred O.

Brooks, Captain, December 6, 1862; First Lieutenant Daniel W. Lee, Captain, January 14, 1863; Second Lieutenant Charles A. Carpenter, First Lieutenant, September 13, 1862; Second Lieutenant George W. Taylor, First Lieutenant, September 13, 1862; Second Lieutenant Augustus D. Ayling, First Lieutenant, December 6, 1862; Second Lieutenant Henry S. Braden, First Lieutenant, January 27, 1863; Second Lieutenant John B. Pizer, First Lieutenant, January 11, 1863; Second Lieutenant William W. Pray, First Lieutenant, January 14, 1863; Second Lieutenant James H. Atherton, First Lieutenant, March 22, 1863; Sergeant Peter Winsor, Second Lieutenant, September 13, 1862; Sergeant George H. Long, Second Lieutenant, November 23, 1862; Sergeant George W. Pope, Second Lieutenant, December 6, 1862; Sergeant Thomas Conant, Second Lieutenant, December 6, 1862; Sergeant William H. Phillips, Second Lieutenant, November 2, 1862; Sergeant George D. Williams, Second Lieutenant, January 27, 1863; Sergeant Frank Goodwin, Second Lieutenant, January 11, 1863; Sergeant William F. Pippey, Second Lieutenant, January 14, 1863; Sergeant Thomas F. Darby, Second Lieutenant, March 22, 1863; Sergeant Chas. G. Boswell, Second Lieutenant, March 22, 1863.

On the 25th of February, the corps was reviewed on the old parade-ground — where the Twenty-ninth had often drilled in, times past — by General John A. Dix, then in command of the department of Fortress Monroe, the review occupying from ten o'clock in the morning till three o'clock in the afternoon. The corps was destined for active service in the West, and the six weeks spent at this place were almost wholly occupied by company and regimental drills. No duty in the army was so odious to the veteran as that of drilling; he considered it the worst form of the "red tape" regulations of military life, and always went about it reluctantly. There was no little ground for this belief; the majority of the soldiers were very proficient in these matters, and when their pride was strongly appealed to, they never failed to acquit themselves creditably.

On the evening of March 17, there was great excitement in camp because of an order from headquarters for each man to be supplied with forty rounds of cartridges and twenty extra rounds, two days' cooked rations and two days' uncooked, and the regiment to be ready to move at a moment's warning. This gave the rumor manufacturers plenty of business; immediately the story spread through the camp that the troops were to move up the Peninsula; that the Army of the Potomac was falling back to Aquia Creek; and another, that the corps was going to Suffolk; and while these wild stories were passing from mouth to mouth, an order came countermanding that part of the former order in regard to the cooking of rations. There was a slight abatement of the excitement for two days, when (19th) the regiment struck its tents and marched down to the Landing, expecting to go on board the steamer "City of Richmond," which was lying in the river. Only a part of the officers and men went on board the boat that night, the rest taking up their quarters in the old log barracks formerly occupied by the Second New York. Those who remained on shore had a cold, wet time, for it snowed hard all night and part of the next day. Every preparation having been made, on Saturday the 21st, the balance of the regiment went on board, and in the afternoon of the same day the boat started down the river. Colonel Pierce, who had long been absent in Massachusetts, and Captain Leach, who had but recently recovered from his sickness, contracted in June, 1862, joined the regiment this day; and Major Chipman, whose health had again become seriously impaired, left for home on a short leave of absence, Captain Doten assuming the duties of Major.

On the 23d, the steamer reached Baltimore, and the regiment immediately took the cars for the West, travelling all night, and the next morning reaching Harper's Ferry, where a pause of two hours was made for breakfast. After leaving Harper's Ferry everything was new to the men, many seating themselves upon the tops of the cars in order to get a better view of the country. Massachusetts soldiers could not be satisfied with passing through any section of the country for the first time without being close observers of every house and garden on the route, and every striking feature of natural scenery; the letters of the comrades written about this time are filled with interesting accounts of their journey. They were passing through a region where the people were loyal to the old flag, and as the train swept along, the occupants of the houses and the lonely forest huts greeted them by waving their hats and shouting words of welcome. Whenever a pause was made at the villages, the people turned out in mass and treated the troops with food and drink; at Grafton, West Virginia, some of the men made the important discovery that whiskey was selling at the moderate price of five cents a glass.

On the 25th, the train reached Parkersburg, on the Ohio River, and here the regiment left the cars and embarked on the river-boat "Eclipse," for Cincinnati. The sail on the river, which occupied about twenty-four hours, was greatly enjoyed. Though there were other New England and Eastern regiments in the Ninth Corps, yet it is stated that the Twenty-ninth was the first from either of these sections to enter the department of the West during the war. The fact that Massachusetts ranked first among all the States of the Union in its devotion to the cause of the Government, as well as its prominence in the earliest days of the war, added greatly to the curiosity of the people of Cincinnati to look upon a regiment bearing the time-honored and historic Pine-tree flag; when the steamer, therefore, hauled up to the levees in that city, and it became known that she had on board a Massachusetts regiment, thousands of people left their homes and thronged about the landing, eager to obtain a glance at the soldiers. What is still more pleasant to record, is the fact that the thousands of men and women who had gathered here were actuated by a better motive than mere curiosity, as nearly every one seemed eager to confer some favor upon the soldiers. The giving of food, which is always the first prompting of human hospitality, was the principal thought of the people; and as the men filed off the steamer and marched up the broad avenue into the city, they were feasted at every step. The regiment proceeded to a large hall, where a banquet of the most substantial character was spread before them; and when the dinner was over, the committee of citizens under whose direction it had been served, bid the soldiers take with them to the steamer the remnants of the feast. The appearance which they presented as they marched down to the boat, every soldier bubbling with joy and satisfaction, and carrying in his hands or slung over his shoulder a loaf of bread or a large ham, was indeed very ludicrous, and furnished an occasion for much mirth. During their brief stay in the city, several of the officers availed themselves of the opportunity of doing a little trading at the stores, which were well filled with a fine assortment of goods. One of these relates the following incident: Knowing that the regiment was going again into the field, he obtained a prescription from the Medical Director for several varieties of medicines needed by soldiers in that climate. Taking his prescription to one of the best druggists in the city, it was faithfully filled; but when he presented the druggist with money, was blandly told by the latter, that they "took no pay from Union soldiers at that store." The same officer made other purchases, such as clothing, and in every instance received the articles either at cost or gratuitously. At that time troops were constantly entering and leaving the city, and every incoming and outgoing regiment was treated in this liberal manner.

On the evening of the day alluded to (March 26), the regiment crossed the Ohio and landed at Covington, Ky., where, after a brief delay, on the same night, it took the cars on the Kentucky Central Railroad and started for Paris, eighty miles distant. A night's ride brought the regiment to the outskirts of the city, but it did not enter the place till the third day of April following. On the way to Paris, two companies were left at one of the railroad stations, where they served as a guard for several days, finally joining the regiment in Paris.

The entire corps had been ordered into Kentucky for the sole purpose of repressing the operations of certain bodies of guerillas under the notorious partisans, Morgan, Wheeler, Pegram, Clute, and others. These bands had for more than a year previous to the arrival of the Ninth Corps, been constantly engaged in raiding over this portion of Kentucky, known as the "Blue Grass" region, the most fertile part of the State, and consisted of bodies of irregular volunteer cavalry, principally Kentuckians. These guerillas made it their object to plunder every Union man within their reach, of cattle, horses, and grain, and conveying the captured property into the lines of the Confederate General Bragg; in other words, they were engaged in foraging for the Confederate army. When pursued, they would retire into the mountain fastnesses of East Tennessee and Southwestern Virginia, where they became reasonably secure from molestation.

Only a year before the arrival of General Burnside at Cincinnati, these irregular Confederate troops were in occupation of Paris and other places in central Kentucky, and lorded over the people in the most despotic manner, persecuting the Unionists, laying contributions upon them whenever their fancy or avarice dictated; and although some of the larger places, such as Paris and Somerset, had been for some months garrisoned by Federal troops, yet these guerilla bands were moving over the country far and near, sometimes even dashing up to our picket lines and firing upon them.

Here and there throughout the region were wealthy planters, who, from the selfish desire to save their property, or from fealty to the Confederate cause, harbored and protected these roving bands, giving them food and quarters. These persons who harbored armed enemies were included in the terms of the famous General Order, No. 38, issued by General Burnside, and by the terms of that order were reckoned as spies and traitors. The particular clause which covered these planters was as follows: "All persons within our lines, who harbor, protect, conceal, feed, clothe, or in any way aid the enemies of our country."

The camp of the regiment was formed quite near the village, and in the vicinity of two important railroad bridges. Its location also commanded the Lexington Road, over which large amounts of stores were daily transported. On Sunday the 29th, a large majority of the men marched with their officers to church, in the village, an incident that at once gave them a high reputation among the good people of the town, and opened the way for the very friendly relations that afterwards existed between them and the inhabitants. On the first of April, an order came for the regiment to pack up and march to Lexington, capital of Fayette County, twenty-five miles south of Paris, on the Covington and Lexington Railroad, and General Ferrero's brigade was to take the place of the Twenty-ninth and the other troops at Paris. At this juncture, the kind feelings of the citizens for the regiment served it in good stead; for as soon as it became known that it had been ordered away, a meeting of the people of the town was called, at which it was decided to request General Burnside to countermand the order. A telegram to this effect was sent to him, and this generous action was supplemented by the circulation of a petition of the same import, which, after being numerously signed by the citizens, was at their request forwarded to the General at Cincinnati, by a committee headed by one Dr. Griffin. The petition was favorably considered, and General Ferrero's brigade was sent to Lexington instead. On the 3d of April, the regiment moved into the town, seven of the companies occupying the court-house, and the others adjoining buildings. Colonel Pierce was given charge of the post, and Colonel Barnes had command of the regiment, with his quarters near the court-house.

The people of Paris were intelligent and cultured, and the place was the residence of some of the finest and the wealthiest old families in the State. The Hon. Garrett Davis, United States Senator from Kentucky, Cassius M. Clay, and Brutus Clay, had their homes here; and among many others worthy of mention were Major Duncan, a most intense Unionist, Drs. Griffin and Barnes, and the mayor of the town. All these gentlemen became much devoted to the officers and men of the regiment, and showed them numerous attentions. Mr. Davis repeatedly called in person upon Colonel Barnes, and cordially invited both him and his officers to dine; and Major Duncan and many other citizens did the same. It was but natural that these educated people of Paris, who had been accustomed to associate a uniform with a guerilla or a loafer, should, upon acquaintance, have had their feelings of respect for the soldiers of Massachusetts greatly increased, for they found, even in the ranks, graduates of our high schools, academies, and normal schools; and among the officers, several graduates of colleges, gentlemen of the learned professions, of the trades, and of the arts.

One of the duties imposed upon the regiments here was to break up and capture the marauding bands of which we have spoken, and to arrest every person who aided or abetted their lawless acts. Two or three of the persons who had been conspicuous for their excesses had been singled out by name, and their arrest expressly directed by the commander of the department. It was in pursuance of these directions that several expeditions were formed from time to time, one of which we deem of sufficient importance to describe with considerable detail.

On Saturday the 4th of April, Colonel Barnes received information that a small party of guerilla chiefs, who had been engaged for some time past in firing upon our videttes, killing and wounding several, were quartered at the house of one Talbut, a wealthy farmer, who lived several miles from Paris. Just after nightfall of the 4th, the Colonel called for twenty volunteers to accompany him on a secret expedition. The men readily volunteered, and, together with Lieutenants Ripley, Taylor, and Long, and a guide, the party started upon their excursion. The night was not altogether favorable for such an enterprise, as the moon was shining brightly, and every object upon the white, shelly roads could be seen at a long distance. After proceeding several miles on the pike, they reached a covered bridge. The guide informed the officers that the house of Talbut was on the opposite side of the river, and close by. To facilitate the surprise, and create as little bustle as possible in the neighborhood, which was known to be the favorite haunt of a large body of the guerillas, the officers dismounted and picketed their horses in the bushes near the stream, and all silently passed over the bridge. The house of Talbut, a large farm mansion, sat back from the highway an eighth of a mile, while between the house and the road was an extensive corn-field.

The guide pointed out the place, and a sergeant and squad of men were directed to proceed carefully to the house and guard each door and window; and when this was done, Colonel B. and Lieutenant Ripley, and several of the men, went up to the front door and knocked. After some delay, Mr. Talbut came to the door and demanded to know who was there. Colonel B. replied, "Federal officers." Talbut said he should decline to admit them. The house was immediately entered, however, and in the front room was found a bed, and lying in it a whiskered man, apparently fast asleep. "Who is this?" Answer: "A Mr. Sullivan from Ohio, the teacher of our village school; he is our boarder." "Get up, Mr. Sullivan, and dress yourself!" was the command; and a guard was left in the room to see that the order was obeyed. Then followed a search of the other rooms, which promised to be fruitless, the party once giving it up and returning with the family to the lower part of the house, Mrs. Talbut in the meantime engaging the officers in conversation, endeavoring to encourage the belief in their minds that her husband was a strong Unionist, while both herself and her daughter sympathized with the Confederates, though she protested that they had never in a single instance given them aid or shelter. Upon consultation, the officers concluded to make another search, and calling for a light, ascended the stairs. Going into one of the back chambers, they discovered a small door in one corner of the room, that, upon examination, proved to open into a clothes-closet. The place was dark, and the small hand-lamp threw but a feeble ray of light into the room. Colonel B. took a musket from one of the guard, and thrusting the bayonet upwards to the ceiling, removed a scuttle door. Mr. Talbut was then called up-stairs to explain matters. He became much excited, and exhorted the officers not to enter the closet with the lamp, and insisted that there was no room above the one they were in. A chair and table were brought, and a soldier climbed up through the opening in the ceiling; the lamp was handed to him, and after some delay he discovered two men crouching under the eaves. He called to them, but they made no answer, evidently thinking that the soldier called at random, as it was difficult to distinguish objects in the dim light. "Order them down, and if they refuse, shoot them!" shouted the Colonel. "I surrender! don't shoot!" cried some one in the attic, who began crawling on his hands and knees towards the scuttle, and, with the assistance of the soldier, came down. This man had been wounded in one of his legs, and upon being questioned, confessed that he belonged to Colonel Clute's guerillas, and had been wounded only a few days before while attempting to pick off the Federal pickets near Paris. The second command brought from his hiding-place a tall, well-built, proud-looking man of about thirty-five years, who came down the opening rather leisurely, saying, "I am only an inoffensive citizen, and I ask why I am hunted in this way." "Why do you hide in this way, if you are inoffensive and guiltless?" was the reply. This was a poser, and elicited no response. The "inoffensive citizen" was evidently a character. His movements were quick and nervous, and he seemed to be studying the character of his pursuers, and measuring his chances of escape. Mr. Talbut was ordered under arrest, and preparations were being made for immediate departure, when one of the guard came hurriedly into the house, and, going to the Colonel, whispered something, and darted back to his post. The soldier had come in to inform the Colonel that a body of Confederate cavalry had just that moment driven across a portion of the farm, and some of them had been seen to go to the stables. Standing at the door were the whole family, and three prisoners, all talking and protesting their innocence. Silence was commanded, the wounded prisoner was paroled, the two others and Talbut were ordered to "fall in," and the whole party at once started for camp, making the best time possible, and arriving at our outer picket station just before the break of day on Sunday the 5th. No pursuit on the part of the Confederate cavalry was attempted, or if attempted, was too tardy to be observed, and the adventurous little band came in safely with their prisoners, who proved to be of more importance than was then supposed. They were sent to Cincinnati, where they were tried and convicted by court-martial. The man "Sullivan" turned out to be an officer in Clute's guerilla band, and the "inoffensive citizen" no less a person than a famous spy in the Confederate service.

General orders from the headquarters of the department authorized the taking of private property for military purposes; but in every instance where such property was taken, the owners were given receipts which enabled them to recover pay from the Government, on proof of loyalty. The guerillas, who learned of this practice of our officers, and who seemed to have had a waggish turn, on one occasion seized a lot of fine horses belonging to some of the farmers of Bourbon County, and gave the owners receipts over the forged signature of Colonel J. H. Barnes.

On the 12th of April, information was brought by one of

the Government spies, that a body of Confederate cavalry was contemplating a raid upon the Union citizens of Middletown and vicinity. After dark, Colonel Barnes set off with about one hundred men, and by a rapid march reached Middletown by daylight the next morning. The Confederates had actually started upon their raid, but learning of the approach of the Federal troops, suddenly fled. This affair caused a wide-spread feeling of alarm among the Unionists, and when our men reached the town, the greatest excitement prevailed. The people were overjoyed at the arrival of our troops, and came thronging into the streets to meet them, each one reciting his or her complaint of abuse and robbery by the guerillas, and telling their well-grounded fears of future molestation. This was a new and strange experience for our comrades, and gave rise to a greater feeling of responsibility than they had ever known before. The terrible situation of these defenceless people, liable at any moment to be plundered of all they possessed, and perhaps murdered also, appealed strongly to the sympathies of the soldiers; and when the time arrived for them to return to Paris, it was with difficulty that they could resist the entreaties of the inhabitants of the town to remain longer. This furnishes a fair illustration of the condition of things in some of the border States during the late war; families were divided among themselves, actually at war with each other, and no man retired at night with a feeling of security.

Not long after the Middletown affair, orders were received to arrest three guerilla officers, one of whom was especially notorious. The parents and wives of two of these men lived some ten miles from Paris, and it was known that they frequently visited there; several night expeditions had been planned for capturing them, but without success. One of these excursions, participated in by twelve mounted officers of the regiment, nearly resulted in the capture of the officers by the guerillas, instead of the capture of the guerillas by the officers. On this occasion, an attempt was made by our officers to search a house occupied by the family of one of these guerilla chieftains; but as they were entering one of the chambers, the wife of the hunted enemy interfered by stating that there was a very sick woman in the room. To avoid any impropriety whatever, Surgeon Cogswell, who was of the party, was called to examine that chamber; but he had scarcely stepped over the threshold, when another of the officers, who was stationed outside as a guard, came rushing into the house, and gave the alarm that a large body of horsemen were rapidly approaching. There was no time for consultation; the same thought, namely, that of getting away from the premises as soon as possible, came into the minds of all at once, and away they dashed for the pike road, eighty rods away, and on which the hostile party was moving. The night was dark, and our officers being well mounted and good horsemen, managed to make their escape, though they were several times nearly overtaken. The good-hearted Doctor probably never left the house of a sick person in so much haste as he did that night.

On the 16th of April, the Paymaster arrived, and the regiment, to the great joy of the men, received four months' pay, ending March 1. At about this time there were some changes made in the roster of the regiment: First Lieutenant Nathan D. Whitman was appointed Quartermaster; First Lieutenant Henry S. Braden, Acting Adjutant; and Sergeant George H. Morse of Company C, Sergeant-Major.

Several public sales of negro slaves had been advertised since the regiment had arrived in Paris, but only one actually occurred. This was witnessed by a number of the men, and it made such an impression upon them, that they moralized upon the subject in their letters and diaries. This sale took place in connection with some mules and other stock, which seemed to add to its offensiveness.

On the 25th of April, the regiment received orders to join its brigade, but did not march till noon of the following day. The departure of the regiment again brought forth many expressions of kind feeling from the people of Paris. "They could not have exhibited more feeling," says an officer, "if the regiment had been composed of their own sons, husbands, and brothers; and the officers and men looked and acted as if they were leaving home."

The regiment, commanded by Colonel Barnes, — Colonel Pierce remaining in command of Paris, — took cars on the Kentucky Central Railroad to Nicholasville, and proceeding two miles beyond the town, encamped for the night. On the morning of the 27th, it broke camp and marched till four o'clock in the afternoon, spending the night at Camp Dick Robinson. By successive marches, it proceeded to Lancaster (28th) and Stanford (29th). At the latter place, the Brigade was found, and after shaking hands all around, the men, weary from constant marching, lay down for the night. The following morning the Brigade broke camp, and after a very fatiguing march of eighteen miles, during which the men were forced to throw away their knapsacks, went into camp at Carpenter's Creek. The spot occupied by the regiment at this place was very remarkable in its physical features; the ground where the tents were pitched was a deep depression in the earth, formed like the bottom of a bowl, covered with a rich carpet of grass, while surrounding this vale were steep hills several hundred feet high, the sides of which were covered with a heavy growth of trees. As a tarry of some five days was made here, the officers and men occupied the most of their time in endeavoring to ascertain where they were. One of the officers, in a letter written here, stated that they were "seven miles this side of Liberty," which was probably incorrect, but as near the fact as any of them reached. The Brigade at this spot was about three miles south of Houston, nearly fifty miles from any railroad, and was under General Carter, the major portion of whose command, together with the General himself, were at this time absent "raiding."

Reveille was beaten at one o'clock on the morning of the 5th of May, and the order given to strike tents and prepare for a long march; a little coffee was made and some food prepared, and after snatching a hasty breakfast, the regiment started off in the midst of a drizzling rain. That day's march was indeed a hard one; the roads all along the route were muddy and uneven; at least twenty streams were forded, and numerous rugged hills (knobs) climbed during the day; the whole distance performed was not far from twenty miles; and although a march of this length in Virginia would have proved very monotonous, yet through this country, unscathed by war, covered with fine farms, and bearing every evidence of peace and plenty, the journey, though long and wearisome, was very interesting. The camp was formed at night at a spot called Fishing Creek. On the following day, during a severe rain-storm, the regiment marched to within four miles of Somerset, the capital of Pulaski County, remaining here till Friday the 8th.

The people living in the country through which the troops had marched were almost wholly farmers, and favorably disposed towards the Government, not having been much disturbed by the political excitement that raged in the large towns and cities of the State.

Some of the soldiers of the regiment, while resting at this camp, visited the farm-houses near by, and in nearly every instance were made welcome, and invited to partake of food. One of the soldiers who supped with an old farmer named Lester gives the following as the bill of fare: Warm wheat biscuit, "corn dodgers," milk, coffee, molasses (a native production), sugar made from the maple, and plenty of "hog" (the natives never speak of pork; it is either "hog," "shote," or "pig meat"). The house in which Lester lived was built of logs, and had but two rooms. All the clothing worn by the family was manufactured by Mrs. Lester, from wool, flax, and cotton of their own raising; and after supper she commenced work on a piece of cloth in the loom, and these Massachusetts soldiers witnessed, for the first time in their lives, the good old custom which at one time prevailed in every home throughout New England. The family of Lester was an old-fashioned one in point of numbers; there were ten children. The average Kentucky family, however, is about twelve; and on the march from Carpenter's Creek, one family was found which numbered nineteen children, twenty-one heads, including the prolific parents, who were represented as being very contented with their lot and proud of their family.

On Friday the 8th, the regiment broke camp and marched to the suburbs of Somerset, a town of two thousand inhabitants, containing some fine private residences and several churches. The town had been twice occupied by the enemy, and many of its citizens plundered of their property; and although few, if any, of the houses had been burned, yet an indescribable air of dreariness and loneliness seemed to pervade the whole place. The citizens appeared to be living under a constant apprehension of danger, kept themselves concealed in their houses much of the time, and so nervous were they, that one day when our batteries were engaged in target practice, the whole population was thrown into a state of great excitement, under the belief that a battle was in progress.

The camping-ground selected for the regiment was on the side of a hill, near the village, in the immediate neighborhood of which were other troops, two light batteries, one of mountain howitzers, the Twenty-seventh New Jersey Infantry, and a portion of Colonel Woodford's Kentucky Cavalry. The latter was a very singular body of troops, and had a fame that extended throughout both Kentucky and Tennessee; it has been said that every name on its roll was represented by three men, two of whom were always at home, tending and watching their own and their companions' crops. Their service in the regiment was by turns, relieving each other as do guards. This peculiar method of rendering military service was practicable, because the regiment rarely left the State, and was necessary on account of the constant liability of devastating raids of guerilla bands among the farming districts. Every man in this famous regiment was a rare character, and its commander pre-eminently so. Some of the orders which this officer was accustomed to give to his men could scarcely be found in any manual of tactics, the following being a specimen: "Prepare to git onto yeer creeturs! Git!" instead of, "Prepare to mount! Mount!"

There were still other troops in this vicinity beside those already mentioned, and it was generally supposed at the time that the Government could, with a few hours' warning, concentrate at least 20,000 troops here.

A force of Confederates, variously estimated as to strength, was on the south bank of the Cumberland River, four miles from Somerset. The north bank of the stream was kept constantly and well picketed, and occasionally the river was crossed by our troops, and a raid made into the enemy's lines. One of these expeditions, made by the Twenty-seventh New Jersey, of Christ's Brigade, was attended by a painful accident; the stream was very rapid, and when the regiment was returning, one of the flat-boats capsized, and thirty-three men, one captain, and one lieutenant were drowned.

The mails had been extremely irregular, and the soldiers felt quite lonesome and unhappy in consequence; they were in truth more isolated from the rest of the world than ever before in their service. There being no railroad nearer than eighty miles, it was seldom that they saw a newspaper, or obtained any reliable intelligence of passing events at the various seats of war. All the rations for the entire army were drawn in wagons from Stanford, a town in Lincoln County, thirty-five miles away; and as no food could be bought in Somerset, the men were obliged to subsist wholly upon army rations; a real blessing to them, but it was nevertheless counted as a great hardship.

On the 12th of May, the regiment received orders to march, and each man was required to have two days' rations in his haversack; but they did not march. The order doubtless originated from one of the numerous alarms which were constantly stirring up excitement, the Confederate General Morgan being south of the Cumberland with a considerable force of cavalry and mounted infantry.

On the 25th, a more serious alarm arose; the enemy crossed the river and captured about forty of Colonel Woodford's cavalry while the latter were on picket. One of the regiments of the Brigade was sent to the river with the howitzers; but the enemy made their escape.

While the regiment was in camp at this place, Captain Thomas W. Clarke reported for duty, after several months' absence from sickness; and here, also, Assistant Surgeon Jameson joined us for the first time.

CHAPTER XXI.

THE REGIMENT LEAVES SOMERSET AND IS ORDERED TO VICKSBURG — MARCH OVER THE COUNTRY TO NICHOLASVILLE — RECEPTION AT PARIS, KY. — GOES TO CINCINNATI — THE JOURNEY TO CAIRO AND MEMPHIS — DOWN THE MISSISSIPPI — A BRUSH WITH THE GUERILLAS — SIEGE OF VICKSBURG AND SURRENDER OF THE CITY — THE "DAILY CITIZEN."

It seems to have been understood, from the day the regiment reached Somerset till it was finally ordered away, that its stay there was to be brief; scarcely a day passed that was not attended with rumors that the regiment was going to Paris, Cincinnati, Vicksburg, and many other places. Towards the latter part of May, all the sick of the Brigade were sent to Lexington, Ky., and an order promulgated reducing each officer's baggage to thirty pounds (they were formerly allowed eighty), and restraining the enlisted men from carrying more than a single change of underclothing. On the 3d of June, another order came for the regiment to be ready to march at a moment's notice, the men to take eight days' rations. The movement was begun on the 4th, at about daylight in the morning, resulting in a long march (eighteen miles), and terminating at Waynesborough, in Lincoln County, — a little hamlet containing one tavern, three whiskey-shops, and five dwelling-houses. The pause here was only for the night, and the distance accomplished was but a small part of the long and weary journey yet to be performed.

On the morning of the 5th of June, the regiment was again ordered forward, making a brief halt at noon for dinner at a place known as "Hall's Gap," a pass in the mountains. The entire line of march from Somerset, north, lay through that portion of Kentucky so famous for its beautiful landscapes; some of the finest of these views were had from the summits of the hills. The plains were covered with extensive fields of waving wheat of a bright emerald hue, and large areas of the famous blue grass, the varied shades of green contrasting richly with each other, and especially with the patches of red soil where the young corn was growing. Here and there, in the midst of this vegetation, were comfortable-looking farm-houses, surrounded by groups of towering sugar-maples in full leaf, the whole forming a picture of peace and beauty very tempting to the eyes of the foot-sore soldiers.

A march of three hours in the afternoon brought the regiment to Stanford, where it went into camp for the night, upon the same ground which it had occupied on the 29th of April. Here the Paymaster met the regiment and paid off the men, and here also a large mail was received. There was considerable straggling during the following day, the men not being contented to subsist upon the wholesome rations of the army; and having plenty of money, strayed about the country, visiting the farm-houses, buying milk and home-made bread. At night, when the regiment halted at Camp Dick Robinson, it was met by its sutler, one Mr. Sheepe, who had learned that the men were in funds, and had provided himself with a large stock of pies, cakes, and other "'lection truck." He had been told only the day before that he must not sell intoxicating liquors; but despite these orders, the audacious Sheepe galloped off to a neighboring town and procured about eight dozens of Kentucky whiskey, which he now offered for sale, actually disposing of nearly a case at the enormous price of three dollars a bottle before the fact of his transgression became known at headquarters. Military law was often executed with as much swiftness as it was made; it was so in this case, and the greedy sutler's unscrupulous speculation came to a speedy and profitless conclusion. The officer of the day (a member of the regiment) was equal to the occasion; the sutler's team was instantly seized, and a guard set over it; Colonel Barnes was informed, and the officer of the day was directed to destroy the whiskey. Every remaining bottle was broken, and the contents spilled on the ground, the entire regiment and the most of the Brigade being deeply-interested spectators. The other goods were confiscated.

During the march of Sunday the 7th, the regiment acted as rear guard, and passed through a region which was more thickly settled than that already traversed. As was often the case on a long march, the soldiers were ignorant of the fact that this was the Lord's Day, only being reminded of it by passing a church just as the congregation was dismissed.

Early in the afternoon Nicholasville was reached, and here the column halted for the rest of the day. A distance of seventy-one miles had been performed in less than four days, making an average march of over eighteen miles each day. Nicholasville was on the line of the railroad, and at an early hour on the morning of the 8th the men were aroused and ordered to take the cars for Cincinnati.

The people of Paris had learned that the regiment was to pass through their city, and they at once made preparations to receive them on a generous scale. The houses were gayly trimmed with flags and bunting, and a large concourse of people assembled at the depot. When the train arrived, the soldiers were greeted with hearty cheers, and invited to partake of a tempting collation prepared expressly for them. The pause here was very brief,—only an hour,—and by five o'clock that afternoon, the regiment was for the second time in Cincinnati, meeting with a reception scarcely less cordial than their first, and partaking of a good supper at the celebrated Market Building, the soldiers' restaurant. It was generally known in the city that the regiment and its brigade had been ordered to join the besieging army of Vicksburg, and the desire of the people to see those who were bound on such an important mission, as also to render them some kindness, was so great, that they thronged around the building where the soldiers were supping in such numbers, that, when the time came for the regiment to leave, it was impossible to form the line in the streets. As soon as the men emerged from the building, hundreds of people rushed toward them, offering them food, flowers, and flasks of whiskey. So great was the confusion thus created, that it required all the efforts of the officers to form the line, and finally it became necessary to sternly order the citizens to clear the streets. This being done, the regiment at once took up its line of march for the depot of the Ohio and Mississippi Railroad, followed all the way by dense throngs of excited people.

Soon after dark, the men took the cars and started on their eventful journey. The patriotic spirit of the people living along the route was manifested in a manner that caused the soldiers great joy, and strengthened their purposes to do their duty; wherever the train paused, the citizens crowded about the cars and regaled the men with food and drink; and at several stations, choirs composed of young ladies stood upon the platforms of the depots, singing patriotic songs as the train passed by.

At Washington, in Indiana, the train was stopped at the request of the people of the town, and a collation served; the committee of ladies that waited on the soldiers at the tables presented each with a bouquet and a nice lunch to take with them on their trip.

On the 10th, the train arrived at Cairo, Ill., and at three o'clock in the afternoon of the same day the various regiments embarked on river-boats, — the Twenty-ninth and Roemer's New York Light Battery on the steamer "Mariner," — and started down the Mississippi River. A stop of nearly three days was made at Memphis, it being supposed that the Brigade was waiting for orders. While here, the men made the most of their chance to study the city, strolled about its streets, and talked with its people. The statue of General Jackson, which stood in one of the parks, had been mutilated by the mob while the city was occupied by the Confederates; the historic words of General Jackson, "The Union — It must and shall be preserved," inscribed upon its base, having been removed by a stone-hammer. Memphis was a busy place in those days; steamers laden with army stores, cotton, and troops, were constantly arriving and departing; and the city was filled with war rumors of every description.

The weather was pretty hot at this time, and the soldiers — whose destination was Vicksburg, some four hundred miles still farther south, in the midst of an unhealthy region — dreaded the experience in store for them, and expressed many hopes that the order sending them there might be countermanded; but no such good fortune was to be theirs; they were destined to breathe the poisonous malaria of the swamps of the Yazoo, infinitely worse than those of the Chickahominy, and share in the hardships and glories of that wonderful campaign.

On Sunday the 14th, the steamer "Mariner" and the other transports cast off from the pier and headed down stream, and now the question of destination became certain. Two river gunboats (tin-clads, boats covered with boiler-plate iron, musket but not cannon proof) accompanied the steamers as convoys, one going in advance, and the other following, a mile astern. At night the boats tied up to a tree, at White River Junction, where Sherman made his famous raid.

The next morning, the steamers cast off and continued their voyage down the river; Captain Leach was officer of the day, and two of the companies assigned to guard duty about the decks. The other officers of the regiment and the most of the men were below, the day being warm, when suddenly, about ten o'clock in the forenoon, a great commotion was heard on the upper deck. Colonel Barnes hastened to the deck, and observed that the transport just ahead of his, having on board a New York regiment, was sheering off towards the opposite bank, and at the same time the firing of musketry was heard. The captain of the boat began at once to get out his iron shutters, or casings, to place about the wheelhouse, as a protection from balls; the commander of the battery, a fine officer, had taken the precaution to mount one of his pieces at the bows. The gunboats had become separated from the transports by quite a distance, and now the bullets were whistling about the decks of the steamer "Mariner" in a lively manner. A party of guerillas, concealed under the levee, were attempting, as they had often done before, to pick off the soldiers. The captain was directed to run the boat in-shore as close as the depth of water would permit. The commander of the battery loaded his gun with shell, and as soon as the boat got within fair range of the bank, fired, the shell exploding right among the enemy. The shell had no sooner burst, than the guerillas were seen scampering away, evidently much terrified, and not a little surprised that what they had taken to be an unarmed transport was supplied with a savage weapon in the shape of a cannon. This was the only interruption which the boats encountered during the trip, but greater watchfulness was afterwards observed. The night of the 16th was passed near a place called Providence, a very desolate region. On the afternoon of the arrival here, a strong wind, accompanied by rain, prevailed, and the boat was blown upon a sand-bar, in which position it remained the most of the night.

At daylight on the 17th, the little fleet commenced on the fourth and last day of the voyage. Towards noon, just as a sharp bend in the river was passed, the gunboat in advance changed its course, and in a few minutes the whole fleet had left the Mississippi and was plowing the dark and sluggish waters of the Yazoo. The land on either side was low and swampy, covered with a thick growth of cypress and other trees, from the boughs of which were hanging long locks of greenish gray moss, giving the place a sombre appearance. In about two hours from this time, the boats reached a clearing on the right bank, when the white tents of a vast army were suddenly revealed. This was Snyder's Bluff, or Milldale; the troops here encamped forming the extreme right flank of General Grant's besieging army before Vicksburg. As the boats neared the landing, the soldiers on shore came flocking down to the bank to inspect the new-comers, and observing that their uniforms appeared to be new, immediately took them to be recently-mustered troops, and accordingly indulged in some disparaging remarks, little knowing that they were deriding the sunburnt veterans of the Peninsula, and the heroes of Antietam,—soldiers whose subsequent services before Vicksburg and at Jackson those rough but good-hearted men of the West learned to appreciate. Upon landing, a camp was formed about a fourth of a mile from the river, the Twenty-ninth occupying a position on the extreme right of the Brigade. A large portion of the Ninth Corps had been ordered here from Kentucky, and had arrived a few days in advance of the Brigade of Colonel Christ. The camp of the corps extended all the way from Haine's Bluff to Snyder's Bluff, and the service at first required of it was that of observation, rather than direct contact with the enemy. The army of General Johnston was hovering in the rear of Vicksburg, ready to strike our besieging army at any exposed and vulnerable point, and every precaution against such a misfortune became necessary.

No sooner had the corps arrived than the work of constructing fortifications commenced, and two entrenched lines were formed. The first extended along Oak Ridge, guarding the roads that crossed the Big Black River; and the second in the rear of the first, extending from Haine's to Snyder's Bluff, through Milldale and the high ground east of Vicksburg, commanding all the approaches from the north and east; of this work the regiment did its full share. The weather was extremely hot, the sky for the most of the time cloudless; and it seems miraculous that men, natives of a northern clime, should have proved themselves able to toil under the rays of an almost torrid sun; yet such was the fact, and, stranger still, the health of the troops was unexceptionably good while here.

This labor was not constant, the regiments of the Brigade relieving each other at regular intervals, and working by details of one and two hundred men at a time. There was little of any other work to perform except the necessary camp guard and police service, and consequently the men had a large amount of "spare time" on their hands; but the life here was not monotonous, however, for although the corps was nearly eight miles from Vicksburg, the booming of Grant's cannon was distinctly heard night and day, and the camp flooded with startling rumors.

The regiment was encamped in the midst of a fruitful region; peaches, plums, and blackberries were very abundant, and of these the men had plenty. As an offset to these advantages, there were many poisonous insects and reptiles. One soldier relates, that, upon awakening one morning, he found a rattlesnake snugly coiled up under his knapsack, upon which he had rested his head during the night. It was by no means seldom that these and other reptiles equally venomous were killed in and about the camp.

On Sunday the 28th, the regiment received orders to prepare and keep constantly on hand five days' rations and sixty rounds of cartridges, and to be ready to move at short notice. On the morning of the following day, it was ordered to pack knapsacks and start immediately; a distance of five miles was marched, and a halt made beside the road. Toward night the wind rose to a hurricane, and then came on a severe storm of rain, with thunder and lightning, actually flooding the earth, which a few minutes before had been parched and dusty. The storm continued till morning, and the night was spent in the forest, without tents. The next day was warm and sultry, and a halt, for the greater part of it, was made near the place of the previous night's encampment for the purpose of proceeding with the formalities of mustering the regiment for pay. The Twenty-ninth, together with other portions of the corps, were heading towards Vicksburg, moving along by short and slow marches till the morning of the 4th of July, when, at an early hour, the men were hurried out of their tents, and a rapid movement began in the direction of Grant's front lines. The corps had approached to within a short distance of the city, when couriers came riding from the front bearing the cheering news that Vicksburg had fallen. Then followed a scene of the wildest joy; the exultant soldiers threw up their caps and cheered loud and long for Grant and the Union.

There was now no need of the regiment at the front; indeed, the only enemy left was at the rear, and a halt was immediately ordered, several of the officers and men taking advantage of the pause to visit the captured city.

At three o'clock in the afternoon, the regiment had orders to march, and proceeding some four miles towards the Big Black, halted on the side of a hill. Here the tents were pitched, and during the afternoon the whole of the division came up and went into camp about the hill. When the night came on, the celebrations of the day were revived; each company kindled a huge bonfire, and each man lighted a candle throughout the whole division. The effect of this illumination was extremely fine, and in keeping with the grand events of the day. The members of the regiment who went to Vicksburg returned, giving very full accounts of the things they had witnessed there, and some of them brought to camp copies of the "Daily Citizen," a paper printed in Vicksburg (for the last time), July 2, 1863. The author has before him one of these copies, and as it is a very interesting relic of the war, and tells a part of the story of the siege, he will conclude this chapter with a description of the paper, and a few quotations from it.

The Vicksburg "Daily Citizen" was printed during the last part of the siege (having exhausted its supply of paper) upon any kind of material available, often appearing upon common brown wrapping-paper. The specimen in the author's possession is printed on the plain side of a piece of common wall-paper, ten inches wide and sixteen inches long. Among the articles which it contains is an exaggerated account of General Lee's campaign in Maryland, from which we quote :—

"We lay before our readers in this issue an account of Lee's brilliant and successful onslaught upon the abolition hordes, and show, even from their own record, how our gallant boys of the cavalry have fleshed their swords to the hilt with their vaunting foes, and how each musket of our infantry has told its fatal leaden tale. To-day Maryland is ours, to-morrow Pennsylvania will be, and the next day Ohio — now midway, like Mahomet's coffin — will fall. Success and glory to our arms! God and right are with us."

"ON DIT. — That the great Ulysses — the Yankee generalissimo, surnamed Grant — has expressed his intention of dining in Vicksburg on Saturday next, and celebrating the Fourth of July by a grand dinner, and so forth. When asked if he would invite General Joe Johnston to join, he said, 'No, for fear there will be a row at the table.' Ulysses must get into the city before he dines in it. The way to cook a rabbit is 'first to catch the rabbit.'"

"VICTIMIZED. — We learned of an instance wherein a 'knight of the quill' and a 'disciple of the black art,' with malice in their hearts and vengeance in their eyes, ruthlessly put a period to the existence of a venerable feline that has for a time, not within the recollection of 'the oldest inhabitant,' faithfully performed the duties to be expected of him, to the terror of sundry vermin in his neighborhood. Poor defunct Thomas was then prepared, not for the grave, but for the pot, and several friends invited to partake of a nice rabbit. As a matter of course, no one would wound the feelings of another, especially in these times, by refusing a cordial invitation to dinner, and the guests assisted in consuming the poor animal with a relish that did honor to their epicurean tastes. The 'sold' assure us the meat was delicious, and that pussy must look out for her safety."

"MULE MEAT. — We are indebted to Major Gillespie for a steak of Confederate beef, alias mule. We have tried it, and can assure our friends that, if it is rendered necessary, they need have no scruples at eating the meat. It is sweet, savory, and tender, and so long as we have a mule left, we are satisfied our soldiers will be content to subsist upon it."

As stated, the city was surrendered on the morning of the 4th of July, and the army of General Grant marched in and took possession. Some of the Federal soldiers who went into the city entered the office of the "Citizen," and finding the type for the paper all set in the forms, added the following note, and struck off a large number of copies, which were extensively distributed among our troops: —

"NOTE (at foot of last column).—July 4, 1863.

"Two days bring about great changes: the banner of the Union floats over Vicksburg; General Grant has '*caught the rabbit*'; he has dined in Vicksburg, and he brought his dinner with him. The 'Citizen' lives to see it. For the last time, it appears on wall-paper. No more will it eulogize the luxury of mule meat and fricasseed kitten, or urge Southern warriors to such diet nevermore. This is the last wall-paper edition, and is, excepting this note, an exact copy of it. It will be valuable hereafter as a curiosity."

The author, deeming this paper a curious chapter in the history of the siege of Vicksburg, has thought it not improper to quote thus fully from its columns.

CHAPTER XXII.

The Regiment Marches on Jackson — Jefferson Davis's House — Siege of Jackson — The Regiment Under Fire — Evacuation of the City — A Part of the City is Burnt by the Enemy — Return to Vicksburg — A Hard March — "French Joe's" Mule — The Dead of the Regiment — Return to Cincinnati — March Over Cumberland Mountains to Knoxville, Tenn.

As soon as the siege was concluded, General Grant immediately turned his attention to General Johnston, who up to this time had held the line of the Big Black, watching for a chance to strike our besieging army. The time had now arrived for the Ninth Corps to perform its part of the work of that memorable campaign. As soon as General Johnston learned of Pemberton's surrender, he began to fall back to Jackson, the capital of the State. The Ninth Corps under General Parke, together with General Smith's division of the Sixteenth Corps, and General W. T. Sherman's own corps, all under command of General Sherman, were ordered by General Grant to pursue the retreating enemy. This movement began as early as the evening of the 4th of July, but the Brigade of Colonel Christ did not commence to move till the afternoon of the 7th, the Twenty-ninth leaving camp at two o'clock in the afternoon. Toward nightfall the Big Black was reached, the men crossing the river on a floating bridge which had been constructed by the advance forces. The march was continued far into the night, no halt being made till twelve o'clock. The day had been severely hot, and a large number of the men were left beside the road, where they had fallen, stunned and bewildered, by the overpowering rays of the sun. When the night came on, it began to rain, and for a space of two hours the overcharged clouds poured torrents of water upon the soldiers, who were toiling along over the muddy roads so faint from exhaustion that they could scarcely drag one foot after the other. As soon as the halt was made, fires were kindled, and the men contrived to dry their clothing and steep a little coffee, the solace of the soldier. That was a wet and intensely uncomfortable bivouac; there was no recourse left the men but to spread their rubber blankets upon the flooded earth, and, lying down upon them, cover themselves with the half of a shelter-tent. They had barely fallen asleep when the storm broke out afresh, and the rain came down upon them in great sheets. Sleep was wholly banished, and huddling around the smouldering fires, the "poor boys" thus passed the balance of that gloomy night. The day which followed this was also very hot, and the officers having learned that the troops could not endure the sun, wisely concluded to allow them to remain quiet till near nightfall. At four o'clock, P. M., the order came to break camp, and a long march was performed, the Brigade marching till one o'clock on the morning of the 9th. On the 9th, the line was formed as early as six o'clock in the morning; but the men were not hurried through the day, being allowed to make frequent but brief halts. The troops halted at nine o'clock in the evening near the plantation of Jefferson Davis, where the regiment was ordered on guard for the remainder of the night.

A part of the regiment on this occasion was posted very near the house of Davis, and though the men were led by curiosity to visit it, yet they refrained from destroying the property of this prominent traitor, or committing any acts unbecoming a regiment of Massachusetts soldiers. As early as seven o'clock on the following morning, the men having had no sleep during the preceding night, and scarcely any for three consecutive nights, the regiment was ordered to start. At two o'clock that afternoon the rear guard of the retreating enemy was suddenly encountered, a line of battle was quickly formed, and slight skirmishing ensued; but the Twenty-ninth, though very near the front, did not become engaged. Toward evening the Confederates retreated, and our troops started in pursuit, the Brigade proceeding only about two miles, when it halted for the night on the plantation of Mr. Hardeman, on the line of the Mississippi Central Railroad.

Early the next morning, while the regiments were resting, the order was given for the Brigade to go to the front, taking position on a ridge of land upon which stood the State Lunatic Asylum, about five miles from Jackson. On the previous day, the enemy had occupied this place, but were driven from it by the First Division under General Welch. The Confederates on the 11th held another line of works a little nearer the city of Jackson, but within easy range of this ridge; the place was thickly wooded, and the Brigade lay concealed among the trees during the day, the Twenty-ninth supporting Captain Edward's Rhode Island Battery, which did but little firing, however.

When it grew dark, shovels were called into requisition, and every man in the Brigade was set to work throwing up entrenchments, laboring till daylight the next morning; but our men were not to be allowed to enjoy the fruits of their night's labor, for in the early morning, they were ordered out of the works, up to the extreme front, in support of our skirmish line. Fortunately they were not obliged to endure the scorching rays of the sun, but found shelter in a piece of woods; it was only a shelter from the sun, however, for the enemy, knowing our position, poured into the woods a continuous fire of shell, canister, and spherical case during the whole of the two days that the regiment was here. The other regiments in the Brigade suffered more or less loss, but the Twenty-ninth escaped without a single casualty. In addition to the storm of larger missiles, many of the musket-balls fired from the enemy's lines found their way into the woods, and so severe was the fire, that nearly every tree along our line bore the marks of the leaden tempest. Many of our comrades had narrow escapes from death and wounds, one soldier in Company K especially, a ball passing through his tin dipper, upon which he was resting his head.

On the morning of the 11th, the Brigade was relieved and ordered to the rear, resuming its former position near the lunatic asylum; but in the afternoon of the same day it was again ordered forward, and again supported Captain Edward's battery. Here it remained till the morning of the 16th, when an advance of the whole line was made, the Twenty-ninth passing up under a heavy fire to within forty rods of the enemy's works, bristling with cannon, the right of the regiment going into the rifle-pits. Once in the pits, there was no such thing as leaving them while it was daylight, and here the "boys" spent the day, constantly engaged with the enemy's sharpshooters. Though considerably exposed, there was but one casualty during the day, Private John Scully of Company A being instantly killed, the ball penetrating his brain. The regiment in this position held the extreme left of the picket line of our army, its right resting in the rifle-pits, and its left in dense woods, retired so as to form nearly a half-circle.

The night of the 16th was dark, and hence favorable for secret movements by both besiegers and besieged. About nine o'clock, unusual noises were heard within the enemy's lines, resembling the rattling of wheels. Colonel Barnes became anxious to learn the cause of these noises, and Captain Clarke was requested to use every effort to ascertain what, if any, movement was going on in the enemy's camp. That officer had no difficulty in carrying out his instructions, for one of his men, a fearless soldier, named David Scully, unhesitatingly consented to undertake the perilous task of approaching the hostile picket line. The ground descended quite rapidly from Clarke's line towards that of the Confederates. Scully was left to execute his adventure in his own way. Prostrating himself upon the ground, he rolled slowly down the hill, till he approached within a few yards of the enemy's pickets, and then pausing, overheard their conversation, which was to the effect that their army was retreating, and that they were soon to be relieved. Listening here, Scully heard more distinctly than before, the noises in the enemy's camp. They were evidently removing their guns from the works; and, beside this, the regular tread of marching men was plainly distinguishable. In due time Scully returned, making this report. About this time, a similar report was brought in by Charles Logue of Company F, who went forward into the woods, very near the enemy, exhibiting great courage. In order to verify the statements of Scully and Logue, Colonel Barnes, with one or more of the captains, advanced some distance beyond our picket line, when they soon became convinced that the whole body of the enemy was moving. Thereupon one of the sergeants was despatched to General Ferrero, who was in command of the trenches, with information that the enemy was moving in large numbers, and shortly after a lieutenant was sent, with the message that the enemy was abandoning his works and retiring from the city.

The night was intensely dark, and the ground over which these officers were obliged to pass, in delivering their messages, beset with difficulties, being broken, and in some places covered with fallen timber and a thick growth of bushes. But, like faithful soldiers, they persevered till they found General Ferrero, when they delivered their messages. The substance of the reply that was sent back was, "The movements of the enemy are well understood at headquarters. The enemy are not retiring." The rumbling of the enemy's trains and the neighing of their horses continued; and the Colonel and his comrades stood at their posts all night, listening to these sounds, which grew fainter and more distant every hour, as the Confederates were slipping out of the grasp of General Sherman, and retiring beyond the Pearl River. When the night was almost gone, a message was received from General Ferrero, that the regiment might move forward in the gray of the morning, if Colonel Barnes thought it advisable.

When the morning came, a flag of truce was seen waving from the enemy's works, and at the same time the city appeared to be in flames. During the night, General Johnston retired with his whole army, artillery, and baggage, and even the large guns upon his works. As soon as it was fairly day, the whole line was ordered forward, and the regiment entered the city. The works were found to be deserted, and the railroad depot and several public buildings in flames; but the fire was quickly extinguished by our troops, and thus a large portion of the city was doubtless saved from destruction. After the regiment had finished its part of the generous work of subduing the flames, the men were dismissed for a couple of hours, during which time they contrived to "do" Jackson quite thoroughly. The gardens were filled with melons and fruits, but of other and more desirable food there was a small supply. Everything of much value had been removed, and many of the deluded inhabitants had followed in the steps of the retreating army, taking with them their personal effects, thus giving the place the appearance of a deserted town. The negroes had the good sense to stay, and, as was invariably the case, they were overjoyed at the appearance of the Union soldiers, testifying to their happiness in the way peculiar to their race.

In the afternoon of the 17th, the regiment had orders to leave the city, marching back to the ground occupied on the 14th. Here it remained, enjoying much-needed rest, till Monday the 20th. Another severe march was before them, a march needlessly hard; and at an unreasonable hour in the morning of the 20th, the reveille aroused the men from their slumbers.

Before the movement began, an order was issued from headquarters, detailing Colonel Barnes Provost Marshal of the corps, and the whole of the regiment as provost guard, with orders to move in the rear of the corps, and to keep everything — men, horses, and wagons — in front. This was the hardest duty the regiment ever performed in the same number of days. For some reason, the march was a forced one; the weather was of the same tropical character that it had been during the three weeks previous, and water not only scarce, but of poor quality. The story among the men was, that the corps was racing with another, the Sixteenth (?); but the more probable statement is, that the corps reaching Vicksburg first would take the transports to go North, there being only a sufficient number of steamers for the transportation of a single corps. The imperative orders given to Colonel Barnes to prevent straggling, required constant watchfulness and almost superhuman efforts, not only on his part, but on the part of his brother officers and the men. Many soldiers gave out, from the combined effects of over-exertion and the enervating influence of the weather. On the second day out, matters in this respect became so bad, that it became necessary to impress into the service, ox-carts, horses, and vehicles of all descriptions which could be found about the country, and use them for the conveyance of the invalids, many of whom had received fatal sunstrokes. The spectacle which the corps presented on the road was wholly unbecoming a victorious army; nearly every regiment had lost even the semblance of an organized body; everybody was straggling along the roads, some riding in carts, and others mounted upon horses and mules, while miles in the rear of this mob was the gallant old Twenty-ninth Regiment, driving the crowd before them. Violent menaces, and sometimes absolute force, were required to keep the stragglers in motion.

For want of ambulances, nearly all the wounded in the battles and skirmishes before Jackson were carried the whole distance from the latter city to Vicksburg on litters or stretchers by details of men. To protect these unfortunate soldiers from the sun, hoods made of pieces of tent cloth were placed about their heads, and green boughs arranged at the sides of the litters.

A large number of disabled horses and mules were left about the country, in the track of Johnston's retreat, and these were systematically gathered up by General Sherman, when he returned from Jackson, and driven along to the various landings in the vicinity of Vicksburg and Milldale, where, together with the horses and other animals captured by the soldiers on the march, they were delivered up to the quartermasters. Nearly every company of the Twenty-ninth had a large number of saddle and pack animals, which they had ridden and used for the conveyance of their baggage during the march. Company A had some twenty horses and mules, and Company G nearly as many, when they returned to Milldale, having, as they swept along the stragglers of the column, as the extreme rear guard, collected these animals, as well as the jaded and tired-out men, and their work was much lightened by these mounts. As the rear guard approached the Big Black, the soldiers on foot were sent forward into camp, and then about thirty or forty mounted men came in together, most of the latter being men who had fallen out or got footsore, and had been picked up and mounted to keep them along with the army.

When one of these motley crowds came in, the commander of the regiment, who was somewhat indignant at the appearance of the thing, hailed the captain in command, "I should like to know, sir, what this means; what sort of a command is this for an infantry officer?" "Irregular mounted infantry, I should think," replied the leader, as he looked at his crew.

It was on this march that Captain Richardson's man, nicknamed "French Joe," came to the conclusion that his captain's mess kit might just as well be carried by a mule as by Joseph, and, in fact, that the mule might carry "Joe" too, and took one of the mules for this purpose. He had only his belt and some old scraps of rope for a tackling; but this he thought might serve well enough. He contrived a pad out of his own and the Captain's blankets, and, warned by the example of John Gilpin, he attempted to balance his load and to tie it securely to the sides of the mule, which were well festooned with pots, pans, gridirons, camp kettles, and tin dippers, giving the animal the appearance of the "hawker's" donkey. After all this varied assortment of wares had been piled upon the animal, Joe kindly allowed a knapsack or two to be strapped on behind, and then mounted, guiding the mule with a rope halter. He had not proceeded far before some of the knots began to slip, for Joe was not a sailor, nor was he a very skilful disposer of weights. Very soon one of the knapsack straps got loose and insinuated itself on the inside of the mule's hind leg. It tickled him — he kicked. This displaced a camp kettle, which slipped under his belly — he "buck-jumped," and unseated Joe. Then all the load shifted, the most of it getting under the beast's belly. He curveted and pranced, he reared and kicked, and cleared the road right and left for more than a mile. The men scattered on every side, for the mule was in earnest, and was no respecter of persons, kicking just as viciously at the officers as at the men. Captain Richardson had no dinner that day, save what he got through the kindness of others; for his coffee, hard bread, and bacon, tin plates and cups, flour, butter, and roasting corn — all the materials of many a savory feast — lay in the dust.

On the 22d, the Ninth Corps reached the Big Black River. General Parke and his division commanders now deemed it impossible, as it certainly was disgraceful, for the corps to continue to march in this manner. The different regiments were here, on the banks of the river, gathered together, and forced to resume their organization. One whole day was spent in this work, during which the men were permitted to rest.

Toward evening of the 22d, the corps moved out of camp, and marching slowly, crossed the Big Black on a pontoon bridge, in the midst of a pouring rain; the troops camped near the river for the night, and the next morning started for Milldale. The regiment was the last to arrive, in consequence of its peculiar duty, and by being the last, lost the first chance to go on board the transports, and was thus forced to remain here till the 12th of August.

During the campaign now closed, the roll of the regiment's dead had been somewhat increased; and this, with a few exceptions, had been occasioned by disease contracted in the sickly regions of the Yazoo and Vicksburg. Private John Scully of Company A, a faithful soldier, was the first to fall in the campaign, having been killed by a bullet while bravely doing his duty in the rifle-pits before Jackson, July 16. Second Lieutenant Horace A. Jenks of Company E came next, dying of malarial fever, July 26. Lieutenant Jenks had at one time been a sergeant in his company, and was promoted to be second lieutenant for his good soldierly qualities. His death was mourned by all the members of the regiment. First Lieutenant Ezra Ripley of Company B, who died of fever at Helena, Ark., July 28, was a member of the Middlesex Bar before entering the service. He was a gentleman of liberal culture and rarest qualities of both heart and mind. No sacrifice for his country was too great in his estimation, and though not of a robust constitution, yet he never shrank from any exposure or hardship. He performed the terrible march to Jackson, but the seeds of disease sown during those days, already described, soon ripened into death. Private Lyford Gilman of Company B also died of disease at Vicksburg, August 2. He was also a victim of the exhaustive march.

When the Ninth Corps was about to leave Vicksburg, General Grant, desirous of recognizing its services in the late campaign, issued the following order: —

"HEADQUARTERS DEPARTMENT OF THE TENNESSEE,
"VICKSBURG, MISS., July 31, 1863.

[EXTRACT.]

"SPECIAL ORDERS, No. 207.

" In returning the Ninth Corps to its former command, it is with pleasure that the general commanding acknowledges its valuable services in the campaign just closed.

"Arriving at Vicksburg opportunely, taking position to hold at bay

Johnston's army, then threatening the forces investing the city, it was ready and eager to assume the aggressive at any moment.

"After the fall of Vicksburg, it formed a part of the army which drove Johnston from his position near the Big Black River, into his entrenchments at Jackson, and after a siege of eight days, compelled him to fly in disorder from the Mississippi Valley.

"The endurance, valor, and general good conduct of the Ninth Corps are admired by all; and its valuable co-operation in achieving the final triumph of the campaign is gratefully acknowledged by the Army of the Tennessee.

"Major-General Parke will cause the different regiments and batteries of his command to inscribe upon their banners and guidons, 'Vicksburg' and 'Jackson.'

"By order of

"MAJOR-GENERAL U. S. GRANT.

"P. S. BOWEN, *A. A. A. G.*"

The time spent at Milldale, after the return from Jackson, was occupied by the ordinary duties of camp life. The weather continued very warm, and the destructive effects of the campaign now became manifest. Deaths were very frequent among the troops here during this time, burial parties were almost constantly engaged, and the funeral notes of the fife and drum could be heard nearly every hour in the day. None save the strongest came out of that campaign in sound health.

On the 12th of August, the regiment embarked on the steamer "Catahoula," one of the slowest boats on the river, to go North; the steamer left Milldale without a sufficient supply of fuel, and accordingly frequent stoppages on the route, to gather wood, became necessary. The trip to Cairo, including one day spent at Memphis, occupied eight days, the boat reaching its destination on the 20th.

At midnight on the 20th, the regiment took the cars for Cincinnati, reaching that city on the afternoon of Sunday the 23d, and receiving the same kind treatment as on its two former visits.

At night, the regiment left the city, crossed the Ohio to Covington, Ky., and went into camp on the outskirts of the town, and remained here till the 27th. At this time, probably nearly half of all the members of the regiment were on the sick-list, and unable to do duty. In the course of a few days they had come from the tropical climate of the South into the cool bracing air of the West, and now the chills and fever broke out among them to an alarming extent.

While here, Colonel Barnes left the regiment on a furlough to his home in Massachusetts; he was very sick from the effects of a malarial fever and overwork; from the eighteenth day of May, 1861, till he was seized with this sickness, he had never been off duty, for any cause, a day, — a fact that is not only remarkable, but, considering the great hardships to which he had been subjected, one that shows him to have been possessed of an iron constitution.

The author, in the preparation of this work, has endeavored, as far as possible, to avoid the diary form of narrative, because he is aware that such does not interest the general reader; but the record of the regiment would be incomplete if it did not give somewhat in detail the events of long and memorable marches, and the various localities visited by it.

The march from Covington, Ky., into East Tennessee, which we are about to describe, was one of the longest which the regiment ever performed, and, for the reasons stated, we shall give a very particular account of it. On the 27th, it broke camp, under the command of Major Chipman, went to the railroad station in Covington, took the cars for Nicholasville, arrived there at seven o'clock the next morning, and camped near the depot. On the 29th, Colonel Pierce, who had for several months been absent on special duty in Massachusetts, joined the regiment and assumed command, and on the same day a march on the Lancaster pike of about four miles was performed.

August 31. The regiment was mustered for pay; Colonel Pierce ordered to the command of the Brigade; the Second Michigan Infantry joined the Brigade, and Major Chipman again took command of the regiment.

September 1. Reveille at four o'clock, A. M. Started for Crab Orchard, in Lincoln County; spent the night for the third time at Camp Dick Robinson.

September 2. Reveille at an early hour; marched all day; camped near Lancaster.

September 3. Another early start. Reached Crab Orchard, a place of five hundred inhabitants, and abounding with mineral springs. Here and at Nicholasville convalescent camps were established, and during the time which the regiment remained at these places, a very large number of its members went into the hospitals, where not a few of them subsequently died.

September 10. The Brigade left Crab Orchard, and had a hard march of about fourteen miles, and went into camp at a place called Mount Vernon. The road for a considerable portion of the way was very rough and mountainous, being so steep in some places that the horsemen were obliged to dismount and lead their animals. The men were in light marching order, having left the most of their extra clothing at Crab Orchard, and had eight days' rations served out to them, being thus prepared for a long march.

September 11. The reveille sounded at half-past three o'clock in the morning, and at half-past four the column was in motion. At night, after a very fatiguing march, the camp was formed near Wild Cat Mountain, Kentucky.

September 12. The men were routed out early in the morning, and the day's march began at five o'clock, but the road was good all day. The weather, which had been fine ever since the march began, became stormy at the end of this day, and at night it rained hard. The camp was formed at Loudon, Laurel County, Ky. On this march the regiment passed over the battle-field of Mill Spring, where the notorious Zollicoffer was killed.

September 13 was Sunday. The men were paid off and allowed to rest all day. Since this famous march began, the Brigade had passed through and into three counties; namely, Gerrard, Rock Castle, and Laurel. The country through which they had travelled was thinly populated, and with the exception of a few wild fruits and nuts which they found on the journey, the men were obliged to subsist upon their rations. It has been stated, that the wild fruits which the men ate on this march proved very beneficial to their health, and resulted in curing them of the complaints they had contracted in the sickly swamps of the Yazoo.

September 14. The march was resumed at five o'clock in the morning, and at night a halt was made at Laurel Spring.

September 15. Only a part of the day was occupied by

marching, a halt being made at the town of Barboursville, in Knox County, Ky.

September 16. Marched from Barboursville to Flat Lick; a long march, pausing till the 19th.

September 19. A distance of about ten miles was travelled this day; the camp was formed at Log Mountain. The column was nearing the far-famed Cumberland Gap, and the roads were growing rougher and more broken at every advance in that direction. The night was very cold, water froze, and the crops of tobacco, sugar-cane, and cotton in that region nearly all destroyed. When the sun rose the next morning, it revealed the earth white with frost.

September 20. At ten o'clock in the morning, the Brigade reached Cumberland Gap, and entered the State of Tennessee. After passing into this gap, which was defended by a small force of infantry and cavalry, the road became more and more elevated, till at last it reached the summits of the mountains. The view from these heights well paid the men for all their toil in climbing their rugged and broken sides. In the far distance, ridge after ridge seemed to rise up toward the heavens, the highest actually invading the clouds, which, with a beautiful curtain of blue, hid from sight the lofty peaks. The night was spent in the mountains near the gap.

September 21. Sycamore, Tenn. Camped for the night. An inquiry having been made at one of the mountain huts, regarding the distance between this place and Tazewell, the answer was, "Two rises to go up and two rises to go down and a right smart plain."

September 22. Morristown, Tenn. Here the Brigade remained till the 24th.

September 24. Marched to New Market.

September 25. Marched to Holston River and forded it.

September 26. Entered the city of Knoxville.

The distance marched between the first of September and 26th was something over two hundred miles. The march over the mountains has furnished the theme of many interesting conversations among the men who performed it. The hardships of the road were manifold and serious. It was enough to be compelled to climb day after day the rugged and precipitous path along the side of these mountains; it was enough, indeed, to bivouac on their cold and barren summits, with only a single woollen blanket to protect the foot-sore soldier from the searching and chilling night-air; but when we add to these discomforts, that of intense and unsatisfied hunger, which was actually endured during the entire march, the measure of the sufferings of our comrades seems full to overflowing. They endured these sufferings and hardships, however, for a good purpose. Together with the troops which had gone on before them, they had wrought the long-prayed-for deliverance of East Tennessee. On the 3d of this month, General Burnside, together with the Twenty-third Corps and other troops, had entered the city of Knoxville, the Confederate General Buckner retiring from the place with his army and retreating toward Chattanooga.

The people of this region had long suffered from rebel rule, and the barbarities which had been practised upon them have never been fully related to the world. Some had been imprisoned, others tortured, and others murdered. Their property had been mercilessly confiscated, and not a few had been forced to perform military duty in the service of a cause that they loathed and hated. When the army of General Burnside appeared bearing the old flag, and the colors of the cruel foe departed in haste and confusion, the loyal people were overwhelmed with joy. The flag of the Union, which had been carefully hid under carpets, concealed in cellars and between mattresses, to save its owners from persecution, was now brought forth from its hiding-places, and flaunted on every hand; from windows and liberty-poles, it floated to the breeze.

A considerable part of General Burnside's army was composed of loyal Tennesseans, who had been forced to fly into Kentucky during the continuance of the enemy's rule. These native troops, among which was the cavalry under Lieutenant-Colonel Brownlow, son of the famous parson, "were kept constantly in advance, and were received with expressions of the profoundest gratitude by the people. There were many thrilling scenes of the meeting of our Tennessee soldiers with their families, from whom they had so long been separated. The East Tennesseans were so glad to see our soldiers, that they cooked everything they had and gave it to them freely, not asking pay, and apparently not thinking of it. Women stood by the roadside with pails of water, and displayed Union flags. The wonder was, where all the stars and stripes came from. Knoxville was radiant with flags. At one point on the road from Kingston to Knoxville seventy women and girls stood by the roadside waving Union flags and shouting, 'Hurrah for the Union.' Old ladies rushed out of their houses and wanted to see General Burnside and shake hands with him, and cried, 'Welcome, General Burnside, to East Tennessee.'"*

These constitute but a small part of all the demonstrations of loyalty by this intensely loyal people, and this brief account of their wrongs but a trifling part of the manifold abuses heaped upon them by a merciless and savage soldiery,— abuses and wrongs of the same barbarous nature as those perpetrated at Andersonville and Belle Isle, forming as they do the saddest chapter in the history of the war. It should be among the proudest boasts of the people of Massachusetts, that in the persons of her soldiers of the Twenty-first, Twenty-ninth, Thirty-fifth, and Thirty-sixth regiments, she helped deliver a people loyal to the old flag from a thraldom such as has been imperfectly depicted in this chapter,—a thraldom worse than death itself.

* "Rebellion Record," Vol. VII., pp. 407, 408.

CHAPTER XXIII.

BATTLES OF BLUE SPRINGS, HOUGH'S FERRY, AND CAMPBELL'S STATION — SIEGE OF KNOXVILLE — THE SUFFERINGS OF THE MEN — BATTLE OF FORT SANDERS — GALLANT CONDUCT OF THE REGIMENT — IT CAPTURES TWO BATTLE-FLAGS — THE SIEGE RAISED — GENERAL SHERMAN RE-ENFORCES BURNSIDE.

During the early part of October, a portion of the Ninth Corps under General Potter, and a large body of cavalry under General Shakleford, were sent up the valley some fifty miles in the direction of Morristown, Jefferson County. A force of the enemy had crossed into Eastern Tennessee from Virginia, and were threatening our communications with Cumberland Gap. This movement on the part of the Federals was made for the purpose of clearing the enemy away from the flank of our army.

On the 8th of October, the regiment with its brigade was ordered forward from Knoxville to join the rest of the corps, and on the night of the 9th halted at Bull's Gap, a pass in the mountains near the line between Jefferson and Green counties.

The movement of the enemy was a very important one; they had reached and occupied Greenville, and moved out beyond as far as Blue Springs. Foster's brigade of cavalry and mounted infantry was sent out from Knoxville, up the valley of the French Broad River, to turn the right of the enemy and get upon his rear, which movement was accomplished on the 9th. Foster got himself into position, and on the 10th, General Custer with his mounted infantry came up with the enemy at Blue Springs, and began to skirmish. Ferrero's division of twelve small regiments, of which the Twenty-ninth was one, arrived about noon, and went into position a half-mile from the field, where they had a good view of the skirmish for nearly half an hour. At the end of this time, two brigades of the division — namely, Humphrey's and Christ's — were sent forward.

The enemy had a battery well supported on the left of the main road leading to Greenville, on a high hill. They had thrown forward their first line and skirmishers well advanced to a distance of perhaps three-quarters of a mile from their battery, across the road and across a rivulet, and had advanced another body of skirmishers through a corn-field to the crest of a hill about three hundred yards from where the Twenty-ninth was lying. Custer's men had slowly retired before the Confederates, and passed to our rear, when the order came for our two brigades to charge. The men rose to their feet and went forward at a rapid run, with arms aport and bayonets fixed, up the hill. The enemy, closely followed by our men, fell back rapidly down the hill, across the rivulet, into and through a belt of woods, where the pursuit ended by the direct orders of our generals. Here Colonel Christ re-formed his Brigade, to carry one of the Confederate batteries that had begun to fire shell into our lines. The enemy, seeing the preparations for a charge, wheeled their guns about and fled; and at this stage in the affair, it became so dark that all further hostilities ceased. Captain Leach, then sixty-three years of age, led his company on this charge; and when the rivulet was reached, which was some eight feet wide, sprang into it and scrambled up the opposite bank as actively as the youngest of his men, refusing the proffered assistance of Major Chipman, who was leading the regiment.

Captains Leach and Clarke messed together; their negro servants, Bob and Isaac, were left in the rear of the field, where this fight had occurred, with their rations and baggage, and when the battle was over, were sought to prepare supper; but the darkies could not be found, — neither the rations nor baggage. Upon investigation, it appeared that a rumor had spread to the rear that both these officers had been killed in the fight. The negroes had of course heard of it, and, considering themselves absolved from all further obligations as servants, had gone back towards Bull's Gap, taking the effects of the officers with them, where at night they held a sort of barbecue, feasted on the rations, and concluded their entertainment with an auction sale of the baggage. These recreant negroes were found the next morning and subjected to a severe questioning. " Where are our rations ? " "Where's the coffee-pot ?" "What has become of our blankets ?" Bob acted as spokesman: "De rations and blankets is done gone; de coffee-pot is done gone, too. — dey's stole." This ended the examination, and these two unfortunate captains had short rations and hard fare for the rest of the march. The enemy retired during the night, and soon after daylight our army started in pursuit. After marching a mile or two, the infantry halted, and Shakleford's brigade of mounted men, with several horse batteries, swept by the head of the column, and then the infantry marched again. The most annoying information came from the farmers along the road. They scarcely knew which were our enemy, — the troops that had passed the night before, or the mounted column of Shakleford, — and these were some of the answers they gave in reply to questions of the whereabouts of the Confederates: "They are just ahead"; "Not far from an hour ago, they went by"; "A good gallop off"; and so forth.

When our troops reached Greenville, they learned to their surprise that the enemy had passed through there six hours before, and that they had a sharp engagement with General Foster's men a few miles out at Henderson's. The tired troops pressed on; at Henderson's, they saw some signs of a fight, but the bridge was intact. General Foster had refrained from destroying it, and the enemy had neglected to do so. Toward night the regiment went into camp at Rheatown, twenty-one miles from Blue Springs. Shakleford and Foster followed the enemy into Virginia, inflicting upon them great injury, and, upon returning, took up the line of the Watauga, to cover the passes from Virginia into East Tennessee.

One of the abandoned wagons of the Confederates, found near Rheatown, furnished our regiment with a liberal supply of excellent bread and some other food. At this place our troops had two full days' rest, and it was much needed, for the men had performed a forced march hither, and in the course of it had an encounter with the enemy.

At the close of the second day, the columns were turned towards Bull's Gap, making the distance by easy marches, and upon arriving there the regiment took the cars, but had proceeded but a short distance when an accident rendered it necessary for them to march six miles to Morristown, at which place they again took the cars and went to Knoxville, reaching there on the 15th of October.

While the Confederates held East Tennessee, a merciless conscription had been enforced by them, to avoid which many of the male population had abandoned their homes and taken refuge in the deep forests, or fled into Kentucky. After the country had been occupied by Burnside, many of these loyal people returned to their homes, and signified their willingness to enlist in the Federal army. Burnside issued an order encouraging such enlistments, and especially into the veteran regiments of the Ninth Corps, which had been greatly depleted by their recent campaigns. Shortly after the Twenty-ninth returned to Knoxville, Captain Clarke and Lieutenant Atherton were detailed for this recruiting service, and ordered to station themselves at Rheatown, where they spent several weeks, and secured a number of recruits. On the 11th of November, a force of Confederates again invaded Tennessee from Virginia, and evading the left of our army on the Watauga, attacked with about 3,500 cavalry our post at Rogersville, and captured its small garrison. This, and other hostile movements at various points, rendered necessary the evacuation of Rheatown, and the drawing in of all our forces in that part of the State, nearer Knoxville. Our recruiting party, therefore, returned to the latter place, and went on after their regiment, which, in the meantime, had gone out to Lenoir's Station.

A serious invasion of East Tennessee, by General Longstreet, had already begun. That officer, with a large force, had early in November been detached from Bragg's army, in the vicinity of Chattanooga, and was now marching up the valley towards Knoxville. On the 20th of October, the Ninth Corps left Knoxville and went to Campbell's Station, fifteen miles southwest of the city, on the East Tennessee and Virginia Railroad; on the 21st, it moved down the railroad to Lenoir's Station, and remained there, with the exception of a few days, till the 14th of November. On the night of the 13th of November, Longstreet made his appearance on the south side of the Holston River, at Hough's Ferry, about six miles below Loudon, and where was stationed General White, with one division of the Twenty-third Corps. November the 14th, early in the morning, General Potter, in a hard rain-storm, started with the whole of the Ninth Corps to re-enforce General White. The Twenty-ninth with its brigade (Christ's) was in advance, and toward noon arrived at a point five miles from the ferry, when rapid and heavy firing was distinctly heard. Now the clouds parted and the storm slackened, but the roads were as heavy and broken as before, making it exceedingly difficult to get the artillery along, and rendering the progress of the troops very slow. It was nearly dark when the Brigade reached the ferry; by this time the battle there had nearly ceased, nothing save an occasional musket-shot indicating the near presence of the enemy. Immediately upon its arrival, the regiment was ordered to the right of the line, marched nearly two miles through a thick woods, and formed in line of battle within one hundred yards of that of the enemy. The night soon came on, and early in the evening the storm broke out again with increased fury; the wind blew with the force of a tornado: the trees swayed to and fro in the blast, threatening to fall upon the heads of the men, who stood to arms all night without fires.

Very early the next morning (15th), when the men were expecting to march against the enemy, the order came to fall back, and taking the same track by which it had entered the gloomy forest, the Brigade picked its way back to the place where it had first halted the night before. All along the way brightly-burning camp-fires were passed, but no troops were seen; these had already left, and were well under way towards Lenoir's. At noon the regiment reached the latter place. The men had tasted no food for several hours, and were nearly worn out with fatigue; during the march here, they had managed to pluck a few ears of corn from the fields by the roadside, and as soon as a pause was made and the arms stacked, the place was ablaze with fires: every man at once went to work making coffee and preparing little messes for dinner. Happily the poor, hungry men had time to finish their meal, but they had barely finished it when they were ordered under arms. The enemy had just then appeared a half-mile away on the Kingston Road, and thither the Brigade was hurried at the double-quick. This movement of the Confederates was at once checked, and the rest of the day passed without any further hostile demonstrations, except a night attack upon our pickets.

The morning of the 16th was sharp and cold; as early as two o'clock the regiment was ordered to march. The roads that had been muddy the day before were now frozen; the artillery horses were pinched with cold and hunger, and quite unable to drag the heavy cannon. It was resolved to sacrifice a portion of the baggage train, which, to the number of many wagons, was parked at Lenoir's. The horses and mules were detached and harnessed into the guns; the spokes of the wagon-wheels were hacked, and, with their contents, set on fire, — not, however, till the soldiers had replenished their haversacks with a goodly quantity of smoked pork, coffee, sugar, and hard bread.

The whole corps was in full retreat soon after daylight, and the enemy at once began the pursuit, harassing our rear guard continually. The road from Lenoir's Station to Knoxville intersects at Campbell's with the road from Kingston, and Longstreet had detached a column on his left to seize the junction of these roads. The possession of Campbell's Station was, therefore, of great moment to Burnside, for should the enemy arrive there before him, his retreat to Knoxville would surely be cut off. A division of troops under Hartranft, by rapid marching, succeeded, in the early part of the forenoon, in reaching Campbell's, and going out on the Kingston Road deployed across it, his left on the Loudon Road, along which our army and trains were moving. Hartranft was just fifteen minutes ahead of the enemy; he had only time to form his line, when the Confederate column appeared hurrying up the Kingston Road. A sharp engagement ensued; but the enemy was foiled in his attempt, and driven back in confusion. Soon after, all our trains passed this dangerous point in safety, and moved on to Knoxville. At about noon, the rest of the army came up, and went into position on "a low range of hills about a half-mile from the cross-roads." The Ninth Corps was posted on the right of the field, which was nearly a mile broad, and extended a half-mile along the main road, and was bordered by heavy woods, passable for infantry. Christ's brigade was on the right of the corps, and the Twenty-ninth on the right of the Brigade, fifty yards from the woods in front, while its right flank actually touched them.

The lines had been formed but a short time, when the blue uniforms of our rear guard were seen, and finally our skirmishers,— the latter crossing the fields, creeping along the fences, and coming up the road, guns in hand, occasionally pausing to load and fire. Now and then a soldier in gray showed himself on the edge of the woods, but he would soon dart back out of sight. Colonel Pierce, now in command of the regiment, had orders to cover his front and flank with skirmishers, and Companies A and I, under Captain Clarke and Lieutenant Williams, were detailed for this purpose. The companies had proceeded but a short distance into the woods, when they came upon the enemy, who were approaching stealthily from tree to tree, evidently attempting what Colonel Christ had feared; namely, to flank the Brigade. A brisk fire began at once, but our men kept their line intact, and maintained perfect coolness. After the lapse of about an hour, the officers on the skirmish line discovered that the enemy were gradually overlapping the right of the Brigade, and promptly informed Colonel Christ of the fact. The skirmishers were ordered to come in at once, and the Brigade changed front and began to fall back. This movement was not made a moment too soon, for a dense mass of the enemy's infantry immediately poured out of the woods in the rear of the retreating Brigade ; while his flanking party, which had not yet lapped over our old position, also at the same moment, emerged from the woods, and, with loud yells, joined in the pursuit, firing an occasional shot, and with terrible oaths, shouting to our men to surrender and lay down their arms.

Our men, loading as they marched, halted by files, turned about and fired, and again took their places in the ranks. At last, the regiment, which was in the rear, reached a sunken road, and, leaping into it, moved rapidly to the left of our lines; while over the heads of the men, now fully protected by the high bank, played the cannon of our reserve batteries, at last free to fire without endangering the lives of our own troops. The slaughter wrought upon the pursuing enemy is described as terrible; and as the Twenty-ninth came up the hill, gaining the plateau of the Knoxville side, Generals Burnside and Ferrero, standing on either side of the road, clapped their hands as it filed proudly between them.

It was now, perhaps, five o'clock in the afternoon, and the battle degenerated into an artillery duel on our side, varied by the enemy with occasional charges, by which they took nothing but disaster. One by one, as it grew dark, the batteries retired, and after nightfall the Brigade moved off and took up its weary march for Knoxville, where it arrived at about three o'clock the next morning, and lay down for a few brief hours to rest upon the bleak hillside near Fort Sanders.

During this battle, Charles H. Dwinnell of Company A, a worthy comrade and brave soldier, was killed, and William O'Conner of Company H was captured. Dwinnell was shot through the brain by a sharpshooter stationed in a tall pine. The ball was probably aimed at Captain Clarke, who was quite conspicuous at the time; the sharpshooter was instantly marked and shot by two of Dwinnell's comrades, who fired simultaneously, the enemy's body being seen to fall out of the tree.

The siege of the city commenced on the 17th, and progressed rather gradually, beginning on the west and northwest, and finally extending around the entire city, from river to river. As the work of investing the place continued, our pickets were constantly pressed in close upon the main works, so that by the 29th of November we scarcely held more than the slope of the plateau crowned by our main fortifications, and in some cases not even that.

To the right of Fort Sanders, named after a brilliant cavalry general who was killed early in the siege, and west of the city, Humphrey's and Christ's brigades picketed one side of the railroad cut, and the enemy the other.

On one occasion, before the pickets were drawn in, a little squad of the Twenty-ninth assaulted a house in front of them, and driving away the enemy's pickets there stationed, captured it, and brought in the supplies, which consisted of a small sack of meal, a few pounds of bacon, a box of tobacco, an eight-gallon keg of blackberry brandy, and two boxes of cartridges. The enemy re-formed and recaptured the house, but our men brought their booty safely into camp. There was meal enough to give each man in the company to which these adventurers belonged, a dish of hasty-pudding, and tobacco enough to furnish every man in the regiment with a good-sized piece. The brandy and cartridges were accounted for during the night by some of the wildest picket-firing that occurred during the siege. There was by no means a large supply of food in the city when the siege began, but long before it concluded, all kinds of provisions became extremely scarce.

On the 19th, the Confederates drove in our outer pickets and took possession of the woods. On the evening of the 23d, they attacked our picket line in front of the Brigade, and seemed to be on the point of bringing on a general engagement. The order was given to set fire to a long line of buildings between the two armies. This was done to break the enemy's lines and unmask their movements, and resulted very successfully. The conflagration that followed was both grand and awful. The dark wintry sky was lighted up by the flames, which roared and crackled with an unearthly sound, casting a broad belt of dazzling light over the fields and into the forests. In the round-house of the railroad, there was stored a large amount of condemned ammunition, and when the flames reached that, there was an explosion that shook the earth, and startled the anxious residents of the city.

The 26th of November was Thanksgiving Day. The men got a full ration of bullets, but only a half-ration of bread.

About midnight of the 28th, the picket line near the river on the southwest was driven in, and could not be re-established by the brigade which furnished it. The line in front of Fort Sanders had also been assailed and taken by the enemy, and about nine o'clock in the evening an order was sent to take the regiment out of the lines and place it in the immediate rear of the fort for special duty; Major Chipman had command. A little later in the evening, Companies A, C, D, and K were detached, and ordered to our lines near the river, where the enemy had a few hours before captured our rifle-pits.

The night had nearly gone, and the first glimmer of day had appeared, when the familiar charging yell of the enemy was heard directly in front of the fort. Our pickets at this point were forced in, and in a moment more a large body of the enemy's infantry were swarming at the very edge of the ditch. The battalion of the Twenty-ninth, under Chipman, were hurried into the fort, and the four detached companies at once sent for. The latter had a perilous experience in joining their comrades, and though exposed to the fire of the enemy's cannon, reached the works without the loss of a man, and in ample time to lend a hand in the severe contest which was now well under way. The Confederates, led by fearless officers, crowded the ditch, and crossing it on each other's shoulders, began to ascend the bank; one of their standard-bearers came running up and planted his colors upon the parapet, in the very faces of Major Chipman's men; but he had hardly performed his deed of daring, when one of our soldiers shot him through the heart, and he fell forward into the works. Inspired by the example of their color-bearer, a large body of the Confederates, led by a gray-haired old officer (Colonel Thomas of Georgia), with wild shouts made a dash up the bank. All seemed lost; but at this moment Companies A, C, D, and K of the regiment came running into the fort, and ranging themselves along the parapet, opened a deadly fire upon the assaulting party. The gray old leader of the enemy, while waving his sword and shouting to his men to come on, was shot dead. Many of his brave followers suffered the same fate, and the handful of survivors fell hurriedly back into the ditch. At the same instant, like scenes were transpiring all along the works. The Seventy-ninth New York was sharply engaged, and the artillerymen, not being able to use their pieces, busied themselves by tossing among the enemy lighted shell with their fuses cut to a few seconds' length. Finally a sergeant of one of the batteries, observing a renewed preparation of the enemy to charge up the bank, slewed one of the large guns about so as to make it bear upon the edge of the ditch, and, with a single charge of canister, raked it for a distance of several yards with deadly effect. About this time the assault slackened; but in a few moments another column of the enemy came rushing towards the fort, and with almost sublime courage faced the withering fire of our troops, and large numbers of them gained the bank. The first terrible scenes of the battle were re-enacted; three of the enemy's standards were planted simultaneously upon the parapet, but they were quickly torn away by our men. The resistance was as desperate as the assault: officers used freely their swords, the men clubbed their muskets, others used their bayonets, and others still axes and the rammers of the cannon. A struggle so severe as this could not be otherwise than of short duration. In a few minutes the enemy's soldiers began to falter and fall back into the ditch. Seeing this, General Ferrero, who was in command of the fort and closely watching the fight, ordered one company of the Twenty-ninth on the left, and one company of the Second Michigan on the right, to go through the embrasures and charge the disorganized enemy. Sweeping down the ditch, these commands captured about two hundred of the enemy, and drove them into the fort, the little squad of the Twenty-ninth following their captives and bearing triumphantly two battle-flags of the foe; the capturers of which were Sergeant Jeremiah Mahoney of Company A, and Private Joseph S. Manning of Company K, both of whom afterwards received the medals of honor voted by the Congress of the United States.

The fight immediately died away in front of Fort Sanders, and the remnant of the enemy's charging column shrank back within their lines in dismay and confusion. But on the left, where the Federal rifle-pits had been captured on the afternoon of the 28th, a fierce battle was heard. Hartranft's division was sharply engaged with the enemy in its efforts to recapture the pits, and the effort was soon successful. The Confederates were everywhere routed, our entire line re-established, and by ten o'clock that Sunday morning quietness had settled down over the whole field. The enemy seemed appalled by the dreadful calamity that had overtaken him, — a calamity, as we shall presently see, that practically ended the siege. Ninety-eight dead bodies were taken out of the fatal ditch from a space of four hundred square feet around the salient. General Humphrey, who commanded the Mississippi brigade, was found dead on the glacis, within twenty feet of the face of the ditch. Lying among the dead in the moat, in every conceivable condition, were the wounded; and scattered all over the open space in front of the fort, through which telegraph wires had been stretched from stump to stump to impede the movements of the assailants, were scattered hundreds of both dead and wounded, and among them not a few of the enemy's soldiers unhurt, who, dismayed at the awful storm of shell and grape that poured upon them, had lain prone upon the earth until the battle was over,' only too willing to be captured. Nearly five hundred stand of small arms were collected on the field within our picket lines. Pollard states the enemy's loss in this battle at seven hundred.

The great bravery of this charge entitles those who participated in it to honorable mention. The troops who engaged in this assault "consisted of three brigades of McLaw's division; that of General Wolford,—the Sixteenth, Eighteenth, and Twenty-fourth Georgia regiments, and Cobb's and Phillips's Georgia legions; that of General Humphrey,—the Thirteenth, Seventeenth, Twenty-first, Twenty-second, and Twenty-third Mississippi regiments; and a brigade composed of Generals Anderson's and Bryant's brigades, embracing among others, the Palmetto State Guard, the Fifteenth South Carolina Regiment, and the Fifty-first, Fifty-third, and Fifty-ninth Georgia regiments." * The troops that garrisoned the fort were Benjamin's United States Battery, Buckley's Rhode Island Battery, a part of Roemer's New York Battery, the Seventy-ninth New York Highlanders, and, at the very beginning of the fight, a battalion of the Twenty-ninth under Major Chipman, and before the repulse of the assault on the salient, Captain Clarke's and the other companies of the regiment already named. When the battle was well advanced, and affairs had assumed a serious aspect, the One Hundredth Pennsylvania was moved up in the rear of the fort, and a few minutes before the close of the fight, the Second Michigan was ordered into the works on the right, one of its companies being detailed to sweep the ditch. Our loss in the fort was eight killed and five wounded, and among the former

* Pollard's "Third Year of the War," pages 161, 162.

were two members of the Twenty-ninth; namely, Sergeant John F. Smith of Company H, and Corporal Gilbert T. Litchfield of Company K, both most excellent soldiers. The loss of the enemy in this encounter doubtless exceeded greatly that given by Mr. Pollard; one of our officers engaged stating it to be fourteen hundred.

When Longstreet had drawn off his troops from the scene of his defeat, General Burnside kindly directed General Potter to send out a flag of truce, granting the enemy permission to remove his dead and wounded from the field. The flag was courteously received, and for the space of several hours there was a complete cessation of all hostilities. As a reward for its services in this action, the regiment was retained in Fort Sanders as a part of its garrison, and consequently relieved from much severe picket duty, only occasionally going on to the line immediately in front of the fort. But the duties of the fort, while not so arduous as those of the rifle-pits, were very important, and called for the exercise of constant vigilance. By day, one-third of the men were allowed to sleep in camp, one-third to rest in the fort with their belts on, and one-third stood to arms at the parapet; while at night all the men except a camp guard were required to be in the fort, one-half under arms and one-half resting with their belts on. At three o'clock each morning, the whole garrison was called up and stood to arms till six o'clock. One-half of the officers could be in camp by day, one-fourth must be at the parapet, and the remainder at rest in the works; and at three o'clock in the morning, all the officers were ordered to stand to arms with their men.

The casual mention, in the course of this chapter, of the telegraph wires which were stretched over the field in front of the fort, leads the author to speak of another device employed by our engineers who constructed these fortifications, — a defensive preparation, as ingenious in its nature as it was destructive in its results. The whole open space within our lines, directly in front of the fort, had been carefully plowed, with furrows leading generally to the work, not parallel, but converging towards a point opposite the main battery. It is natural for men when passing over broken ground to avoid the ridges and seek the smooth places and hollows. The furrows were quite wide and well defined, and when the enemy's column charged in the gray of the morning, his men coming suddenly upon the plowed ground, were thrown into great confusion. They took to the furrows, as was expected, and by the time they had reached the point where the furrows converged, the whole of the first battle line, consisting of a brigade, was huddled together in a disorganized mass, and in this condition received the concentrated fire of every gun on the works, which poured into them several very destructive charges of canister and grape.

At midnight on the 4th of December, as our men in Fort Sanders were standing to arms, something of an unusual nature was observed to be going on in the enemy's camp. Lanterns were seen flitting about in their batteries; night signals were at work, a fixed lantern low down near the ground and a movable one above it bobbing about from right to left. Our pickets all along the siege line were doubled, and the troops in the fort ordered to the parapets. All sorts of speculations were indulged in by our officers and men; some thought the enemy was preparing for another and final assault upon our works, and others that he was retreating.

General Sherman had for some days been marching to the relief of Burnside, and a rumor was prevalent that his cavalry had already attacked the rear of the enemy's army. The army of General Bragg, of which Longstreet's forces were a part, had fallen back from Chattanooga, and was then moving South. These circumstances, together with the hopeless nature of the siege, forced upon Longstreet the abandonment of his undertaking. Daylight revealed the fact that the enemy had gone. "Stack arms! All but the camp guard may rest!" was the order given to the garrison of Fort Sanders, when this state of things became officially known. The order was indeed a welcome one, for our soldiers in Knoxville had not tasted the pleasure of absolute repose for many long weeks. The termination of the siege was an important and joyful event to the whole nation; it was also a great crisis in the lives of the soldiers there, and what they said and did on this important occasion, our readers may be curious to know. The answer shows how utterly unromantic and prosaic were the Yankee soldiers who made so much history during the four years of war. "Thank God! now I can have a good snooze," said one, in no irreverent spirit. "Captain, can I go down to the run and wash my shirt?" said another. "Sergeant, has the company got any soap?" asked a third. Probably the thought of one-half of the men in Knoxville, at that moment, was sleep, and of the others, a wash, either of clothes or person. A few officers of the staff, a few orderlies, and surgeons rode out to visit the deserted camp, while our pickets were thrown out to capture the stragglers. In the course of an hour the loiterers and laggards of the late besiegers began to come into our lines in crowds. Some of them had overslept, others had strayed away, and others still had lost heart and skulked in the woods.

A report reached the ears of General Ferrero about noon, that a full regiment of the enemy had been left behind their main army, at a point about five miles distant. Colonel Christ's brigade, with the Twenty-ninth, was ordered out at once to capture these troops, and a forced and fruitless march was the result. No enemy, save a few worthless stragglers, were found, and the Brigade toward the close of the day returned, tortured with the conviction that they had been made the victims of a practical joke. The men had taken just so much wear out of their last pair of shoes, so travel-worn already, and had been brought just ten miles nearer to raw-hide moccasins. On the same day (December 5), Major-General Sherman, with his own corps and that of General Granger and a portion of General Howard's, arrived at Marysville (near Knoxville), and sent by his aid-de-camp to General Burnside the following hearty message: —

"I am here, and can bring twenty-five thousand men into Knoxville to-morrow; but Longstreet having retreated, I feel disposed to stop, for a stern chase is a long one. But I will do all that is possible. . . . Send my aid, Captain Audenried, out with your letters to-night. We are all hearty, but tired. Accept my congratulations at your successful defence and your patient endurance."

The endurance of the men had indeed been patient, and their sufferings and privations very great; but they had saved to the Government the stronghold of East Tennessee, and consequently both East Tennessee and Kentucky.

CHAPTER XXIV.

MOVEMENTS AFTER THE SIEGE — THE REGIMENT LEAVES KNOXVILLE — THE CONDITION OF THE TROOPS — BLAINE'S CROSS-ROADS — THE MEN RE-ENLIST — STRAWBERRY PLAIN — FIGHT WITH THE CONFEDERATE CAVALRY — THE REGIMENT GOES TO KNOXVILLE — ERIN STATION — THE CORN EXPEDITION — TRANSFER OF NON-RE-ENLISTING MEN TO THE THIRTY-SIXTH MASSACHUSETTS REGIMENT — LONG MARCHES — THE SNOW-STORM — ORDERED HOME — MARCH OVER THE CUMBERLAND MOUNTAINS — THE REGIMENT REACHES BOSTON — THE RECEPTIONS.

Early in the morning of the 7th of December, the Brigade started with other troops of the Ninth Corps in the direction of Morristown, in pursuit of the retreating enemy.

As showing the decimation which disease and suffering had wrought in the ranks of the regiment, one of its companies was able to muster that morning but one commissioned officer, one sergeant, one corporal, and three privates. Nearly one-quarter of the Ninth Corps remained in Knoxville for these and equally good reasons. There were over a thousand men of the First Division in camp there, who had done duty through the siege, but who could not march at this time because of their sick and enfeebled condition and lack of suitable clothing. All who were not absolutely sick and destitute were put in readiness for active duty in the course of ten days, and sent to their regiments. In order to fit out these men, the sutlers' shops and stores of the town were ransacked for clothing, blankets, etc. If boots and shoes could not be found at the commissary department, or furnished by it, the men purchased them with their own money, and set out for the front; and when these articles could not be bought, the old shoes were tapped in camp with leather or raw-hide; and when the latter resource failed, as it often did, raw-hide moccasins were cobbled up. Coats and trousers were patched with old blankets or the capes of overcoats; coverlids and bed-quilts were bought of the inhabitants of Knoxville, and issued to those who were destitute of blankets. This was the motley character of the outfit of the large majority of the soldiers who took part in that distressing winter campaign of which we are about to speak. On the 8th of December, the regiment reached a place called Blaine's Cross-Roads, where it remained only one day. On the next day it marched to Rutledge, pausing here till the 15th; on the latter day returning to Blaine's Cross-Roads.

Before entering upon a description of the life passed in this memorable camp, it seems proper to speak of some of the special duties performed by the soldiers in this department, and especially by the members of the regiment. Nearly every man in Company K of East Boston, and many members of other companies, were handy with tools. The East Boston men were acquainted with calking and graving and ship-carpentry; and the engineer officers of the corps were not slow in finding it out. Since our army had entered East Tennessee, a large portion of its pontoon train had been destroyed. The army was now operating in a country full of rivers, and at this, the rainy season, few could be forded; railroad bridges had been destroyed by both armies, and to enable the army to move, these must be rebuilt; no flour or meal could be found in the country except what the army could grind in the mills from wheat and corn foraged. Many of these mills had been broken down, and it was necessary to repair them. Skilful mechanics were hence in great demand, and as the wants of the army grew more pressing, the soldier who could repair a mill or build a boat came to be more esteemed than a major-general. As we have stated, the Twenty-ninth was very fortunate in having a large number of mechanics in its ranks, and consequently many details were made from it for these purposes. At one time nearly a whole company was engaged in building pontoon boats. The men felled the large trees, cut them into plank with two-handed saws and a saw-pit, and with this green lumber, built large, clumsy "dories" and strong ferry-boats, calking them with cotton, and graving them with gum (obtained in the forests).

At one time nearly a third of the regiment was set at engineering-work of one sort or another; and in this and other like labors, were kept employed through the rest of the month of December. This handiness of the men was in part the result of their native Yankee ingenuity and strong self-reliance. While few, if any, were professional engineers or millwrights, yet their knowledge of carpentry and of the use of mechanics' tools enabled them to do a fair piece of work of almost any description, and led them to attempt many things that they had never seen done.

The author does not wish to create the impression that this handiness and mechanical skill was wholly confined to the Twenty-ninth Regiment. It was quite general in the whole Ninth Corps, in which were several other Massachusetts regiments. It was about this time that the coffee-mill was introduced, with the outfit, to grind corn and wheat. Who originated the idea, cannot now be known; but it was a happy one, and saved the men from much destitution and labor, Christ's brigade having two or three of these machines in every company. "There must have been a corner," says an officer, "in this article of ironmongery, at that time, in East Tennessee. But the Twenty-ninth was superior even to a corner, for when these articles became scarce from having been worn out, one of the men got a file, and gathering three or four discarded coffee-mills, recut their scores, and fitted out his friends and comrades with something almost as good as new."

The favorite theory of some, even professional military men, that a good soldier should be, and is, a good machine, never using his reasoning faculties, or exercising his own judgment, finds no corroboration in the history of this campaign. But for the intelligence and sterling common-sense of our soldiers here, giving them complete adaptability to all the varied circumstances of their situation, they would have perished from the cold and hunger of that mountainous and terribly destitute country.

A knowledge of the laws of health taught them that the practice of getting a full meal as often as the rations would allow, though it be but once a day, was a better way of sustaining life and health, than that of taking three or four scanty meals, and being hungry all the time; they learned for themselves the beneficial effect of sleeping as much as possible by a blazing fire, and taking every precaution to keep the body warm. But neither intelligence, good judgment, nor the use of cunning devices, nor all combined, could wholly avail the soldiers against the absolute want that prevailed in that dreary winter camp. Blaine's Cross-Roads was the Valley Forge of the Rebellion. It was a bleak, mountainous plain, some twenty miles from Knoxville. The ground was for much of the time well covered with snow and ice. Many of the men were without shoes or stockings, and to supply this want, raw-hides were issued, which the destitute soldiers fashioned into rude moccasins. The garments of both officers and men were in tatters, and all sorts of expedients were resorted to, to protect themselves from the cold; some whose trousers were ragged, cut up their overcoats for patches; others still were without blankets. The army was quartered in shelter-tents; nothing except the abundance of wood saved the men from freezing. The suffering from want of food was, if possible, even greater than that which arose from a lack of clothing and shelter. "At one issue of rations, each man received for his mite eight ounces of flour for nine days. One tablespoonful of coffee was issued once in from three to five days."[*] It was not possible for men to exist upon such a small quantity of food, and hence they resorted to foraging. The food-hunting excursions that grew out of this state of pinching poverty often extended far into the surrounding country, but they commonly resulted in sore disappointment.

The loyal farmers had been stripped of nearly all their supplies by the army of the enemy; but they were touched by pity at seeing our hungry men, and listening to their earnest requests for food, and occasionally some large-hearted planter would share with them his meagre stock of provisions, and send them away from his door with a small piece of bacon or a few pounds of meal. The pangs of hunger are not easy to be endured. After the teamsters had fed their animals at night, the half-famished soldiers would creep stealthily to the pens, steal the corn upon which the poor animals were feeding, and then betaking themselves to their tents, spend

---

[*] Adjutant-General's Report, Massachusetts, 1863.

a large part of the night in grinding and cooking it. So general did this practice of stealing the food of the animals become, that guards were regularly stationed over them whenever they were fed; but the guards, as hungry as their fellows, stole the corn themselves.

The author is well aware of the distressing nature of these details, but the story of Blaine's Cross-Roads has never before been published to the world, so far as his knowledge extends, and showing as it does that the sufferings of our soldiers in this campaign were not surpassed by those of our revolutionary soldiers even at Valley Forge, he has deemed it important to give a somewhat minute account of these privations. The story is well calculated to disprove the favorite theory of many, that the habits of luxury of the Americans of to-day have resulted in both physical and moral degeneracy. Washington's soldiers at Valley Forge were mutinous, and at times could not be commanded,* but the Union soldiers at Blaine's Cross-Roads were obedient, and so far forgetful of their sufferings, that, without murmuring, they performed every task assigned to them, and whenever their brave old enemy made his appearance, they were ready to fight. Pack and draught animals died by scores here and at other places in the department, by reason of the scarcity of food. This state of things made it necessary to lessen the number of mounts usually allowed in the army. Only one pack mule was allowed to a regiment for officers' baggage and mess kit, and two to the brigade headquarters. Writing concerning the experiences of this winter, an officer of the regiment says: "It is well known that a mule will thrive on fence rails, but it may be a benefit to future campaigners to know that sassafras twigs are very nourishing and satisfactory to a hungry horse, and that he can be kept fat on them."

The law of Congress which provided for the payment of large bounties to re-enlisting veterans, was designed to retain in the service an army of trained and skilful men. In pursuance of this law, the War Department issued an order just before the close of the year 1863, promising, in addition to the bounty, a furlough of thirty days, provided a sufficient

---

* Irving's "Life of Washington," Vol. III., p. 354.

number of men enlisted in each regiment to constitute an organization of that size, the furlough to be given before the expiration of the original term. Strange as it may seem, a very large majority of the members of the Twenty-ninth re-enlisted under this order, while they were enduring the famine, toil, and nakedness of Blaine's Cross-Roads. On the first day of January, 1864, they were mustered into the service of the United States for another term of three years, as the Twenty-ninth Veteran Regiment of Massachusetts Volunteer Infantry. But they were doomed to disappointment as to receiving at once the promised furlough.

On the 16th of January, the whole corps was ordered out of camp, and moved to Strawberry Plain, a station on the East Tennessee and Virginia Railroad, crossed the Holston River, and went into camp upon the banks. General Sheridan, who was in command of the Fourth Corps (also engaged in this movement), assumed command of all the troops. This march, though only of seven miles, was one of the hardest of the campaign: the roads, which were frozen at night, thawed during the day, producing mud several inches in depth; and the men were so feeble from the effects of their suffering, that it required nearly all the strength they possessed to get along. The regiment was now under the command of Colonel Barnes, — Pierce having the command of a brigade. During the siege of Knoxville, Barnes reached our forces at Cumberland Gap, on his way to his regiment, and here he remained till the siege was raised, on duty as a member of the staff of the general in command there. He reached his regiment on the 26th of December, at Blaine's Cross-Roads.

On the expedition above spoken of, the Twenty-ninth went no farther than the first halting-place, on the Holston. Its camp was formed near a famous trestle railroad bridge, that spanned the river at this point. The bridge was famous because of its great value and skilful construction, and from the fact that it had been repeatedly destroyed and rebuilt by both armies. While the bulk of the army was operating far beyond, in the direction of Virginia, the regiment, with a few other troops of the Ninth Corps, seemed to be left here for the purpose of protecting this bridge. In the course of several days afterwards, the expeditionary army began to return, moving towards Knoxville; and at midnight of the 20th, the regiment was ordered to recross the river. Falling back about three miles from the bank, it halted, and remained in camp till the 22d, other troops taking its place as a guard at the bridge, where, on the 21st, a sharp skirmish was had with the enemy, who attempted to cross.

The First Division of the Ninth Corps was assigned to the duty of covering the retreat of our army. At midnight of the 22d, the regiment marched two miles to the rear, and halted for the troops that had been in advance to pass. These troops had with them two brass pieces of artillery, drawn by the men. The regiment followed on behind the artillery till daybreak, when one of these guns, having been abandoned, they took charge of it. "The men, without much complaint, formed along, took up the cold, stiff rope attached to the cannon, and were soon on the march again, dragging the heavy piece after them, over the frozen road, that had been badly cut up by the passing trains. Up and down hills, over streams, and through fields and forests, the men dragged the gun, exerting all their strength."* When within twelve miles of Knoxville, the regiment was met by horses sent out to take in the artillery, and were thus relieved of their charge. During this movement, the Seventy-ninth New York Highlanders acted as rear guard, with the Twenty-ninth as a support, Colonel Morrison of the Seventy-ninth being in command of both regiments.

At about noon (22d), when ten miles from Knoxville, word was sent to the Twenty-ninth regiment, from the headquarters of the Ninth Corps, then two or three miles away, that a halt was to be made for dinner, and that the Twenty-ninth and Seventy-ninth might govern themselves accordingly. All seemed comparatively quiet at the moment, and Colonel Barnes ordered his regiment to halt. The staff-officers removed the saddles from their horses, to give the weary animals a little rest, while both men and officers stretched themselves upon the ground. They had scarcely settled down to rest, when a number of sharp shots were heard from

* Soldier's letter.

the direction of the skirmish line, indicating that the enemy
had struck our rear. The horses were quickly saddled, and
the line formed. Shortly the Seventy-ninth was seen coming
down the hill, steadily but rapidly. "Here they come!"
cried one of the officers, and in a moment more the enemy
made their appearance. The two regiments now formed in
the field. A large body of the enemy's cavalry, with drawn
sabres, shouting and screaming, dashed down the road. Our
men brought their pieces up instantly and fired a well-aimed
volley, and the troopers fell back into the woods. But in a
few moments they again appeared, this time in the field.
Our troops now took the road and the edge of the woods that
skirted the field, and as the cavalry came across the open
space at a rapid run, shouting to our men to surrender, they
received both a front and flank fire at the same moment.
The line was thoroughly broken, and the horsemen instantly
scattered and fled for the woods in their rear, under a heavy
fire. As soon as the battle began, word was forwarded to
the corps, and orders were sent back for the regiments to
retire gradually, and hold the enemy in check. The enemy
almost wholly disappeared, and the officers began to suspect
an extensive flanking movement. Our men fell back rapidly
for the distance of a mile, halted, and sent out a line of skirmishers. The Confederates appeared in front in small squads,
firing a few shots to attract our attention, but presently, as
had been anticipated, their main body appeared on our left
flank. The two regiments now began to retreat in line of
battle, — through woods, over fences, across streams and
meadows, — keeping up a constant skirmish, till they arrived
within three miles of Knoxville, where they made a stand and
drove their pursuers back.

On the 24th of January, the regiment passed through
Knoxville, flying its tattered flags, and marched about five
miles southwest of the city, to a beautiful place known as
Erin Station, on the Virginia and East Tennessee Railroad.
The scarcity of food for both men and beasts was now, notwithstanding the raising of the siege, nearly as great as it
had been during the preceding autumn and early winter, and
all troops not required for actual field service were being

employed in gathering such supplies as the already much-exhausted country afforded.

On the 25th, Colonel Barnes was ordered to forage south of Clinch River, and taking with him a large number of wagons and all his men fit to march, set out in the direction named. A halt for the night was made at Mr. Black's plantation, Black's Ford, on the Clinch. Black was a farmer of means, and possessed a large store of corn, a portion of which was taken the next morning, Mr. Black receiving therefor a written receipt enabling him to obtain pay for it from the Government, upon proof of his loyalty. The trains then forded the river and divided, Major Chipman taking charge of one division and Colonel Barnes of the other. Chipman, who had a less number of wagons to load, reached the camp of the regiment at Erin Station in advance of the other detachment, which had a long journey, but returned on the 28th with well-filled wagons.

After moving about the country considerably, Colonel Barnes came to the plantation of one Sheriff Staples, whose corn-fields were very extensive. Upon entering the fields, it appeared that the corn had been gathered, and as the battalion was about leaving, some keen fellow ventured upon a further examination, resulting in the discovery that the corn on the outside rows had been plucked, while in the centre of the field there was great abundance of it. This plan had been devised to deceive foragers, but it failed to operate successfully this time. Members of the regiment speak of a certain family named "Crow," whose place they visited on this march, and whose conduct and appearance were so suspicious, that they deemed it unwise to lodge or eat in the house. Much of the country travelled over on this march had never before been visited by the regiment, and in searching for the large farms, the officers were often obliged to inquire the way of the country people. One familiar answer to such inquiries was, "Two looks and a screech"; and another, "Six bends and a go-over"; the meaning of which latter expression was, you will pass six bends or turns in the road, and cross one bridge — "go-over" — before reaching the place inquired about. The extreme ignorance of some of the people of this region is well shown by a conversation which

Lieutenant Whitman had with a farmer's wife, to whom he said that he came from Boston, Massachusetts. "I come from them parts myself," said the old lady. "Ah! whereabouts, Madam?" asked the officer. "Tarry Haute, Indianny." was the intelligent answer.

January 29. A written order from division headquarters directed the regiment to make immediate arrangements to proceed on their veteran furlough, and that the non-re-enlisting members of the regiment, about one hundred in number, should at once be transferred to the Thirty-sixth Massachusetts Regiment. The order was an unjust one, and contemplated a complete dissolution of the connection of these men with the Twenty-ninth, and forcing them, wholly against their will, to become members of the Thirty-sixth Regiment. It was in effect a severe punishment for not being willing to serve the Government for a longer term than that which they had originally agreed to. If it had been simply an assignment to duty with the Thirty-sixth Regiment, there would have been no cause for complaint, and no injurious consequences would have resulted from it; but their names were to be dropped from the rolls of the Twenty-ninth, and as some of the transferred men were absent in hospitals and on detached duty, the names of the latter were not taken up on the rolls of the Thirty-sixth, and much confusion and difficulty as to their pay and discharge came from it. Colonel Barnes, who commanded the regiment at the time of the order, clearly foreseeing its baneful effects, attempted to have it modified; but he was unable to do so, and all the evils predicted by him finally became apparent. It was not till the midsummer of 1864, that the Government discovered this blunder, and then orders were issued directing the re-transfer of all non-re-enlisting men to their old regiments. At this time both the Twenty-ninth and Thirty-sixth regiments were at the front, engaged in the severe duties of an active campaign. Books and papers had been lost in the terrible marches and battles from the Wilderness to the James; officers and men had been killed; and not a few of the old officers of the Twenty-ninth had been discharged. The execution of the last-named order devolved on the Thirty-sixth Regiment; but they were, for the reasons already given, utterly unable to comply with it; and though every effort was made to set the matter right, and the commanding officer of the Twenty-ninth rendered all the aid in his power, yet the order could not be, and never was, fully executed. One of the most serious results of the original order of transfer was the loss of the final record of some of the transferred men, including several who were actually killed in battle while serving in the Thirty-sixth Regiment. The aged mother of one of these poor fellows, who was killed at the Wilderness, applied for a pension, and was informed by the pension officer that the rolls of the Twenty-ninth showed that the name of her son had been dropped, and that as the rolls of the Thirty-sixth Regiment did not bear it, the conclusion was he had deserted.

The movements of the regiment during February and March were so numerous, that we cannot describe them with much detail, but will speak of them briefly under their dates.

February 15. Moved camp to a place near Knoxville, in a drenching rain-storm. A part of the march was performed during the night, which was very black and wild.

February 18. Again moved, keeping near the city, however. The night was very cold.

February 24. The regiment and corps, including the Thirty-sixth Regiment, broke camp at daybreak, marched three miles beyond Strawberry Plain, and camped in the woods. During this march the officers were without horses, tents, or blankets.

Under the date of February 26, the diary of a field-officer of the regiment, from which we quote, has the following:—

"Same place. Sent the tents, etc., to the bridge to be taken to Knoxville. Move to-morrow, at daybreak. The little the 'mess' had to eat was destroyed by fire last night. I have no money, no horse; clothes in rags; boots worn through on the soles, and burnt; no tobacco; no chance to buy anything if I had money; couldn't get forage if horses were here. Slept on the ground in front of a fire, with one ragged blanket. Very cold."

If a field-officer was thus destitute, how much greater must have been the destitution of the men! The regiment had not been paid for more than six months.

February 27. Moved to Strawberry Plain. Crossed the

Holston River in boats, and moved forward two miles into the woods. Encamped for the night.

February 28. Sunday. The horses were returned to the officers. The whole corps moved through New Market to Mossy Creek, a distance of eleven miles, and formed a camp.

February 29. Marched to Morristown. It rained in torrents all day and night. An attack by the enemy was rumored, and the troops received orders to be prepared for it.

March 1. In camp all day. Severe, cold rain. Many of the soldiers agree in saying, that this was one of the most uncomfortable days spent in the army.

March 2. Moved at half-past four, A. M., to Mossy Creek. At midnight the order came for the whole corps to retire across the creek. The blundering and confused manner in which the orders were given, indicated "that somebody in authority was badly frightened, without cause."

March 3. Moved forward across the creek again, and camped.

March 5. The regiment had a skirmish with the enemy's cavalry while on picket.

March 12. Colonel Barnes was placed in command of the Brigade, the command of the regiment devolving upon Major Chipman. Moved to Morristown.

March 13. The enemy attacked our pickets, causing some excitement, but nothing serious resulted.

March 14. The regiment and brigade marched with the First Brigade to a cross-roads, as a support to the latter, in their movement towards the enemy's lines. While here the First Brigade dashed upon the enemy, and scattered and broke up one of his camps.

March 17. The regiment and corps moved through the woods and fields to New Market. The day was very cold, and the march extremely hard.

March 18. Marched to within seven miles of Knoxville, crossing the Holston on pontoons. The day was very cold. On the next day the regiment went into camp near Fort Sanders.

March 21. The corps and regiment marched to Clinton, nineteen miles, and encamped upon the banks of the Clinch River.

The regiment had already received orders to go to Massachusetts on its veteran furlough. It had been arranged for a part of the men — those who were the most destitute and unfit to march — to go by rail by way of Chattanooga and Nashville; while the balance, by far the minority, were to perform the march over the Cumberland Mountains. Captain Richardson was placed in command of the railroad party, and started on his trip about March 20. The mountain party under command of Major Chipman — Colonel Barnes having been assigned to the command of the Brigade — were provided with six pack mules and saddles, with which to transport their baggage over the mountains. The allowance was indeed scanty, for the march was to be a long one; no food could be obtained on the road, and these animals were to carry all the necessary stores, tents of officers, mess kits, and other baggage.

On the 22d of March, the Brigade was ferried across the Clinch River in scows. Here a furious snow-storm came on, which grew so severe as to prevent the balance of the corps from crossing. Colonel Barnes was ordered to move on without waiting for the rest of the troops; the air was biting cold and raw, and the roads frozen and slippery. The officers were compelled to dismount and lead their horses; while the men, many of whom were poorly off for shoes, suffered intensely from cold feet. Worn out, tired, and miserable as men could be, the camp was formed early in the afternoon in a forest near the roadside. To add to their misery, a heavy rain-storm set in soon after nightfall, continuing till morning. "Even the climate of East Tennessee seems to grudge us our departure, and to place all its impeding powers in the way of our passage homeward," says an officer of the regiment in his diary, under this date.

March 23. The balance of the corps came up, and the march over the Cumberland Mountains was begun. From this time till the 27th, the troops were passing along over the mountain roads. On the 24th, the regiment camped at "Chitwoods." It snowed all night, and the men slept upon the ground. On the 25th, the regiment marched all day, from early morning till late evening, in a hard rain-storm, and lay down upon the cold wet earth at night. The roads were in a most shocking condition; so bad that the officers were obliged to dismount. The rain gave birth to innumerable torrents, which, rushing down the mountain-sides, plowed open great furrows in the road-bed, in some instances so wide that they could only be crossed by bridging. On the 27th, the troops reached Point Isabel, in the mountains, where there was a camp called "Camp Burnside." The sutler stationed at this place, hoping to make a fortune in a day, very imprudently trebled the price of his goods. A murmur of disapproval arose among the men, which resulted in the whole of Ferrero's division turning out and sacking the greedy trader's booth, and making among them a distribution of his goods. There was a sort of wild justice about this performance, that so far commended itself to the officers of the corps, that the men were not interfered with or punished. At noon of this day, the regiment crossed the Cumberland River on pontoons, and at night went into camp at Somerset, Ky.

March 28. The march was commenced early in the morning, a halt being made for dinner on the same spot of ground where the regiment stopped for the same purpose in June, 1863. At night, camped (the third time) at Waynesborough. The men had a wet bivouac; it rained hard all night.

On the night of the 29th, the camp was formed at Hall's Gap. A severe snow-storm set in as the sun went down, and continued all night, rendering the condition of the "boys" intensely miserable.

March 30. Marched through Stanford, and halted for dinner at Lancaster. The roads were covered with snow, and the weather was very cold. Went into camp about three miles from Camp Dick Robinson. The camp was made on the farm of an eccentric character, named Robert L. Route. He was the owner of a large plantation, and was in that region a sort of "land king,"— a man to whom the neighboring people always went for advice, and whose word was law; there were many such throughout the South. Route kindly invited the brigade commander and staff to spend the night at his house, a genuine country palace, where they were hospitably treated. During the night, some of the men very thoughtlessly cut down one of his fine black locust-trees. When the old planter discovered the mischief, the next morning, he became exceedingly angry; but instead of going to the officers and making known his grievance, he knelt down under the windows of their bedroom, and in their hearing, invoked, in a long prayer, upon the heads of the soldiers who destroyed his locust-tree, the Divine wrath, — prayed that they might be suddenly removed from the earth, and consigned to the torments of the damned.

The officers feared an unpleasant reception at the breakfast table that morning; but Mr. Route's hospitality was superior to his passions, and as though nothing of an unpleasant nature had happened, greeted them courteously.

After supper (the night before), Route brought in his little son, a youth of some nine or ten summers, whom he introduced to the officers as Robert L. Route, Jr., and standing him upon the table, made the following exhibition of his precocity : " Robert, my son, who was the greatest man that ever lived?" "Jesus Christ," said the youth. "Right, my son; who is the next greatest man that ever lived?" "Abraham Lincoln," was the answer. "Right, my son; and who is the next?" "Robert L. Route, my father." answered the boy, with increased assurance. "Right, my son; and, gentlemen, isn't this a boy to be proud of?" said the delighted parent. The officers increased the father's happiness by saying that they thought the boy a very remarkable one indeed, and that his high estimation of his father's worth was well grounded.

March 31. The regiment arrived at Camp Nelson at noon. Here four days' rations were distributed among the men of the Brigade, after which it moved to Nicholasville, and took the cars for Cincinnati.

April 1. The Brigade arrived at Covington (opposite Cincinnati), and Major Chipman had orders to proceed with the regiment to Cincinnati. Crossed the Ohio to the city, and took up quarters in the Sixth Street barracks. Colonel Barnes gave up his command of the Brigade and joined his regiment. Colonel Pierce, who had been in Massachusetts for several weeks prior to this, upon learning of the arrival of the regiment at Cincinnati, came to that city on the 3d of April, assumed command, and on the 7th started with the regiment for Boston, arriving there about five o'clock on Saturday afternoon, April 9.

The regiment came home so unexpectedly, that no preparations were made to receive it, and the men, except those who belonged in the city, went into the barracks on Beach Street, while the officers took up their quarters at the United States Hotel. The Boston papers of Monday the 11th of April duly noticed the arrival of the regiment, the "Journal" devoting nearly a half-column to a description of it, the names of its officers, an account of the battles and campaigns in which it had been engaged, and said of it, among other pleasant things, "The Twenty-ninth has as good a record as any in the service, and deserves a hearty welcome."

According to the report above alluded to, the regiment at that time numbered one hundred and sixty-six enlisted men. On this day the regiment was formally received by the State and city authorities. Escorted by the Cadets, it marched through the principal streets of the city. Dinner was served at the American House, to which all, both men and officers, were made welcome. Governor Andrew was present at the dinner, and made a most pleasing address. Speeches were also made by Colonels Pierce and Barnes, and by Captains Clarke and Leach. The command was dismissed at the close of the day, and the men, weary with the formalities of a public reception, went to their several homes, there to be received in a manner that more keenly touched their hearts; for there they were to be greeted by those who loved them, had a deep personal interest in their welfare, and who had waited and watched for them for nearly three long, weary years.

On the evening of the 19th of April, a reception levee was given to the members of the Bay State Guards, in the City Hall of Charlestown. The hall was elaborately decorated for the occasion, and fine music enlivened the guests. His Excellency Governor Andrew, and His Honor Mayor Stone, were present, and both made speeches to the veterans, welcoming them to their homes and the festivities of the evening. The levee ended with dancing and a collation.

Company C of East Bridgewater was also accorded a public reception soon after its return. The good people of Plymouth and Sandwich paid similar honors to their returning soldiers; but there was mingled with all these receptions and kind greetings, much that tended to repress joy and gladness. The war-cloud still hovered over the land, darkening every hearth and every home. Even while the furloughed soldiers were listening to the strains of welcoming music, the booming of Grant's cannon in the Wilderness was heard, and the knowledge that their own comrades, so unjustly separated from them, were fighting there, tinged all their enjoyment with sorrow, and filled them with troublesome apprehensions.

CHAPTER XXV.

THE TRANSFERRED MEN IN THE THIRTY-SIXTH REGIMENT—THEY MARCH OVER THE CUMBERLAND MOUNTAINS—GO WITH THE NINTH CORPS TO ANNAPOLIS, MD.—THE CORPS ORDERED TO THE FRONT—MARCH THROUGH WASHINGTON—BATTLES OF THE WILDERNESS AND SPOTTSYLVANIA—A LIST OF THE KILLED—THE TRANSFERRED MEN SENT HOME—THEY MEET THEIR BROTHERS OF THE TWENTY-NINTH REGIMENT IN WASHINGTON—THE REGIMENT AGAIN IN THE FIELD—ASSIGNED TO THE FIFTH CORPS—BATTLE OF BETHESDA CHURCH—A SURPRISE AND NARROW ESCAPE—RE-ASSIGNED TO THE NINTH CORPS—BATTLE OF SHADY GROVE CHURCH—TO THE JAMES—A LONG MARCH—BATTLE OF JUNE SEVENTEENTH—TRAGIC DEATH OF THE THREE COLOR-BEARERS—THE FLAG RESCUED—THE DEAD AND WOUNDED.

The Thirty-sixth Massachusetts Regiment had been in the service since September 2, 1862, and had earned for itself a proud record. It was at the battle of Fredericksburg, in December, 1862, but lost only two men, wounded. It was attached to the Ninth Corps, and in February, 1863, accompanied the Twenty-ninth Regiment and the other troops of the corps to Newport News, and after spending about six weeks here in drill, went into the department of Ohio; did duty in Kentucky and Tennessee, and in June went to Vicksburg, taking part in the siege of that city, and later, in July, in the siege and battles about Jackson, losing several men killed and wounded. The regiment returned with the corps to Tennessee, in August, where it was engaged in the battles of Blue Springs and Campbell's Station, and the siege of Knoxville. It was likewise at Blaine's Cross-Roads, in December, 1863, and January, 1864, and suffered all the privations there endured by our army.

On the 21st of March, 1864, it commenced the march over the Cumberland Mountains to Nicholasville, Ky., a distance of about two hundred miles, where it arrived on the first day of April.

The regiment, containing the transferred men of the Twenty-ninth, reached Annapolis, Md., April 6, and went into camp. The corps had been ordered to this place to recruit, and during the seventeen days that it remained here, its numbers were considerably increased. The old regiments were filled up, to some extent, by re-enlistments and new levies; five cavalry and twelve infantry regiments, and five batteries of artillery, beside an entire division (Fourth) of colored troops, were added to the corps, making its strength about twenty-five thousand men. General Burnside was again assigned to the command of the corps, while General Ferrero was placed in command of the division of colored troops.

At an early hour in the morning of the 23d of April, the removal of the corps from Annapolis began. The Thirty-sixth broke camp before sunrise, and taking the track of the Elk Ridge and Annapolis Railroad, marched some thirteen miles, halting in some fields near the track for the night. Another very early start was made on the morning of the 24th, and in the course of six hours the regiment struck the Washington and Baltimore Turnpike. A brief halt was made for dinner, after which the march was resumed, the camp being formed at sunset about ten miles from Washington. Reveille sounded at four o'clock the next morning, but in consequence of the severe rain, the regiment did not break camp till four hours later, passing through Bladensburg on the march, and arriving in Washington at about mid-day, in advance of the other troops of the corps.

The report had reached Washington that the Ninth Corps was to pass through the city, and that among the troops was a division composed wholly of colored soldiers, and a large body of people gathered in the streets to witness this grand, and at that time novel, military parade. President Lincoln and his party, including General Burnside, had taken a position in the balcony of Willard's Hotel. The streets were free from dust, and "a cool wind breathed through the soft air of the early spring"; the sky was cloudless, the bright rays of the sun lending beauty to the scene. A loud shout went up from the assembly when the head of the long column made its appearance. The veteran soldiers had exchanged the ragged garments that they wore home from Tennessee for bright new uniforms; but they carried the same old tattered flags, which told a story of toil and suffering, that brought flowing tears to the eyes of many spectators. The appearance in the column of the colored division of General Ferrero produced the most intense excitement, and gave birth to rounds of cheers; for although these black men had been but a few weeks in the service, they manifested considerable excellence in marching. When this division reached Willard's Hotel, and the eyes of the men fell upon "Massa Lincoln," "a spirit of wild enthusiasm ran through their ranks; they shouted, they cheered, they swung their caps, in the exuberance of their joy." Towards sundown, the Thirty-sixth crossed Long Bridge, and went into camp near Alexandria with the rest of the corps.

April 27. After a day's rest, the movement into Virginia was again commenced. The regiment started on the road at ten o'clock in the morning, and marched all day, passing through Fairfax, and halting at night three miles beyond the village.

April 28. Broke camp at five o'clock in the morning, waded Bull Run about noon, and camped at night near Manassas Junction.

April 29. Turned out early in the morning, and after getting breakfast, packed up, marched about thirty rods, halted, stacked arms, marched and countermarched all day, and finally went into camp at night within a quarter of a mile from the place of the previous night's encampment.

April 30. Started out of camp early in the morning, marched up the Alexandria and Orange Railroad about four miles, to a point about three miles from Catlett's Station, and relieved a battalion of the Seventeenth Regulars, there stationed. The whole of the corps was stationed at various points along this railroad.

May 1. The regiment was mustered for pay. The camp was formed about twenty rods from the railroad, half-way between Catlett's and Bristoe's stations.

May 4. Orders were issued for the men to strike tents early in the morning, and soon after the regiment started up the track, marched all day, and camped at night near Bealton Station.

May 5. Started at six in the morning, crossed the Rapidan on a pontoon bridge, and went into camp a mile beyond the river, in the woods.

May 6. The regiment was ordered out at an early hour, and started toward the Wilderness battle-field, joining the corps which was stationed near the Wilderness Tavern, and becoming hotly engaged in that terrible battle. Three times during the day the regiment with its division charged the enemy's lines, manifesting the greatest bravery, but suffering serious loss. Major Draper and Captain Marshall were wounded; eleven of the men were killed, and fifty-one wounded. The regiment was also engaged May 7, but escaped without loss.

On the 8th and 9th, it marched a distance of about ten miles, to Chancellorsville, and on the following day marched from Chancellorsville to near Spottsylvania Court-house, where it went into the rifle-pits. Early in the morning of the 12th, General Hancock's corps made a gallant assault upon a salient of the enemy's works, carrying them, capturing General Johnston and his entire division and twenty pieces of artillery. The Thirty-sixth regiment, with the rest of the Ninth Corps, early engaged in the battle, which lasted for nearly three hours. The assault on the enemy's works was followed by a counter assault upon our lines, which was many times repeated, but without success. The Thirty-sixth was stationed in thick pine woods, and the share which it took in the battle is well shown by its dreadful loss. Captain Bailey and Lieutenant Daniels were killed, and Captain Morse severely wounded; twenty of the men were killed, and fifty-six wounded, and among the killed, the following members of the Twenty-ninth Regiment: Sergeant William H. Mosher, Company B, who had but two more days to serve in which to complete his three years' term; First Sergeant William T. Hamer, Company A; Edward P. Mansfield, Company C; James Ward, Company D; John K. Alexander and Lemuel B. Morton, Company E; and John E. Fisher, Company K. The term of service of the six last-named soldiers would have expired on the 22d, and in the cases of all, it seems to have been a most cruel fate, that spared them through so many months of hardship and danger, and just as the end of their faithful service was near at hand, and the bright prospect of a happy return to their homes was rising up before them, cut them down upon the battle-field, and sent them to unknown graves. Probably there is no official record of their deaths, owing to the unfortunate circumstances attending their transfer; and but for the fact, that some of their comrades who fought with them escaped the battle and brought back to their friends these sad tidings, the author would not have been able to present this account of them, however meagre, nor to pay this deserved tribute, however poor, to their memory.

The diary of a soldier of the Twenty-ninth Regiment,* who was engaged in these battles, states that twenty-eight members of the latter regiment were wounded in this campaign; but it does not give their names, and the author has been unable to learn the names of only those of his own company, as the records of neither the Twenty-ninth nor Thirty-sixth regiments contain any information upon this point. For several days after the battle of May 12, the Thirty-sixth Regiment remained at the front, in the rifle-pits, almost constantly under fire. The term of service of the members of companies I and B (Twenty-ninth Regiment) expired on the 14th, and that of the others on the 22d. On the afternoon of the 17th, Sergeant-Major George H. Morse of the Twenty-ninth Regiment, who was serving with the transferred men, proceeded to the headquarters of General Burnside, upon a pass signed by the commanding officer of the Thirty-sixth Regiment, for the purpose of laying before the General the facts in regard to the transferred men, and obtaining from him an order for their discharge. Morse, who was somewhat noted for his persistency as well as his personal bravery, encountered great difficulty in obtaining an audience with General Burnside. The Adjutant-General informed the Sergeant-Major that he could not be permitted to see the General, and that his extraordinary request could not then be granted; but Morse was not to be put off even by a positive denial: he

---

* Diary of Preston Hooper, Company C.

insisted upon seeing the General, painted in strong colors and with eloquent words the wrongs of his comrades, and finally so far excited the interest of the Adjutant-General in his case, that he was admitted into the presence of the Commander. This point gained, Morse was certain of success; the good-hearted General listened with his customary patience to all the Sergeant-Major had to say, and then taking his pen, wrote an order directing that these men be immediately relieved from duty, and coupled the order with a pass to Washington. Proud of his triumph, Morse proceeded to the lines, took charge of the men, and immediately started with them for Belle Plain Landing.

The thirty days of furlough were gone before the re-enlisted men fully realized it. On the 16th of May, the Twenty-ninth Regiment was summoned to the front. The tattered old flags, having on their folds the battle record of the regiment, written by shot and shell, were turned over to the State authorities, and replaced by new ones, bearing in bright, golden letters the same proud inscriptions.

On the 18th, the regiment reached Washington, and went into barracks; on the following day, the transferred members of the regiment arrived in the city from the front, meeting their old comrades, from whom they had been separated for several months. This happy meeting was wholly accidental, and the greetings which followed were therefore all the more cordial. Since their sad parting in East Tennessee, their experiences had been widely different; for while some were fresh from their homes, others had just escaped from the tumult and carnage of the battle-field. The recounting of the hardships of the campaign then in progress, the recital of the thrilling incidents of these battles, the sorrowful tidings brought back by the returning veterans of the loss of this and that old brother, together with the painful certainty that some of those now going to the field would in the course of a few days be sleeping in soldiers' graves, all operated to invest this meeting with an air of strange sadness, and to inspire in those who engaged in it the deepest feelings of fraternal love. On the morning of the 20th, the boys were compelled to separate, the regiment having received orders to march.

According to a roll prepared by Sergeant-Major Morse, the transferred men under his charge numbered eighty-three; namely, seven members of Company A, four of Company B, sixteen of Company C, eighteen of Company D, nine of Company E, one of Company G, three of Company H, one of Company I, and twenty-four of Company K. If this roll is correct, and the author has no reason to doubt it, then including Morse and the seven who were killed at the Wilderness and Spottsylvania, it appears that ninety-one members of the Twenty-ninth actually served with the Thirty-sixth Regiment in this campaign. But this does not include all of the men who were actually transferred, as some of them were absent in hospitals and on special duty at the time of the transfer, and never joined the Thirty-sixth Regiment. The order of General Burnside directed that these men should proceed to Washington, there to be mustered out and paid; but not having been furnished with descriptive lists by the commanders of companies in the Thirty-sixth Regiment, it became impossible to properly execute this order. Encountering this difficulty, Sergeant-Major Morse applied to the Secretary of War, who, upon a representation of the facts, issued an order directing Morse to proceed to Boston with his men, and directing Major Clark, U. S. A., there stationed, to muster out and pay Morse and the members of his command. The squad arrived in Boston, May 23, but, upon the presentation of the order, Major Clark declined to comply with it, for the reason that the men were without descriptive lists, and it was therefore impossible to determine what amount was due them. The men were, however, dismissed, and allowed to return to their homes, when, after the expiration of several weeks, descriptive lists having been patched up, with the assistance of the officers of the Twenty-ninth Regiment, these worthy soldiers, who had had so little difficulty in entering the service, but so great trouble in leaving it, were finally mustered out and paid. They were among the best soldiers of the Twenty-ninth, and are deserving of a full share of its honors.

On the 20th of May, the Twenty-ninth Regiment took a government transport at Washington, and went down the Potomac, arriving at Belle Plain on the afternoon of the same day.

The regiment had recruited but little during its stay in

Massachusetts, and having been greatly reduced in strength by a variety of causes, some of which have already been named, the number of commissioned officers was now greatly out of proportion to the number of its enlisted men, and in excess of that allowed by law. Accordingly, on the 22d of May, several of the old officers whose terms expired that day, were relieved of command, and left for Washington, there to be honorably mustered out of the service.

Among these faithful soldiers was Captain Lebbeus Leach, then about sixty-three years of age, whose hair was white as "the driven snow." The loss of his companionship was deeply felt by those who remained to share still longer the fortunes of the regiment. In every place of peril, he had stood like a rock, chiding, by his manner, rather than words, all faint-heartedness, and setting an example of bravery that never failed to animate all about him. The sort of stoical indifference which this old man manifested, not only towards danger, but extreme physical suffering, was remarkable, and has been often spoken of by his comrades.

Captain Samuel H. Doten, who left the regiment a little later, May 30, with the deserved brevet of Major, was another soldier of the Puritan type, and was fifty-one years old at the time of leaving the service. He was a man of strong religious convictions, and impressed all his comrades with a sense of his candor; his natural dignity and self-respect won for him that treatment which these qualities always secure, and he left the army deeply beloved by all who had enjoyed his acquaintance and friendship.

The departure of these and other officers furnished another occasion for sorrowful farewells, and was another breaking-up of old army associations,—relations that were sacredly cherished, as they had been formed amidst scenes of danger and suffering.

A provisional brigade of five regiments, among which was the Forty-sixth New York, the old friends of the Twenty-ninth, was formed from among the fresh arrivals at Belle Plain, and placed under the command of Brigadier-General Lockwood. On the 23d of May, these troops broke camp and marched to Falmouth, opposite Fredericksburg, and went into camp.

May 24. Crossed the Rappahannock on pontoons; took the "Bowling Green" road, and went into camp at one o'clock in the afternoon.

May 25. Moved at four in the morning, and halted for dinner at Bowling Green. Crossed the Mattapony River; marched through General Ferrero's division of colored troops, into camp.

May 26. In camp all day. Rained during the night. In the midst of the night, the camp was alarmed, and the Twenty-ninth was sent out to reconnoitre, the men realizing that they were again soldiers in the field; the alarm proved to be unfounded.

May 27. The Brigade moved through a beautiful section of the country, and camped near Penola Station.

May 28. Passed through Aylettstown and camped near a place rejoicing in the euphonious name of "Cat-tail Church."

May 29. Came up with the Army of the Potomac after crossing the Pamunkey River, and bivouacked in a field with other troops. The army of General Grant was then moving away from the North Anna River, and the enemy being in his immediate front, skirmishing was of daily and almost hourly occurrence.

May 30. The regiment was assigned to the Fifth Corps, First Division, Third Brigade, and the fact, that, upon being assigned to this corps, it should retain the same numbers, having been in the First Division and Third Brigade of the Ninth Corps, seemed a little strange. Both officers and men were, however, alike disappointed at this assignment, it having been their expectation to return to the old Ninth, with whose history their own was singularly identified.

On the first day of June, the whole line moved forward. The Twenty-ninth Regiment was ordered to send out one hundred men on the skirmish line, and Captain Thomas W. Clarke was placed in command of this force, which formed the extreme right of the corps line of skirmishers. On the immediate right of the line was a dense growth of woods and a morass, which the staff-officer who directed the movement said were "impassable"; but Clarke, who, during his three years' service, had acquired a familiarity with the enemy's ways of fighting, was not satisfied with the staff-officer's statement; there was a certain ominous silence about the dark woods especially, that greatly excited the Captain's suspicions. His right was wholly unconnected with other troops, and his men too few to justify him in extending his line into the forest; if the enemy were lurking there, as he had reason to believe, his men were in imminent danger of being flanked, and he accordingly despatched an officer and squad of men to examine the place. The squad had scarcely entered the woods when the enemy commenced a violent attack all along the corps front, and at the same moment a large body of them came pouring out of the "impassable" woods, in the very faces of our men who had invaded their hiding-place. But for the starting into the woods of the squad, who could at best only give the alarm, the one hundred skirmishers would have been lost, and this result might have been attended with serious consequences to the whole line. As it was, an immediate and rapid retrograde movement became necessary, with a change of front, to prevent the enemy from moving directly to the rear of our line. The position of our men was both awkward and perilous, but they proved themselves equal to the emergency; changing front with great rapidity, they then fell back to the main line, firing deliberately as they did so, but suffering considerable loss. This movement resulted in a severe general engagement. The regiment formed in line at the breastworks, next the Eighteenth Massachusetts, and became hotly engaged, expending nearly all its ammunition. Toward night, the enemy were driven back, when the skirmish line was re-established and properly protected on the right. Considering the exposed situation of our hundred men, it is remarkable that their loss was not greater.

The death of private John C. Lambert of Company C was a shocking affair; he was wounded in the legs while in the edge of the woods, and left in that position by his comrades, who had no opportunity to remove him. Later in the day, the woods were set on fire, probably by exploding shell, and the poor fellow actually burned to death, his crisped and lifeless body being found by his comrades after the battle. Captain George H. Taylor and First Lieutenant George H.

Long,* both of whom behaved themselves with great gallantry, were severely wounded. Martin Jefferson of Company F, and Charles Drake and Henry A. Osborne of Company C, were captured: and the following enlisted men were wounded: Sergeants Richard Harney of Company A, and Francis J. Cole of Company K; Privates Thomas Hawes and Charles Bassett of Company A; Thomas Manning and John Connolly of Company B; John A. Holmes of Company C; Perez Eldridge of Company D; and Abram Hascall of Company F.

Captain Taylor, though unfit for duty for some time, returned to the regiment, and served till it was mustered out, in 1865. The battle of this day has been called the battle of Bethesda Church.

June 2. About four in the afternoon, the regiment moved to the rear, the corps being engaged in a flank movement to the left. The enemy made a desperate attack upon our division during a severe rain-storm late in the day, and while the division was in a very disadvantageous position. Nothing save "the magnificent fighting" of the Regulars prevented serious disaster; they checked the enemy in his headlong charge, until the First Division could get into position in the rear. The Regulars then fell back in good order upon the division line, followed hotly by the enemy, who were met by a destructive fire, and after a long, hard fight, were repulsed with loss. The one hundred skirmishers of the Twenty-ninth were relieved at the front by a good Pennsylvania regiment of about two hundred men, which lost in this battle nearly half its number; showing how severe was the engagement, and how exposed the situation in which our comrades had been placed only the day before.

June 3. A welcome order from the headquarters of the Army of the Potomac transferred the Twenty-ninth Regiment from the Fifth to the Ninth Corps, and the regiment reported to General Burnside in the afternoon. On this day was fought the terrible battle of Cold Harbor, in which the Ninth

---

* Lieutenant Long was severely wounded, losing a portion of the ulna bone of his right arm. He was promoted to Captain, June 8, 1864, and discharged for this wound, October 8, 1864. He was subsequently commissioned in the Veteran Reserve Corps, and served to the end of the war.

Corps bore the brunt of the battle on the right, losing in the engagement over one thousand killed and wounded. Owing to the lateness of the hour on which the order of transfer reached the regiment, it did not arrive at Burnside's lines in season to take a very active part in the battle; but it moved promptly, however, and lay in support behind some old breastworks. One of our batteries, which was posted in the rear of these works, engaged in shelling the enemy, wounded Lawrence T. Chickey and Conrad Homan of Company A. Sergeant Samuel C. Wright of Company E was also wounded here by a rifle-shot from the enemy's lines.

June 4. The enemy moved from our corps front, and the corps moved to the left along the rear of the army.

June 5. The corps moved in the afternoon and threw up breastworks. There was some hard fighting on the left, but the regiment did not become engaged.

June 6. The enemy opened a sharp fire on the corps front, but the men being well covered, no harm resulted.

June 7. Flag of truce to bury our dead in front of the Eighteenth Corps.

June 8. The Brigade relieved a brigade of the Second Division on outpost.

June 10. The regiment went out on the picket line.

June 11. On picket. All quiet.

June 12. The corps left its lines and marched rapidly all day and all night.

June 13. Moved along the south side of the Chickahominy, making a rapid march, and went into camp at eleven o'clock in the night, at Jones's Bridge.

June 14. Passed Providence Forge, crossed the Chickahominy River in the forenoon, and bivouacked at Charles City Court-house.

June 15. At about half-past ten o'clock in the night, the regiment crossed the James River on a pontoon bridge, and marched the remainder of the night.

June 16. Marched till six o'clock in the afternoon, when the regiment reached the lines in front of Petersburg, and formed the third line of battle in the woods, under a fire of both musketry and artillery. The march since the night of the 15th had been terribly severe; the roads were dusty, and during the day the mercury had stood at nearly 100°. Many men of the regiment — and of all the regiments — had been left on the road in an exhausted condition, so that when our lines were formed on the night of this day, the corps was but a skeleton compared with its former strength. An attack having been determined upon, orders were given to assault the enemy's works early the following morning. General Potter's division was selected to lead the assault.

June 17. At the first blush of day, the charge was made; the enemy's lines were rapidly swept for nearly two miles, and four pieces of artillery, with their caissons and horses, a stand of colors, fifteen hundred stands of small arms, a quantity of ammunition, and six hundred prisoners, were captured.*

At daylight, the regiment and its brigade moved up, under a severe fire, and occupied one of the works that had just been captured by Potter's men. Affairs remained in this condition till afternoon, when General Willcox made an attack, but he was repulsed with heavy loss. Shortly after this repulse on the right, and quite late in the afternoon, the division (General Ledlie's) was moved forward into a ravine, where it was protected from the fire of the enemy. Colonel Barnes was placed in command of the Second Brigade, in which was the Twenty-ninth, with Captain Clarke as his Assistant Adjutant-General, while the regiment was commanded by Major Chipman. Colonel Barnes was told by General Ledlie, that the division was to assault the enemy's works directly in its front, the First and Second brigades to charge in line of battle, and the Third Brigade to act as a support. The officers and men of the two brigades then crept up out of the ravine towards the enemy, — who were well entrenched and lay behind their works, — and formed one long line of battle, all lying flat upon the ground, waiting for the order to spring to their feet and dash forward. At this moment, an aid of General Ledlie's crept out of the ravine, and approaching Colonel Gould of the Fifty-ninth Massachusetts, commanding the First Brigade, beckoned Colonel Barnes to him, and then stated to the two colonels, "in plain language," that the pro-

---

* "Burnside and Ninth Army Corps," pages 409, 410.

posed assault had been abandoned; that the men were to remain in their present positions till dark, when they would be retired into the ravine from whence they started. The two brigade commanders, Gould and Barnes, upon the reception of the above order, at once called to them their respective regimental commanders and communicated these instructions, and the latter crept back to their regiments and gave them to their men. The order not to advance was received with much satisfaction, for all realized fully the desperate nature of the undertaking. But the order had hardly been imparted to the troops, when suddenly there came an imperative order from General Ledlie to advance instantly. No time could be given for explanation; the order, "Forward!" was shouted along the line, and the men with cheers started on a rapid run. They had scarcely emerged upon the open plain, when the whole crest of the Confederate works was fringed with fire and smoke; grape, canister, and musket-balls filled the air. The first fire staggered the whole line, but for a short distance it struggled on, when without absolutely breaking, suddenly both brigades, as by one impulse, fell rapidly back. As the line was retiring, the Third Brigade, not having changed its position, rose up with cheers and moved forward. This checked the backward movement, and the three brigades, in one confused mass, with terrific shouts and yells, dashed over the field and into the enemy's first line of works and captured them. The division had lost heavily in this action, and darkness soon coming on, all further offensive movements here ended.

Instances of great courage and individual daring are rarely wanting in a battle; but an exhibition of almost sublime courage, which occurred in this engagement, cannot with justice to the living and the dead be passed by in silence. Color-Sergeant John A. Tighe of Company K had permission from his officers to remain at his home in East Boston for a few days after the departure of the regiment. During the absence of Tighe, Sergeant Silas N. Grosvenor, Company C of East Bridgewater, had carried the national colors. As the regiment was preparing to move out of the ravine to charge the bristling works of the enemy, Tighe, who had just that moment reached the front, fresh from home, came up, and being color-bearer of the regiment, demanded of Grosvenor the flag. Grosvenor had carried the colors during all the long marches from Belle Plain to Petersburg, and being a high-spirited soldier, declined to give them up right on the eve of a battle, and thereupon a contention arose between the two brave men as to which should perform that most perilous service. Major Chipman, who was only holding temporary command of the regiment, as an act of courtesy, referred the matter to Colonel Barnes, who was near at hand. The decision was, that Grosvenor should carry the colors during the battle.

The regiment moved out upon the field; at the first fire, a musket-ball pierced the brain of the valorous Grosvenor, and he fell a bleeding corpse upon the ground. The colors had scarcely touched the earth before the hands of Tighe, who was in the color-guard, grasped the staff, and, proud of his soldier-trust, shook them defiantly towards the foe. His exultation was short-lived, for in a moment more another well-aimed ball laid low in death the heroic bearer. Again the flag went down, but only for an instant, for immediately it was seized by Sergeant-Major William F. Willis of Charlestown. A short advance in the hurry and tumult, and a third shot brought both flag and bearer to the ground. Now the line faltered and went backward, and the gallant old regiment for the first and only time in its history left the battle-field without its flag, but in the terrible confusion of the moment the loss was not discovered. When the fact became known, a minute later, a loud cry arose through the ranks, "We've lost our flag!" "We've lost our flag!" It was at this critical juncture that Major Chipman called for volunteers to rescue the colors; Corporal Nathaniel Burgess, Company E of Plymouth, and Private Patrick Muldoon, Company A of Boston, * quickly responded, and the second brave trio dashed out of the line and over the field, under the fire of a thousand muskets. The prostrate flag was seen just before them. But can they ever reach it?

---

* The author has been unable to learn that any others actually engaged in this brave exploit, and, though several slightly different versions have been given him, he has chosen this as being in his opinion the correct one. This statement is based upon that of three very reliable soldiers of the regiment, who were present and witnessed the affair.—AUTHOR.

It is said that the enemy, filled with admiration for the daring of our men, perceptibly slackened their fire, and when the little squad bore off the flag in triumph, mingled their generous cheers with those of our own men.

The hands of poor Willis were found clutching the staff so firmly, that his comrades, who saved the flag he died to honor, were obliged to pry open his fingers in order to loosen his death-grasp, while the folds of the silken banner completely enveloped his body.

The conduct of Major Chipman and his comrades, which was witnessed by a large number of troops, caused them to be very conspicuous for their bravery; while Corporal Burgess, who actually bore off the flag from the field, for the part he took in the affair, was made a first lieutenant as soon as a vacancy occurred. The colors were found to be badly shot, and the staff broken in two places.

Captain Clarke, of whose good conduct the author has several times before had occasion to speak, was in the thickest of this fight, and was untiring in his efforts not only to urge, but to lead on the men. As the line fell back and melted away under the terrible fire from the batteries, Colonel Barnes, as commander of the Second Brigade, suddenly found himself at the front, without troops. It was at this critical moment that Clarke's bravery shone out so brightly. Observing the perilous situation of his commander, he hastened to his side, to share with him the dangers and responsibilities of his position. "The supports will move forward, and we shall be all right yet," was his confident remark. True enough, the supports did move, but not too soon to save the day.

A little more than three years before this day, these two officers, as Captains of companies A and K, both of Boston, were prominently engaged at Great Bethel, the first pitched battle of the Rebellion; and here, after all the vicissitudes of war, and a service peculiarly eventful, as Brigade Commander and Adjutant-General, they stood together on one of the bloodiest battle-fields of Virginia, — a field made famous alike by the valor of our soldiers and the revolutionary memories that clustered around the historic day.

The regiment went into this action with less than one hundred men, and suffered a loss of twenty-nine officers and men killed and wounded,—about one-third of its number. The following is a list of the casualties:—

KILLED.

First Sergeant SILAS N. GROSVENOR, Company C.
Color Sergeant JOHN A. TIGHE, Company K.
Sergeant and Acting Sergeant-Major WILLIAM F. WILLIS and Corporal RICHARD GURNEY, Company H.
Privates JOHN C. STEWART and MARTIN MINTON, Company B.

WOUNDED.

First Lieutenant GEORGE W. POPE, Company G, mortally.
First Lieutenant CHARLES A. CARPENTER, Company H.
First Sergeant JOHN LUCAS, Company B, badly in wrist.
Sergeant H. B. TITUS, Company G.
Sergeant JOHN H. HANCOCK, Company H, arm shot off.
Corporal JOHN M. THOMPSON, Company B, both legs broken, and afterwards died.
Corporal WILLIAM H. TINDAL and Musician JAMES LIFFIN,* Company F.
Privates THOMAS W. CASHMAN, Company A; EMERY HODGKINS, Company B; WILLIAM H. BURNS, JOSEPH W. GLASS, NAPOLEON MASON, JOHN HARVEY, TIMOTHY HAYES, and GEORGE F. BROWNE, Company F; DANIEL WHITMORE, RICHARD OWEN, PHILIP A. LAWALL, WARREN CROWELL, and EDWARD CARNEY, Company G; WILLIAM JONES, Company H; and WILLIAM H. HOWE, Company K.

It is said on good authority, that every third man in the attacking column was either killed or wounded, a fact that shows how sanguinary was the battle.

* James Liffin was mortally wounded, and died July 29, following.

CHAPTER XXVI.

Movements After the Battle of June 17 — Battle of the Mine — A List of Killed and Wounded — Various Movements of the Regiment — Death of Major Chipman — Battle of Blick's House — Poplar Grove Church — A Reconnoissance — Colonel Barnes Leaves the Army.

On the day following the 17th of June, the regiment, with the other troops of the First Division, retired a short distance to the rear to rest, and overcome as much as possible the bewildering and disorganizing influences of the battle. It was usual to grant this poor privilege to troops that had been severely engaged, the amount of rest given them depending upon the severity of their losses and the strength of the reserve forces, or, in other words, the means of the commanding general to supply their places at the front with fresh troops. The extended nature of our lines in front of Petersburg, and the activity of the enemy, required the presence of a vast army there, and the strength of our army at that time did not afford a large reserve, hence the regiment enjoyed but a brief respite from duty.

During the night of the 20th, the division moved forward to the front line, relieving a division of the Second Corps.

June 21. Same place, skirmishing.

June 22. The enemy made a sortie on the division skirmish line, but were repulsed.

June 23. Severe skirmishing in the night; the weather very warm and oppressive.

June 24. Same place; the Brigade moved to the extreme front line.

June 25. Severe skirmishing all night; the regiment was in line of battle till near daylight.

June 26 and 27. Same place.

June 28. This day the regiment was ordered to deploy near General Ledlie's headquarters, and advance through the woods to drive up stragglers. About three hundred of these faithless soldiers were found hiding in the forest, fifty of whom were arrested by our men, the rest making their escape. The Tenth Corps advanced their picket line at night, which caused considerable skirmishing, but after awhile everything became quiet; the regiment moved to the rear during the night.

July 1. The enemy threw several mortar-shell directly into the regimental camp, but no one was injured.

July 2. The regiment had orders to move to the vicinity of brigade headquarters, to act as provost guard of the division. Major Charles Chipman was detached from the regiment and assigned to the command of the Fourteenth New York Heavy Artillery. This was a large regiment, then acting as infantry; its Colonel, Lieutenant-Colonel, and three Majors were absent, the first two officers by reason of wounds. It was regarded as a great compliment to Major Chipman, that he should have been selected from among the many able officers of the corps and division to take the command of this excellent regiment; but it was a well-deserved mark of respect. The men were kept busy nearly all day throwing up a line of works to protect them from the enemy's bullets; the weather was extremely warm, and the earth hard and difficult to work with the shovel.

July 3. The men were kept at work on the entrenchments nearly all day, which was equally as warm as the preceding one. During the day a patrol was sent out from the regiment, and arrested seventy Federal soldiers, who were found without proper passes; toward night the enemy opened a severe artillery and musketry fire upon our whole line, making it dangerous for a man to show his head above the breastworks.

July 4. A part of the regiment were at work shovelling, while a detail was made for patrol duty; eighty-nine more stragglers were apprehended and sent back to their respective regiments. The enemy seemed to be engaged in observing the anniversary of American Independence, and allowed our army to do the same. The officers of the Twenty-ninth had a modest little celebration of the day on their own account.

We have given enough of the daily experiences of the soldiers on the front line to enable the general reader to understand the nature of the life which troops thus situated, led. But we have another purpose in occasionally adopting the diary form of narrative. These dates form so many initial points in the history of the regiment, and lead its members on to the recollection of a great variety of incidents, not of sufficient importance to chronicle, but of peculiar importance to them personally.

On the 21st, there were some indications of a battle; the Second Brigade, of which the Twenty-ninth was a member, was ordered up during the night to the support of General Willcox's division. On the following day, the Brigade, Colonel Barnes in temporary command, was reviewed, and highly complimented. General William F. Bartlett arrived and assumed command of the First Brigade, and Colonel Marshall of the Fourteenth New York (H. A. Vols.) having also reported for duty, was assigned to the command of the Second Brigade. The regiment was transferred to the First Brigade.

July 24. The regiment again went to the front line.

July 26. Ordered to the rear.

July 27. Orders were received to be in readiness to move at any moment.

July 28. The entire First Brigade moved to the front line.

It seems necessary to pause here and state certain facts closely associated with the thrilling events of which we must directly speak. In the various assaults made upon the enemy's lines on the 16th, 17th, and 18th of June, the Ninth Corps obtained an advanced position, "beyond a deep cut in the railroad, within about one hundred and twenty-five yards of the enemy's lines. Just in rear of that advanced position was a deep hollow," . . . where any work could be carried on without the knowledge of the enemy. In the course of a few days after this ground had been taken by the corps, Lieutenant-Colonel Henry Pleasants of the Forty-eighth Pennsylvania Volunteers waited on General Potter, who commanded one of the divisions of the Ninth Corps, and suggested to him, that in his opinion a mine could be run under one of the enemy's batteries, by which means it could be blown up, and a breach thus made in the enemy's lines. General Potter seems to have thought favorably of the plan, and in turn suggested it to General Burnside, by whom it was fully approved.

On the 25th of June, Colonel Pleasants commenced the work of excavation, employing none but members of his own command, which then numbered about four hundred. This project was not looked upon with any favor by General Meade, and nearly every application made to headquarters for the tools and materials necessary for the carrying on of the work was wholly disregarded. Colonel Pleasants says in his testimony before the Committee of Congress on the Conduct of the War, "Whenever I made application, I could not get anything, although General Burnside was very favorable to it. The most important thing was to ascertain how far I had to mine, because if I went short of or went beyond the proper place, the explosion would have no practical effect. Therefore, I wanted an accurate instrument with which to make the necessary triangulations. I had to make them on the farthest front line, where the enemy's sharpshooters could reach me. I could not get the instrument I wanted, although there was one at army headquarters; and General Burnside had to send to Washington and get an old-fashioned theodolite, which was given to me." Not having been supplied with wheelbarrows with which to remove the earth, he was compelled to use common cracker-boxes, with pieces of hickory nailed on them for handles. Notwithstanding all these obstacles, the worthy and energetic Colonel and his no less worthy officers and men kept at their work night and day. To remove all chance of discovery by the enemy of what was going on in his camp, Colonel Pleasants had the fresh earth brought from the mine covered with bushes and the boughs of trees. The mine was completed July 23, and consisted of one main gallery $510\frac{8}{10}$ feet in length, with two lateral galleries, the left being thirty-seven feet long, and the right thirty-eight feet. The two galleries ran directly under the enemy's works, a part of which consisted of a six-gun battery, with a garrison of about two hundred men. As this work had been carried on within the lines of the Ninth Corps, General Burnside had naturally enough assumed not only the responsibility of it, but had matured plans for the explosion of the mine and the assault upon the enemy's works, that was immediately to follow. The plan that had been adopted by Burnside, was to explode the mine just before daylight in the morning, "or at about five o'clock in the afternoon; mass the two brigades of the colored division in rear of my first line in columns of division, 'double columns closed in mass,' the head of each brigade resting on the front line; and as soon as the explosion has taken place, move them forward, with instructions for the division to take half distance as soon as the leading regiment of the two brigades passes through the gap in the enemy's line by the right companies 'on the right into line wheel,' the left companies 'on the right into line,' and proceed at once down the enemy's works as rapidly as possible; and the leading regiment of the left brigade to execute the reverse movement to the left, running up the enemy's line; the remainder of the columns to move directly towards the crest in front as rapidly as possible, diverging in such a way as to enable them to deploy into column of regiments, the right column making as nearly as possible for Cemetery Hill; these columns to be followed by the other divisions of the corps as soon as they can be thrown in." *

The reasons given for the selection of the colored division to lead the assault, were, that they had been less exposed to the hardships of the campaign than any of the white divisions, the latter having been kept on the front line ever since the commencement of the campaign. Beside this, the colored division had for several weeks been drilled with great care for this special duty.

When the time came to put into execution this novel plan of dislodging the enemy from his works, General Meade, as he had a right to do, by reason of his rank, assumed the entire direction of the movement, wholly changing several of Burnside's plans, and directed, among other things, that one of the white divisions, instead of the colored, should lead the assault; "and the order of assault was also changed, in respect to sweeping down the enemy's lines to the right and left of the crater by the leading regiments of the assaulting column."

---

* Letter of General Burnside to General Meade, dated July 26, 1864.

These instructions were not communicated to General Burnside till the afternoon of the 29th of July, at which time General Meade issued his battle order. There were reasons equally strong for assigning each one of the three white divisions of the Ninth Corps to the important service of leading the assault; and to leave no ground of complaint, and avoid the appearance of being needlessly arbitrary, General Burnside determined to decide this question by the drawing of lots. Accordingly, on the afternoon of the 29th of July, the several division commanders were summoned to headquarters for the purpose above indicated. The lot fell upon General Ledlie's division, of which the Twenty-ninth Regiment was a member.

The mine was charged, and by the order of Meade, it was to be sprung at half-past three in the morning of the 30th; and as soon as this was done, the assaulting column was "to move rapidly upon the breach, seize the crest in the rear, and effect a lodgment there." Major-General Ord was to support the right of this column, and Major-General Warren the left.

During the night of the 29th, the division moved into position at the extreme front, so as to be ready to make a rapid and sudden movement towards the enemy's lines. At a little before five o'clock in the morning of the 30th, the mine exploded; and the regiment was in a position to witness the whole of this memorable scene. First, there was heard a deep, prolonged rumble, like the sound of distant thunder, then the whole surface of the ground for many yards in the immediate vicinity of the galleries of the mine began suddenly to heave and swell, like the troubled waters of the sea. The Confederate line, which up to this moment had been silent, was now thoroughly aroused; and their men lining the breastworks, were seen peering over the parapets, filled with wonder and alarm at the terrible sounds that were issuing from the earth. In front of Ledlie's division, directly under a Confederate work, the ground seemed to swell into a little hill, and presently there burst from its summit a huge volume of smoke and flame. Eight tons of powder had exploded directly under a six-gun battery of the enemy and its garrison of two hundred men. Large masses of earth, guns, caissons, tents, and human bodies filled the air. The first explosion was quickly followed by others of lesser magnitude, but it was all over in a few minutes. As soon as the explosion occurred, a heavy cannonading began on our side, which has been said by some to exceed in intensity that at Malvern Hill or Gettysburg. It will be observed from the foregoing statement, that the mine was not fired at the time designated in the order of General Meade. The match was applied promptly at the hour named, but owing to a defective fuse, the process of firing was not then accomplished; the fuse was in short pieces, spliced together, and "ceased to burn at one of the points of junction. The additional precaution had been taken to lay the fuse in a train of powder, but the powder had become damp by being so long laid, some thirty or more hours, and that also failed to ignite." For awhile it was supposed by our officers that the experiment was destined to be a failure; but after waiting nearly an hour, Lieutenant Jacob Doubty of Company K, and Sergeant Henry Rees of Company F, Forty-eighth Pennsylvania Regiment, volunteered to enter the mine and determine by actual inspection the cause of the failure; and while in the mine, relighted the fuse, producing its final explosion at 4.42, A. M. The great bravery of this deed secured for Sergeant Rees a promotion to second lieutenant, and both were prominently mentioned in the report of the Joint Committee of Congress on the Conduct of the War.

In the course of ten minutes after the final explosion, the division of General Ledlie charged. The explosion produced a crater from one hundred and fifty to two hundred feet in length, about sixty feet in width, and thirty feet deep; the bottom and sides of which were covered with a loose, light sand, furnishing scarcely a foothold, and for this reason, as well as that of the narrowness of the place, it was with great difficulty that the troops could pass through it. From these causes, as might well be supposed, the division lost its organization as soon as it entered the narrow gorge, and the confusion which ensued was soon heightened by the enemy opening fire upon them from a battery upon the right, and another upon the left, and before long from a battery directly in their front, upon Cemetery Hill. Another division was thrown forward with the same results as the first; the men taking

" shelter in the crater of the mine and the lines of the enemy adjacent thereto." The Third Division followed in the same hopeless task, and finally the Fourth (colored) Division, under a very heavy fire, passing in confusion the white troops already in the crater, and then re-forming, charging the hill in front, but without success, breaking in great disorder to the rear.

This was the state of things about four hours after the explosion; namely, 8.45, A. M. At half-past nine o'clock in the forenoon, General Burnside received orders from General Meade to immediately withdraw his troops, and informing him that he had likewise ordered the cessation of all offensive movements on the right and left. As the order could not be executed at once without exposing the troops to even greater losses than those which they had already suffered, the order to withdraw was so far modified as to allow General Burnside to exercise his judgment as to the time when it should be attempted. Here the troops remained till nearly three o'clock in the afternoon, under a galling fire, shielding themselves as best they could, but suffering intensely in the meantime from the heat of the sun and choking thirst. At about this time, Generals Hartranft and Griffin directed their men to withdraw; and almost simultaneously with this movement, the enemy again charged, capturing nearly all the wounded lying in the crater, and some who were not. Those who escaped were obliged to run a race with balls and bayonets, and many who attempted it, fell dead or wounded before reaching our entrenchments. The loss sustained by our army during that day's operations amounted to between four and five thousand in killed, wounded, and missing. This loss included twenty-three commanders of regiments, — four killed, fifteen wounded, and four missing; and two commanders of brigades, — General William F. Bartlett, who was disabled by the destruction of his artificial leg, and Colonel E. G. Marshall, were taken prisoners.

The losses sustained by the regiment were as follows: —

KILLED.

Sergeant EBENEZER FISK, Company G.
Corporal PRESTON O. SMITH, Company F.
Private WILLIAM S. COLLINS, Company B.

WOUNDED.

Captain CHARLES D. BROWNE, Company C.
Sergeants GEORGE TOWNSEND, Company F, and HENRY CAMPBELL, Company G.
Corporal SAMUEL C. WRIGHT, Company E (very badly in the head, and reported as dead).
Privates CHARLES F. BOSWORTH, Company F; LEMUEL CHAPIN, Company G; and JACOB H. DOW, Company H.

CAPTURED.

First Sergeant JOHN SHANNON, Company E.
Corporal THOMAS W. D. DEANE, Company G.
Privates GEORGE THOMAS, Company A; BENJAMIN B. BROWN, Company B; DANIEL WHITMORE, Company G; and JOHN MOORE, Jr., Company K.

Corporal Wright was promoted to Sergeant after this battle for his brave and meritorious conduct manifested during the engagement. Probably no event of the war excited so much discussion, and called forth so much bitterness of feeling among the officers of our army, as did this. The conduct of the First Division and its commander has been made the subject of the severest criticism. Henry Coppee, A. M., who wrote a book entitled "General Grant and his Campaigns," in giving an account of this affair, uses this language: "But the attack must be instantaneous. What delays it? Ten minutes pass before Ledlie's division, which had been selected by lot to lead the charge, has moved; when it does, led by the gallant General Bartlett, instead of complying with the order, it halts in the crater." In another part of his book, he says: "The storming party was then thus organized. Ledlie's division of white troops was to lead the assault, charge through the crater, and then seize the enemy's works on Cemetery Hill." As these and other statements, to which reference will be made, reflect great discredit upon the division, the author has deemed it important to quote from a carefully-written paper in his possession, prepared by one of the field-officers of the division, who took an active part in the battle.

"It will be seen that Coppee states that Ledlie's division was 'to charge through the crater and seize the rebel works on Cemetery Hill,' but that, instead of complying with the order, the division 'halts in the crater.'

Ledlie's division had no such order. It was not a part of the plan of the battle for that division to advance after reaching the crater. The orders issued to the division were distinctly, ' *not to advance.*' General Bartlett's First Brigade consisted of seven regiments. On the afternoon of the 29th of July, the seven regimental commanders assembled at brigade headquarters by direction of the General, and were then informed by him that the mine was to be fired the next morning; that Ledlie's division had been selected by lot to lead the assault; that the division was to move forward immediately after the explosion and occupy the enemy's front line of works; that the division would be promptly followed by another division of the corps, which would move beyond, ' over the heads of Ledlie's division, to be followed by the remaining divisions of the corps.' "

This statement comes, not only from a reliable source, but is very reasonable upon its face. In the nature of things, the leading division would necessarily be badly cut up in carrying out its part of the work; and after having secured the front line, it was reasonable to suppose — and, under the circumstances, its regimental officers were justified in supposing — that the other divisions in the corps would follow and finish the work. The other divisions, with the exception of the Fourth, followed, but they did not advance beyond the lines of the First Division. Remaining in the crater, they added to the confusion, and finally rendered any movement impossible.

Another historian, if such he may be called, has said that the assault upon the enemy's lines "*failed because it was led by the worst division in the army.*" This writer could not have been familiar with the record of the brave men whose courage he thus flippantly assails. Among the troops of this division were the Twenty-first, Twenty-ninth, Thirty-fifth, Fifty-sixth, Fifty-seventh, and Fifty-ninth Massachusetts regiments, Third Maryland, an old and excellent regiment, and the One Hundredth Pennsylvania. The Twenty-first regiment entered the service as early as August, 1861. It fought with Burnside in North Carolina, was engaged in the second battle of Bull Run, Chantilly, Antietam, and Fredericksburg, and afterwards in East Tennessee. Its record is a very bright one. The Twenty-ninth regiment had served in nearly every department, and contained the oldest three years' troops from New England. The Thirty-fifth regiment had been in the service since August, 1862, and was engaged at South Mountain and Antietam before it had been a month in the service, in both of which actions it had behaved with signal bravery. The Fifty-sixth, Fifty-seventh, and Fifty-ninth regiments, though they had not been long in the service, were composed chiefly of veteran soldiers. The many silent mounds scattered all the way from the Wilderness to the James, beneath which repose their dead, tell more eloquently the story of their bravery and devotion, than can any words of praise. The One Hundredth Pennsylvania was a most superior regiment, and was the equal of any in the army. Many of the field-officers of the division were most gallant soldiers, while General Bartlett was without his superior in our army for courage and daring. To speak of such regiments and such officers as these as being *the worst in our army*, is wholly unjustifiable, and not susceptible of palliation or excuse.

The Committee of Congress, which made a patient examination into this unfortunate affair, closed their report with these words:—

" . . . Your Committee must say, that, in their opinion, the cause of the disastrous result of the assault of the 30th of July last, is mainly attributable to the fact, that the plans and suggestions of the general who had devoted his attention for so long a time to the subject, who had carried out to a successful completion the project of mining the enemy's works, and who had carefully selected and drilled his troops for the purpose of securing whatever advantages might be attainable from the explosion of the mine, should have been so entirely disregarded by a general who had evinced no faith in the successful prosecution of the work, had aided it by no countenance or open approval, and had assumed the entire direction and control only when it was completed, and the time had come for reaping any advantages that might be derived from it." *

The Committee, in the same report, pay a most deserved tribute to the white troops of the Ninth Corps, and speak as follows:—

" They are not behind any troops in the service in those qualities which have placed our volunteer troops before the world as equal, if not superior, to any known to modern warfare. The services performed by the Ninth Corps on many a well-fought battle-field, not only in this campaign, but in others, have been such as to prove that they are second to none in the service. Your Committee believe that any other troops

* Report of Committee on "Conduct of the War," Vol. I., pp. 11, 12, 1865.

exposed to the same influences, under the same circumstances, and for the same length of time, would have been similarly affected. No one, upon a careful consideration of all the circumstances, can be surprised that those influences should have produced the effects they did upon them."*

If loss of life is any evidence of the bravery of a corps in battle, that of the Ninth on this occasion would seem to speak most eloquently in this regard. Its entire loss in killed was 52 officers and 376 men; wounded, 105 officers, 1,556 men; missing, many of whom were killed, 87 officers, 1,652 men.

On the evening after the mine affair, Colonel Barnes took command of the First Brigade, General Bartlett having been captured; and on the following day, the regiment moved to the rear, taking up its former position, Captain Willard D. Tripp being assigned to the command, and retaining it till the 14th of September.

The regiment was greatly reduced in numbers at this time, having scarcely men enough to form a full company; yet, during a large part of the time that followed, it was required to perform the same kind and amount of duty as other and larger regiments, being one day at the front in the rifle-pits, exposed to the deadly fire of the enemy's sharpshooters, and the next in the rear, doing fatigue duty, and both night and day, whether at the rear or the front, under almost constant fire from the enemy's lines.

Late in the afternoon of the 7th of August, the enemy opened a furious fire upon our entrenchments. The fire was particularly heavy on that part of our lines occupied by the Fourteenth New York Heavy Artillery, which was still commanded by Major Chipman. Great confusion ensued, and the troops were ordered to form in line of battle. The faithful Major, who was never missing in time of peril, hastened from his quarters to attend personally to the formation of his regiment; but while engaged in the performance of this duty, he was mortally wounded by the fragment of a large mortar-shell which exploded near him. From this time till eleven o'clock the next forenoon, he lingered, apparently uncon-

* Report of Committee on "Conduct of the War," Vol. I., pp. 11, 12, 1865.

scious, when life became extinct. His body was carefully embalmed and sent to his home in Sandwich, Mass., for burial, where it was received by a heart-broken wife and children, and many sorrowing neighbors and friends.

Major Charles Chipman was a true man and most gallant soldier. He possessed some advantage over the most of his fellow-officers in the Twenty-ninth Regiment, at the outset, by having had, during his earlier life, the benefits of the strict discipline and thorough training of the regular army, in which he had served as a Sergeant; at one time under Colonel Gardner, who, during the war, commanded the Confederate forces at Port Hudson. The esteem in which Major Chipman was held by his comrades found a fitting expression at a reunion of the survivors of the regiment, held at Plymouth, Mass., on the 14th of May, 1873, when the fine oil-portrait of this officer, which had constituted a part of the collection in the "Gallery of Fallen Heroes," having been purchased by Sergeant Samuel C. Wright, was re-purchased by the Association, and by it presented to his widow and children, together with a kind and highly-appropriate letter from the President of the Association, as a token of the love and regard of his comrades.

During the night of the 14th of August, 1864, the Ninth Corps was relieved by the Eighteenth, and on the 15th, the Ninth moved to the left and relieved the Fifth Corps, the latter having moved out towards the Weldon Railroad. While remaining here (some five days), the regiment with its brigade was placed on the front line as skirmishers. There were no trenches or works of any kind, and the men were considerably exposed.

On the 19th, the whole division moved to the left to connect with the Fifth Corps, which was in position on the Weldon road. While the division was on the march, in the midst of a blinding rain-storm, the enemy dashed out of the woods at a place called Blick's House, and began a fierce assault upon the right flank. For a short time it looked as though all would be lost. The fierceness of the assault, and the unfavorable situation of our troops, threatened a serious disaster. But our men had been too long accustomed to such scenes to be disconcerted or alarmed. The line was quickly formed, though under a terrible fire, and the enemy routed at every point. It was a great victory, apart from the good fighting of the men. The enemy were engaged in a secret, well-planned movement to cut off the Fifth Corps from the main body of our army; but the division, by its gallantry, wholly frustrated their plans.

Great praise was awarded the division for its conduct on this occasion. General Julius White, a fine officer, was in command, and manifested great skill in handling his troops. Colonel Joseph H. Barnes, who commanded the First Brigade in this battle, by his good conduct, earned promotion to Brevet Brigadier-General.*

An incident of the battle worthy of mention, is, the regiment captured one of the enemy's captains, who fought the battalion at Great Bethel, June 10, 1861.

The regiment did not escape this battle without some loss. Sergeant Curtis S. Rand, Company A; Privates John B. Smithers, Company B; David A. Hoxie, Company D; William McGill and Edwin C. Bemis, Company H; and First Lieutenant George D. Williams, Company F, were wounded. Sergeant Rand had been a wagon-master during the most of his term; just before this battle, he requested permission to go into the ranks, saying that he was desirous of performing active service. Poor fellow! his wounds proved mortal, and he died a few days after the battle.

From this time till the 21st, everything remained in the same condition as at the close of the battle, except that our troops had entrenched themselves, the Ninth Corps "occupy-

---

* The following recommendation was sent forward for Colonel Barnes's promotion:—

"HEADQUARTERS THIRD DIVISION, NINTH ARMY CORPS,
September 13, 1864.

"Captain JOHN C. YOUNGMAN, A. A. Gen., Ninth Army Corps.

"CAPTAIN: I have the honor to forward Brigade Commanders' lists of recommendations for brevet.

"I beg permission to add my own recommendation in favor of . . . . Lieutenant-Colonel Joseph H. Barnes, Twenty-ninth Massachusetts, lately commanding brigade, First Division, Ninth Army Corps, for distinguished gallantry and success in action, at Blick's House, Weldon Railroad, resisting enemy's attack on Ninth Corps' right.

"Very respectfully, your ob'd't serv't,
"(Signed) O. B. WILLCOX, Brig. Gen. Com'd'g Div.

"Official: W. V. RICHARDS, Capt, and A. A. A. G."

ing the line extending from the Fifth Corps on the Weldon Railroad to the left of the Second Corps, near the Jerusalem plank road."

The enemy had manifested great uneasiness ever since this ground had been occupied by our troops, and had more than once threatened an attack. On the 21st, he made a spirited assault upon our works, charging up to the breastworks several times in quick succession, but was repulsed with great slaughter. The regiment, though exposed to a severe enfilading fire, was not actively engaged in this battle.

The great losses sustained by the First Division, in the various battles in which it had engaged, rendered a reorganization of the corps necessary. The troops of this division were accordingly, on the first of September, merged with those of the Second and Third. The Twenty-ninth, Fifty-seventh, and Fifty-ninth Massachusetts Regiments, Third Maryland, One Hundredth Pennsylvania, and Fourteenth New York composed the Third Brigade of the First Division.

On the 10th of September, eighty-three recruits from Massachusetts reached our regiment.

On the 14th, Colonel Barnes was relieved from the command of the Brigade by the arrival of Colonel McLaughlin of the Fifty-seventh Regiment, and again assumed command of the Twenty-ninth Regiment, relieving Captain Willard D. Tripp, who had been in command since the battle of July 30.

On the 24th of September, an order was issued from the headquarters of the Ninth Corps, directing Brigadier-General Hartranft, commanding First Division, to garrison Fort Howard with one hundred and fifty men. On the same day, General Hartranft designated the "Twenty-ninth Regiment Massachusetts Veteran Volunteer Infantry . . . as a permanent garrison to be placed in Fort Howard," and Colonel N. B. McLaughlin, commanding the Third Brigade, was directed to "see that the camp of the regiment is placed in the immediate vicinity of the fort."

For a period of nearly two weeks, the regiment was happily exempt from the hardships of the field; but the necessities of the service finally required its presence at the front, and on the 5th of October, it was ordered out of the fort, and on the same day rejoined its brigade on the front line at Poplar Grove Church.

On the 8th of October, there was a reconnoissance in force on the left of the army by the First Division, but the regiment, though engaged in the movement, was not under fire.

On the 9th, Colonel Barnes was mustered out of the service, very much against the wishes of his superior officers, who had learned to appreciate his many excellent soldierly qualities. But his motives for leaving the army were of the most honorable character. His commission as Captain bore date of the 27th of April, 1861. He had been in the service of the United States since the 18th of May, 1861. During a large part of this time, he had had the actual and responsible command of the regiment, and for much of the time that of a brigade.

In taking leave of this excellent officer, who was so long and so honorably connected with the regiment, we deem it but an act of simple justice to him and his comrades as well, to quote some of the kind words spoken of him by several officers of the Ninth Corps. In 1864, General N. B. McLaughlin said of him: "During his term of service, Lieutenant-Colonel Barnes commanded his regiment nearly two-thirds of the time, and commanded a brigade for nearly two months in the present campaign. I consider him a cool, reliable officer, courageous, and of good judgment and conduct, both in action and in camp, a fine disciplinarian, and capable of commanding either a regiment or brigade."

Major-General Orlando B. Willcox said: "I consider Colonel Barnes a man of great coolness and gallantry, of considerable experience as a regimental and brigade commander, and every way qualified." Major-General Parke, commanding the corps, also expressed his high appreciation of this officer in the following language: "I consider Colonel Barnes a most excellent soldier, and a very efficient commander. He is eminently qualified for command."

The soldiers of the Twenty-ninth, though they sometimes fretted over the stern discipline of this officer, both loved and respected him. The same qualities that made him a good soldier have made him a good and useful citizen, and in the important civil office which he now holds, he displays the same good judgment and strong sense of duty which marked his career in the army.

CHAPTER XXVII.

MOVEMENT TO WELLS'S FARM—THE CAMP AT PEGRAM'S FARM—BUILDING OF WINTER QUARTERS—ORDERED BACK TO PETERSBURG—DISAPPOINTMENT OF THE MEN—THE REGIMENT OCCUPIES BATTERY NO. 11—FRIENDLY RELATIONS BETWEEN THE PICKETS—BATTLE OF FORT STEDMAN—THE REGIMENT MAKES A GALLANT FIGHT—THE PRISONERS SENT TO LIBBY—CLOSING SCENES BEFORE PETERSBURG—THE REGIMENT ENTERS THE CITY—DUTIES PERFORMED AFTER THE BATTLE—DEATH OF ABRAHAM LINCOLN—ORDERED TO ALEXANDRIA, AND FROM THENCE TO GEORGETOWN—PROVOST GUARD—THE GRAND REVIEW—REGIMENT GOES TO TENALLYTOWN, MD.—SOLDIERS OF THE THIRTY-FIFTH MASSACHUSETTS ASSIGNED TO THE TWENTY-NINTH REGIMENT—ORDERED TO MASSACHUSETTS—PARADE IN NEW YORK—IN CAMP AT READVILLE, MASS.—THE LAST ORDER—DISCHARGED THE SERVICE—CLOSING REMARKS.

The last chapter left the regiment at Poplar Grove Church. Here it remained till the 27th of October, when, very early in the morning, the Brigade advanced in line of battle to and a little beyond Wells's Farm, halted for the night, and the next morning fell back to Pegram's Farm, between the Squirrel Level and Vaughan roads, the regiment covering the latter movement as skirmishers.

It was supposed that the corps was to pass the winter at this place, and the regimental commanders were ordered to prepare winter quarters for their men. No duty which the soldier is required to perform is so pleasant as that of erecting a house to live in. Such orders after a fatiguing campaign, promising both comfort and rest, are peculiarly welcome, and always cheerfully obeyed. In this, as in every other similar instance, the soldiers worked with great zeal, manifesting much ingenuity in the construction and arrangement of their houses. The rude idea of the negroes of building a chimney with sticks and clay, was adopted by the men, with some improvements of their own, while each hut was provided with comfortable bunks, spacious fire-places, and shelves for their guns and clothing.

This was the first time in nearly two years that the regiment had even seen the prospect of winter quarters, and was the first time in many months that it had been out of the range of the enemy's sharpshooters and picket-firing. The camp was very unlike the ones it had occupied in front of Richmond, or in Tennessee, but was upon a dry, sandy knoll, well supplied with good water, and in full sight of Fort Sampson, a strong redoubt, named after the brave Captain Sampson of the Twenty-first Regiment of Massachusetts Volunteers, who fell there in the battle of September 20, with the colors of his regiment in his own hands, gallantly leading his men in a charge. Though the camp was very pleasantly located, yet winter was near at hand, the trees had already lost their foliage, and the cool autumn winds found their way through the cracks and crevices of the humble huts of the soldiers, often reminding them of the necessity of applying a little more of the "sacred soil" of Virginia, if they would be wholly comfortable. Thus quartered, it was natural that they should compare their present lot with that which fell to them the winter before in East Tennessee, where cold, hunger, nakedness, and danger were daily experienced for a dreary succession of weeks and months. But the soldier's fondest dreams of comfort are often rudely dispelled, and so these anticipations of ease and quiet were never fully realized; the men were scarcely ensconced in their winter homes, before they were ordered to leave them. Any one who has heard a soldier grumble, and has noted some of his expressions, can understand what was said by the men about this change of location. Captain Taylor, who was of a positive temperament, rose to the sublimity of the occasion by swearing that "he would never lift another handful of dirt as long as he remained in the army"; while some of the soldiers declared that the officers were "a mean set," and were bent on ruining the health and destroying the comfort of the men as a mere pastime.

As usual, all this rage was utterly impotent, and indulged in as a sacred privilege. It operated something like a cushion, however, lessening the severity of impact with a hard surface; to use less elegant language, it "let them down easily." The lesson of implicit obedience to orders — not unquestioning, for volunteer soldiers were never without their mental reservations as to the propriety of every military movement — had already, and long since, been thoroughly learned. On the 29th of November, when the weather was quite cold and cheerless, the Ninth Corps was ordered to march. The men little dreamed that they were going back to the old bloodstained trenches in front of Petersburg, where they had borne the heat of the summer, and faced the shells of a hundred mortars and as many cannon. Here, however, they soon found themselves, and as they moved along over the battlefield of the 17th of June, and among the graves of their brothers who died for their country there, more than one eye was wet with the tears of manly sorrow. The regiment was ordered to do duty as the garrison of Battery No. 11, a small *ravelin* covering about three-fourths of an acre, having embrasures for two guns, but no guns being mounted. About two hundred yards from this work was Battery No. 12, a large redoubt mounting four cohorns, garrisoned by a portion of the First Connecticut Heavy Artillery. On the right of Battery No. 11, one hundred and twenty-five yards distant, was Fort Stedman, held by the Fourteenth New York Heavy Artillery; and a little to the rear and left of Battery No. 11 was the Fifty-ninth Massachusetts Volunteers; while to the left of Battery No. 12, and between it and Fort Haskell, was the One Hundredth Pennsylvania Volunteers; and at the right of Fort Stedman, the Fifty-seventh Massachusetts Regiment.

The pickets of both armies were stationed in rifle-pits large enough to hold several men, midway between the respective lines, and these were approached by covered ways.

Though under fire much of the time, the men found opportunity to build quarters, and so far as protection from the cold was concerned, were quite comfortable during the winter. As in the winter of 1863, while the regiment was before Fredericksburg, the pickets of the two armies became friendly; but as these familiarities were strictly forbidden, they were never indulged in except at night.

The members of our regiment performed their full share of

picket service, and, like all the rest of our troops, had frequent parleys with the Confederates. A member of the regiment has furnished the writer with a detailed statement of several of the interviews which took place on the picket line, from which it appears that this service was a source of more amusement than danger.

When everything was quiet, one of our men would call out, "Johnnies, have you got any tobacco?" "Yes Yanks; have you got any hard-tack?" was the common answer. "Meet you half-way." says the Confederate. "All right; come on!" say our men. Then three or four men from each side would leave the pits, crawl out over the space between the two lines, shake hands, have an exchange of tobacco, hard-tack, and talk, crack jokes, and separate with the understanding, that, as soon as each party got back to the pits, they should commence firing, for the purpose of misleading their respective officers.

This state of things was finally discovered by the Confederate and Federal officers, and was terminated by strict orders forbidding the practice under severe penalties. But the practice, though not worthy to be encouraged, resulted in bringing about numerous desertions from the enemy's camp.

The proclamation of General Grant, encouraging desertions among the Confederates, was, by means of these forbidden interviews, extensively circulated, and scarcely a night passed, during the months of January and February, which did not witness more or less of these desertions.

The Twenty-ninth had been very much reduced in numbers, having less than two hundred muskets; and yet, because of its long and conspicuous service, General Parke, commanding the corps, refused to consolidate it with some other larger Massachusetts regiment, and allowed it to retain a full list of field-officers, only one of whom, under the then existing rules of the War Department, could be mustered. Captain Willard D. Tripp, who had been commissioned as Lieutenant-Colonel, October 12, 1864, had been mustered out on the 13th of December, 1864, his term of service having expired. Captain Charles D. Browne was promoted to Lieutenant-Colonel, October 14, 1864; Captain Charles T. Richardson commissioned as Major, August 9, 1864, and mustered as such;

and Captain Thomas William Clarke commissioned as Colonel, November 8, 1864. During the winter, Colonel Clarke was assigned to duty upon the staff of General Hartranft, commanding the division; Lieutenant-Colonel Browne made Inspector of the division; and Major Richardson had command of the regiment.

No event of particular significance occurred till the 25th of March, 1865. Long before daylight in the morning of this day, a large force of the enemy — afterwards learned to be the corps of General Gordon, supported by the division of General Bushrod Johnson — crossed the level plain between Fort Stedman and the Appomattox River, fully a quarter of a mile to the right of Battery No. 11, and the entire storming party effected a wide breach in the works, and moved directly upon Fort Stedman, entering the rear sally-port almost undiscovered. So complete was the surprise, that the fort was captured at once. Slight firing was heard from this direction by the garrison in Battery Eleven; whereupon Major Richardson caused the men to be aroused, but the firing was so slight, that when the regiment was ordered to "fall in," the sentinel stationed on the top of the parapet called out that there was "no attack." The men were not dismissed, however, and stood silently in line for some time, peering into the gray, frosty air of the morning, the Major taking a position on the top of the works, listening intently, and looking down into the ravine below, where he saw his trusty pickets standing quietly by their fires, apparently unaware of any disturbance on the main line. But the commanding officer soon became satisfied that there was an attack in the direction of Fort Stedman; the right curtain of Battery Eleven was re-enforced, and the bugler Pond having sounded the alarm, the garrison was wholly prepared to repel any attack. Up to this time, no general alarm had been sounded along the line, and no word from any source, indicating an attack, had been received by Major Richardson; much less that the line had been broken, or that any danger lurked in his rear. The regiment had remained in line of battle nearly thirty minutes, when suddenly the men in the right curtain commenced firing; they were ordered to cease, lest they should shoot our own pickets, who had begun to come in. The latter order had hardly been given, when some of our soldiers cried out, "The Johnnies are coming in at the rear sally-port!" This was the first positive information that the garrison had received of an attack; but the worst was revealed now,—the enemy had actually captured Fort Stedman, and though our pickets under Lieutenant Josselyn had not been disturbed, yet at least five hundred of Gordon's and Johnson's troops had suddenly appeared in our rear. These veteran soldiers of the Confederacy were destined, however, to meet with a stubborn resistance; a hand-to-hand encounter at once began; a Massachusetts battery stationed at the left joined in the desperate conflict, which, in the course of fifteen minutes, ended in the capture by our regiment of three hundred and fifty of the storming party, at least one hundred and fifty more than the whole number of the Twenty-ninth, and the temporary closing of the gap in this part of our lines.

During this encounter, the officers and men behaved with signal bravery. Captain Taylor was especially conspicuous, using a musket, and dealing powerful blows with its breech. Major Richardson, mingling with his men, was in the thickest of the fight, and received a terrible blow on the head from an enemy's musket, sufficient to overcome an ordinary man; but he was not an ordinary man, and so far from quitting the fight, he kept on in the desperate struggle, cheering his men, and assuring them that the day was theirs.

The enemy now disappeared, the fort was cleared of the prisoners, and word sent to brigade headquarters of the state of affairs at the camp of the Twenty-ninth Regiment. General McLaughlin, commander of the Brigade, soon came up, with the Fifty-ninth Massachusetts Regiment as a re-enforcement, and was greatly surprised at the sight of so large a number of prisoners as he found standing in the rear of the fort. The General gave Major Gould, commanding the Fifty-ninth, imperative orders to assist the Twenty-ninth in holding the fort, and then, with his staff, rode over towards Fort Stedman; he had, probably, not been gone five minutes, before he and all his staff fell into the hands of the enemy. The best possible disposition was now made of what remained of the garrison (for it is true that some had been captured in the first assault and others had been killed and wounded) to resist the attack of the enemy, which he was now preparing to make, having collected his main assaulting column in a ravine in the rear of the battery. Major Gould was offered the command of the forces here, being the ranking officer, but declined; Major Richardson concluded to establish a strong picket line in the rear of the battery, and, with Captain Taylor, went personally to superintend the work. The enemy were already in sight, and firing soon began; on returning to the fort, to their great surprise these officers found the work nearly deserted, and saw in the dim light of the morning the command of Major Gould, and some of their own regiment, moving away down the ditch towards Fort Haskell, which was still held by our troops. During the brief absence of Major Richardson, Major Gould, who had discovered the approach of the enemy in his rear, gave orders to his men to "Leap the breastworks, and retreat between the rebel works and our own to Fort Haskell."* No resistance was now possible; in a few moments the enemy swarmed into the battery, and Major Richardson, Captain Taylor, and a number of their faithful men were captured. This was a cruel fate for these brave soldiers, who had striven so zealously to beat back the enemy; and had their example been followed by others who held equally responsible positions, the little fort would probably have not been lost.

By this time the alarm had spread far and near, and though it was scarcely light, yet the entire corps was under arms and in motion.

The left column of the enemy, passing down the line to Battery No. 9, drove the Fifty-seventh Massachusetts from the works. It next encountered the Second Michigan, and though the regiment was surprised, and some confusion followed, yet it soon rallied, and held its ground against the most determined efforts of the enemy. Re-enforcements arriving at this point, the enemy were repulsed, and fell back towards Fort Stedman, in which their right column was now huddled, having been checked in its further movements by our troops on that part of the line.

* Report of Fifty-ninth Regiment in Report of Adjutant-General, 1865, page 595.

The Twenty-ninth rallied about this time, near brigade headquarters, where a regiment of General Hartranft's command arrived; and the two regiments at once charged and occupied a line of works about one hundred yards in the rear of Battery Eleven, thus completely stopping the opening in that part of the line.

At about seven o'clock, an advance was ordered upon the enemy, in all directions. Battery Eleven was soon retaken by our men, Conrad Homan, the color-bearer of the Twenty-ninth, being the first man who entered the works; and for his distinguished gallantry on this occasion, was promoted to be First Lieutenant, and received one of the medals of honor voted by Congress. The only works now held by the enemy were Fort Stedman and Battery No. 10, which, shortly after eight o'clock, General Hartranft's division was ordered to attack. The Two Hundred and Eleventh Pennsylvania, though composed wholly of raw troops, was chosen to lead the assault. A finer display of bravery was never witnessed in the army, than that of these untrained soldiers. With great impetuosity, they rushed upon the fort in the face of a blaze of musketry, and in a few minutes were masters of the situation. At the same instant other troops of the division stormed Battery No. 10, and captured it.

The retreat of the enemy was now cut off by the fire from our other works, and one thousand nine hundred and forty-nine of their number, of whom seventy-one were officers, nine stands of colors, and a large number of small arms, fell into our hands. And thus ended this brilliant and well-conceived movement of the enemy. It was, to a great extent, a fair offset to the mine affair, but the disadvantages under which our troops labored could never have been overcome, except by hard fighting and good generalship, which characterized our movements from the beginning.

The events of this terrible battle were mostly sad and distressing; but the affair was not without its ludicrous features. A soldier of Company C,* who was captured in the early morning, made an involuntary exchange of hats with a Confederate officer. The soldier's hat was nearly new, while

---

* Horace Ripley, an excellent soldier.

that which he received from the officer was exceedingly shabby. The soldier broke away from the guard and ran into our lines, taking a gallant part in the charge just mentioned. While circulating among the captured enemy after the battle, he discovered the identical officer who had taken his hat from him. The soldier, in a very droll manner, approached the officer and said: "Well, Mister, if you please, I'll take my hat now, and here's yours back again, just as good, and no better, than when I took it about three hours ago." The two again exchanged hats, and shaking hands "on it," indulged in a hearty laugh.

The following-named soldiers of the regiment were killed in this action, which is known as the "Battle of Fort Stedman": Company B, Edward J. O'Brien (he was terribly bayoneted in the breast and killed by one of the enemy, after he had been badly wounded, and was found in this mutilated condition after the battle); Company C, Sergeant C. Francis Harlow; Company E, First Lieutenant Nathaniel Burgess, Sergeant Orrin D. Holmes, William Klinker, and Ruter Moritz; Company F, Preserved Westgate; Company G, Nelson Cook, George E. Snow, and John Cronin.

Lieutenant Burgess of Plymouth had been promoted for his great bravery on the 17th of June. Orderly Sergeant Harlow was overpowered, and ordered to surrender; he replied with spirit that he would not, fired, and shot his antagonist; but another Confederate, standing near, seized his gun, and shot the courageous Harlow through the head. After the battle, the dead body of Harlow was found in the fort, lying upon that of a dead Confederate officer, from which fact it was inferred that Harlow shot the officer, and upon being himself killed, fell in the position in which he was found. One of the comrades, who witnessed this sad affair, states that the officer was one Captain Gordon, who led the assaulting party. The death of Burgess causes us to remark, inasmuch as he was the last officer in the regiment killed during its term of service, that the first and last officer in the regiment who fell in battle, were citizens of the historic old town of Plymouth.

NOTE.—The chief facts concerning this battle are somewhat in dispute; two or three distinct and conflicting accounts of it having been published. The version here given, so far as it relates to Battery Eleven, was furnished

The real mettle of the officers and men of the regiment was fairly tested in this battle, and the result shows that they were among the bravest soldiers in the army. In the depressing adversities of the early morning, as well as in the success which followed later in the day, their courage was equally conspicuous. Stubborn and unflinching when the enemy burst upon them in greatly superior numbers, they were impetuous and daring while on the charge.

Captain Clarke, as Adjutant-General of the Brigade, led a large body of re-enforcements on the charge at six o'clock. Lieutenant-Colonel Browne, while carrying an order from the commander of the division, dashed on horseback directly through the lines of a Confederate regiment. Captain Pizer, Lieutenant Josselyn, Lieutenant McQuillan, and Lieutenant Scully, who were captured, all escaped, and fought with great gallantry in the latter part of the battle, and for their bravery were afterwards brevetted.

The captured of the regiment, who did not manage to escape, were carried to Petersburg, and confined in a small room till nine o'clock in the morning. They were then transferred to a large hall in the village, where they were all searched, and their overcoats taken from them. Towards noon they were marched from the hall, together with a number of other prisoners, to an open field on the outskirts of the town, and were kept there under guard till night, when they took the cars for Richmond. During the day it rained and snowed by turns, and the wind was cold and piercing, the poor soldiers, stripped of their overcoats, suffering intensely. No food was given them till about noon of the following day; and then nothing but a small quantity of bean soup, without any seasoning, brought to them in dirty iron kettles. The men were confined together in one room at the notorious Libby Prison; and, as further illustrating the barbarous nature of their treatment, it should be stated, that crowded into the same apartment, which was filthy in the extreme, alive with vermin, and poorly ventilated, were nearly two hundred other prisoners. The quantity and quality of the

the writer by Major Chas. T. Richardson of Pawtucket, R. I.: the comments upon that officer, and Captain Taylor, being those of the author, based upon the statements of reliable persons.—AUTHOR.

food dealt out to them was such as hardly to sustain life: the breakfast consisted of a small ration of smoked pork; for dinner they had bean soup; and at night a small loaf of bread, with water. All the food was of the most inferior quality; the meat especially, which frequently emitted a nauseating odor.

Happily, these men were not compelled to endure such privations for many days; but they were days of anxiety and suffering, as the author well knows from his own experience. The life of the wicked Rebellion was fast ebbing away; a few days before Lee's surrender the men were released, and sent to the prison depot at Annapolis, Maryland, afterwards joining the regiment at Georgetown, District of Columbia.

After the repulse of the enemy on the 25th of March, and the recapture of our works, the regiment again occupied Battery No. 11. supported by the Fifty-seventh and Fifty-ninth Massachusetts regiments. The final movements of our army, which resulted in the surrender of General Lee, were close at hand. A state of feverish excitement prevailed among both armies in front of Petersburg. The enemy were disposed to be belligerent, and for nearly a week kept up a constant fire upon our lines.

On the 27th of March, General Sheridan began his grand movement on the left, and the whole army had orders to be ready to march at a moment's notice.

On the 30th, General Parke, commanding the corps, was ordered to assault the enemy's works in his front at four o'clock the next morning, but the order was subsequently countermanded by General Meade.

On the 1st of April, the order for an assault was renewed. At ten o'clock that night our artillery opened all along our line, and at the same time a heavy force of skirmishers was sent forward. General Griffin's brigade captured the enemy's picket line, opposite Forts Howard and Hayes, and a number of prisoners. During these movements our whole line was forming for the assault, which was made at about four o'clock in the morning of the 2d. The contest was a bloody one, but was very successful.

At the close of the day, during which the enemy made

repeated attacks, General Parke was in possession of several hundred yards of the enemy's lines, on each side of the Jerusalem Plank Road, including several formidable works. In the meantime a determined attack on the left had been made by the Sixth, Second, and parts of the Twenty-fifth corps, capturing a considerable number of prisoners.

During the battle on this part of the line, General A. P. Hill of the Confederate army was killed. He was one of the most distinguished officers of the long list of able and brilliant Southern Generals. The tragic account of his death, given by E. A. Pollard in his "Lost Cause,"* is probably incorrect, and is of the same sensational character as much else that this pseudo historian has written.

The night of the 2d of April was passed by the Ninth Corps on its advanced line with heavy skirmishing, continuing till near midnight. The regiment did not become seriously engaged during the 1st and 2d of April, though it took part in the demonstrations which were made in front of Fort Stedman.

At four o'clock in the morning of the 3d of April, all our troops were put in motion, no opposition was encountered, the enemy having deserted their lines. The Brigade was among the first to pass the Confederate works; the Third Maryland Regiment having the honor of being the first to enter the city of Petersburg. The Twenty-ninth, with other troops, soon followed, but at once passed out on the Richmond Stage and Chesterfield roads, where it was placed on picket.

From this time till the 5th, the regiment had its headquarters at a place called Violet Bank, a fine old Virginia plantation, the house of which had been long occupied by General Lee. "There were two pianos in the house, and for two days one would have thought that some impressario had his troupe there, in rehearsal of all the known, and some unknown, operas." The regiment recrossed the Appomattox on the 5th, and, with its brigade, "was deployed across the country, from the river to the Boydton Road," with headquarters at Roger A. Pryor's, "preparing to advance and cover

* The "Lost Cause," page 692.

the reconstruction of the railroad, and to guard that and the Cox Road, as the army advanced."

In the afternoon of the 6th, the regiment marched to Sutherlands, remaining there till midnight, and then moving out on the Cox Road to Beazeley's. By short marches, made at different times, it finally proceeded to Wilson's Station, "about twenty miles from Sutherlands, and at the junction of the Grubby and Cox roads."

While remaining here, the men received the sad news of the death of Abraham Lincoln. Every soldier felt that he had lost a dear friend in the lamented chief magistrate, whose heart always beat with joy at their successes in the field, and sorrowed with the truest sorrow over their reverses and misfortunes. Of all the many true men who stood at the helm of the nation during the stormy days of the war, Abraham Lincoln was pre-eminently the soldier's friend; he always frowned upon the harsh punishments inflicted by military law, and by his sympathy for the erring, saved from death many who had been thus doomed by the inexorable decrees of courts-martial.

On the 21st of April, the Ninth Corps was ordered to Washington, and the men bid good-by forever to these scenes of their strifes and sufferings. The regiment reached Alexandria on the 28th, and on the next day was ordered to Georgetown, where it was detached from the division and made provost guard at this place, and furnished all the details for General Willcox's district headquarters.

On the 23d of May occurred the grand review in Washington. The Twenty-ninth was not permitted to participate in this triumphal march of our noble army, but as provost guard, was assigned to the duty, on this memorable day, of keeping the streets of Georgetown clear of obstructions, and of guarding the various "approaches to the route of the procession." Several of the officers of the regiment, however, who were on staff duty, were in the column, and Colonel Clarke was intrusted with the formation of the First Division line, a duty that he performed with great ability and credit to himself and the State.

On the 7th of June, Colonel Clarke was relieved from

duty as Assistant Adjutant-General of the division, and assumed the command of the regiment.

On the 9th, a large portion of the Thirty-fifth Massachusetts Regiment was transferred to the Twenty-ninth. These men were mostly Germans and Belgians, whose term of service did not expire before October 1, 1865. They were asked by their commanding general to which regiment they desired to be transferred. Much attached to their officers, they replied, that "they preferred to go where their officers could go with them." By an arrangement made with the War Department, eleven officers were transferred with these men, and it speaks well for the regiment that these officers chose to be transferred to the Twenty-ninth. Both officers and men were superior soldiers, and the commanding officer of the Twenty-ninth, in his last report to the Adjutant-General of Massachusetts, speaks of them in terms of high praise.

On this day, the regiment marched to Tenallytown, Md., remaining here till the 29th of July. The formalities of mustering the regiment out of the service were completed on the 29th of July, and on the same day it started for Massachusetts.

Upon its arrival in New York, it became the guest of the New England Association, as also did the Fifty-seventh Massachusetts Regiment, which left Washington at the same time. The Association asked the regiments to parade in the city. The request was granted, and Brevet Brigadier-General McLaughlin (Colonel of the Fifty-seventh) assuming command, marched the troops through Broadway, from the Battery to Union Square, and from the Square again to the Battery. The veterans were greeted with cheers everywhere on the line of their march, and at the close were met by General Burnside, who addressed them in a cordial manner.

At the conclusion of the parade, the Association invited the soldiers to partake of a dinner, at which were present, Major-General Joseph Hooker, the patriotic Colonel Howe, President of the Association, and the Rev. M. H. Smith (Burleigh). It has been said that this was the last parade of Union troops in New York City.

Taking the cars on the Connecticut Shore road, the regiment reached Massachusetts the next morning; but not having been paid or discharged the service, still further delay became necessary, and it was for this purpose ordered into camp at Readville.

It was wholly natural for soldiers who had been so long in the service as had the members of the Twenty-ninth, and were now, at the close of their protracted term, almost within sight and sound of their homes, to feel a disagreeable sense of restraint at being thus detained. They found some fault with this state of things, which they characterized as "the last crop of red tape"; but their soldierly instincts and self-respect kept them from the commission of any act which they or their friends will ever have occasion to regret. Their conduct was so exemplary under these perplexing circumstances, and this event in their career in every sense so historical, that their commanding officer was moved to address them upon the subject. This address was termed, "General Orders, No. 12," and was the last order issued to the regiment from any source, or by any officer. As it is a well-written paper, alike touching and soldierly in its tone, and altogether a pleasing feature of the record of the regiment, we here give space for it : —

"GENERAL ORDERS, NO. 12.

"HEADQUARTERS TWENTY-NINTH MASSACHUSETTS VETERAN VOLUNTEERS,
"READVILLE, MASS., August 3, 1865.

"You hold the musket for the last time. From May, 1861, to August, 1865, we are a part of the history of the Republic. The very number of the regiment was prophetic; for twenty-nine battles will be inscribed on the flag which we carry.

"To be soldiers who have never lost a color, have never left the field without orders, have always cheerfully performed the requirements of the service, is indeed a cause for pride. But of one thing we should be prouder yet! Few regiments have had so few desertions, so few dishonorable discharges, so little punishment, of all who have served the Republic in the last four years.

"During the past three days, your conduct has been deserving of all praise. In receiving their welcome home, no men could have proved themselves more worthy of the honors paid them. Trying as the delay has been, anxious as you all were to return to the Commonwealth, no single thing was done unbecoming the good soldier.

"Around you cluster the memories of the two great armies of the Republic: that which fought four long years for Richmond, and that which opened the Mississippi to the commerce of the Northwest.

"You hold in your hands the last muskets of the army of the Potomac,—the last muskets of the army of Sherman. Remember, then, the brilliant record which is yours; and remember hereafter not to tarnish it." *

In concluding this narrative, which the writer fears has already been extended beyond the point which, in the estimation of a purely disinterested person, might be regarded as its proper limit, it seems essential to allude briefly, in review, to certain prominent and remarkable features of the record given in the foregoing pages. The seven companies of Captains Clarke, Wilson, Leach, Chipman, Doten, Chamberlain, and Barnes, were among the first in the country to enter the service for three years; while the regiment was among the last of all the volunteer forces to disband: serving, including the term of these original companies, a period of four years, two months, and twenty days, which is rather more than the whole period of the active hostilities of the war. During this time it served under thirty-one general officers, of more or less distinction, in three army corps, namely, the Second, Fifth, and Ninth; did duty in the States of Massachusetts, Maryland, Virginia, Kentucky, Mississippi, and Tennessee, and in the District of Columbia: while it carried its flags into fifteen States of the Union, travelling, in the course of fourteen months, a distance of four thousand two hundred and seventy-seven miles. Two of the companies participated in the first pitched battle of the Rebellion; and the regiment was engaged in one of the last battles of the war, which took place just seven days before the surrender of General Lee and his army. The regiment was, therefore, practically, present at the birth — it was also present at the death and funeral — of the Rebellion. It took part in the four great sieges of the war, namely, Richmond, 1862; Vicksburg, 1863; Knoxville, 1863; and Petersburg, 1864–5; was enengaged in twenty-nine pitched battles, beside a large number of skirmishes, picket fights, and artillery duels. It is chiefly in connection with the battle record of the Twenty-

---

* The author does not vouch for the statement, that the regiment held the last muskets of the armies of the Potomac and Sherman, as he believes there were regiments of both of these armies, that were mustered out even later than the Twenty-ninth.—AUTHOR.

ninth, that its surviving members have the greatest cause for feelings of profound gratitude; the comparatively small losses sustained by it in all these numerous encounters with the enemy forming, perhaps, the most remarkable feature of its entire career as a regiment. And what seems most singular, is the fact that this good fortune attended the regiment, with two or three exceptions, from the beginning to the close of its term. The time of its arrival at Gaines' Mill, though it did not operate to prevent it from performing valuable service, — a service that aided in rescuing from destruction Porter's troops, — alone saved it from the slaughter that covered that sanguinary field with several thousand wounded and dead.

At Antietam it chanced to be placed in a favorable position, while two other regiments of the same brigade, on its right and left, were nearly annihilated; at Fredericksburg it secured exemption from dreadful loss by a timely transfer to another corps of the army, made in the ordinary course of military changes, without the efforts of its officers, or the knowledge on the part of any one as to what results would follow.

Even a cursory glance at the records of some of our Massachusetts regiments which lost heavily in the war, will show that their losses were mainly the fruits of unfortunate positions, and, in some instances, that the major part of all their losses were sustained in a single battle, as was the case of several at Ball's Bluffs, Antietam, and Gettysburg. While we have shown that this exemption of the regiment from heavy battle casualties was in the main the result of accident, yet, from the nature of things, it cannot be wholly so.

The death-lists of many new regiments were often largely increased by the mere inexperience of the troops, and the insane idea sometimes possessed by their officers, that recklessness and wanton exposure were evidence of valor.

The Twenty-ninth was long in the field; its soldiers, for the last three years of their term, were in every sense veterans, having learned, by actual experience, the many little arts and devices always employed by old soldiers to protect themselves while in perilous positions, — a knowledge that the

Confederate officers imparted to their soldiers early in the war, and resulted in the saving of life, and the winning of more than one important victory over our armies. The romantic notion which for awhile possessed the soldiers, that it was unmilitary and unsoldierly to make any effort to be comfortable, or to shield themselves from the death-dealing minie, or the howling cannon-ball, soon gave place to more sensible ideas; and long before the close of the war, a rock, a fence, a log, a tree, or even a stump or bush, were often used with great effect for defensive purposes, and saved more than one soldier his life; while his cover, slight as it was, enabled him to fire with greater precision and coolness.

Notwithstanding the remarkable escape of the regiment in many battles, yet its list of the dead, as the reader will perceive, is by no means insignificant; and though but a small part, it yet constitutes a precious part, of the terrible price of human life which the Republic paid for its final victory over treason and rebellion.

A regiment of soldiers is in some respects like a family, having its own quarrels and jealousies, which family pride usually keeps hidden from the knowledge of the world, and which family sufferings and common interests finally cause, in a large measure, to be buried and forgotten.

To his comrades, the author, in closing, would say, let us all, as members of the same regiment, forever forget the petty bickerings and jealousies of the war, if they are not already forgotten; forgive with a generous spirit all who wronged us, — even those who fought against us in the field, — and turn our eyes upon the pleasant spectacle of a Republic and a nation rescued from anarchy and ruin, in part by our own efforts; and, finally, let us hope, that the record of our deeds as volunteer soldiers, saved, it may be, from forgetfulness by this printed volume, — humble as the deeds which it chronicles, — may in the years to come serve, as has that of our fathers of the Revolution, to keep bright and warm the fires of patriotism, and nourish a love for the nation's flag, and the principles it symbolizes, that neither suffering nor danger can quench.

THE ROSTER OF THE REGIMENT.

NOTE.

There are some facts about the rolls of the regiment that demand explanation. The published rolls of the Adjutant-General of Massachusetts give the Twenty-ninth a total membership of eighteen hundred and twenty commissioned officers and enlisted men. Of this number, fourteen commissioned officers* and three hundred and thirty-four enlisted men were transferred to it from the Thirty-fifth Massachusetts, June 9, 1865. A large proportion of these enlisted men are placed upon the rolls of the Twenty-ninth, without remark or note indicating that they were transferred, and appear upon our rolls as recruits for 1864. As they joined our regiment after the close of the war, and have their record with the Thirty-fifth for all except about a month of their entire service in the army, there seems to be no reason for publishing their names in this volume. The Twenty-ninth is charged with the desertion of some of these men, while in point of fact it derived no benefit from their service.

Besides these men, and those who are placed upon the following company rolls, there are found, as recruits for 1864, the names of about ninety men on the published rolls of the Twenty-ninth. After a careful consideration of all the facts, I have concluded to print the names of seventy of these soldiers, though it is very doubtful whether all of them actually served with the regiment. I print them in a roll by themselves, for the reason that it does not appear with certainty with what companies of the regiment they were connected. Five of these men are reported to have died in the service, and I have placed their names at the end of the roll of our dead.

The names of the following soldiers of the regiment do not appear at all upon the Adjutant-General's rolls: Thomas Burt, Edwin H. Hosmer, Charles Kleinhans, Edward L. Pettis, of Company E; Leander Clapp, Henry W. Pettee, of Company F; John Usherwood, Charles Young, George S. Welsch, of Company H; Ira A. Clark of Company I; and Martin Bird, Joseph A. Brown, David Dockerty, and William H. Moore, of Company K. The name of Moore does not appear upon any of the rolls of the regiment which I have been able to find.

* On page 337, the number of officers transferred from the Thirty-fifth Massachusetts to the Twenty-ninth Regiment, is erroneously stated as eleven.—AUTHOR.

The reader will observe that I have noted upon the following rolls the death and wounding of certain soldiers. This has been done because their names were omitted from the list of casualties given in the narrative portion of the work.

The published rolls of the regiment give a list of forty-nine "Unassigned Recruits." There could not have been any unassigned men who actually joined the regiment for duty, and the publication of this list only shows the unsatisfactory condition of the records of both the War Department and of our own State. With the help of kind comrades in each company, I have closely examined this list, and taken from it all identified names, and placed them with the companies to which they belonged; and it may interest the comrades to know that, but for this examination, some of the best soldiers in the regiment would have suffered the mortification of seeing their names printed in a list of "unassigned recruits." After all the labor bestowed upon this matter, there are still several soldiers in the list referred to whom we have not been able to identify, and the conclusion is they were never members of the regiment.—AUTHOR.

THE ROSTER OF THE REGIMENT.

FIELD AND STAFF

At Date of Organization of Regiment, December 13, 1861.

Ebenezer W. Pierce,	Colonel.
Joseph H. Barnes,	Lieutenant-Colonel.
Charles Chipman,	Major.
Orlando Brown,[1]	Surgeon.
George B. Cogswell,[2]	Assistant Surgeon.
Henry E. Hempstead,[3]	Chaplain.
First Lieut. John B. Collingwood,	Adjutant.
First Lieut. Joshua Norton, 3d,	Quartermaster.

NON-COMMISSIONED STAFF.

Henry S. Braden,	Sergeant-Major.
William W. Davis,	Quartermaster Sergeant.
John B. Pizer,	Commissary Sergeant.
John Hardy,	Hospital Steward.

MEMBERS OF STAFF

Appointed Subsequent to Date of Organization of the Regiment to Fill Vacancies, Whose Names Do Not Elsewhere Appear Upon the Rolls.

George King,[4]	Surgeon.
Robert E. Jameson,[5]	Assistant Surgeon.
Albert Wood,[6]	Assistant Surgeon.
James C. Bassett,[7]	Assistant Surgeon.
Gustavus P. Pratt,[8]	Assistant Surgeon.
Edgar L. Carr,[9]	Assistant Surgeon.

[1] Resigned.
[2] Promoted Surgeon, August 7, 1862. Discharged for disability, March 15, 1864.
[3] Appointed January 4, 1862.
[4] Mustered March 18, 1864. Discharged May 15, 1865.
[5] Mustered May 27, 1863. Discharged as Assistant Surgeon, July 29, 1864.
[6] Mustered July 31, 1862. Promoted to Surgeon First Mass. Regt. Cavalry, July 6, 1863.
[7] Mustered August 20, 1862. Resigned February 27, 1863.
[8] Mustered July 20, 1863. Transferred to Nineteenth Mass. Regt., Dec. 7, 1863.
[9] Mustered September 26, 1864. Expiration of term, July 29, 1865.

Note.—Promotions from Companies to the Field and Staff will be found on the Company rolls.—Author.

ROLL OF COMPANY A.

The following soldiers originally composed this Company, enlisted April 20, 1861, and were mustered into the United States service, May 21, 1861 :—

Thomas Wm. Clarke,[1]	Captain.	James Brent,	Private.
Joshua Norton, 3d,[2]	1st Lieut.	Malachi Coullahan,	"
John E. White,[3]	2d Lieut.	Joseph J. Crosby,	"
William W. Pray,[4]	1st Sergt.	Lawrence T. Chickey,	"
William W. Davis,[5]	Sergeant.	Henry Carson,	"
Albert H. De Costa,	"	John Cunningham,[8]	"
Albert N. Morin,	"	Hiram Cole,	"
Lysander A. Howard,	"	Thomas W. Cashman.[6]	"
Solomon B. Smith,[6]	Corporal.	Henry G. Chase,	"
William T. Hamer,[7]	"	Jeremiah J. Crowley,	"
Thomas Bacon,[6]	"	Barton De Costa,	"
William Coots,	"	Charles Dwinell,	"
Henry Alexander,	"	Daniel A. Dailey,	"
Charles T. Lovell,	"	Timothy D. Donovan,[3]	"
Charles H. Thayer,	"	Michael Edmands,	"
Horace Damrell,	"	Matthew T. Fitzpatrick,	"
Hiram B. Butler,	Musician.	Albert E. Frost,	"
James McGovern,	"	Thomas Foley,	"
Charles N. Drake,	Wagoner.	Levi B. Gaylord,[5]	"
Myron E. Alger,	Private.	Edward L. Gunnison,	"
Cornelius Ahern,	"	James Golden,	"
Alexander Bassett,	"	Charles D. Hodge,	"
Henry Blackstone,	"	John Hollihan,	"
Alexander T. Barri,	"	Conrad Homan,[4]	"
Edward C. Blossom,	"	John Hardy,[9]	"
Sylvester F. Blake,	"	Frank M. Hobart,	"
Tom Brooks,[6]	"	William M. Hobart,	"
Oscar H. Bassett,[8]	"	Thomas Hawes,[8]	"
Charles Bassett,[4]	"	Joseph E. Holbrook,	"
Albert Butler,	"	William Henry,[5]	"
Michael A. Brady,[8]	"	Richard Harney,[7]	"
David Bly,	"	Alanson K. Joslyn,	"

[1] Promoted to Colonel. [2] Appointed Assistant Quartermaster Volunteers.
[3] Resigned July 31, 1861. Captain Ninety-ninth New York Volunteers.
[4] Promoted to First Lieutenant. [5] Promoted to Second Lieutenant.
[6] Promoted to Sergeant. [7] Promoted to First Sergeant.
[8] Promoted to Corporal. [9] Promoted to Hospital Steward.

TWENTY-NINTH REGIMENT.   349

Henry C. Joslyn,[1].	Private.	Edward L. Pickard,		Private.
Holden Johnson,[2].	"	Isaac H. Perry,		"
Edward Kelley,	"	Henry P. Pitcher,		"
Joseph Leeds,[7]	"	Byron Rice,		"
James Lyman,[3]	"	Sandford M. Richardson,		"
Charles P. Locke,	"	Charles Ross,		"
Joseph McAlery,	"	George F. Simpson,		"
James McGlinchy,	"	John Sullivan,		"
John McCarthy,	"	Charles H. Shaw,		"
John W. McCarthy,[4]	"	John M. Sweeny,		"
Patrick Muldoon,[4]	"	John Scully,		"
Jeremiah Mahoney,[3]	"	David P. Scully,[6]		"
Martin C. Mullen,	"	Frederick C. Shaw,[4]		"
John W. Morse,	"	George G. Towne,		"
Edward O'Donnell,	"	George Thomas,[3]		"
Edward B. O'Donnell,	"	Charles Vaughan,		"
Daniel Owens,	"	Levi S. York,[3]		"
Dennis O'Connor,	"	George H. Wise,		"
Chandler H. Poud,[5]	"			

JOINED IN 1861 (July 31).

George H. Taylor,[1]   .   .   2d Lieut.

JOINED IN 1862.

Joseph J. Farrell,[2]   .   Private.   T. D. Sullivan,   .   .   Private.
Philip Sullivan,   .   .   "

JOINED IN 1863.

James L. West,   .   .   .   Private.

JOINED IN 1864.

Morris Connor,   .   .   Private. | Robert Grace,   .   Private.

[1] Promoted to Captain.
[2] Promoted to First Sergeant.
[3] Promoted to Sergeant.
[4] Promoted to Corporal.
[5] Promoted to Principal Musician.
[6] Promoted to First Lieutenant and Adjutant.
[7] Promoted to Commissary Sergeant.

ROLL OF COMPANY B.

The following soldiers originally composed this Company, enlisted April 18, 1861, and were mustered into the United States service, May 14, 1861 : —

Jonas K. Tyler,[1]	Captain.	John Hancock,	Private.
Samuel A. Bent,[1]	1st Lieut.	Lawrence Hayes,	"
Thomas H. Adams, 2d,[2]	2d Lieut.	Frank Hall,	"
Walter Frost,[2]	1st Sergt.	Thomas Hayes,	"
Emery Hodgkins,	Sergeant.	Dennis Hanley,	"
James Freel,	"	James B. Johnson,	"
Benjamin B. Brown,[4]	"	Thomas Kelley,	"
Joseph L. Mitchell,[5]	Corporal.	Delevan Kimball,	"
Warren Goodwin,[6]	"	John J. Lynch,	"
Charles F. Bowen,	"	John Lucas,[6]	"
William Gray,	"	Mathias Leonard,[8]	"
William H. Baker,	Musician.	Henry Lynch,	"
John D. Atkinson,	Private.	George Mahann,	"
Ira D. Bryant,	"	William H. Mosher,[5]	"
George Barnes,	"	Martin Minton,	"
Stephen H. Caverly,	"	Patrick Moran,	"
John Clark,	"	Charles McNulty,	"
Harrison C. Campbell,	"	William H. Murphy,	"
Thomas Cruse,	"	Theobald M. O'Brien,[5]	"
Michael Dorgan,	"	Thomas S. O'Brien,	"
John Donnelly,[7]	"	Thomas O'Dell,	"
Stephen H. Egan,	"	John Riley,	"
Patrick F. Feeney,	"	John D. Ratchford,	"
Richard R. Furbush,	"	John G. St. Clair,	"
Thomas Finnerty,	"	John H. Hodder,	"
Lyford J. Gilman,	"	Charles F. Hearns,	"
William Graham,	"	Patrick Thompson,	"
William H. Goss,	"	John M. Thompson,	"
John Gordon,[7]	"	Otis S. Whiting,	"
Samuel Grant,	"	George S Whiting,	"
John Gallagher,	"		

JOINED IN JULY, 1861.

Israel N. Wilson,	Captain.	John B. Anderson,	Private.
Ezra Ripley,	1st Lieut.	George B. Andrews,[7]	"

[1] Resigned July 18, 1861.
[2] Mustered as Ensign. Promoted to First Lieutenant.
[3] Unjustly reported as a deserter.
[4] Promoted to Second Lieutenant.
[5] Promoted to Sergeant.
[6] Promoted to First Lieutenant.
[7] Promoted to Corporal.
[8] Promoted to First Sergeant.

Thomas Brady,[1]	Private.	George Hale,	Private.
William C. Babcock,[2]	"	Dan E. Higgins,[1]	"
James Brogan,	"	William Havilin,	"
William Baker,	"	Albert N. Johnson,	"
Henry W. Brigham,	"	Robert Little,	"
W. F. Britten,	"	Anthony La Rochelle,	"
Oscar F. Carleton,[1]	"	Timothy J. Mahony,	"
James Cable,[3]	"	Bernard Molino,	"
William Carlin,	"	James S. Messer,	"
Edward T. Collier,	"	Henry E. Magee,	"
Thomas Conway,	"	Edward J. O'Brien,[1]	"
Horace A. Dean,	"	Francis D. O'Riley,	"
William D. Emerson,	"	Aaron L. Pearsous,[2]	"
Timothy Fenton,	"	Philip Sullivan,	"
George H. Gammons,	"	John B. Smithers,[2]	"
C. E. Getchell,	"	Henry H. Savage,	"
Allen Hingston,[4]	"	Henry Tufts,[4]	"
Thomas Harris,	"	William Williams,	"
James Hill,	"		

Joined Later in 1861.

George O. Bent,[2]	Private.	John Holton,	Private.
John Bellam,	"	Joseph Kelly,	"
William S. Collins,[1]	"	Ward Locke,	"
James Campbell,	"	Thomas Manning,	"
Ezra A. Chase,[4]	"	Herman Marshall,	"
August Dickman,[1]	"	John J. O'Brien,	"
Stephen E. Flood,	"	James Read,	"
John B. Gravlin,[1]	"	James W. Shepard,	"
George F. Gorham,	"	William E. Short,	"
John Gorham,	"	John C. Stewart,	"
Foster Ham,	"		

Joined in 1862.

George W. Fairbanks,	Private.	John J. Ryan,	Private.

[1] Promoted to Corporal.
[2] Promoted to Sergeant.
[3] Appointed Musician.
[4] Transferred to U. S. Battery.

ROLL OF COMPANY C.

The following soldiers originally composed this Company, enlisted April 20, 1861, and were mustered into the United States service, May 22, 1861:—

Lebbeus Leach,	Captain.	Preston Hooper,[6]	Private.
Nathan D. Whitman,	1st Lieut.	James W. Harding,	"
Elisha S. Holbrook,[1]	2d Lieut.	Charles H. Hayden,[7]	"
Silas N. Grosvenor,	1st Sergt.	Damon Hoyt,	"
Thomas Conant, Jr.,[2]	Sergeant.	John A. Holmes,	"
George H. Morse,[3]	"	C. Francis Harlow,[8]	"
Joshua E. Hayward,	"	John S. Howard,	"
Francis M. Kingman,[4]	Corporal.	Emery Jaquith,	"
Alfred B. Cummings,[5]	"	James G. Johnson,	"
Levi Wright,	"	Charles E. Jordan,[6]	"
Lawrence V. Poole,	"	William H. Johnson,	"
Abner H. Holmes,	Musician.	William F. Keith,	"
Walter M. Holmes,	"	David H. Lincoln,	"
George W. Allen,[6]	Private.	Eugene A. Lincoln,	"
Thomas Arnold,	"	James H. Leonard,	"
James A. Bates,	"	Neil McMillan,[5]	"
Isaac N. Bourne,	"	William H. Morse,	"
Asa W. Bates,	"	Henry A. Osborne,	"
George D. Brown,	"	Edward S. Osborne,	"
Irving Bates,[6]	"	William H. Osborne,	"
Minot S. Curtis,[5]	"	Ebenezer H. Pratt,	"
John Conant,[6]	"	Edward P. Packard,[9]	"
Edward F. Drohan,	"	Horace A. Ripley,[5]	"
Charles Drake,	"	Wallace R. Ripley,	"
Benjamin F. Edson,	"	Joshua S. Ramsdell,	"
Curtis Eddy,	"	William F. Rounds,	"
George W. Fisher,	"	William W. Smith,	"
Henry M. Folsom,	"	William B. Smith,	"
Robert C. Fellows,[8]	"	John T. Sturtevant,	"
Henry K. Gould,[6]	"	Ira C. Shaw,[9]	"
Caleb L. Hudson, Jr.,	"	James W. Siddall,	"

[1] Mustered as Ensign.
[2] Promoted to Second Lieutenant.
[3] Promoted to Sergeant-Major.
[4] Promoted to Sergeant and Color-Sergeant.
[5] Promoted to Sergeant.
[6] Promoted to Corporal.
[7] Transferred to U. S. Battery.
[8] Promoted to First Sergeant.
[9] Appointed Musician.

TWENTY-NINTH REGIMENT.

Benjamin Siddall,	Private.	Charles C. Whitman,	Private.
Elijah H. Tolman,[1]	"	Nehemiah White,	"
Charles H. Turner,[1]	"	Thatcher P. Wright,	"
Daniel W. Tribou,[1]	"	Edward Williams,	"
Freedom Whitman,[1]	"	James E. White,	"
Asa W. Whitman,	"		

JOINED IN SEPTEMBER AND DECEMBER, 1861.

William B. Hathaway,	2d Lieut.	Harvey Lucas,	Private.
Algernon S. Brett,[2]	Private.	Edward P. Mansfield,	"
David Blakeman,	"	John M. Nason,	"
Marshall M. Chandler,	"	Alpheus Packard,	"
Thomas G. Clark,	"	Edmund T. Packard,[2]	"
James W. Cooper,[1]	"	John G. Sampson,	"
Elbridge R. Curtis,	"	Alonzo Sharp,	"
George R. Dyer,[3]	"	Hugh Stran,	"
Isaac W. Drinkwater,	"	Sylvanus Thomas,	"
Timothy W. Fisher,	"	Vernon M. Thompson,	"
Charles W. Flagg,	"	James L. Washburn,	"
Granville H. Gould,[4]	"	Herbert O. White,	"
Daniel W. Harding,	"	Cyrus L. Williams,	"
John C. Lambert,	"		

JOINED IN 1862.

Henry T. Manchester,[2]	Private.	Theodore C. Rodman,	Private.
Isaac H. Bates,	"	Patrick Frawley, 2d,	"
Rodney Churchill,	"	William J. Stanley,	"
Amos L. Dorr,	"		

[1] Promoted to Corporal.   [2] Promoted to Sergeant.
[3] Promoted to First Sergeant and Brevet Second Lieutenant.
[4] Appointed Bugler.

ROLL OF COMPANY D.

The following soldiers originally composed this Company, enlisted April 20, 1861, and were mustered into the United States service, May 22, 1861: —

Charles Chipman,[1]	Captain.	Benjamin Fuller, .	Private.
Charles Brady,[2] .	1st Lieut.	John H. Gray,	"
Henry A. Kern,[3] .	2d Lieut.	James M. Getchell,	"
William Stuart, .	1st Sergt.	James Guiney,	"
James H. Atherton,[4]	Sergeant.	John Gordon,	"
William H. Woodward,	"	Samuel W. Hunt, .	"
Edward Brady, .	"	Alden P. Hathaway,	"
David B. Coleman,	Corporal.	Charles Harkins, .	"
George F. Bruce,[5] .	"	Michael Heslin, .	"
Benjamin H. Hamlin,[6] .	"	James H. Heald, .	"
William Breese, .	"	David A. Hoxie,[6] .	"
George E. Crocker,[7]	Musician.	Charles H. Hoxie,	"
Christopher B. Dalton,	"	Zenas H. Hoxie, .	"
George W. Badger,	Private.	Samuel N. Haskins,	"
Gustavus A. Badger, .	"	Charles E. Jones, .	"
James Ball, .	"	William D. James,	"
John T. Collins,[7] .	"	David S. Keen, .	"
James Cox,[9] .	"	Martin L. Kern, Jr.,[9] .	"
James Cook, .	"	Patrick Long, .	"
Patrick Clancy, .	"	Peter McNulty, .	"
Thomas W. Chapman, .	"	John McAlaney, .	"
Alfred Cheval, .	"	William McDermont, .	"
John Campbell, .	"	Michael McKenna,[9]	"
Thomas F. Darby,[10] .	"	Patrick McElroy, .	"
Timothy G. Dean, .	"	Isaac H. Phinney, .	"
Warren P. Dean, .	"	Peter Russell, .	"
Edward Donnelly,[9] .	"	Caleb T. Robbins, .	"
Joseph W. Eaton, .	"	Philip Russell, .	"
Perez Eldridge, .	"	William J. Smith,[11] .	"
John Fagan, .	"	Francis C. Swift, .	"

[1] Promoted to Major.   [2] Promoted to Captain.
[3] Mustered as Ensign. Promoted to First Lieutenant.
[4] Promoted to First Lieutenant.   [5] Promoted to Hospital Steward U. S. A.
[6] Promoted to Sergeant.   [7] Promoted to Principal Musician.
[8] Commissioned Lieutenant-Colonel U. S. Colored Troops.
[9] Promoted to Corporal.   [10] Promoted to Second Lieutenant.
[11] Wrongly reported as a deserter. Entered United States navy, and received an honorable discharge.

TWENTY-NINTH REGIMENT.

Martin S. Tinkham,	. Private.	John Woods,	.	. Private.
Joseph Turner,	. . "	Francis Woods,	.	. "
Charles G. Wright,	. "	William H. Woods,	.	"
Anderson Wright,	. "	James H. Woods,	.	"
John Weeks,	. . " .	James Ward,	.	. "

JOINED IN JANUARY, 1862.

Augustus D. Ayling,[1]	. 2d Lieut.	James G. B. Haines,	. Private.
Frank G. Bumpus,	. Private.	Joseph J. C. Madigan,[1]	"
Nathaniel F. Ford,	. "	Edmund L. Pray, .	. "
Andrew Gaffney,	. "		

[1] Promoted to First Lieutenant.

356   ROSTER OF THE

ROLL OF COMPANY E.

The following soldiers originally composed this Company, enlisted May 6, 1861, and were mustered into the United States service, May 22, 1861:—

Samuel H. Doten,[1]	Captain.	Timothy E. Gay, .	Private.
John B. Collingwood,[2]	1st Lieut.	Thomas W. Hayden,[6]	"
Thomas A. Mayo,[3]	2d Lieut.	James S. Holbrook,[5]	"
Edward L. Robbins,	1st Sergt.	Orrin D. Holmes,[5]	"
Horace A. Jenks,[4]	Sergeant.	Seth L. Holmes, .	"
John M. Atwood, .	"	Samuel H. Harlow,[6]	"
George S. Morey, .	"	William H. Howland, .	"
Peter Winsor,[4]	Corporal.	John F. Hall,[6]	"
Benjamin F. Bumpus, .	"	Alexander Haskins,	"
Ichabod C. Fuller,[5]	"	Henry W. Kimball,[5]	"
Samuel D. Thrasher, .	"	Thomas P. Mullen,	"
Charles Atwood, .	Private.	Charles E. Merriam, .	"
Columbus Adams,	"	William R. Middleton, .	"
John K. Alexander,[6]	"	Lemuel B. Morton,[6]	"
Winslow C. Barnes,	"	William Morey, .	"
Antonio Beytes, .	"	Isaac Morton, Jr.,	"
Nathaniel Burgess,[7]	"	John E. Morrison,	"
Moses S. Barnes,[6] .	"	John A. Morse, .	"
Simeon H. Barrows,	"	William T. Nickerson, .	"
Ellis D. Barnes, .	"	George F. Pierce, .	"
George E. Burbank,	"	Seth W. Paty,[6]	"
George F. Bradford,	"	William H. Pittee,	"
Andrew Blanchard,	"	John H. Pember, .	"
Charles C. Barnes,	"	Otis W. Phinney, .	"
Lawrence R. Blake,	"	Henry H. Robbins,	"
Cornelius Bradford,	"	Albert R. Robbins,	"
Sylvanus L. Churchill, .	"	Winslow B. Standish,[6] .	"
Thomas Collingwood,[6] .	"	Albert Simmons, .	"
Barnabas Dunham,	"	Frank H. Simmons,	"
Henry F. Eddy, .	"	Miles Standish,	"
Philander Freeman,	"	William Swift, .	"
William P. Goodwin,[6] .	"	John Shannon,[4]	"

[1] Promoted to Brevet Major.
[2] Appointed Adjutant.
[3] Mustered as Ensign.
[4] Promoted to Second Lieutenant.
[5] Promoted to Sergeant.
[6] Promoted to Corporal.
[7] Promoted to First Lieutenant.

TWENTY-NINTH REGIMENT. 357

Patrick Smith,	. Private.	Alfred B. Warner,[2]	. Private.
James E. Stillman,	. "	John Washburn,	. "
Walter Thompson,	. "	David Williams,	. "
Frank A. Thomas,	. "	Joseph B. Whiting,	. "
Francis H. Vaughan,	. "	Samuel C. Wright,[1]	. "
Leander M. Vaughan,	. "	William Williams,	. "
George E. Wadsworth,[1]	"		

Joined in 1862.

Benjamin F. Bates,	. Private.	Justus W. Harlow,	. Private.
Thomas Burt,	. "	Charles Kleinhans,	. "
Patrick Cain,	. "	George H. Partridge,	. "
Elisha S. Doten,	. "	George S. Peckham,[2]	. "
Edwin R. Eaton,	. "	James L. Pettis,	. "
Charles A. Faunce,	. "	Charles E. Tillson,	. "
Edwin H. Hosmer,	. "	Albert C. Wilson,	. "

[1] Promoted to Sergeant.   [2] Promoted to Corporal.

ROSTER OF THE

ROLL OF COMPANY F.

The following soldiers originally composed this Company, enlisted in the autumn of 1861, and were mustered into the United States service, December 30, 1861: —

Willard D. Tripp,[1]	Captain.	Leander W. Caswell,	Private.
John A. Sayles,	1st Lieut.	Linus E. Caswell,[4]	"
Thomas H. Husband,[2]	2d Lieut.	Leander Clapp,	"
Joseph O'Neil,[2]	1st Sergt.	Hugh D. Conaty,	"
Robert Clifford,	Sergeant.	Joseph Davis,	"
Charles S. Packard,	"	Benjamin F. Dean,	"
Bela H. King,[2]	"	Charles Dolan,	"
George D. Williams,[3]	"	James Dugan,	"
George W. Child,	Corporal.	Philip Dennehy,[9]	"
George E. Westgate,	"	Charles Dunn,	"
Lyman N. Caswell,[4]	"	Thomas Dixon,	"
Arthur Clifford,	"	Alonzo Garvin,	"
John N. Perry,	"	Michael Geary,	"
Stephen Hodgkins,	"	Benjamin T. Godfrey,	"
Baylies R. Chase,	"	John Goodwin,[7]	"
William H. Phillips,[5]	"	Peter Harrington,	"
Ira Bryant,	Musician.	John Harvey,[10]	"
James Booth,	"	Ephraim Haskell,	"
George A. Alexander,	Private.	Martin V. Haskell,[7]	"
James Black,	"	William Haskell,	"
Edward Belcher,	"	Timothy Hayes,[11]	"
Darius Bonny,[6]	"	Albert D. Hunt,	"
Philip H. Borden,	"	Otis S. Hewatt,	"
Charles G. Bosworth,[2]	"	Martin F. Jefferson,	"
Alexander Brickell,	"	John Kelly,	"
David P. Brooks,	"	John Kearvin,	"
Kendall Brooks,	"	Martin Lackore,	"
George W. Brown,[7]	"	William Lang,	"
George W. Burns,	"	Charles Logue,	"
Joseph Boyden,[5]	"	John McCarty,	"

[1] Promoted to Lieutenant-Colonel. [2] Promoted to First Lieutenant.
[3] Promoted to Captain. [4] Transferred to U. S. Battery.
[5] Promoted to Second Lieutenant. [6] Appointed Musician.
[7] Promoted to Corporal. [8] Promoted to First Sergeant.
[9] Transferred to Veteran Reserve Corp. [10] Wounded June 17, 1864. Lost an arm.
[11] Promoted to Sergeant.

TWENTY-NINTH REGIMENT.

Owen McMannus,	. Private.	Solomon H. Smith,	. Private.
James McQuillan,[1]	. "	Charles Stone,	. . "
Thomas Murphy,[2]	. "	Benjamin F. Stowell,	. "
Timothy O'Sullivan,	. "	John Sullivan,	. . "
George Pierce,	. . "	Edward W. Tarbox,	. "
Lewis R. Pierce,	. "	Leander Tripp,	. . "
James Pittsley,	. . "	Silas Townsend,	. . "
William Pittsley,	. . "	George Townsend,[4]	. "
Edward Ratigan,	. . "	William H. Tyndal,[5]	. "
Granville T. Records,	. "	George W. Welch,[3]	. "
Culbert Reynolds,	. "	Cornelius Westgate,	. "
Charles E. Robertson,[3]	. "	Elisha Westgate,	. . "
Mason Rogers,	. . "	Elisha B. Westgate,	. "
Thomas Rooney,	. . "	John Westgate,	. . "
Joseph Short,	. . "	Joseph L. Westgate,	. "
James S. Sherman,	. "	Preserved Westgate,	. "
Francis H. Simmons,	. "	Oliver A. White,	. . "
James Simmons,	. . "	Edward Wilbur,	. . "
James W. Smith,	. . "	John Wragg,	. . "
Preston O. Smith,	. "		

JOINED IN 1862.

John Booth,	. . . Private.	Albert R. Pittsley,	. Private.
William H. Burns,[6]	. "	Henry W. Pettee,	. "
Joseph Hamer,	. . "	Edward H. Pierce,	. "
Abraham Haskell,	. "	John B. Pizer,[1]	. . "
Henry L. Hill,	. "	Joseph Westgate,	. "
Michael Mahoney,	. "		

JOINED IN 1863.

David Cohn, . . . Private.

JOINED IN 1864.

James Liflin, . . . Private.

[1] Promoted to Captain.
[2] Wounded at White Oak Swamp, June 30, 1862.
[3] Promoted to Corporal.
[4] Promoted to Sergeant.
[5] Promoted to Corporal, and made Color-Corporal.
[6] Promoted to First Lieutenant.

ROLL OF COMPANY G.

The following soldiers originally composed this Company, enlisted in the autumn of 1861, and were mustered into the United States service, December 31, 1861 :—

Charles T. Richardson,[1]	Captain.	Hiram F. Chace, .	. Private.
Freeman A. Taber, .	1st Lieut.	Edward Carney, .	. "
Charles D. Browne,[2]	. 2d Lieut.	Henry Campbell,[6]	. "
George W. Pope,[3] .	. 1st Sergt.	James F. Clark, .	. "
Charles A. Carpenter,[4] .	Sergeant.	Lafayette W. Carpenter,	"
A. Baylies Richmond, .	"	Patrick Cullen, .	. "
Robert L. Watts, .	"	Charles W. Clifford, .	. "
James C. Allen, .	"	Francis Clark,[7] .	. "
Lemuel Capen, .	. Corporal.	Albert Cobbett, .	. "
George D. Hodges, .	"	William E. Cobbett, .	. "
Joseph Bunker, .	"	George C. Cobbett, .	. "
Ephraim E. Follett,[5] .	"	James H. Cram, .	. "
Charles D. Hodge, .	"	Charles Debelino, .	. "
Ebenezer Fisk,[6] .	"	Joseph Duxbury, .	. "
Edward W. Greene, .	"	George E. Darling,[2]	. "
Robert E. Harris, .	"	Patrick Duffy, .	. "
Samuel A. Wilkinson, .	Musician.	Willard Drake, .	. "
John F. W. Clark, .	"	Thomas W. Dean,[8]	. "
James H. Ladd, .	. Wagoner.	Edmund Davis, .	. "
Henry Austin, .	. Private.	Elijah H. Esty, .	. "
Daniel B. Blaisdell, .	"	John Field, .	. "
Joseph Baker, .	"	Albert E. Follett, .	. "
Robert Burns, .	"	Henry H. Fairbanks, .	. "
George W. Burnham, .	"	Solomon R. Foster, .	. "
William Brophy, .	"	Barney Galligar, .	. "
John Bartlett, .	"	Charles B. Griffin, .	. "
William A. Burrill, .	"	William H. Hudson, .	. "
Joseph Bosell, .	"	Henry Ide,[9] .	. "
Nelson Cook, .	"	Talbot Jenks, Jr., .	. "
Charles N. Cotton, .	"	Daniel A. Jillson,[3]	. "

[1] Promoted to Major.
[2] Promoted to Lieutenant-Colonel.
[3] Promoted to First Lieutenant.
[4] Promoted to Captain.
[5] Promoted to Second Lieutenant.
[6] Promoted to Sergeant.
[7] Reported "Absent without leave," but he afterwards returned to duty.
[8] Wrongly reported as a deserter; received an honorable discharge.
[9] Wrongly reported as a deserter.

TWENTY-NINTH REGIMENT.

Roger Kennedy, .	. Private.	Albert W. Smith,[4]	. Private.
Patrick McManimay, .	"	George W. Sprague, .	"
Daniel H. Morey, .	"	Orange S. Stearns,[5]	"
George E. Miller, .	"	George E. Snow, .	"
Patrick McLoughlin,[1] .	"	Charles H. Smith,	"
Lorenzo Macomber, .	"	John Thayer, .	"
Richard Owen, .	"	Nathaniel I. Thurber, .	"
John O'Neil,[2] .	"	Levi Trumbull, .	"
Henry J. Paine, .	"	Henry B. Titus,[6] .	"
Hiram Porter, .	"	Thomas Ward, .	"
Minot E. Phillips, .	"	Daniel Whitmore,[7]	"
James P. Parker, .	"	Roland T. J. White, .	"
William H. Perry, .	"	Cornelius L. White, .	"
Nelson N. Randall, .	"	Henry Walker, .	"
Franklin L. Ramsell,[3] .	"	James Wood, .	"
William B. Richards, .	"		

JOINED IN 1862.

Charles M. Dunn,[6]	. Private.	Charles F. Roberts,[8]	. Private.
Albert Lincoln,[3] .	"		

JOINED IN 1864.

Wesley L. Beals, .	. Private.	John Cronin,[9] .	. Private.
George Burns, .	"	Philip P. Lawall, .	"

[1] Did not desert as reported.
[2] Received an honorable discharge; wrongly reported as a deserter.
[3] Promoted to Second Lieutenant.   [4] Improperly reported as a deserter.
[5] Promoted to First Lieutenant.   [6] Promoted to Sergeant.
[7] Promoted to Corporal.
[8] These two soldiers enlisted in the autumn of 1861; but were rejected, as being too young, by Captain Ames, U. S. A. Mustering Officer. They were taken as orderlies by Colonel Pierce to Newport News, and afterwards, by his order, placed on the rolls of Company G.   [9] Killed March 25, 1865; Fort Stedman.

ROLL OF COMPANY H.

The following soldiers originally composed this Company, enlisted in the autumn of 1861, and were mustered into the United States service, January 13, 1862:—

Henry R. Sibley,[1] .	. Captain.	James Culter, .	. Private.
Daniel W. Lee,[2] .	. 1st Lieut.	John H. Clark, .	. "
William R. Corlew,	. 2d Lieut.	William Coakley,.	. "
T. W. Wrightington,	. 1st Sergt.	Edward E. Dearing,	. "
Ansel B. Kellam, .	. Sergeant.	Theodore W. Dearing,[7]	"
George H. Long,[2] .	. "	Edward L. Daniels,	. "
William F. Pippey,[3]	. "	Jacob H. Dow, Jr.,	. "
Charles F. Colburn,[4]	. "	Chris. C. Eldridge, Jr.,	"
George Merritt, .	. Corporal.	Obed H. Ellis, .	. "
William F. Willis,[5]	. "	Daniel C. Easton,[5]	. "
Edward M. Hastings, .	"	William P. Farnsworth,[3]	"
Lorenzo L. Billings,[6]	. "	Henry W. Fuller,.	. "
Joseph Dominick,	. "	William H. Gould, Jr.,	"
George Curtis, .	. . "	John H. Galloway,	. "
Waldo F. Corbett,[6]	. "	Rufus H. Gurney,.	. "
Robert F. Greenough, .	"	Joseph P. Gardner,	. "
Alonzo F. Howe, .	. Musician.	Malvin Gear, .	. "
James A. Forbes,.	. "	Albert E. Gear, .	. "
George C. Wheeler,	. Wagoner.	Richard Gurney,[5] .	. "
Charles H. Almeder,	. Private.	John H. Hancock,[5]	. "
John H. Aldrich, .	. "	Albert A. Hill, .	. "
Lyman H. Bigelow,	. "	Alanson S. Howe,[5]	. "
Edwin F. Bassett,	. "	William E. Hadlock, .	"
George G. Brigham,	. "	John F. Hoit, .	. "
David Barnes, .	. "	Benjamin F. Hall,	. "
Ezra C. Bemis, .	. "	William Keith, .	. "
Charles W. Bates,	. "	Ira W. Keyes,[9] .	. "
Nathaniel L. Battles, .	"	George H. Leman,	. "
Jeremiah Barnett,	. "	Edward L. Loveland, .	"
Charles E. Brown,	. "	Henry O. Lawrence,	. "
Edwin C. Bemis,[5] .	. "	William Henry Lee,	. "
Eben B. Clifford, .	. "	Ephraim Lucas, .	. "
Edward A. Clark,	. "	William McGill, .	. "

[1] Promoted to Colonel U. S. Volunteers.   [2] Promoted to Captain.
[3] Promoted to Second Lieutenant.   [4] Promoted to First Sergeant.
[6] Promoted to Sergeant.   [7] Transferred to U. S. Cavalry.
[6] Commissioned in U. S. Colored Troops.
[5] Erroneously reported as a deserter; was wounded at White Oak Swamp, and received an honorable discharge.   [9] Promoted to Corporal.

TWENTY-NINTH REGIMENT.

John E. McDonald,	. Private.	John H. Spear,	.	. Private.
John C. Martin, .	. "	Artemus Sylvester,	.	"
Daniel McDonald, Jr.,.	"	Silas S. Smith,	.	"
Nathaniel S. Mellon, .	"	George W. Smith,	.	"
James Neville, .	. "	Joseph Staples,	.	"
Charles L. Nightingale,[1]	"	John F. Smith,[5]	.	"
Daniel B. Perkins, Jr.,.	"	Timothy Sullivan,	.	"
Frederick Peabody,	. "	George W. Swain,	.	"
John S. Pulsifer, .	. "	Henry A. Stephens,	.	"
Henry Proctor, .	. "	John Schow,	.	"
Horace H. Packard,	. "	Isaac H. Taylor,[2] .		"
Darius Perry,	. "	John B. Thomas, .		"
Albert H. Prouty,	. "	George L. Woodbury,	.	"
Lewis Prescott, . .	"	Chris. H. Westphal,	.	"
George S. Preble,.	. "	Jacob W. Wasch,	.	"
John S. Robinson,[2]	"	Ebenezer Whiting,	.	"
Alonzo C. Richardson,[3]	"	Charles Young, .		"
Thomas H. Sylvester,[4] .	"			

JOINED IN 1862.

Etheridge Bryant,	. Private.	Mathew Kerwin, .		. Private.
Abel W. Burroughs,	. "	Ira F. Martin,	.	"
Patrick Boland, .	. "	William McGaughlin,	.	"
George A. Bryant,	. "	Franklin J. Noyes,	.	"
Edward Carroll, .	. "	William O'Conner,	.	"
Caleb Clark,.	. "	George B. Perkins,	.	"
Ira W. Clark,	. "	Bernard Rooney, .	.	"
Nathaniel Cobb, .	. "	William Story,	.	"
Joshua G. Fuller,.	. "	James E. Sanborn,	.	"
Charles J. Hale, .	. "	John Usherwood,.	.	"
Michael Harrington,	. "	Francis Wyman, .	.	"
William Jones, .	. "	George S. Welsh, .	.	"

JOINED IN 1864.

Henry A. Glines, . . . Private.

[1] Promoted to First Lieutenant.
[2] Promoted to Corporal.
[3] Promoted to Quartermaster Sergeant.
[4] Erroneously reported as a deserter.
[5] Promoted to Sergeant.

ROLL OF COMPANY I.

The following soldiers originally composed this Company, enlisted April 17, 1861, and were mustered into the United States service, May 14, 1861 :—

Wm. D. Chamberlain,	Captain.	Charles S. Dow,	Private.
Abram A. Oliver,[1]	1st Lieut.	John C. Dow,	"
John E. Smith,[2]	2d Lieut.	Joseph A. Dow,	"
William H. Burns,	1st Sergt.	John A. Durgin,	"
Elbridge G. Kemp,	Sergeant.	George W. Forsyth,	"
John W. Barnicoat,	"	George P. Fowler, Jr.,	"
Aaron O. Atwill,	"	Thomas S. Glass,	"
Frank Goodwin,[3]	Corporal.	Lucius B. Grover,	"
Gardner Parker,	"	William P. Green,	"
Henry E. Hay,	"	Daniel Gould,	"
Nathaniel J. Downing,	"	John H. Hall,	"
Alvin Moulton,[4]	Musician.	George H. Hammond,	"
Samuel L. Eaton,	"	Charles E. Harris,	"
William H. Adams,	Private.	Alonzo Hollis,	"
Thomas Ashcroft,	"	George Horton,	"
George W. Armstead,	"	George W. Jewett,	"
Joseph M. Badger,	"	Joseph W. Knights,	"
Charles I. Betton,	"	David Lee,	"
William W. Bowman,	"	George A. Lindsey,	"
Augustus A. Blaney,	"	Joseph A. Millett,	"
Charles C. Bonner,	"	John B. Moulton,[5]	"
George L. Brown,	"	Solomon Moulton,	"
James L. Brown,	"	John S. Miller,	"
Charles A. Carroll,	"	James W. Noyes,	"
Joseph P. Caldwell,	"	Jacob Phillips,	"
Isaac H. Childs,	"	William Phillips,	"
William Chesley,	"	Thomas Pickett,	"
Charles Chamberlain,	"	Edmond C. Poland,	"
Edward F. Chase,	"	Elbridge M. Rawson,	"
John H. Cummings,	"	George H. Rich,	"
Willard P. Dailey,	"	Curtis S. Rand,[5]	"
James G. Dearmid,	"	Clifford I. Rogers,	"
Charles Dodge,	"	George Seeley,	"

[1] Promoted to Captain.
[2] Mustered as Ensign.
[3] Promoted to Second Lieutenant.
[4] Promoted to Corporal.
[5] Promoted to Sergeant.

John H. Shaw, . . Private.	George Townsend,[2]	. Private.
David A. Swan, . . "	Benjamin E. Thompson,	"
William R. Swan, . "	William K. Williams, .	"
James M. Swan, . . "	Isaac O. Willey, . .	"
George Sullivan, . . "	Addison B. Young, .	"
Andrew H. Tarr,[1]. . "		

Joined in 1862.

Walter A. Kezar,[2] . Private.	Oliver H. P. Doak,	. Private.
Edward G. Bachelder, . "	Orrin Fields, . .	"
John Q. Bachelder, . "	Benjamin S. Gardner, .	"
Thomas R. Bartol, . "	James F. Goodwin, .	"
Ira A. Clark, . . "	Charles F. Gove, . .	"
Frederick A. Clark, . "	Eben T. Heath, . .	"
Melvin F. Clough, . "	Joseph A. Short, . .	"
Tennison P. Collins, . "	Lyman B Williams, .	"
Andrew Dinsmore, . "		

Joined in 1863.

Harvey G. Smith, . . . Private.

[1] Killed at Malvern Hill, Va., July 1, 1862. [2] Promoted to Sergeant.

ROLL OF COMPANY K.

The following soldiers originally composed this Company, enlisted April 20, 1861. and were mustered into the United States service, May 22, 1861 :—

Joseph H. Barnes,[1]	Captain.	John E. Fisher,	Private.
James H. Osgood, Jr.,[2].	1st Lieut.	Frederick A. Godbold,.	"
William T. Keen,[3]	2d Lieut.	Isaac S. Hill,	"
William Pray,[2]	1st Sergt.	James T. Holmes,	"
Henry S. Braden,[4]	Sergeant.	Abiel R. Henry,	"
Francis J. Cole,	"	William H. Howe,[8]	"
James N. Greenwood,	"	Richard Howes,	"
Henry A. Hunting,[5]	Corporal.	Joseph F. Hooper,	"
David Warren, Jr.,[6]	"	Nathaniel J. Huntress,	"
John B. Keen,[6]	"	John R. Hume,	"
George R. Rumney,[7]	"	Freeman Hall,	"
Jason L. Blodgett,	Private.	Thomas W. Kenny,	"
Edward Boston, Jr.,	"	Benjamin Loveland,[6]	"
Robert M. Blackhall,[9]	"	Abijah Lane,	"
Loring Baker,[9]	"	Gilbert T. Litchfield,[9]	"
Thomas M. Bride,	"	Augustus Leavitt,	"
John P. Burbeck,[5]	"	Charles H. Leavitt,	"
John F. M. Burk,	"	John A. Linnell,[6]	"
James Brownlow,	"	William P. Lander,[9]	"
William R. Barker,	"	Charles Laslie,	"
Horace Colby,	"	John A. McKie,	"
John H. Crafts,	"	William McAllister,	"
John L. Chapman,	"	Jesse Morris,	"
Benjamin L. Clark,	"	William McFarland,	"
William G. Chambers,	"	Hiram A. Mosher,[9]	"
Henry F. Creighton,[10]	"	Samuel F. G. Newton,	"
Edgar Curry,	"	Frederick G. Parsons,	"
David Dockerty,	"	Meltiah T. Remick,	"
Charles A. Daggett,[7]	"	Elisha Ranks,	"
Joseph Drugan,	"	Charles Ramsell,	"
Andrew P. Fisher,	"	Henry E. Stewart,	"
Alonzo B. Fisk,[9]	"	William W. Sanborn,	"

[1] Promoted to Brevet Brigadier-General. [2] Promoted to Captain.
[3] Mustered as Ensign. Promoted to First Lieutenant.
[4] Promoted to First Lieutenant and Adjutant.
[5] Promoted to Second Lieutenant. [6] Promoted to Sergeant.
[7] Promoted to First Sergeant. [8] Promoted to First Lieutenant.
[9] Promoted to Corporal. [10] Sergeant in Howard's U. S. Battery.

Joseph K. Stafford, . Private.	Charles Walker, .	Private.
John Tierney, . . "	George Wright, . .	"
John A. Tighe,[1] . . "	Charles H. Winslow, .	"
Ezra Vinal, Jr.,[2] . . "	George Wood, . .	"
Benjamin F. Valpey, . "	George P. Woodis, .	"

Joined in 1861.

John Ewart,[3] . . Private.	Alexander McKinnan, .	Private.
John B. Hibbert, . . "	Joseph S. Manning, .	"

Joined in 1862.

Joseph A. Brown, . Private.	John Moore, Jr.,[4] . .	Private.
Martin Bird, . . "	James H. Powers, .	"
Thomas F. Dolan, . "	Theodore S. Robinson, .	"
James A. Fisher, . . "	Nelson H. Snow, . .	"
Joshua Grimes, . . "	J. Sturgis Wright, .	"
Joseph H. Locke, . . "		

Joined in 1863.

Sydenham Dumington, . . Private.

Joined in 1864.

William H. Moore, . . . Private.

---

[1] Promoted to Sergeant and Color-Sergt. [2] Promoted to Corporal.
[3] Promoted to Second Lieutenant. [4] Promoted to Sergeant.

A list of soldiers whose names are not borne upon the foregoing rolls, some of whom are known to have served, and others are reported as having served in the Twenty-ninth Regiment for short periods during the last few months of the war :—

Jeremiah Austin.	James Doherty.	Napoleon Mason.
Otto Beyer.	George Eaton.	Henry Moonshine.
John Brown.	Martin Esk.	Daniel Murphy.
Patrick Boyle.	John Easy.[2]	Patrick Murphy.
Gerhard Briggerman.[1]	Francis Flora.	Joseph Miller.
John P. Brennan.	Louis Fruger.	Robert Nelson.[2]
William Barrett.	Frederick Graven.	Alexander O'Brien.
Larin R. Curtis.	Frederick Gradholf.	James O'Bierne.
Maurice Cronin.	Joseph F. Glass.	Leopold Obreiter.
John Conly.	Edward Hazen.	Manuel Portello.
William Cunningham.	Christian Holdt.	William H. Phillips.
Morris Collin.	David Hannaford.	Isaac Patton.
William Claman.[2]	John H. Harbourne.	Henry Rose.
Francis Cassidy.	Michael Hilly.[2]	Frank A. Roberts.
William Chapman.	William Klinker.[4]	Charles E. Robertson.[1]
Maurice Christian.	David Labonne.	Andrew J. Rider.
William Coulter.	John G. Moore.	John Raftes.
Peter Doherty.	Michael McFarland.	Henry J. Sweet, Jr.
Parker Dwight.	Louis Monplaiser.	Hezekiah S. Sargent.[5]
Otto Duger.[3]	James McLaughlin.	John Smith.
William Doody.	Herman Meier.	Emile Taubert.[6]
Jeremiah Dwyer.	Thomas Mooney.	George Townsend.
Thomas Dyer.	Ruter Moritz.[4]	Eli Wigglesworth.

[1] Corporal. [2] Discharged by order of War Department.
[3] Sergeant; discharged by order of War Deparement.
[4] Killed March 25, 1865.
[5] Died of wounds, January 2, 1865. [6] Died February 13, 1865, of disease.

THE DEAD.

"True to their Country and God,
To meet at the last reveille."

NOTE.

In deciding what names should appear upon the rolls of the dead, I adopted this rule, which is that of the Pension Department in the matter of granting pensions: First, those who died in the service from disease, wounds, or injuries contracted while in the service and in the line of their duties as soldiers; second, those who died after their discharge from the service, of disease, wounds, or injuries contracted while in the service and in the line of their duties as soldiers.

I feel confident that the following rolls, under the rule mentioned, give the names of all the regiment's dead, and that the name of no soldier appears upon them which ought not to be stated, though I regret that in several instances I have not been able to give the place and date of death.

Having had access to the rolls of the dead prepared by the Quartermaster-General of the United States Army, I have made a careful search for the names of all members of the regiment borne on these lists, and where I have been able to find their place of burial have stated it opposite their names, hoping that the information may not only prove comforting but useful to their friends and relatives.

The several company rolls of the dead show a total of one hundred and seventy-three, including the Chaplain. Of these, twenty-two only found a Christian burial at their homes; thirty-five are shown to have been identified and buried in National Cemeteries; leaving one hundred and sixteen who rest, and probably must forever rest, in unknown graves. All of the comrades, five in number, who died at Andersonville, Ga., were identified, and their graves suitably marked by a marble block; but the name of comrade Theodore W. Dearing of Company H, who fell a victim to the filth and exposure at Salisbury, is not found in the long list of 3,538 Union soldiers buried at that place. Such is also the case of Minot E. Phillips and Levi Trumbull of Company H, who suffered martyrdom at Belle Isle, Va., and Isaac S. Hill of Company K, at Florence, S. C. The facts in regard to the management of the three last-named prison-pens relieves one of all wonder at not finding the name of the soldier for which he may be searching. Over 5,000 Union soldiers were orginally buried at Salisbury, in thirteen long trenches, "without coffins or boxes, and without any means of identifying them (except sixteen belonging to the Masonic Fraternity), ...
. . . . who died while confined in the Salisbury prison and in the hospitals near the 'stockade,' during the Rebellion. The burial of these soldiers in so inhuman a manner was done by one Sergeant Harris, under the orders of Major Gee, both of the rebel army. Out of nine or

ten thousand soldiers confined there, over five thousand fell victims to the cruelty of the Rebels then in charge, by starvation and disease."*

As further showing how the rules of civilized warfare were disregarded by the enemy, Major Dana, who makes the above report, says, that in the Lutheran Cemetery, near the principal prison-pen, were buried fourteen Union soldiers, "who, upon taking the oath of allegiance to the Rebel Government, were admitted into the Rebel hospital, where they afterwards died." It seems by this, that the only way by which a Union prisoner at this loathsome and accursed place could secure the medical treatment which common humanity would extend even to a savage, was by forswearing allegiance to his Government. Among the unfortunate fourteen, however, not one belonged to the Twenty-ninth regiment.

The grave of William H. Murphy of Company B, and that of Sergeant Wm. T. Hamer of Company A, who were killed in the battle of Spottsylvania, May 12, 1864, and buried on the field under the names of "William Murphy" and "William H. Hamer," were found, and their bodies afterwards removed to the National Cemetery at Fredericksburg, Va. None of the other members of the regiment killed in that battle were found and recognized by those who gathered up the dead for burial. This is not in the least surprising, for the sad words, "Unknown United States Soldier," were placed upon the headboards of many hundreds who fell on that bloody field. Large numbers who were killed in this battle were not buried at all until General Sherman marched through the country in May, 1865, when an agreement to that effect was made by that officer with one Mr. Sandford, who resided near Spottsylvania Court-house. "It was no unusual occurrence" says Assistant-Quartermaster Moore of the United States Army, who had charge of the work of removing the dead from this place, "to observe the bones of our men close to the abatis of the enemy; and in one case several skeletons of our soldiers were found in their trenches. The bones of these men were gathered from the ground where they fell, having never been interred, and by exposure to the weather for more than a year, all traces of their identity were entirely obliterated."

In the National Cemetery at Knoxville, which is one of great beauty, ornamented with trees and shrubs, and situated about three-fourths of a mile north of the city, were found the graves of four members of the regiment; namely, Orrin Fields and Sergeant Henry G. Smith of Company I; Sergeant John F. Smith of Company H; and Corporal Gilbert T. Litchfield of Company K. In the cemetery are two graves, marked "Sergt. John F. Smith, Co. H, 29th Mass.," the date of death of one being given November 29, 1863, and of the other, March 11, 1864. How this mistake arose, or what the explanation of it is, I am unable to say, but mistakes of a similar character appear throughout all the rolls of the Quartermaster-General. For instance, Frank Hall of Company B,

* Report of J. J. Dana, Major and Quartermaster U. S. A., Brevet Brig. Genl. Roll of Honor No. XIV., page 134.

buried in the Richmond National Cemetery, is buried under the name of "T. Hall, Co. D, 29th Mass.," but the date of his death is given correctly, and this was one of the means by which I recognized him. In the Mount Olivet National Cemetery at Frederick City, Md., was at one time buried a soldier whose grave was marked, "Charles F. Adams, Private, 29th Mass., Co. D, date of death Oct. 2, 1862." No such soldier ever belonged to Company D, or any other company of the regiment. In the same cemetery is buried a soldier whose grave is marked, " Walter W. Horner, 29th Mass., Co. D," and another called " Benj. Godfrey, Co. H, 29th Mass." There were no such soldiers in the regiment. Again, in the Knoxville Cemetery is a grave marked, "George Gault, Co. I, 29th Mass., died Mar. 4, 1864." This is also an error.

In the Hampton, Va., National Cemetery, were found the graves of seven members of the regiment, and in the same yard the graves marked respectively, " Patrick Cain, Co. K, 29th Mass.; P. Finnigan, Co. A, 29th Mass.; C. C. Hadden, Co. C, 29th Mass., and J. C. Williams, Co. H, 29th Mass. Vols." The names of neither of the three last-named soldiers are found upon the rolls of the regiment, though it is probable that " C. C. Hadden" is Charles H. Hayden of Company C, who died in that department. Mistakes of this nature frequently occur throughout the rolls of the Quartermaster-General, not only in regard to the Twenty-ninth, but other regiments also, leaving in the minds of those familiar with the subject, very grave doubts as to even the general correctness of these lists.

AUTHOR.

THE DEAD.

Rank.	NAME.	Place.	Cause.	Date.
Chaplain,	Henry E. Hempstead,	Falmouth, Va.,	Disease,	Dec. 21, 1862.

COMPANY A.

Rank.	NAME.	Place.	Cause.	Date.
Private,	Henry G. Chase,	Harper's Ferry, Va.,	Disease,	Nov. 18, 1862.
"	John McCarthy,	Newport News, Va.,	Accidentally killed,	June 3, 1861.
"	Timothy D. Donovan,[1]	Smoketown, Md.,	Wounds,	Oct. 26, 1862.
"	Edward O'Donnell,	Antietam, Md.,	Killed in battle,	Sept. 17, 1862.
"	Charles H. Dwinell,	Campbell's Station, Tenn.,	"	Nov. 16, 1863.
"	Matthew T. Fitzpatrick,	Great Bethel, Va.,	"	June 10, 1861.
"	William M. Hobart,[2]	Newport News, Va.,	Disease,	Sept. 19, 1862.
1st Sergt.,	William T. Hamer,[3]	Spottsylvania, Va.,	Killed in battle,	May 12, 1864.
"	Richard Harney,	Near Petersburg, Va.,	Wounds,	June 27, 1864.
Com. Sergt.,	Joseph Leeds,	Knoxville, Tenn.,	Disease,	Jan. 20, 1864.
Private,	T. D. Sullivan,	Antietam, Md.,	"	Sept. 17, 1862.
"	John Scully,	Jackson, Miss.,	Killed in battle,	July 15, 1863.

COMPANY B.

Rank.	NAME.	Place.	Cause.	Date.
Private,	William S. Collins,	Near Petersburg, Va.,	Killed in battle,	July 30, 1864.
"	Edward T. Collier,	Washington, D. C.,	Disease,	July 3, 1863.
Musician,	James Cable,[4]	Point Lookout, Md.,	"	July 31, 1862.
Private,	Lyford J. Gilman,	Vicksburg, Miss.,	"	Aug. 2, 1863.

TWENTY-NINTH REGIMENT.

Rank	Name	Place	Cause	Date
Private,	Frank Hall,[a]	Richmond, Va.,	Disease,	Apr. 14, 1864.
"	Ward Locke,	Billerica, Mass.,	"	9, 1864.
"	Martin Minton,[6]	Near Petersburg, Va.,	Killed in battle,	June 17, 1864.
Sergeant,	William H. Mosher,	Spottsylvania, Va.,	"	May 12, 1864.
Private,	William H. Murphy,[7]	Spottsylvania, Va.,	"	12, 1864.
"	John J. O'Brien,	Antietam, Md.,	"	Sept. 17, 1862.
"	Edward J. O'Brien,	Near Petersburg, Va.,	"	Mar. 25, 1865.
1st Lieut.,	Ezra Ripley,	Helena, Ark.,	Disease,	July 28, 1864.
Private,	James W. Shepard,	Newport News, Va.,	Killed by burst'g of a cannon,	Feb. 11, 1862.
"	John C. Stewart,	Near Petersburg, Va.,	Killed in battle,	June 17, 1864.
"	John M. Thompson,	Annapolis, Md.,	Wounds,	June 27, 1864.

COMPANY C.

Rank	Name	Place	Cause	Date
Private,	George D. Brown,	Fair Oaks, Va.,	Killed in skirmish,	June 15, 1862.
Sergeant,	Alfred B. Cummings,[8]	Andersonville, Ga.,	Starvation and neglect,	May 22, 1864.
Private,	Marshall M. Chandler,	On transport, James River, Va.,	Disease,	July 31, 1862.
"	Edward F. Drohan,	Washington, D. C.,	"	Jan. 13, 1863.
1st Sergt.,	Silas N. Grosvenor,[9]	Near Petersburg, Va.,	Killed in battle,	June 17, 1864.
Private,	Caleb L. Hudson, Jr.,[10]	Camp Dennison, Ohio,	Disease,	Sept. 11, 1863.

[1] Wounded September 17, 1862. [2] Buried in National Cemetery at Hampton, Va. Row 12. Section C. Number of grave, 5.
[3] Buried under name of "Sergeant William H. Hamer," in Fredericksburg National Cemetery, Va. Terrace Section No. 8. Number of grave, 167. Body removed from Beverly's Farm, Spottsylvania County. [4] Buried in National Cemetery at Point Lookout, Md. Number of grave, 62.
[5] Buried in Richmond National Cemetery, Va., under the name of "T. Hall." Number of grave, 1,272.
[6] Buried in Poplar Grove National Cemetery, Va. Division D. Section D. Number of grave, 218.
[7] Buried under name of "William Murphy," in National Cemetery at Fredericksburg, Va. Terrace Section No. 4. Number of grave, 230. Originally buried on farm of Harris, Spottsylvania County, Va. [8] Buried in National Cemetery at Andersonville, Ga. Section C. Number of grave, 1,290.
[9] Buried in Poplar Grove National Cemetery, Va. Division D. Section D. Number of grave, 215.
[10] Buried in National Cemetery at Camp Dennison, Ohio, under name of "C. D. Hudson." Number of grave, 240.

THE DEAD.—COMPANY C—Continued.

Rank.	NAME.	Place.	Cause.	Date.
2d Lieut.,	Elisha S. Holbrook,	Fortress Monroe, Va.,	Disease,	Aug. 20, 1861.
1st Sergt.,	C. Francis Harlow,[1]	Near Petersburg, Va.,	Killed in battle,	Mar. 25, 1865.
Private,	Daniel W. Harden,	Annapolis Junction, Md.,	Disease,	Sept. 22, 1862.
"	Charles H. Hayden,	Suffolk, Va.,	"	July 31, 1862.
"	John C. Lambert,	Bethesda Church, Va.,	Killed in battle,	June 1, 1864.
"	David H. Lincoln,	Antietam, Md.,	Disease,	Sept. 17, 1861.
"	Edward P. Mansfield,	Wilderness battle-field, Va.,	Killed in battle,	May 6, 1864.
"	John M. Nason,	Camp Nelson, Ky.,	Disease,	1863.
Sergeant,	Edmund T. Packard,	Annapolis, Md.,	"	Apr. 24, 1864.
Private,	Wallace R. Ripley,[2]	Newport News, Va.,	"	July 9, 1862.
"	Joshua S. Ramsdell,[3]	Mill Creek Hospital, Va.,	"	Oct. 6, 1862.
"	Charles H. Turner,	Fort Wood, New York Harbor,	"	Dec. 19, 1862.
Corporal,	Elijah H. Tolman,	Antietam, Md.,	Killed in battle,	Sept. 17, 1862.

COMPANY D.

Rank.	NAME.	Place.	Cause.	Date.
Major,	Charles Chipman,[4]	Before Petersburg, Va.,	Killed in battle,	Aug. 8, 1864.
Private,	Thomas W. D. Chapman,		Disease,	Sept. 22, 1862.
"	Edward Donnelly,	Sandwich, Mass.,	Wounds received in the battle of the Wilderness,	1865.
"	Joseph W. Eaton,	"	Disease,	July 15, 1869.
"	Benjamin Fuller,		"	Aug. 20, 1864.
"	James G. B. Haines,		"	July 18, 1862.
"	James H. Heald,	Annapolis, Md.,	"	Oct. 11, 1862.

TWENTY-NINTH REGIMENT. 377

Private,	Charles E. Jones,	Newport News, Va.,	Killed by the bursting of Sawyer gun,	Feb. 11, 1862.
"	David S. Keene,	Camp Dennison, Ohio,	Disease,	Oct. 18, 1863.
"	Patrick Long,[3]	Newport News, Va.,	"	Aug. 15, 1862.
"	Martin S. Tinkham,	"	"	Sept. 28, 1861.
"	John Weeks,	"	"	1862.
"	William H. Woods,	"	"	Jan. 16, 1862.
"	James Ward,	Wilderness battle-field, Va.,	Killed in battle,	May 12, 1864.

COMPANY E.

Corporal,	John K. Alexander,	Battle of Spottsylvania, Va.,	Killed in battle,	May 12, 1864.
1st Lieut.,	Nathaniel Burgess,	Near Petersburg, Va.,	"	Mar. 25, 1865.
Private,	Lawrence R. Blake,	Antietam, Md.,	"	Sept. 17, 1862.
"	Thomas Burt,	Washington, D. C.,	Disease,	Oct. 31, 1862.
1st Lieut.,	John B. Collingwood,	St John's Hospital, Cincinnati, Ohio,	"	Aug. 21, 1863.
Corporal,	Thomas Collingwood,	Camp Parke, Ky.,	"	31, 1863.
Private,	Patrick Cain,[6]	Craney Island, Va.,	"	Feb. 3, 1864.
Corporal,	Thomas W. Hayden,	Camp Parke, Ky.,	"	Sept. 4, 1863.
Sergeant,	Orrin D. Holmes,[7]	Near Petersburg, Va.,	Killed in battle,	Mar. 25, 1865.
Private,	Justus W. Harlow,[8]	Mill Creek Hospital, Va.,	Disease,	Sept. 15, 1862.

[1] Buried in Poplar Grove National Cemetery, Va. Division A. Section C. Number of grave, 103.
[2] Buried in National Cemetery at Hampton, Va. Row 9. Section B. Number of grave, 39.
[3] Buried in National Cemetery at Hampton, Va. Row 3. Section D. Number of grave, 4.
[4] While in command of the Fourteenth New York Heavy Artillery Volunteers.
[5] Buried in National Cemetery at Hampton, Va. Row 9. Section B. Number of grave, 23.
[6] Buried in National Cemetery at Hampton, Va. Row 20. Section B. Number of grave, 17.
[7] Buried in Poplar Grove National Cemetery, Va. Division A. Section C. Number of grave, 102.
[8] Buried in National Cemetery at Hampton, Va. Row 1. Section E. Number of grave, 27.

THE DEAD—COMPANY E.—Continued.

Rank	NAME	Place	Cause	Date
2d Lieut.,	Horace A. Jenks,	Milldale, Miss.,	Disease,	July 26, 1863.
"	Thomas A. Mayo,	Gaines' Mill, Va.,	Killed in battle,	June 27, 1862.
Corporal,	Lemuel B. Morton,	Spottsylvania, Va.,	"	May 12, 1864.
Private,	William Morey,	Plymouth, Mass.,	Disease,	1862.
"	Thomas P. Mullen,	Washington, D. C.,	"	Jan. 9, 1863.
"	Charles E. Merriam,	Harper's Ferry, Va.,	"	Nov. 12, 1862.
"	George S. Peckham,	Lenoir's Station, Tenn.,	"	1, 1863.
"	Henry H. Robbins,	Washington, D. C.,	"	Dec. 4, 1863.
"	Albert R. Robbins,	Plymouth, Mass.,	"	Mar. 5, 1864.
"	Frank A. Thomas,[2]	Mill Creek Hospital, Va.,	"	Sept. 15, 1862.
"	Charles E. Tillson,[3]	Andersonville, Ga.,	Starvation and neglect,	July 24, 1864.
Sergeant,	George E. Wadsworth,[4]	Camp Parke, Ky.,	Wounds,	Aug. 31, 1863.
Private,	David Williams,	Camp Dennison, Ohio,	Disease,	Sept. 14, 1863.
"	William Williams,	Plymouth, Mass.,	"	

COMPANY F.

Rank	NAME	Place	Cause	Date
Private,	James Black,[5]	Andersonville, Ga.,	Starvation and neglect,	July 5, 1864.
"	Hugh D. Conaty,	Harrison's Landing, Va.,	Disease,	28, 1862.
Corporal,	Arthur Clifford,	On transport from Fortress Monroe North,	"	
Private,	Benjamin T. Godfrey,	Philadelphia, Penn.,	"	Aug. 7, 1862.
"	Joseph Hamer,	Mill Creek Hospital, Va.,	"	Sept. 7, 1862.
"	Abraham Haskell,	Long Island, N. Y.,	"	9, 1864.
"	James Liffin,[6]	Near Petersburg, Va.,	Wounds,	Oct. 4, 1864.
				July 29, 1864.

TWENTY-NINTH REGIMENT.

Rank	Name	Where Buried	Cause of Death	Date
Private,	Edward Ratigan,	Antietam, Md.,	Killed in battle,	Sept. 17, 1862.
"	Granville T. Records,[7]	Mill Creek Hospital, Va.,	Disease,	" 12, 1862.
"	Culbert Reynolds,	Harrison's Landing, Va.,	"	July 18, 1862.
"	Solomon H. Smith,	Bolivar Heights, Va.,	"	Oct. 24, 1862.
"	Francis H. Simmons,	Hospital at Georgetown, D. C.,	"	Sept. —, 1862.
"	James Simmons,	"	"	"
Corporal,	Preston O. Smith,[8]	Near Petersburg, Va.,	Killed in battle,	July 30, 1864.
Private,	George E. Westgate,	Somet House Hosp., Alexandria, Va.,	Disease,	Dec. 19, 1862.
"	Cornelius Westgate,[9]	Regimental Hospital, Falmouth, Va.,	"	" 26, 1862.
"	Joseph Westgate,	Frederick City, Md.,	"	Oct. 9, 1862.
"	Joseph L. Westgate,	Alexandria, Va.,	Wounds,	" 21, 1862.
"	Preserved Westgate,[10]	Near Petersburg, Va.,	Disease,	Mar. 25, 1865.
"	Edward Wilbur,[11]	Camp Nelson, Ky.,	Killed in battle,	Nov. 16, 1863.

COMPANY G.

Rank	Name	Where Buried	Cause of Death	Date
Private,	Henry Austin,	White Oak Swamp, Va.,	Killed in battle,	June 30, 1862.
"	William A. Burrell,[12]	Covington, Ky.,	Disease,	Aug. 16, 1863.
"	Charles W. Clifford,	Bridgewater, Mass.,	"	July 29, 1862.
"	George C. Cobbett,	Craney Island, Va.,	"	Aug. —, 1862.

[1] Buried in National Cemetery at Chattanooga, Tenn., under the name of "G. T. Peckham." Section II. Number of grave, 159. Originally buried at Loudon, Tenn. [2] Buried in National Cemetery at Hampton, Va. Row 1. Section E. Number of grave, 1. [3] Buried in National Cemetery at Andersonville, Ga. Section T. Number of grave, 3,808. [4] Wounds received at White Oak Swamp, Va. [5] Buried in National Cemetery at Andersonville, Ga. Section R. Number of grave, 2,568. [6] Wounded June 17, 1864. [7] Buried under name of "G. Record," in National Cemetery at Hampton, Va. Row 14. Section D. Number of grave, 48. [8] "Battle of the Mine. [9] Buried in National Cemetery, Mount Olivet, Frederick City, Md., under the name of "Joseph Tresgate." Number of grave, 250. Wounded in battle of Antietam. [10] Battle of Fort Stedman. [11] Buried in Camp Nelson National Cemetery, Ky., under the name of "Edward Wilber." Section D. Number of grave, 50. [12] Buried in Linden Grove National Cemetery, Covington, Ky. Section C. Number of grave, 104.

THE DEAD.—COMPANY G.—(Continued.)

Rank.	NAME.	Place.	Cause.	Date.
Private,	John Cronin,	Petersburg, Va.,	Killed in battle,	Mar. 25, 1865.
"	Nelson Cook,	Near Petersburg, Va.,	"	25, 1865.
"	Joseph Duxbury,	Fort McHenry, Md.,	Wounds,	Nov. 29, 1862.
Sergeant,	Ebenezer Fisk,	Near Petersburg, Va.,	Killed in battle,	July 30, 1864.
Private,	Charles B. Griffin,	Attleborough, Mass.,	Disease,	Nov. 26, 1862.
Corporal,	Charles D. Hodge,	General Hospital,	"	Feb. 27, 1863.
Private,	Philip P. Lawall,	Arlington, Va.,	"	July 1, 1864.
"	Minot E. Phillips,	Belle Isle, Va.,	Starvation and neglect,	—, 1862.
"	George E. Snow,	Near Petersburg, Va.,	Killed in battle,	Mar. 25, 1865.
Private,	George W. Sprague,	Mississippi,	Drowned,	Aug. 16, 1863.
"	Levi Trumbull,	Belle Isle, Va.,	Starvation and neglect,	1862.

COMPANY H.

Private,	John H. Aldrich,	Long Island, N. Y.,	Disease,	Oct. 22, 1862.
"	David Barnes,	Harrison's Landing, Va.,	"	July 28, 1862.
"	George Curtis,	Charlestown, Mass.,	"	1866.
"	Edward Carroll,	Washington, D. C.,	"	Feb. 22, 1863.
"	Edward E. Dearing,	Charlestown, Mass.,	"	Jan. 22, 1865.
"	Theodore W. Dearing,	Salisbury, N. C. (prison-pen),	Exposure and neglect,	Sept. 22, 1865.
"	Joshua G. Fuller,	Crab Orchard, Ky.,	Disease,	June 17, 1864.
Corporal,	Richard Gurney,	Near Petersburg, Va.,	Killed in battle,	Aug. 13, 1862.
Private,	William H. Gould, Jr.,	Harrison's Landing, Va.,	Disease,	Sept. 17, 1862.
Corporal,	Robert F. Greenough,	Antietam, Md.,	Killed in battle,	21, 1861.
Private,	Henry A. Glines,	Petersburg, Va.,	Killed,	

TWENTY-NINTH REGIMENT. 381

Rank	Name	Place	Cause	Date
Sergeant,	Edward M. Hastings,	Harrison's Landing, Va.,	Disease,	Aug. 12, 1862.
Musician,	Alonzo F. Howe,	Camp Dennison, Ohio,	"	Sept. 20, 1863.
Sergeant,	Ansel B. Kellam,	White Oak Swamp, Va.,	Killed in battle,	June 30, 1862.
Private,	William O. Connor,[1]	Andersonville Prison-pen, Ga.,	Starvation and neglect,	Oct. 17, 1864.
"	George S. Preble,	Charlestown, Mass.,	Disease,	Dec. 16, 1861.
"	Henry Proctor,	Danvers, Mass.,	"	Nov. 5, 1862.
Sergeant,	John F. Smith,[2]	Fort Sanders, Knoxville, Tenn.,	Killed in battle,	" 29, 1863.
Private,	George W. Smith,	White Oak Swamp, Va.,	"	June 30, 1862.
"	John Schow,	On transport, Mississippi River,	Disease,	Aug. 20, 1863.
Sergeant,	William F. Willis,[3]	Near Petersburg, Va.,	Killed in battle,	June 17, 1864.
Private,	Francis Wyman,	Charlestown, Mass.,	Disease,	" 2, 1866.
"	Charles Young,	Craney Island, Va.,	"	" 1862.

COMPANY I.

Rank	Name	Place	Cause	Date
Private,	John Q. Bachelder,	Portsmouth, Va.,	Disease,	Oct. 17, 1862.
"	Joseph M. Badger,		Disease,	June 3, 1862.
"	James L. Brown,	Newport News, Va.,	Disease,	Aug. 7, 1861.
"	John C. Dow,	Near Antietam, Md.,	Wounds,	Sept. 20, 1862.
"	Orrin Fields,[4]	Knoxville, Tenn.,	Disease,	Mar. 4, 1864.
"	George W. Jewett,			Jan. 7, 1864.
"	Thomas Pickett,[5]	Frederick City, Md.,		Mar. 22, 1865.
Sergeant,	Curtis S. Rand,	Near Petersburg, Va.,	Wounds,	Sept. 19, 1864.

[1] Buried in National Cemetery at Andersonville, Ga. Section O. Number of grave, 11,080.
[2] Buried in Knoxville National Cemetery, Tenn. Section 6. Number of grave, 98.
[3] While carrying the flag. Buried in Poplar Grove National Cemetery, Va. Division D. Section D. Number of grave, 220.
[4] Buried in Knoxville National Cemetery, Tenn. Section 7. Number of grave, 54.
[5] Buried in Mount Olivet National Cemetery, Frederick City, Md. Number of grave, 834.

382   THE DEAD OF THE

THE DEAD.—COMPANY I—Continued.

Rank.	NAME.	Place.	Cause.	Date.
Private,	Joseph A. Short,	White Oak Swamp, Va.,	Killed in battle,	June 30, 1862.
"	Harvey G. Smith,[1]	Knoxville, Tenn.,	Disease,	Mar. 10, 1864.
"	Andrew H. Tarr,	Malvern Hills, Va.,	Killed in battle,	July 1, 1862.

COMPANY K.

Rank.	NAME.	Place.	Cause.	Date.
Private,	Horace Colby,	Great Bethel, Va.,	Killed in battle,	June 10, 1861.
"	Edgar Curry,	Boston, Mass.,	Disease,	—
"	Thomas F. Dolan,	Spotsylvania, Va.,	Killed in battle,	May 12, 1864.
"	John E. Fisher,	"	"	12, 1864.
"	Frederick A. Godbold,[2]	Andersonville, Ga.,	Disease and privation,	June 24, 1864.
"	John B. Hibbert,[3]	Fayette, Ky.,	Disease,	May 2, 1864.
"	Isaac S. Hill,	Florence Prison, S. C.,	Disease and privation,	Jan. 30, 1865.
"	Charles Laslie,	Chelsea, Mass.,	Wounds,	—
Corporal,	Gilbert T. Litchfield,[4]	Fort Sanders, Knoxville, Tenn.,	Killed in battle,	Nov. 29, 1863.
"	Hiram A. Mosher,	Boston, Mass.,	Disease,	8, 1862.
Private,	Meltiah T. Remick,	Washington, D. C.,	"	Feb. 17, 1863.
"	Nelson H. Snow,[5]	Camp Nelson, Ky.,	"	Nov. 1, 1863.
"	William W. Sanborn,			
Sergeant,	John A. Tighe,[6]	Near Petersburg, Va.,	Killed in battle,	June 17, 1864.
Private,	Charles W. Winslow,	Newport News, Va.,	Disease,	Oct. 30, 1861.

RECRUITS OF 1864.

William Klinker,	Near Petersburg, Va.,	Killed in battle,	Mar. 25, 1865.
Ruter Moritz,	"	Killed in battle,	Mar. 25, 1865.
Hezekiah S. Sargent,	"	Wounds,	Jan. 2, 1865.
Emile Taubert,	Arlington, Va.,	Disease,	Feb. 13, 1865.

[1] Buried in Knoxville National Cemetery, Tenn. Section 4. Number of grave, 161.
[2] Buried in National Cemetery at Andersonville, Ga. Section G. Number of grave, 2,414.
[3] Buried in Lexington National Cemetery, Ky. Circle 12. Number of grave, 531. Originally buried at Lexington, Ky.
[4] Buried in National Cemetery at Knoxville, Tenn. Section 4. Number of grave, 143.
[5] Buried in Camp Nelson National Cemetery, Ky. Section D. Number of grave, 51.
[6] While carrying the colors. Buried in Poplar Grove National Cemetery, Va. Division A. Section C. Number of grave, 216.

APPENDIX.

REUNIONS OF THE REGIMENT.

The feelings of fraternity which grew out of participation in common dangers and hardships naturally gave rise to a desire on the part of the surviving members of the regiment to occasionally meet each other in a purely social way, exchange greetings, and renew the old and strongly-cemented friendships of army life.

THE FIRST REUNION.

The first of these reunions took place in Boston in June, 1870. A small number of comrades assembled at Evans's Hall, Boston, May 30, 1870; the meeting was called to order by Sergeant John B. Smithers of Company B, and it was voted to form a temporary organization. Captain Charles Brady was elected President, and Hospital Steward John Hardy, Treasurer, *pro tempore*, whereupon the meeting adjourned till June 17, following, at the same place.

On the 17th of June, 1870, the meeting again assembled, Captain Brady in the chair, and a permanent organization was effected as follows:—

President.—General Joseph H. Barnes.
Vice-Presidents.—William H. Osborne, Company C; Sergeants B. B. Brown, Company B; Samuel C. Wright, Company E; William H. Burns, Company I.
Secretary.—Lieutenant John Lucas, Company B.
Corresponding Secretary.—John J. Ryan, Company B.
Treasurer.—Hospital Steward John Hardy.
Executive Committee.—Colonel Thomas W. Clarke; Captain William D. Chamberlain; John J. Ryan, Company B; Sergeant John B. Smithers, Company B; Corporal Martin L. Kern, Jr., Company D.

Some discussion was had concerning the rolls of the regiment, and Colonel Clarke and Lieutenant-Colonel Willard D. Tripp were appointed a committee to revise the regimental roll prepared by the Adjutant-General. At this meeting it was announced that comrade William H. Osborne was engaged in collecting material for the history of the regiment, and Sergeant Hodgkins, Company B; Lieutenant Henry A. Hunting, Company K; and Daniel B. Perkins, Jr., of Company H, were chosen a committee to assist in the matter.*

This meeting was not largely attended, but nearly every company was represented by one or more members.

SECOND REUNION.

In pursuance of a call published in several of the Boston papers, the Association met at the Sherman House, Boston, May 13, 1871. Officers were chosen for the ensuing year, as follows:—

President.—General Joseph H. Barnes.
Vice-Presidents.—Lieutenant-Colonel Willard D. Tripp; Major Samuel H. Doten; William H. Osborne, Company C; Sergeant B. B. Brown, Company B; Colonel Henry R. Sibley.
Recording Secretary.—Lieutenant John Lucas.
Corresponding Secretary.—John J. Ryan, Company B.
Treasurer.—Captain George H. Long.
Executive Committee.—Colonel Thomas W. Clarke; Lieutenant J. O'Neil; Samuel W. Hunt, Company D; Sergeant-Major George H. Morse; Sergeant Samuel C. Wright, Company E.

At this meeting, which was largely attended and of unusual interest, a very valuable paper was read by the President, reviewing an account, written by one Henry Coppee, LL. D., of the battle of the Mine, July 30, 1864, and embracing a particular statement of the facts concerning the transfer of the non-re-enlisting members of the regiment to the Thirty-sixth Massachusetts Regiment.

A vote of thanks was passed to comrades Ryan, Smithers, Captain George H. Taylor, and Lieutenant Lucas, for the interest they had taken in bringing about the reunion of the regiment.

It having come to the knowledge of the meeting that Major-General Ambrose E. Burnside was then in the city, a committee composed of Colonel Clarke, Lieutenant-Colonel Tripp, Captain Long, Adjutant Braden, and comrade Ryan, was chosen to wait on the General, and extend to him the kind greetings and regards of the members of the regiment Action was taken concerning a regimental badge, and Colonel Clarke was appointed a committee to prepare a design for it. This was the first time that the Association dined together, a fine dinner being served at the Sherman House.

THIRD REUNION.

This was Company H's day; the Association assembled at Monument Hall, Charlestown, May 14, 1872. Colonel Clarke reported a design for

---

* This committee never discharged its duties.—AUTHOR.

a regimental badge, which was adopted. It was a rough bronze medal, stamped with the figures of an upraised right forearm, grasping in the hand an uplifted sword; beneath this a row of cannon-balls, and under all the figures "29."

OFFICERS FOR 1872-73.

President.—General J. H. Barnes.
Vice-Presidents.—Major S. H. Doten, Colonel H. R. Sibley, Major Charles T. Richardson, Captain W. D. Chamberlain, Lieutenant J. Lucas.
Recording Secretary.—J. J. Ryan.
Corresponding Secretary.—Lieutenant-Colonel W. D. Tripp.
Treasurer.—Captain George H. Long.
Executive Committee.—Major S. H. Doten; Sergeant S. C. Wright, Company E; Colonel T. W. Clarke; Captain Charles A. Carpenter; Emery Jaquith, Company C.

Lieutenant-Colonel Tripp presented the Association with the two large printed volumes entitled, "The Record of Massachusetts Volunteers," for which a vote of thanks was tendered him.

It was voted to hold the next reunion at Plymouth. A committee of ten, consisting of one member of each company, was chosen to prepare a perfect roster of the regiment.*

FOURTH REUNION.

PLYMOUTH, May 14, 1873.

The meeting assembled in Grand Army Hall, and after listening to the reports of its Secretary and several committees, proceeded to choose officers for the year 1873-74.

The officers elected were as follows:—

President.—General J. H. Barnes.
Vice-Presidents.—Major Samuel H. Doten; Surgeon George B. Cogswell; Adjutant H. A. Braden; Sergeant John H. Hancock, Company H; Sergeant G. Townsend, Company I.
Recording Secretary.—J. J. Ryan, Company B.
Corresponding Secretary.—J. S. Manning, Company K.
Treasurer.—Colonel T. W. Clarke.
Executive Committee.—Captain W. D. Chamberlain; Corporal H. E. Hay, Company I; Captain A. A. Oliver; Sergeant George Townsend, Company I; Sergeant J. F. Smith, Company H.

An act of soldierly love for a dead comrade distinguished this meeting from all that had preceded it; indeed, from all that have since been held. During the latter part of the war, a certain well-known foreigner, with

---
* This committee never did its duty.—AUTHOR.

the aid of the friends and relatives of our dead soldiers of this and other States, established in the city of Boston a portrait gallery, which was known as the "Gallery of Departed Heroes." The friends of Major Charles Chipman had contributed liberally towards an elegant oil-portrait of this worthy soldier of the regiment, which, with a costly frame, had been placed in the aforenamed gallery. Through improper management, leading to the pecuniary embarrassment of the originator, all the portraits in the gallery had become heavily mortgaged, and shortly prior to this meeting, the several mortgages had been foreclosed, and the property not being of a generally saleable character, much of it had fallen into the hands of the mortgagees, including the portrait of Major Chipman.

Previous to this reunion, Sergeant Samuel C. Wright, whose love for his comrades, living and dead, is as pure as refined gold, redeemed at his own expense Major Chipman's portrait, and brought it to Plymouth with the purpose of eventually presenting it to the widow and family of the deceased. The comrades would not suffer him to bear the whole of this burden, but, at this meeting, generously contributed each one his share of the expense incurred, and then, by an unanimous vote, granted the fine portrait, as a token of their love and esteem, to Mrs. Chipman and her children.

The portrait was soon afterwards sent to the donees, accompanied by a touching letter from the President of the Association.

This reunion was the first that was attended by the wives and lady friends of the comrades, and was one of great enjoyment, the citizens of Plymouth doing all in their power to contribute to its success, and by their many acts of kindness, reviving the memory of the unselfishness and flowing bounty of 1861.

Dinner was served at the Samoset House, at which the Plymouth Band, and many of the first citizens of the town, were in attendance.

FIFTH REUNION. — LYNN, MAY 14, 1874.

OFFICERS.

President.—General J. H. Barnes.
Vice-Presidents.—Major S. H. Doten; Colonel Henry R. Sibley; Surgeon George B. Cogswell; Wm. H. Osborne, Company C; Sergeant G. Townsend, Company I.
Secretary.—J. J. Ryan, Company B.
Corresponding Secretary.—Sergeant Samuel C. Wright, Company E.
Treasurer.—Colonel T. W. Clarke.

The business meeting was held in the hall of General Lander Post, G. A. R., at the close of which the comrades and their ladies took carriages and drove to the Relay House, Nahant Beach, where a fine dinner was served. Captain D. W. Lee acted as toast-master for the occasion, and sentiments were responded to as follows: "The President of the United States," by letter from General Banks; "The Day we Celebrate," by Surgeon Cogswell; "The Army of the Union," by General Barnes, who closed by offering this touching sentiment: "Our Heroic Dead: God keep their memory green." This was responded to by all the comrades, who rose in token of respect to their memory. The other sentiments were, "The State of Massachusetts," responded to by the band; "The Twenty-ninth Massachusetts Regiment," by Colonel Clarke and W. H. Osborne. Corporal A. B. Fiske of Company K closed the literary exercises by an eloquent speech.

"The company then spent some time strolling on the shore, enjoying the fine water views and pleasant weather. The day had been warm, and closed like a superb mid-summer day, calm and still, giving the water the appearance of a sheet of silver." At half-past six o'clock the members took the carriages and drove to the Lynn depot, taking the evening train to Boston.

SIXTH REUNION.

The sixth reunion was held at Downer's Landing, Hingham Harbor, September 17, 1875. The comrades and their families, to the number of about one hundred, assembled at the Boston wharf of the Hingham Steamboat Company quite early in the morning, took the boat for the Landing, where, upon arrival, a business meeting was held, and officers for the year 1875-76 chosen, as follows:—

President.—General J. H. Barnes.
Vice-Presidents.—Wm. H. Osborne, Company C; Corporal Alonzo B. Fiske, Company K; Sergeant W. B. Standish, Company E; Sergeant Geo. Townsend, Company I; Sergeant J. B. Smithers, Company B.
Recording Secretary.—Sergeant Sam'l C. Wright, Company E.
Corresponding Secretary.—H. E. Stewart, Company K.
Treasurer.—Colonel Thos. W. Clarke.
Executive Committee.—Colonel H. R. Sibley; Lieutenant John Shannon; Captain D. W. Lee; Lieutenant J. O'Neil; Lieutenant J. Lucas.

Comrade W. H. Osborne was called upon to report what progress he had made in writing the history of the regiment, and when he had reported, Colonel Sibley offered a resolution, which was passed, pledging the assistance of the comrades in publishing the work.

The cold and windy character of the day tended to render this meeting of the regiment less successful and interesting than those of former years.

SEVENTH REUNION. — AMERICAN HOUSE, BOSTON, May 15, 1876.

The Association met at one o'clock, P. M., and chose officers and transacted business.

OFFICERS ELECTED.

President.—General J. H. Barnes.
Vice-Presidents.—Major Chas. T. Richardson; W. H. Osborne, Com-

pany C; Sergeant Geo. Townsend, Company I: Colonel H. R. Sibley; Captain Lebbeus Leach.
Recording Secretary.—Sergeant Sam'l C. Wright, Company E.
Corresponding Secretary.—H. E. Stewart, Company K.
Treasurer.—Colonel T. W. Clarke.
Executive Committee.—Colonel H. R. Sibley; Lieutenant J. O'Neil; General J. H. Barnes; Captain D. W. Lee; Colonel Thos. W. Clarke; Sergeant Sam'l C. Wright; Wm. H. Osborne; Corporal Geo. W. Allen, Company C.

A vote of thanks was extended to comrade Wm. H. Osborne for his services in writing the regimental history, and also for his invitation to the Association to hold its next meeting at East Bridgewater.

At 3 o'clock, P. M., the Association, with its invited guests,—among whom was Governor Rice,—sat down to dinner. Colonel Clarke acted as toast-master, and the first toast, " The President of the United States," was proposed, and a letter read from Collector Simmons in response to the sentiment. " The Commonwealth of Massachusetts " called out Governor Rice, who was received with cheers, and who said, in the course of his remarks, that he considered it a greater honor to have been a faithful soldier of the Union than Governor of Massachusetts; and also, that if the Association found any pecuniary difficulty in publishing the history of the regiment, to call upon him, in which case he would gladly aid the worthy undertaking. Letters were read from Governor Hartranft of Pennsylvania, Mayor Cobb, and others. Speeches were made by the President, Colonel Clarke, Major Doten and Corporal Fiske.

About eighty comrades were present.

EIGHTH REUNION.

The eighth reunion was held at East Bridgewater, June 18, 1877, two hundred, including members and their families, being present.

The day was one of the most lovely in June, and was keenly enjoyed by the visiting comrades, their wives and children, who strolled about the quiet, shady streets of the town, visited the soldiers' monument upon the common, which bears the names of a number of the dead of the regiment, and walked through the adjacent groves. The citizens of the town met them everywhere with smiles and words of welcome, and at one o'clock provided them with a bountiful dinner in the lower hall of the Town-house, where a large committee of the ladies of East Bridgewater were in attendance to wait on the tables and testify by their presence and numerous attentions their respect for these veterans of the war.

At the close of the enjoyments at the table the company assembled in the main hall to listen to some fine singing by members of the East Bridgewater Musical Society. After this came speaking, in which several of the townspeople and comrades took part.

The whole meeting was conducted in a pleasantly informal manner, and was, for that reason, all the more productive of enjoyment and profit.

Nineteen new members were added to the roll of the Association, and in view of the deep interest taken by the wives of the members in the meeting, they were, by vote, made honorary members of the Association.

While the business meeting was in session in the morning, Captain Leach, whose absence all had been regretting, suddenly came into the hall. The members all rose in their seats and gave him three hearty cheers, to which warm welcome the brave old Captain, now slightly bowed by the weight of seventy-seven years, responded by choking words of gratitude and thanks.

One of the saddest and bravest chapters in the history of the old regiment was brought freshly to remembrance by a fine photograph, suspended in front of the speaker's desk, of Major Charles Chipman, Lieutenant Burgess, and the three standard-bearers, Grosvenor, Tighe, and Willis, who lost their young lives on the 17th of June, 1864.

The officers elected for the year 1877-78 were,—

President.—General J. H Barnes.
Vice-Presidents.—Major C. T. Richardson; W. H. Osborne, Company C; Sergeant George Townsend, Company I; Colonel H. R. Sibley; Captain Lebbeus Leach.
Treasurer.—Colonel T. W. Clarke.
Recording Secretary.—Sergeant S. C. Wright, Company E.
Corresponding Secretary.—H. E. Stewart, Company K.
Executive Committee.—Colonel H. R. Sibley; Lieutenant J. O'Neil; General J. H. Barnes; Captain D. W Lee; Sergeant S. C. Wright, Company E; Colonel T. W. Clarke; William H. Osborne; Corporal George W. Allen, Company C.

The author sincerely hopes that the Secretary of the Association will have the pleasure to record the proceedings of many future meetings of his comrades, and that none will prove to be seasons of less joy and gladness than this, the eighth annual reunion.

PARADE OF THE REGIMENT,

September 17, 1877.

The beautiful and costly monument erected by the city of Boston in memory of its heroic dead of the late war was dedicated with imposing ceremonies on the 17th of September, 1877, which was the fifteenth anniversary of the battle of Antietam. The monument, one of the finest in the country, is erected on a little hill on the Boston Common, at the foot of which stood the famous Old Elm, destroyed by wind, February 15, 1876. There was once a powder magazine on the hill occupied by the monument, which, during the siege of Boston, was the site of a British fortification bombarded by Washington. In the war of 1812, a body of troops designed to protect the town was encamped about this very spot.

On the side of the monument, facing the south, cut in bold, square letters, is the following inscription:—

> TO THE MEN OF BOSTON
> WHO DIED FOR THEIR COUNTRY
> ON LAND AND SEA IN THE WAR
> WHICH KEPT THE UNION WHOLE
> DESTROYED SLAVERY
> AND MAINTAINED THE CONSTITUTION
> THE GRATEFUL CITY
> HAS BUILT THIS MONUMENT
> THAT THEIR EXAMPLE
> MAY SPEAK
> TO COMING GENERATIONS.

Honorable Charles Devens, Attorney-General of the United States, delivered the oration; and General Augustus P. Martin of Boston acted as Chief Marshal. Colonel Henry R. Sibley of the Twenty-ninth Regiment was honored with the command of the Suffolk County Division of the Grand Army of the Republic.

At a meeting of the Executive Committee of the Twenty-ninth Regiment Association, held September 1, 1877, it was voted to parade as a regiment on the occasion of the dedication of the monument, and General Joseph H. Barnes was chosen to act as Colonel and Commander, Colonel Thomas William Clarke as Lieutenant-Colonel, Major Charles T. Richardson as Major, Lieutenant Henry S. Braden as Adjutant, and Captain D. W. Lee as Quartermaster On the 7th of September, General Barnes issued a circular letter addressed to the comrades of the regiment, inviting them to parade on the 17th, and requesting them to assemble at 29 Pemberton Square, Boston, at 9 o'clock in the morning of that day.

One hundred and fifty comrades responded promptly to the invitation of their old commander, dressed in dark clothes and wearing their corps and regimental badges. Sergeant Samuel C. Wright, who was wounded in four different battles, was assigned to the proud position of National color-bearer. General Barnes, Colonel Clarke, Major Richardson, Lieutenant Braden, and Captain Lee, were handsomely mounted; elegant wreaths of choice cut-flowers adorning the necks of their fine horses.

The procession moved at a little past 12 o'clock, and the regiment took the position assigned it, in the Second Division, commanded by Colonel Edward O. Shepard; in which also marched the First, Second, Sixth, Ninth, Eleventh, Twelfth, Thirteenth, Twenty-first, Twenty-fourth, Twenty-eighth, Fortieth, Forty-third, Forty-fourth, Forty-fifth Massachusetts Veteran Infantry regiments; also, the Massachusetts Veteran Batteries under Colonel O. F Nims, the hero of many a battle-field; several Army and Navy Associations; the Third Massachusetts Cavalry; Massachusetts members of General Hooker's "Old Brigade," under General Gilman Marston; also the Second New Hampshire Infantry; "Maine Veterans in Massachusetts"; Ninety-ninth New York Infantry, under Colonel David W. Wardrop, and the "Survivors of Rebel Prisons."

The route of the procession was very extended, and the parade was not concluded till nearly dusk. The day was warm and fine, and it seemed as if every town and city in Massachusetts had emptied their entire population into the streets of Boston. Business in the city was wholly suspended, and the buildings along the route of the procession were tastefully decorated with flowers and bunting. The gay plumes and gaudy uniforms of the militia attracted their usual share of attention; but when the veterans went by, with war-like tramp, carrying the shreds of old war flags, many eyes were wet with tears, and many of the adult spectators gazed with half-quivering lips upon these remnants of the Nation's Grand Army of Freedom. The presence in the column of Generals McClellan, Hooker, Burnside, and many other old heroes of the war, tended greatly to increase the enthusiasm of the vast throngs of people along the sidewalks, and when a pause was made, hundreds gathered about the carriages in which these soldiers were riding, and greeted them with cheers and gifts of bouquets of fragrant flowers.

The Twenty-ninth made a fine appearance; its mounted officers riding at the head of its column, and the orderly arrangement of its ranks, reminded one forcibly of the bygone days, when it marched in review before its commanding generals; while the earnest, bright faces of the boys showed plainly enough that they had caught again the old spirit that so often, from 1861 to 1865, led them to triumph over the dangers and toils of the war. Captains Leach and Chamberlain, and Surgeon 'Cogswell, all of whom are somewhat infirm, and were unable to march, and several of the disabled members of the regiment, rode in a carriage in the immediate rear of the regimental column.

The Boston "Home Journal" of September 22 published a very extended and complimentary article concerning the Twenty-ninth Regiment, entitled "Who Are They Now, and Where Are the Rest of Them?" The first part of this question was answered in a manner that must cause its living members and their many friends the keenest satisfaction, while the inquiry, "Where Are the Rest of Them?" which we only have space to quote, touches most tenderly the sweetest and the saddest chords of a soldier's memory :—

"Where are the rest of them? Half of the living men of 1861 were in the line. The other half are scattered. All parts of the State sent up their contribution. Every New England State sent up its quota. From Maine to Oregon, from the great lakes to the Gulf of Mexico, the residue of the living three hundred are scattered. About seven hundred are dead. The killed in action; the men who died of wounds; the men who died of disease while in the service; the men who died, after their discharge, of disease contracted in the service; the men starved to death in rebel prisons; the men incurably weakened by famine and malaria at Knoxville and Vicksburg and Jackson, — they have all gone. It was the strongest of them that we saw on Monday, the best constitutions, the hardest muscles, the toughest fibres, and all of them were prematurely aged, and the boys' faces which most of them wore at the time of enlistment, have now no trace of youth in them. To an old comrade, this age, this worn look, was inexpressibly sad, but sadder yet it was to think of the long roll of dead comrades, and how they died.

"And yet, on every man's face, at some time in the day, in the presence of some old and loved friend, there momentarily returned the transfiguration of youth, and the faces of 1861,— a flash and play of the "battle light" of an earnest, honest, human heart, full of enthusiasm, love, and duty. This was recognizable, and invariably was recognized, no matter how worn and gray the older face and hair might be.

"To have returned to the Commonwealth at least two hundred good citizens, with characters educated by hardships and trials, and by the friendships of the valley of the shadow of death, into a willing and intelligent acquiescence in the rule of law, and the importance of preferring the common weal to mere individual pleasure and profit, is not the least credit of that old regiment; and if the military service has merely succeeded in teaching the necessity of orderly and systematic organization, and the ability to govern one's self, as it has in most instances everywhere, the work of the war can never be undone, and never should be."

50

www.ingramcontent.com/pod-product-compliance
Lightning Source LLC
Chambersburg PA
CBHW032015220426
43664CB00006B/254